EO NA TOA   EO NA TOA, E
THIS IS BATTLE.   YOU MUST RESPOND.

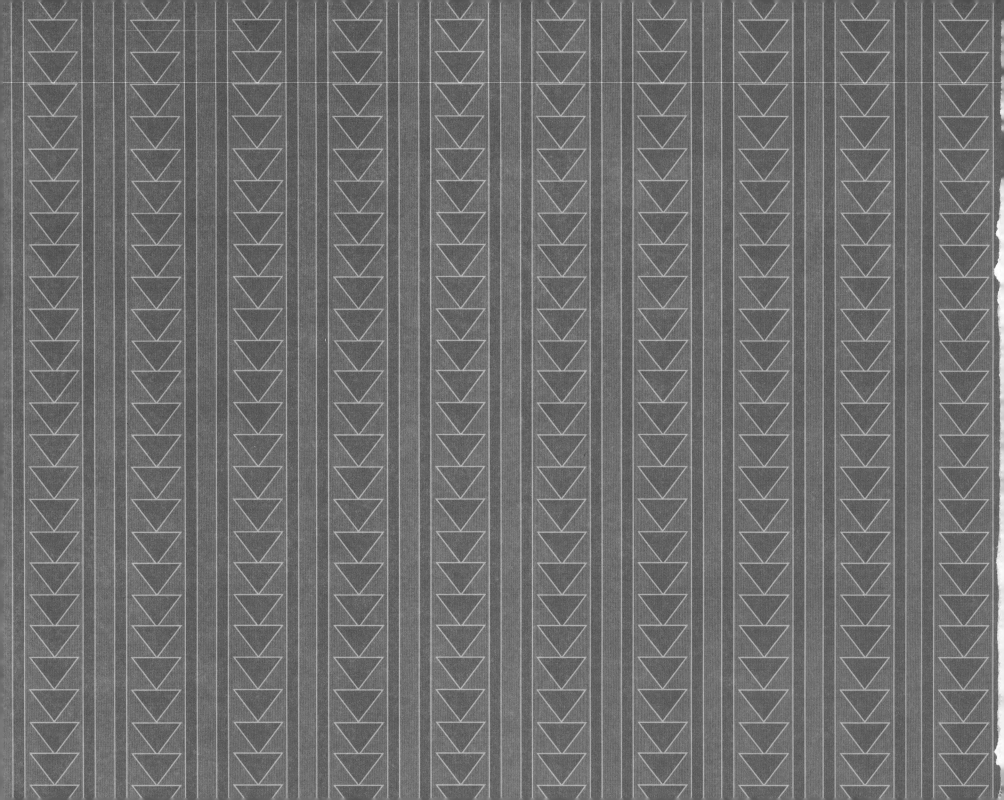

HAWAI'I WARRIOR FOOTBALL

A Story of Faith, Hope and Redemption

J. DAVID MILLER

FOREWORD BY JUNE JONES

3565 Harding Avenue
Honolulu, Hawai'i 96816
phone: (808) 734-7159
fax: (808) 732-3627
e-mail: sales@besspress.com
http://www.besspress.com

THIS IS BATTLE.   YOU MUST RESPOND.

Design: Carol Colbath

Cover photos: top: AP Photo, second: University of Hawai'i Athletics,
third and bottom: Ralph "PBase" Omoto
End sheet photos: Dennis Oda

Cataloging-in-publication data

Miller, J. David.
  Hawaii Warrior football : a story of
faith, hope, and redemption / by J.
David Miller ; foreword by June Jones.
          p.   cm.
  Includes illustrations.
  ISBN 1-57306-282-0
1. Hawaii Warriors (Football team)—
History.   2. University of Hawaii—Football—
History.   3. Jones, June.   I. Title.
GV958.H38.M55 2007   796.33263-dc21

08 09 10   3 4 5 6

Printed in Korea

Contents

RALPH "PBASE" OMOTO

Acknowledgements

I was watching Hawaii football on ESPN in December 2006 when I first turned to my wife Laurie and shared with her my ideas for this book. The fact that *Hawai'i Warrior Football: A Story of Faith, Hope and Redemption* actually happened has required some divine intervention of its own. Rarely does one get to share in a story that encompasses so many miracles, so many people, so many *coincidences* – in the magical backdrop of Hawaii, no less. The powerful tale of June Jones' success could have been told in two ways: The first, by far the easiest, would have been a simple book on Colt, or the recent success of the team. The second, the route we chose, was by far the hardest, but therein is the *real story:* The mosaic of June's life that *explains* the *how* and *why* and *mystery* of Hawaii's current success. It was breathtaking to take all of these tiny little pieces and fit them together; then stand back in awe at the outcome.

Finding all of the 'pieces' required dozens of interviews with scores of people dating back to 1954. We had to document every story and find photos to bring them to life. The fun part was that we did all of the above in 90 days; it wasn't until March of 2007, that Benjamin "Buddy" Bess, president and founder of Bess Press, believed in me and bought into the project. Once he did, just like that, we were on our way. I promised Buddy we could rely on my 24-year friendship with June Jones to make this book happen; once again, June didn't let anyone down. He is the person most responsible for the access, relationships and *insight* that literally transformed this from a local Hawaii book into a story of international interest. To be able to count June among my friends is one of the greatest honors I've ever had.

Mouse Davis was, as always, a thrill. I will spend the rest of my career inventing reasons (*wink, wink!*) to keep interviewing this man until I glean every last drop of knowledge from him. He is far and away the best teacher I've ever encountered in my life, and I hope to share his complete story with the world very soon. The deeper you get into June Jones, the more you realize it's like reading a single story in the *Chronicles of Narnia,* and all roads lead to Mouse. Along the way, I reunited with old friends and made new ones in Artie Wilson, Al Souza, Don Murphy, Jeremy Spear, Pastor Norman Nakanishi, Greg and Heather McMackin, Jeff Reinebold, Sheldon and Marilyn Jones, Leigh Steinberg (and Ellen Goodman), Ruta Aunese, Steve Gerrish, Dave Reardon, Sandi and Steve Bartkowski and Hugh Yoshida. It was very cool to talk to Bobby Hebert again – he was my first-ever feature profile in *Sport* magazine, dating all the way back to 1983.

At Bess Press, it took a tireless, dedicated publishing team – Beverly Motz, Kim Carroll, Carol Colbath, Lee Mottler – to actually *make* a book, in *three* short months — much less one of such *quality*. What they did was akin to turning around a battleship in a bathtub, and the results are everywhere you look. Allen Cordrey built the *Warriors Haka (www.warriorshaka.com)* website, at no charge, to create buzz and co-promote the book.

Our family had many friends who supported us while I took the sabbatical required to do this. Dr. Michael C. Grant pulled an abscess tooth while I was on deadline, and kept me upright and writing. I spent many hours with Frank Urso and Mike LaBanca (and staff) at Beef 'O' Brady's family restaurant, where I ate the best wings in town and engaged a host of special friends, including Mary Williams, John and Cheryl Slivick, and Connor Fox. My theory was that if we could make people in South Florida care about Hawaii football, we could make *anybody* care, and I hope that proves true.

Occasionally, I would take my laptop and sit out on the ocean at the Bilmar Beach Resort in Treasure Island, where Chris Ringwald, Clyde Smith, Kim Laskey, Richie Viera, Jason Replogle, Kate Sailes, Debbie Lee, Theresa Artos, Patrick O'Rourke and Stephen Ridge allowed us to watch endless sunsets, enjoy "free" inspiration and "free wi-fi, as well.

I dedicated my first few books to my mom, whom I love dearly, and I hope she continues to see her teachings in every word that I write. For the first time in nine books, however, my own father read this one cover to cover. I was shocked at how sharing key points in the book drew us closer together.

Laurie, my life partner and wife, is more complex than the Sunday crossword puzzle in the *New York Times.* Only her mom and dad, Ed and Vicki Zifchock, possibly understand; anytime they're ready to offer clues, I'm willing to listen. We are grateful to them, as well as "adopted" parents Will and Diana Hamilton. Laurie can billow like the clouds in an afternoon squall, or shine as bright as a rainbow; what you get depends on how much you love her. I love her unconditionally. She is an amazing mother, friend and help-mate. Laurie, a former bank executive, did every administrative task for this book that fell through the cracks. Finally, each midnight, she would either kiss my cheek and applaud my work; or threaten to kill me if I didn't hurry and give her my undivided attention.

Along with my girls – Chelsea Rhea, Savannah Bey, Kailey and Madison – there is no part of my life that my family has left untouched. In many ways, they live every part of this book along with me, and each one of them individually understands what that means. The very thought of hearing the word *"daddy ...,"* in any of their voices, in any context, bad or good, melts my heart. What an awesome, overwhelming, *satisfying* responsibility. *God – I know you hear me – I love my baby girls!*

Finally, I dedicate this book to my Heavenly Father. I thank Him for second chances, and for the opportunity to live each day. Within these pages, June Jones has given us example after example of what *God* can *do.* Like a gunfighter going into battle, I taped Psalms 45:1 to my mirror, and I read it each morning before I sat down to write: *"My heart is overflowing with a good theme ... my tongue is the pen of a ready writer."*

My ultimate prayer for this book is that you, the reader, find a little *faith, hope and redemption* ... and in doing so, that God gives *you* a Hawaii-size miracle that becomes uniquely your own.

Preface

When Henry Adams said that a *"teacher affects eternity . . . he can never tell where his influence stops,"* he must have been thinking about Mouse Davis.

Without Mouse Davis, you certainly wouldn't be reading this book, and Hawai'i would only be a place where you hope to go someday on vacation, not a team in the top 25 football programs in America.

Without Mouse Davis, there would have been no modern Run 'n' Shoot, June Jones, and probably no Jerry Glanville, at least the version we know now. Without an amazing mosaic of connect-the-dots miracles that now spans decades, there might not be a Colt Brennan, either.

I first met 5-foot-8-inch Darrel "Mouse" Davis in the spring of 1985, when I was a nervous young pro football writer for *SPORT* magazine. He was the new head coach of the USFL's Denver Gold and well into the process of proving to the world that his Run 'n' Shoot offense could win on any stage. We met over dinner, and with him was his beloved bride, Beverly.

COURTESY J. DAVID MILLER

J. David Miller and Darrel "Mouse" Davis

No sooner had we been seated than my condensation-wrapped ice tea slipped through my sweaty hands, spilling across into Davis' lap. *"I hope you don't catch with those hands,"* he said, erupting into laughter. I blushed. It didn't take long for me to never feel more at home. For hours, I enjoyed Mouse and Beverly as they shared their stories, charm and philosophies. That led to the first-ever published national article on Mouse Davis, entitled "The Mouse that Roars."
That story would change my life.

Over the years, I would meet his children, June Jones and his other coaches at their various stops along the way. I learned the offense and installed it in my local Little League as a volunteer coach. For three sea-

sons my quarterback, Kevin Thomas (who was 8, 9 and 10 years old during this span), threw for more than 300 yards seven times, including five touchdowns in a single game. Kevin ended up on the cover of *Disney Adventures* magazine as the most prolific Little League quarterback in history.

Mouse and June, perhaps bemused by a midget version of their offense, rewarded Kevin with a trip to Detroit, where they were coaching at the time. Kevin took a few snaps with the Lions' Silver Stretch offense and even signed an "honorary" contract with the Lions. I became a junior high head coach and eventually a high school offensive coordinator before hanging it up with a record of 37-12.

Mouse even traveled all the way to my old hometown of Chattanooga, Tenn., to host a football clinic. My own quarterback, Mark Lane, would later become a high school coach himself, and he used the Run 'n' Shoot to take a team that once lost 18 consecutive games — *sound familiar?* — to the state playoffs. "This system has a lot to do with positive reinforcement," Lane says. "The Run 'n' Shoot gave me and all the kids I have now coached the capability to change the course of a perennial losing program into a positive one. Whether you have tremendous athletes or not, the Mouse Davis system, and the positive attitudes that come with it, gives your team a chance to compete, win and be part of this legacy that Mouse and June have now created. It is not just the X's and O's that make it work; it is the work ethic and the classroom effort, too. Once the kids understand it and buy into it, you can put a winning product on the field, and we were proud to share in the Mouse Davis vision."

I seized every moment to learn something new from Mouse, including the times I slept on a fold-out sofa in his home on my trips to Detroit. Beverly was the consummate football wife. She had blankets, jackets, scarves, mugs, posters, pennants and necklace charms from every team

Davis had ever coached. In Detroit, their van was silver and blue, full of TVs and warm coffee and the even warmer Beverly. She was the perfect complement — and foil — to Davis, his stories and personality. She also knew defenses better than most coaches I interviewed.

I owe much of my career to Mouse and June, who were never selfish with a quote or a relationship or a referral. They were always there for me, whether it was charity golf tournaments and coaching clinics — where June would bring along Steve Bartkowski — during my three-year radio career, as guests. My years with June in Houston were unforgettable, from watching film, where he discovered Tracy Eaton, to learning to eat fajitas at Pappasito's on Kirby Street.

Mouse introduced me to Neil Lomax, who became co-author of my first book, *Third and Long.* June introduced me to Jerry Glanville, my co-author of *Elvis Don't Like Football.* Through June I met the person who introduced me to NFL legend Hank Stram, with whom I would also collaborate. That success led to the *Super Book of Football,* for *Sports Illustrated.*

Mouse, who wrote the business plan, rules and offenses for the now wildly successful Arena Football League, encouraged me to "walk on" with his friend and coach Joe Haering in Pittsburgh in 1987. Under Joe, I would not only get the chance to play but also to learn pro football in a way few writers could or would — or perhaps, should. Hundreds of national magazine articles poured out of my experiences and relationships that could all be traced back to . . . *Mouse.*

The Run 'n' Shoot is far more than an offense. It is the Mouse Davis aura; it warms you like sunshine. There is a supreme sense of confidence you get from being around him and listening to his teachings.

Always a victim of size itself, Davis and his offense will forever be symbolic of the epic battle of David vs. Goliath, the "it-can't-be-done-this-way" mode of thinking, the "we-will-prove-you-wrong" mindset. Davis, his offense and now his thousands of coaching protégés have allowed more undersized kids to play football in the high school, college and pro ranks than any other system in the annals of football. "My own stature gave me a little bit more incentive," he laughs.

To my four girls — ages 16, 11, 7 and 5 — Mouse and June are as much

storybook legends as Curious George or Lemony Snicket. Countless times when I've heard them tell me a class was too difficult to pass, a school bully too much to take, a circumstance too hard to bear, I answer with a Mouse or June story of positive reinforcement, maintaining your sense of humor, overcoming the odds or *finding* a way to win.

On *mistakes:* "There was the time," I told them, "when Mouse was coaching a really fast guy — Mel Gray — in Detroit. Mouse would tell him the route — *Break it across the safety's face!* — but over and over, and over and over, he'd just run straight down the field. 'Dammit, Mel,' Davis said, grinning, 'at least when you make a mistake, you make it *really fast.*'"

On *repetition* (my favorite): "Whatever you're teaching, whatever you're coaching, it has to be second nature to the players. That's why we do it again and again, and then we do it again. When they finally get it right, we do it again.

Repetition, repetition, repetition."

On *being little:* "Size is relative. When you catch touchdowns, you're the biggest guy on the field."

On *criticism:* "The way to shut up the crowd," says Davis, "is *throw touchdowns.*"

On *failure:* "It only takes one play to change the game."

I don't know if any of this works, but all my kids are honor roll students; two of them attend magnet schools, and one of them even won a kickball tournament by instructing teammates to catch the ball *"in the noose,"* the way Davis and Jones teach their receivers and how I taught her to catch.

Mouse Davis is now a part of football history, but without a trace of vindictiveness, animosity or disdain. It's not often you can prove the entire world wrong, yet remain so humble, so disarming, so subtle that your enemies, however begrudgingly, embrace you. "That's called lathering 'em up while he shaves you," says Glanville.

In 2001, I caught up with Mouse Davis at a hotel in Los Angeles.

He opened the door with a flashbulb smile and bear-hug embrace. I would later write that seeing Mouse again was as comfortable as slipping on your favorite pair of old jeans. We joked, laughed and talked for two hours about the years that had passed, friends, business and the virtues of leadership.

When we came to the subject of Beverly's death to cancer, I saw my greatest mentor cry for the first time in 18 years. It killed me to hear him whisper about the loss of his soul mate, his life-long partner since early adulthood. "That's a tough deal," he said. "Relationships are *all* you have. *Forget money, or anything else.* If you don't have relationships, you don't have *anything.*"

That lesson obviously got through to everybody Davis ever touched: Between Davis, Jones and Glanville, countless thousands of people, coaches and players all over the *world* have been touched by their lessons, lives and efforts. God forbid Davis ever dies, because there isn't a state big enough to hold the funeral.

When Mouse joined June in Hawai'i, followed by Glanville, I watched from 6,000 miles away with intrigue as they retooled the UH program. I had settled in Laguna Beach, Calif., during the Colt Brennan high school era, and I was all too familiar with his story when he wound up in Hawai'i, too, when June extended forgiveness and a hall pass in exchange for Colt's humility.

I will never forget how hollow I felt leaving Mouse's hotel room back in 2001, the last time I saw him before I began this book. I wished then, and now, I'd spent more time making myself a better person. I've been through some tough divorces and some tough situations. I've failed miserably in certain businesses and hurt people I didn't mean to. I've even stopped writing for long periods and disappeared from all my friends while searching for life's answers.

I always seem to wind up back in the same place. "Find what you do well, and do it consistently," Mouse always said. This book, then, also represents some personal unfinished business. I *had* to tie it all together.

One day my girls were playing four-square in the driveway. One of them fell, the ball bounced out of bounds, and she shouted, *"Do-over! Do-over! Do-over!"*

Herein is the story of the biggest do-over in the history of college football, engineered by men whose careers personify the meaning of do-over, and a quarterback whose personal do-over offers hope to generations of children to come.

To Mouse and June: Thanks for showing the world that true friends multiply your joy and divide your sorrow. God determines who walks into our lives. It's up to us to decide who we let walk away and who we refuse to let go.

Godspeed,

J. David Miller

J. David Miller, June Jones and Colt Brennan

Foreword

by Coach June Jones

"Sometimes, it's just a person's destiny"

With a voice as deep and powerful as James Earl Jones, the late Ed Wong uttered words that would ignite my passion to become the 20th head football coach at the University of Hawaiʻi.

What I didn't know was that this decision would become not only the greatest experience but also the greatest challenge I had ever encountered, either personally or professionally.

This was December of 1998.

Just the day before, at 2 a.m., I had received a phone call from Bobby Beathard, my good friend and then president and general manager of the San Diego Chargers. Bobby informed me that owner Dean Spanos had accepted my counteroffer for a five-year deal — two years more than the original three they had proposed.

Furthermore, the Chargers were willing to pay me an additional $2.5 million *above* their original offer. When I hung up the phone with Bobby and laid my head on the pillow, in my mind, the deal was done.

I was going to be the head coach of the San Diego Chargers.

After tossing and turning and unable to sleep, I even called Bobby Beathard *in the middle of the night* to give him my commitment. The next day, we would clean up the arrangements and announce it to the public.

Meanwhile, the day before, the University of Hawai'i had sent eight people to San Diego to interview me for their vacant head coaching job.

I was scheduled to meet with the Hawai'i contingent at 8 a.m., just a few short hours away. Included among them were Edison Miyawaki, part owner of the Cincinnati Bengals; Hugh Yoshida, the athletic director; John Fink, president of K-5 the Home Team; Ed Wong, president of the booster club; and Jim Donovan, the assistant athletic director.

Earlier that night, I had prayed for guidance. Now that I had made up my mind to stay with the San Diego Chargers, my heart panged with guilt for stringing out the hopes of the special people of Hawai'i.

I'd hardly slept when the alarm clock rudely awakened me.

I called Leigh Steinberg, my agent, to tell him of my decision.

"Leigh," I said, "It's a done deal. We're staying in San Diego. The two things you recommended — five years instead of three, the additional $2.5 million — I asked them for everything, and they've agreed."

There was a long pause on the other end of the phone. Looking back, I truly believe that God spoke to me right then through Leigh, and it would change my life forever.

"June," he said, "I've known you . . . what, *20-plus years?* All you've ever talked about is one day being the head coach of Hawai'i. I think *you owe it to yourself* to follow through with that interview this morning."

Two hours later, I went to the meeting. In my back pocket, I had tucked

a blank, personal, hand-written check for $10,000, *to reimburse them* for their expenses and trouble.

That's when something magical occurred. The next thing I knew, I found myself in that very meeting, trying to answer the most obvious question:

Why would an NFL coach want to take over a team that is dead-last in the nation?

The more I answered their questions, the more I began to sound like a guy that wanted the job. A passion rose up inside me that I'll never be able to explain. A fire ignited in my gut, in spite of the fact that Hawai'i was offering me a tenth of the money so generously laid on the table by the Chargers.

If you're going to shock the football world, is there a better place to do it than with the *worst program in America?*

You can't get any more uphill than that. If you're a football coach who is worth his salt, this is just the kind of deal that makes your motor run. Just like that, my paradigm shifted, and Ed Wong tacked on the exclamation point that will forever live in my memory:

"Sometimes, it's just a person's destiny!"

Destiny, indeed.

Eight years later, I'm so proud that we've now developed a winning program with a *tradition* of winning. We've done the impossible. We're winning today with the same budget we had when I got here, when they had just lost 18 straight. Our boys are now the proud holders of countless records. We've got kids all over the NFL. We won a WAC Championship with mirrors. Nobody in this football office ever complains.

We just keep *finding a way to win.*

Our kids have now won four out of five bowl games, against schools that have far, far more resources than we do: Houston, Oregon State, Arizona

State. We've beaten Michigan State, BYU, Purdue, and even Alabama, which must have made Bear Bryant roll over in his grave.

So much has happened to me in the past eight years, I almost don't know where to begin. Some of these moments you will find in the following pages, and a few I've chosen to keep for myself. One fact, however, consistently holds true, and it's something I tell my players every day: The memories we keep are not found in wins and losses but in the eyes of the men in the locker room and in the eyes of those people we meet along the way.

We will all forget the touchdowns and the final scores, but the eyes and the faces and the passion of these men in the locker room and all those who cared about us will live on forever.

This is a love that defines great teams and separates them from ordinary men. When I use the word *"ohana,"* I mean it. *Ohana* means family, and family means nobody gets left behind — or forgotten.

As you read the amazing stories in this book, you'll become a part of our *ohana,* too.

Each of the past eight years had its own positives. Though we struggled during losing seasons in 2000 and 2005, I am still convinced that because of the way we, as coaches, taught our players to stay united as a group, this led to enormous success with the following 2001 and 2006 teams.

Tribulation requires perseverance. Perseverance builds character.

Character blossoms into *hope,* and *hope* does not disappoint.

In those losing years, we built upon the character that would lead future teams to memorable seasons, and now, when you hear about Hawai'i football, you think about *hope,* and I can promise you, we will *always* have a chance to win, regardless of the color of the helmet on the other side of the ball.

In the pages to follow, you are going to hear a lot about *hope* and *redemption.* You will get to relive our magical seasons of 1999 and 2006.

I was unaware, beginning with the second week of January 2000, right up to my birthday on February 19, 2005, how these years would completely change me.

I am so thankful to God that He loved me so much that, over time, I could forgive myself and others for some of the decisions that were made. During my private island moments, I take the time to reflect on my life, like the 18th tee at Hualālai or walking behind the 'Ilikai Hotel and sitting quietly on the rocks by the pier, where I first envisioned what could be one day.

These are the things I think about when I ride my Harley to Hale'iwa for shave-ice; when I stroll the beaches of Lanikai, or a night walk at the Ihilani, or stare into the pounding surf of Mākaha; or even when I simply walk alone behind the Kāhala Resort and lie on the beach chairs and stare at the stars.

These places — and a few dozen more — live in a special place in my heart.

All of these moments have changed the man I've now become.

Hawai'i has allowed me to do what I always wanted to do. We've now proven we can win in a very different way than you'll find in most football playbooks. My goal — from day one — was to throw first and have fun second. We do this every day; in the office, at practice and in the games.

This, truly, is the best job anyone could dream of having.

I'm grateful to have been given this opportunity. I made the decision from day one that we would live on the edge. I knew we would be second-guessed — *winners always are.*

Whether it was throwing the ball on fourth and 1 or faking a punt from our own 15-yard line, this was the way I decided I wanted the game played.

I also knew that allowing God to be a part of the locker room would change lives. Looking back, this is all part of what Ed Wong spoke of —

helping all of these boys become men. This was why I was called back to Hawai'i — to allow God to use me in a way He chose for me.

When I see Hawai'i football and the *haka* being replayed in the living rooms of kids across America, it makes me so proud. No matter where we travel, watching our fans stay until the final gun — *just to be a part of us* — the *haka* took on its own life. It became *"us."* Watching kids from Los Angeles, Oakland, Texas, and wherever else they come from — to see

them now *take* part and *become* part of the culture here, it just makes you smile.

Now we get phone calls every day from Polynesian players who moved away and want to come *home,* to *reconnect with their own.*

How can you not feel good about what has happened here? We have tradition. We have pride.

We have all those intangibles that were lost during those dark years when Hawai'i *couldn't find a way to win.*

I always believed you could be a champion by being a totally positive person.

When I started my football career, berating players was the "in" thing to do — but I always believed a pat on the back could accomplish more. I was determined to build up, not tear down, the people around me. From my very first job, I wanted to *prove* that you could win with positive reinforcement.

Over the past eight years, I have fought some battles along the way that, I admit, I didn't need to fight. But that is who I am. I have always believed in the big picture, which is for Hawai'i football to be thought of on the same level as a PAC-10 team, or Big 12 team. All of the changes I've tried to make here were done with one thing in mind: *To make the University of Hawai'i football program the best it can be.*

We have so many things that need to be changed, but we've begun something now that will last. I believe in my players. I love motivating them, I love showing them I truly care. And I don't judge a single one of them for their past.

RALPH "PBASE" OMOTO

I believe in second chances.

This is why *this story* is now bigger than the game of football itself.

As we open the 2007 season, I am anxious again for *destiny* to happen — and to continue to grow as a man myself.

Frank Gansz taught me a long time ago that what you *give* will grow, and what you *keep*, you will most certainly *lose*.

I have never forgotten those words.

I have given all I have.

My good friend Mike Post once said to me that we should do something for the University of Hawai'i that will live forever, something they will remember long after we're dead and gone. He did, and I've tried, and I will continue to give it my all.

Eō nā toa!
Eō nā toa e!

This is battle!
You must respond!

Mahalo,

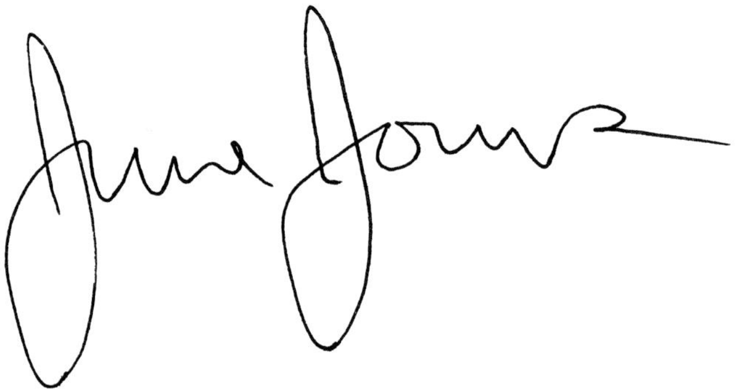

June Jones III

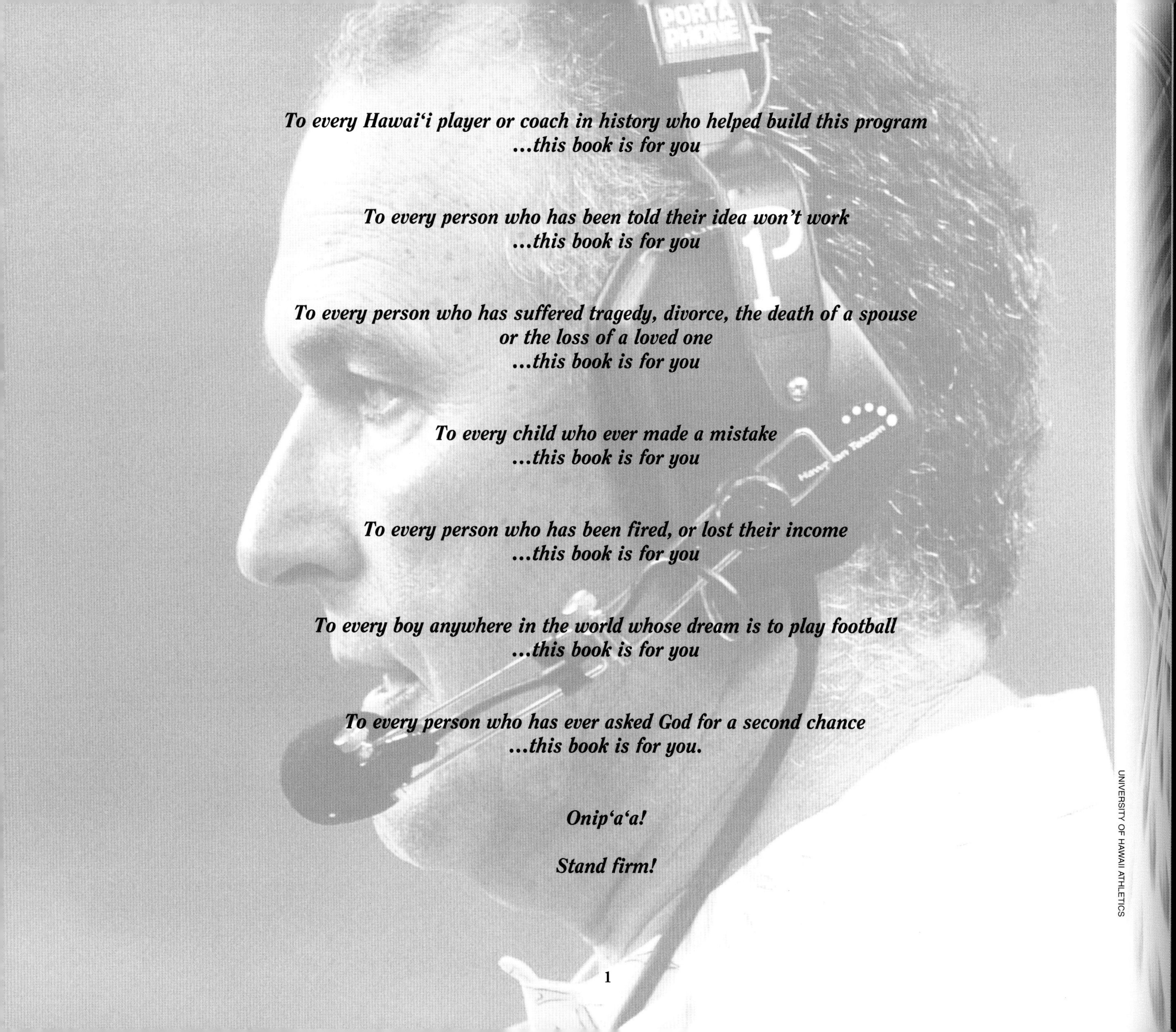

UNIVERSITY OF HAWAII ATHLETICS

To every Hawai'i player or coach in history who helped build this program
...this book is for you

To every person who has been told their idea won't work
...this book is for you

To every person who has suffered tragedy, divorce, the death of a spouse
or the loss of a loved one
...this book is for you

To every child who ever made a mistake
...this book is for you

To every person who has been fired, or lost their income
...this book is for you

To every boy anywhere in the world whose dream is to play football
...this book is for you

To every person who has ever asked God for a second chance
...this book is for you.

Onip'a'a!

Stand firm!

The Warriors' Haka personifies the heart, soul and attitude of University of Hawai'i football

Chapter 1
NEW BEGINNINGS

The island of O'ahu sits in the middle of the Pacific Ocean at about 21 degrees 30 minutes north latitude and 158 degrees west longitude, roughly 2,600 miles west of San Diego, Calif., and 3,850 miles east of Tokyo, Japan. From the air, this island mass appears to be a gigantic chunk of blue-green gemstone, cut whole and set neatly into place. For the 1.3 million people of Hawai'i, its precious land, ocean and culture are sacred and scarcely understood by the 20 million annual visitors whom they allow to briefly sip from its charm and mystery.

On December 24, 2006, the lights of Aloha Stadium twinkled like diamonds in the night sky, beckoning an ESPN audience of more than 2.3 million people to come inside and join the 40,623 in the stands for a Christmas miracle. This, for the record, was exactly a couple million more people to ever watch a Hawai'i football game this late in the season.

Hawai'i? Are you kidding me?

Amidst thick smoke and raucous celebration, the silver-and-black-clad University of Hawai'i Warriors spilled onto the emerald green field. Opposing players wearing the timid yellow and burgundy colors of Arizona State stared cautiously, their wide eyes betraying the fact that the Sun Devils were heavily favored to win.

After all, Hawai'i, you might remember, is a college football anomaly, a team that a college football "expert" said back in 1998 was *"impossible to take seriously."*

On this night, however, Hawai'i — *yes, Hawai'i* — was about to stuff its proverbial boot in the butt of every pundit who had ever voiced disrespect

RALPH "PBASE" OMOTO

for its football program. Arizona State simply had the misfortune of being in the wrong place at the wrong time, like the two little kids wandering around *Jurassic Park,* oblivious to the piercing eyes of the cunning raptors stealthily calculating their every move, waiting for just the right moment . . . *to devour them.*

The Hawai'i football Warriors ringed each other and faced the crowded stadium. Of 105 players, 75 were of Polynesian, Hawaiian or Samoan descent, evidenced by the layers of glistening olive skin that stretched across enormous, muscular physiques and flowing rivers of wavy jet-black hair that obscured the names on the backs of their jerseys. Their names didn't matter, to be honest, for on this night, *they were one.*

Suddenly, like panthers, they crouched, in preparation of the *haka,* a pregame tribal dance based in Maori culture. *Hakas* traditionally have various uses in everyday Maori life.

They typically are used to tell a story or to express emotions and opinions, but they are best known in their most aggressive form. Historically, warriors use the *haka* to prepare for a battle, to focus their strength, to proclaim their powers and to celebrate the triumph of life over death.

Mostly, however, they use the *haka* to challenge and intimidate their opponent.

In unison, the Hawai'i Warriors began to chant and cry aloud in a single, guttural voice:

Ringa pakia!

"A Warrior is many things," teaches June Jones. "A Warrior is a brother. Touchdowns will fade away. Games will disappear. The faces to your right and the left, behind you and in front of you, will live for a lifetime."

Uma tiraha!

Turi whatia!

Hope whai ake!

Waewae takahia kia kino!

The players' rough body movements were accompanied by rhythmically chanting vocals. They screamed into the night air, both crying and grunting. Tears streamed down war-painted faces. Eyes bulged. Together they slapped their thigh pads and beefy forearms, pounded their chests and gripped their mighty biceps. They showed their teeth, poked out their tongues and sniffed through their nostrils, glaring with white-hot intensity.

The poor members of Arizona State, looking very much like missionaries surprised by a tribe of not-so-congenial cannibals, tried to appear disinterested, except for the one player whom you can spot on film gawking at the Warriors while a passed football bounces directly off his head: Helmet in hand, he stares in disbelief — then, *doink!* — is stunned by an errant ball, as he absorbs the fate that awaits him and his teammates.

Tēnei te tangata pūhuruhuru!

Nāna nei i tiki mai whakawhiti te rā!

Ā upane, ka upane!

Ā upane, ka upane!

Whiti te rā, hī!

To be honest, football fans should have seen it coming. The records had been falling at Hawai'i for years, but nobody on the mainland could find time between their precious day planners, cell phones, iPods or e-mail to listen, watch or understand.

Since 1999, Hawai'i has posted a 64-40 record. The Warriors led the country in offense twice, behind six all-Americans and 51 all-conference

RALPH "PBASE" OMOTO

performers. Lest we forget, 16 of these kids would be drafted by the NFL, and another 41 would sign as free agents. Throw in a conference championship, five bowl-game invites and five nine-plus win seasons — *did we mention the* 15 conference *road* wins? — and victories over Alabama, Brigham Young, Oregon State, Michigan State, Northwestern, Arizona State and Purdue.

If you didn't know better, you might think we're talking about the storied programs of Florida or Oklahoma or USC.

In 2006, the Warriors lost three times by a *total* of three touchdowns. Quarterback Colt Brennan — *wow, this quarterback!* — had run and thrown for more yards than Ohio State's Heisman Trophy winner Troy Smith and Michigan's Chad Henne *combined,* and with *fewer attempts.*

Colt didn't just break records, he *shattered* them, but this was no big deal, as he had already done it before — *twice* in three years, to be exact.

And — get this — Colt *didn't play the fourth quarter in six games!* Tyler Graunke, the backup quarterback, ran the offense so well in just these fourth quarters alone that he, too, threatened the record books.

Hawai'i?

Are you kidding me?

ESPN, in its pregame diatribes, scrambled for answers as it attempted to explain in less than a minute and a half this mess that Hawai'i had created for the pious college crowd. While it might be human nature to explain away anything you can't understand or comprehend, some took it to a new level.

Hawai'i was called a *"pass-happy affair . . . yes, they put up numbers, but it's the system."* There were pointed references to the strength of schedule, or in this case, the lack thereof. The Western Athletic Conference, they said, was weak, and the Hawai'i defense. The passing rules of today's game, they said, allowed for this kind of nonsense.

It seemed the focus fell everywhere except the obvious — that Hawai'i would play anyone and everyone, and in doing so, the team was tipping the sanctimonious scales of tradition — and, most certainly, the record books — in favor of a program no one cared about just 10 years before.

Five players would be drafted from this 2006 team alone, and five more would sign free-agent contracts, yielding a harvest the likes of which Hawai'i hadn't seen since farmer John Wilkinson tended its first sugarcane and coffee crops in 1825.

Prior to June Jones, Hawai'i hadn't even had a player drafted *in 11 years*.

RALPH "PBASE" OMOTO

Future Miami Dolphin Tala Esera (right) protects Run 'n' Shoot triggerman Colt Brennan against ASU. Note how far away the nearest tackler is ... which is one reason that Colt has become the most accurate passer in football at any level ...

Yet, the reaction on the mainland remained indifferent.

Beer-bellied sports fans laughed at the thought of football gods like LSU or Michigan being replaced by the football gods of Akua and Kupua.

Hawai'i?

Are you kidding me?

Hawai'i is supposed to be a place you either dream *about* or vacation *to* — certainly not a Top-25 football program that kicks the crap out of your team and sends them back to your continental hometown bellyaching about the officiating, the lopsidedness or the beating they endured.

Prior to January 12, 1999, the day June Jones forsook the NFL to become Hawai'i's 20th head coach, scheduling the team — still the Rainbows — was a vacation: a free trip to O'ahu and a chance to wow the boosters and alumni, with a disrespectful dip or two in its sky-blue waters. So badly was Hawai'i routinely routed through decades past that most games were a next-day paragraph buried on the last sheet of Sunday's sports page. Remember, this was a program that had lost 18 consecutive games before Jones arrived — and had finished dead-last in offense, defense and special teams.

The level of play had descended lower than the volcanic depths of the coal-black rocks that shroud the island; so bad, in fact, that its teams played in front of crowds so sparse that players could have gone into the stands and introduced themselves *individually* during pregame warm-ups. University regents were voting to extinguish the program *altogether*.

Hawai'i football was on the verge of extinction, teetering dangerously between committees and subcommittees that hoped to erase it from the face of the earth, until Jones spurned the NFL and accepted the minuscule offer of $320,000 to become its head coach.

"I think there's a sense of ownership between the people of Hawai'i and that football program that is unique beyond any other program," says ESPN's Neil Everett. "Hawai'i football may not be 'big-time' on the mainland . . . but it's huge to Hawai'i . . . and it takes a special guy to navigate that course."

RALPH "PBASE" OMOTO

Playing against the Hawai'i defense is no longer just another fun day in the sun …

Fortunately, June Jones, the man responsible for this shift of power, had heard it all before. In fact, June Jones and his staff had been listening to misplaced judgment for a collective 300 years: from the levels of Little League to junior high, to high school, to college and an assortment of professional leagues, including the sacred-cow National Football League.

The coaching profession is one of networking and leapfrogging. Promotions are preferred. Lateral moves are acceptable. Backward moves, however, jeopardize a career. Make no mistake: Jones' peers saw his decision as a death wish.

Had anyone taken the time to notice, however, they might have discovered that everywhere that June Jones went, passing records — like Mary's little lamb — were sure to follow. Jones and his offense simultaneously debunk detractors and statistically sink critics like sailboats in an ocean tempest.

The man had a plan when he came to Hawai'i, and all would be revealed in due time. Remember, this was a coach whose quarterbacks have achieved every conceivable honor known to man. And Hawai'i would prove to be no different, as victories, records and championships would quietly fall like autumn leaves each September through December.

On this night before Christmas, all creatures were stirring, *especially* a Mouse; in this case, one Darrel "Mouse" Davis, who was prowling the sidelines, relaying thoughts to his former quarterback-turned-genius head coach. Mouse had invented this offense decades ago, which was now fine-tuned by June Jones and on international stage for the world to witness, and he could *smell* what was about to happen.

Perhaps the biggest difference between amateur and professional football is that the college game is chock-full of pomp and circumstance: the subplots and story lines; the unique campuses, against-all-odds fairy tales, and bouncy co-eds plummeting up-skirt into the arms of spotting cheerleaders. But football has a sideline secret that remains a common denominator, and on this night, it was evident across the white-washed faces of the star-struck Sun Devils, as they tried desperately to avoid the stares of the Hawai'i football Warriors.

Ask any coach at *any level* and they will tell you they can *feel* when something *horrible* is about to happen. All the motivation and encouragement — *Don't look at them! Just play through it!* — won't dispel *the fear you smell* on the sidelines.

Most mainlanders think of Hawai'i as a picture-postcard portrait, as depicted in epics such as *Waikiki Wedding* and *Blue Hawai'i,* which glamorized Hawai'i to mythic proportion. *Waikiki Wedding* even starred Bing Crosby, Bob Burns, Martha Raye, Shirley Ross, George Barker and even bad-singer-turned-worse-actor Leif Erikson.

Truth, however, for those willing to look it up, can be found in *Molokai: The Story of Father Damien.* Paul Cox's 1999 film, about a Catholic priest's struggle to aid victims of leprosy, is a rare example of accuracy in a genre too often suffused with myth and glamour.

Watch the film, as coaches say, and you'll see a heart-wrenching struggle of the Hawaiian people, showing the conflict between the missionaries and the Hawaiians and how they had to learn to *trust* one another and *believe* in one another; how one *culture* helped another *culture,* and how one man *sacrificed* his life and well-being for the sake of a village.

God?

Trust?

Culture?

Sacrifice?

Village?

HAWAII STATE ARCHIVES

Apparently, Arizona State overlooked this in its shuffle of game film.

In short order, this would prove to be the mistake of a lifetime.

The proverbial chip was about to leap off a century of soldiers' shoulders. Decades of disrespect and months of misinterpretations would suddenly boil red-hot.

Like searing, hissing lava, 100-plus boys wearing Hawai'i silver-and-black were about to erupt like the very volcano on which they live, yearning and burning desperately to prove themselves as men . . . in a fight far, far greater than any human opponent that could ever line up against them.

Depending on your indifference, the Hawai'i roster read either like a police blotter or a Polynesian *puaka.*

Either way, these were boys-becoming-men before your eyes, as they portrayed the courage and cunning of the hunt. In the stands, the women danced the *hum-ha.* The bodies of the players were splashed with tattoos, which not ironically is actually a Polynesian word. For each, their patterns confer prestige, power and protection.

This game had it all — energy, color and the excitement of the Pacific Islands' beauty and grace. Arizona State took an early 10-3 lead, and their coaches did their best to scribble, quibble and yell through the obvious, like inane TV weathermen who stand before a quelling storm telling viewers not to fear the hurricane, just moments before its wicked grip rips them en masse from the viewing screen.

RALPH "PBASE" OMOTO

Future Miami Dolphins Samson Satele (left) and Nate Iloa (right) sandwich Hercules Satele

Had the hapless Sun Devils understood the words to the *haka*, they might have called off the hunt at 10-3 and gone home. "We didn't listen to the *haka*," said Arizona State safety Josh Barrett. "We ignored that crap. In fact, we were thinking we were going to go back out there in the second half and do the same thing we did to them in the first half."

Perhaps, if young Josh had listened to the actual words of *"that crap,"* he might have better understood what was about to happen next.

'Tis death, 'tis death
'Tis life, 'tis life
'Tis death, 'tis death
'Tis life, 'tis life

A step upward, another step upward
A step upward, another step upward!

It is death, it is death: it is life, it is life;

This is the man who enabled me to live

As I climb up step by step . . .

Had the hapless Sun Devils read the script, they wouldn't have kicked offensive lineman Tala Esera in the groin, forcing him to rip off his helmet and wave his dreadlocks with rage across the 50-yard line. This, in turn, ignited a daring quarterback named Colt, and further enraged and engaged guys with names like Hercules and Samson.

Hollywood couldn't have written this script, nor cast it better; the last time this many characters gathered in one place, they named it Disney World.

Except, as Jeff Goldblum smirked in *Jurassic Park,* as his character desperately attempted to race away from the pursuing dinosaurs, *"When the Pirates of the Caribbean breaks down, the pirates don't eat the tourists!"*

Bear Bryant once said, *"You cannot be absolutely certain about a boy until you see inside his heart."*

▼▼▼▼▼▼▼▼▼▼▼▼▼▼

To be honest, football fans should have seen it coming. The records had been falling at Hawaii for years, but nobody on the mainland could find time between their precious day-planners, cell-phones, i-Pods or e-mail to listen, watch or understand.

▲▲▲▲▲▲▲▲▲▲▲▲▲▲

Colt Brennan had waited his lifetime for this moment, and this is what the fans had paid good money to watch.

He was about to lay his heart wide open for the world to peek inside. This was a kid, you see, who had told himself he was the best quarterback in America, and who was secure enough in his manhood to snuggle a football in his bed at night while he dreamed of becoming just that.

Toweling beads of perspiration from under his black-streaked eyes, Colt Brennan entered the huddle, which distinctly smelled of athletic tape, liniment and sweat. Colt, of all people, was the most unlikely guy to be in this position, including some teammates who had never even played football until just a few years before. They don't televise games in jail, which is exactly where Colt had been, prior to meeting a guy named June Jones.

None of that mattered now, however, as the upstart Warriors trailed Arizona State, 10-3. Colt, for reasons to be explained later, was superfluous to the situation and frankly could have cared less. Like all great quarterbacks, while the rest of the free world wonders and frets, he — in the words of Mouse Davis — simply *"does what he does."*

As his perspiring linemen heaved in deep gasps, exhaling the thick island air like *nā koholā* (the humpback whales) pluming on the North Shore, Colt took a deep breath and relaxed. Every great quarterback since Johnny Unitas is always described as having *"ice in his veins,"* and Brennan's teammates will once again substantiate this cliché.

Colt breathes. Colt sweats. But Colt is, well, *casual* in the eye of the storm.

Brennan cupped his hands over his helmet's ear-holes, drowning out noise and gathering his thoughts. He approached his teammates.

Funny, but 30 years ago, Mouse Davis had taught June Jones that there are only two kinds of quarterbacks in the world:

One gets better, and one gets worse.

Colt Brennan was about to show the whole world whether Mouse Davis was right — for better or worse.

Brennan's eyes constantly flicker with God-given confidence; a trait that permits him to speak as he does to his Polynesian, Samoan and Hawaiian teammates with their utmost respect. He turned his palms inward-out, touching his teammates and igniting their faith.

Colt inhaled, withdrew, and, staring back into his teammates' smoldering eyes, clicked his chinstrap confidently into place.

"Alright boys . . ."

Brennan smirked, and his teammates instantly fed into his self-assurance.

"Let's do what we do. Let it come to us. Let's go 781 X-15. We'll let these guys get comfortable, we'll move down the field, and we'll do this our way. Once they settle, we're gonna go five-91-Texas for the touchdown.

"Are you with me?"

Few ever stand at the threshold of history; fewer still kick down the door

Colt's visor is a point of contention among coaches. "When Colt doesn't wear the visor," says Mouse Davis, "and he uses his eyes to look-off the safety, he's twice as good as he already is, which is pretty darn good."

when their point in time arrives. Colt, ever comfortable in the role of giant slayer, seized his moment by the throat. Colt is the kind of gunslinger who will let you count to 10, misfire, and shoot you in the leg anyway, even after the fact, and without remorse.

"C'mon fellas," he said, flashing his trademark toothy grin, *"are you ready to have a little fun?"*

Surfers don't decide on their own when to escape Hawai'i's frothy, furious curls; the *waves decide when to let them go.* Likewise, as Colt saddled under center, his right arm was about to capture the hearts of Hawai'i and its ESPN audience: a vortex of football, passion and people that, like the O'ahu surf, *would refuse to let go.*

Had this been a screenplay, someone might have alertly foreshadowed that ASU was overplaying what Hawai'i coaches call "the vertical," or deep-thirds outside, which — *wink, wink* — allows for deep, inside post routes.

"When Colt sees that look," chuckles Mouse, "he can be, let's just say, an *instigator of offense.*"

With 12:29 to play in the third quarter, receiver Jason Rivers used his hips and speed to create space, and Colt casually dropped the ball on his inside shoulder in full stride, like flicking a donut down a chimney into an area roughly the size of a welcome mat.

This score would tie the game.

Furthermore, Colt had just tied the record for most touchdowns — 54 — in a *single season.*

He wasn't finished, either; and the history lesson continued.

Two dusty playbooks might have helped Arizona State on this day, and both could be traced back to 1977. Great football coaches don't reinvent the wheel; they always revert back to what they *know,* and they'll keep inflicting it — *over and over and over and over* — until you figure out a way to stop the pain.

It's rare for a head coach to be able to enjoy a mentor on his own sidelines, and in this case Jones had *two:* Davis on the offensive side and the black-clad Jerry Glanville — *yes, that Jerry Glanville* — calling the defense. It's important to note that both men believe — on either side of the ball — that the word *"relentless"* is both a job title and a job description.

Both were about to recommend to June, in the words of Glanville, to *"dance with who brung ya,"* or, as Mouse says, *"go back to whatcha know."*

So when Hawai'i lined up in *Trips-Right Hap 60 Z Go,* not a single coach in Portland, Ore., was even slightly surprised. Portland, you see, was where Mouse Davis had invented the modern Run 'n' Shoot some four decades ago. Davis had delighted in torturing his opponents with this very play as a primary method of torment, until the lights shorted out on the scoreboards, including one whom he beat — *I kid you not* — 105-0.

Meanwhile, on the defensive side of the ball, Glanville was reverting to *"Sticky Sam,"* an all-out defensive assault that aging Atlanta Falcons' fans might recall as the *"Gritz Blitz."*

Sticky Sam can be traced to the Falcons' 1977 home-opening victory over the former Los Angeles Rams. Against a stationary Joe Namath, Glanville called the safety blitz — *believe it or not* — 46 times. "We sent cornerbacks, safeties, linebackers, even a few ball boys," Glanville says. So rough was the treatment of Namath that the once-great quarterback had to be packed in ice for the four-hour plane ride back to Los Angeles.

Defensive coaches will tell you that this was as unsound as you could get on the field, outside of using more than the allotted number of players. Glanville, on the other hand, endorsed using *extra* players, once telling a reporter that "we like to get 11 hats on the football . . . unless they're near our sideline. In that case, *let's get 13!*"

A football field is 53 and 1/3 yards wide by 100, and as the tension built to a crescendo, June Jones was about to take every lesson he'd ever learned in his life and make Arizona State defend every single inch.

Rain is described 96 times in the Bible, slightly more than twice the number in which June Jones inflicted Colt Brennan's right arm on Arizona State. The outcome, however, was similar to that felt by Noah's neighbors, and for the barren Sun Devils, even an ark wouldn't have helped as the heavens opened and the barrage poured down.

"If you can be accurate with the football in this offense," says former NFL all-pro Bobby Hebert, "it will make an average quarterback pretty good, and a good quarterback, like this kid at Hawai'i, really, *really great.*"

Arizona State, in the meantime, had decided to dumbfound "this kid" with in-and-out, man-to-man coverage.

RALPH "PBASE" OMOTO

Jason Rivers races for the end zone

13

Not a good idea.

With 8:46 left in the third, Colt hit Ryan Grice-Mullins on a perfect flat for a 7-yard touchdown. For the record, that score made Colt the best quarterback to ever play college football — *in history.* On the next series, against the same look with 2:14 to play in the quarter, Colt delivered the same result — on a different route to Grice-Mullins *again,* this time for 36 yards.

This throw — *I implore you to look at the film* — was akin to tossing a football into the sunroof of a moving car in midtown New York traffic. While it's recorded as *only* a 36-yard score, the cross-field throw was in the air 47 yards or so, and it had to be perfect — over a linebacker and between the safeties — and Colt did it as nonchalantly as most people wake up and brush their teeth.

"You would think they'd learned by then," June says. "I knew that as long as we could keep Colt standing up, he was going to deliver that ball, and Colt, trust me, will make you pay the price. If it's not broke, don't fix it. I knew they were going to blitz us, I knew the ball needed to come out early, and I wanted to give Colt solid options of where to go with the ball. Colt went to his first option, which was Ryan in the flat, and Ryan just made unbelievable moves to get in the end zone."

In the event that anyone would ever look back on Brennan's 559 yards and five touchdowns and simply call it dumb luck, Colt — on the next series — delivered one for the training reels that will live forever.

Brennan — with 5:26 to play — effortlessly put the football on the *back shoulder* of speedy wideout Devone Bess in full stride, enabling him to scamper in for the score. "I was open," Bess says, shaking his dreadlocks, "*but that throw — wow!* Colt just gets, like, unconscious out there."

And Colt *still* wasn't finished.

With barely a second more than two minutes remaining in the game, Colt hit Rivers on a quick slant. "We had worked on this play all year," Jones says, "and as soon as I saw they had given up on their zones, I knew they were going to play more man, and I had coached our guys to break the slant flat and run away. Jason did that, broke two tackles, and he was gone."

Seventy-nine yards later, the crowd went wild.

June Jones bowed his head and wiped away tears.

The last shall be first, the scriptures say. . . .

The real fun, though, was happening on defense, where Glanville had all 11 guys on the line of scrimmage, frothing at the mouth in pursuit of Arizona State quarterback Rudy Carpenter, who wouldn't have fared worse had he replaced his jersey with a bulls-eye.

Four sacks. Three forced fumbles. Five tackles for losses.

Defensive end Ikaika Alama-Francis, who didn't even play football in high school, sacked Carpenter to kill one drive; on that play, Ikaika's eyes rolled back, pearl-white, like a shark ripping into its prey. "When Jerry gave us the green light to attack the quarterback," Ikaika says, smiling, "*that's all we needed to hear.*"

Melila Purcell, the other defensive end from Pago Pago, made six tackles, harassed Carpenter into bad throws four times and sacked him twice.

Linebacker Solomon Elimimian, he of Calabar, Nigeria, ran sideline to sideline like a madman, virtually decapitating one runner, hurrying the quarterback, forcing fumbles and recording six solo tackles on the day.

Safety Leonard Peters, a former fire-knife dancer, ignored broken ribs and hit one ASU ball carrier so hard his mouthpiece skittered across the turf. "If football wasn't a contact sport," says Glanville, "Peters would either make it one or quit."

Glanville, true to form, kept sending one linebacker after another — Blaze Soares, Micah Lau, Timo Paepule — until he harassed the Sun Devils into submission.

But the game's greatest untold story is this: Glanville took little-known defensive back Michael Malala and placed him against Zach Miller, Arizona State's famed tight end.

ASU couldn't have prepared for Malala — he had seldom played, except on special teams. But in true Hawai'i form, when Malala's number was called, the Sun Devils would find no way to out-coach his giant heart.

"Malala held their tight end to one catch for three yards," Glanville says. "That kid will spend the rest of his life trying to pronounce *Malala*."

"At one point," Colt says, *"they started playing this in-and-out man technique. We saw that, we know how to beat it really well and we laughed, because they actually put this in to slow us down. It was fun."*

Laughed?

Fun?

Colt, if you ask him, will tell you that it was a very verbal game. "They were playing for pride," he says. "They were wounded. It wasn't a dirty game, just competitive. But we kicked the hell out of them in the second half."

Hawai'i?

Kicking the crap out of . . . anybody?

Are you kidding me?

RALPH "PBASE" OMOTO

Davone Bess escapes another defender

On Salt Lake Boulevard and across the island, *ho'olaule'a,* or street parties, were breaking out everywhere as citizens raucously celebrated their own version of a holiday miracle. People on the mainland were choking on turkey, hams and eggnog as they stared incredulously at their respective flat-screens.

Hawai'i pounded Arizona State to win its fourth bowl game under head coach June Jones

Hawai'i 41, Arizona State 24.

With a recruiting budget one 1/50th the size of the University of Florida?

With dozens of walk-ons who would eventually play in the NFL?

With scores of kids rescued from jail to play NCAA football?

Somehow ranked in the Top 25 football programs in America?

Hawai'i?

Are you kidding me?

Hawai'i finished the season with 27 NCAA all-time records.

Songwriter Martin Smith once penned — in a melody entitled "Not Forgotten" — that *"Love is bigger than oceans / Love is given to me / Grace is bigger than history / Grace is given for free."*

This is a lesson that June Jones III, head coach of the University of Hawai'i, would forever brand on the hide of college football.

As the Hawai'i football Warriors gathered at midfield in the postgame celebration, singing the school alma mater, and then, in a grand finale, repeating the *haka,* history was made.

Tēnei te tangata pūhuruhuru!

It is death, it is life!

This is the man who enabled me to live!

This chapter should end here. However, in the southern deep thirds of the United States lives an old quarterback named Bobby Hebert, who was the Colt Brennan of his era in Louisiana.

Nicknamed the "Cajun Cannon," Bobby is descended from Acadian immigrants from Nova Scotia, a French territory taken over by England in the 18th century. Bobby, you should also know, is in the New Orleans Saints' Hall of Fame, and he will be remembered forever in the National Football League as one of the grittiest gunfighters to ever button up a helmet.

He's also a June Jones protégé, and he watched Hawai'i's dismantling of Arizona State with peculiar interest. While everyone else who saw the game was ready to declare Colt Brennan as the second coming of Dan Marino, the ever-humble Hebert saw a perspective just a little more down-to-earth.

When Hebert speaks, he does so softly, sincerely, and with a deep Cajun staccato.

"Remind that kid," Bobby says, "and I'm not disrespecting him, *but what's his name? Brennan?* Tell him that with June's offense, he can move the *entire defense with his eyes. Tell him to trust June Jones. June doesn't lie to the players.* You can believe this man, I'm telling you.

"Tell him if he pops his eyes, that the flat route underneath is always open. Tell him that second and 4 is always, always better than second and 6 . . . and if he does that, in this offense, *he'll always have the next play to be a hero."*

Hawai'i?

Are you kidding me?

Chapter 2

"WE ARE OUT OF HEROES . . . AND WE ARE OUT OF HOPE"

Hawai'i's rise to football dominance didn't happen overnight. In fact, it almost didn't happen at all.

Insurmountable circumstances seem to be a staple of Hawai'i football history.

From the program's inception, hardly a decade passed without someone questioning if the program would even survive.

No other college football team *but* Hawai'i can use the Empire of Japan's First Air Fleet as an excuse for interrupting the growth of its program, which is exactly what happened on December 7, 1941. On that infamous day, just 11 miles north of the university on what is now Interstate 1, the Japanese sent 49 level bombers, 51 dive bombers, 40 torpedo bombers and 43 fighter planes (183 total) through the misty skies to rain down a fiery hell on Pearl Harbor.

The attack began at 8:30 that morning with the drone of a lone, single-engine Mitsubishi Zero, the lead aircraft in the formation. It was followed by the rattle of machine guns and then intensified as more and more planes in V-shaped formations swarmed like bees across the island.

The ensuing war would suspend Hawai'i football for four years. It was the second time in three decades the program had been ripped asunder, after three seasons were lost due to World War I.

It's hard to believe that, at one time, the Hawai'i football program was arguably as rich in tradition as any program on the mainland.

The first time Hawai'i fielded a football team was in 1909, 40 years to the date after Rutgers beat Princeton in 1869 in the first college football game ever played.

The school changed its name from the College of Hawai'i to the University of Hawai'i in 1920, and three years later upset Oregon State 7-0 as a rainbow appeared over Mō'ili'ili Field. This, by the way, would lead reporters to nickname the team the *Rainbows,* which would result in much consternation in generations and lifestyles to follow.

In 1924 and 1925, the Hawai'i "wonder teams" enjoyed back-to-back undefeated seasons, outscoring opponents 606-29 in 18 games, including wins over Colorado, Colorado State and Washington State. The 1934 team would go undefeated again, and running back Thomas Kaulukukui, who would later become Hawai'i's head coach, set a school record in 1935 with a 103-yard kickoff return for a touchdown.

After years of playing Division II and independent teams, Hawai'i upset Nebraska 6-0 in Lincoln in 1955 in what is still considered to be among the program's biggest wins. Yet the setbacks continued. Just six years later, a lack of finances shut down the program for a *third* time, before new athletic director Young Suk Ko restored it 16 months later.

From 1968 to 1974, under head coach Dave Holmes, the team changed its name to the Rainbow Warriors, won 67 percent of its games and never had a losing season. Its 10-7 upset over Washington, which had been favored by as much as 50 points, was up to that point the biggest upset in school history.

Some 90 percent of Hawai'i's original creatures and plants are found nowhere else on earth. Imagine how breathless white-skinned British explorer James Cook must have been to "discover" Hawai'i's unspoiled beaches and resplendence in 1778, when his boats came upon this luxuriant, velvet volcano in the middle of the ocean.

Prior to Cook, there was nary a single snake, cockroach, deerfly or horse-fly on the islands. Outsiders would eventually introduce Hawai'i to the curses of nonnative plants and bugs and reptiles that still today wreak havoc on the islands' delicate ecosystem.

This is an important bit of history, for it helps one understand why the people of Hawai'i are skeptical toward panderers of their paradise.

This *especially* includes *football coaches,* who historically *took* from Hawai'i more than they *gave* — winners or not.

Perhaps this is *why* the people of Hawai'i carefully choose whom they wish to respect with *aloha.* "Aloha" is generally translated as "hello," "goodbye," or even "love." But often, Western visitors are referred to as haole (pronounced howlee), a term originally describing any foreigner but now applied to whites.

"Haole" can be applied disparagingly to Caucasians. This is because some of the newcomers exhibited cultural arrogance, prejudice and ethnocentric opportunism, and they unintentionally brought disease, devastation and death to the islands.

More than one Hawai'i coach would be remembered as a haole, and a few would be sent packing, being told they could add the word "ass" in front of it as well.

The fortunes of Hawai'i football undulated like the ebb and flow of the frothy surf of Lā'ie Beach for the next 31 years. New coaches thundered in with waves of promise, only to wash out and disappear amidst swirling currents of controversy, more losses than wins or both.

From 1974 to 1976, Larry Price won 15 times but lost 18.

From 1977 to 1986, Dick Tomey would deliver Hawai'i fans a hard-hitting

Larry Price

Bob Wagner

defense and a measure of consistency, winning 63 games against 46 losses. Tomey, however, would leave for *greener pastures* — *get this* — in the *desert,* with the University of Arizona.

The popular Bob Wagner came next, and he would pilot the helm for nine years, posting 58 wins against 49 losses. Wagner had lived in Hawai'i for 19 years, from his hand-to-mouth days as a struggling young coach to the joy of 1992 when he led the team to a share of the WAC title with an 11-win season.

Hawai'i couldn't pay Wagner, much less fund outside *recruiting,* and it was no surprise after he finished 4-8 in 1995 — after his best coordinators had left and after attendance had dropped to an all-time low — that the university cut ties and ushered him to the door.

Regardless, Hawai'i *still* handed him $200,000 to cover his contract. *"That money allowed them to have a clear conscience,"* he told the press.

And so it went, tit for tat. Hawai'i found itself — as usual — *mired* in a whirlpool of frustration, searching for another skipper to right its course.

This dogged program needed *somebody* to *save* it before the decision was made — *again* — to cancel football.

And this was the last chance to save it.

Old-school, ex-military and defensive-minded Fred von Appen became the 19th Hawai'i head coach in 1996. Von Appen was largely unknown; he had mostly bounced around as an assistant under various coaches along the way, including the famed Bill Walsh, yet for some reason he had no head coaching experience.

Granted, there was *one* person who knew von Appen well: Hawai'i Athletic Director Hugh Yoshida. Their relationship, in fact, could be traced back to 1961, when together the two earned all-conference honors at tiny Linfield College in northwestern Oregon.

But before you draw your own conclusions, the *real* reason von Appen

UNIVERSITY OF HAWAII ATHLETICS PHOTO BY EUGENE HOPKINS

Fred von Appen

was hired, for lack of better words, was *pedigree.* The Internet was hardly popular as a method of instant research at that point, and von Appen had been an assistant coach to some powerful men. When phone calls from Dick Vermil, Joe Gibbs, Bill Walsh and other prominent head coaches jammed the phone lines in the Hawai'i Athletic Department, it created more than a ripple in a place not so wise to the ways in which coaches elevate themselves to find such jobs.

Von Appen was firm and boisterous in his interviews, with cookie-cutter answers in a deep voice that mimicked those of his former great coaches, and this further pushed aside other applicants. Finally, Hawai'i regents explained that *yes,* while they were looking for a *head* coach, *no,* von Appen wouldn't be paid as such.

Fred agreed to accept "assistant coach" money, and that was that.

Had anyone dug a little deeper in his resume, they might have discovered an ominous warning.

A few years earlier, as a special teams assistant at Stanford, von Appen's most dubious distinction had been insisting on the squib kick that would allow Cal to weave through Stanford — and its band — for perhaps the most famous, last-second, lateral-filled, game-winning kickoff return in NCAA history.

Sadly, von Appen was about to become another footnote in history — only more of the wrong kind. His Hawai'i teams went 2-10, 3-9, and then 0-12, *losing 18 consecutive games* over his final two seasons.

Everywhere you looked, failure was seeping through the cracks, like urine racing through ceramic grout in the tiny tiles of the coach's bathroom. "We were excited," says one player, *"to just get a first down."* Transfer-quarterback Dan Robinson, who had suffered hairline fractures in *both legs,* fought off all negativity, stumbling around on crutches for three months, watching film, working out his upper body against doctor's orders and gamely vowing to help the team win, someway, somehow.

One spring morning, Robinson — fresh from a weight-room workout — headed up to the football office in his sweat-soaked grays. Looking for extra film time in the hopes of digesting the offense, Robinson bumped into a coach in the hallway, who beckoned him unexpectedly to his cramped office.

Like all boys, Robinson was *excited* to speak with one of his peers. Desperate to play quarterback for the University of Hawai'i, Dan had spent weeks throwing to his own *wife,* because there were no *receivers* around in an off-season program to throw *to.*

Although he was competing with another quarterback for the job, he couldn't wait to tell his coach of his progress; of his understanding of the new offense; of his high hopes for the fall; and how his tight spirals were burning his wife's hands a crimson red.

Coach would be thrilled to hear of the progress of his cracked but healing legs!

"Coach," Robinson said, sitting down in the cramped office, "my legs are doing great —"

The coach interrupted.

"Son," the coach told him, *"I don't think you're ever going to make it here."*

Robinson had to pinch himself, for he couldn't believe what he thought he'd just heard.

Sure, he was little, but he was the *best* they had.

"Why?" he inquired, incredulous, dumbfounded and perplexed by the sudden abandonment, which panged his giant heart, for all this quarterback had ever craved was *acceptance* and *approval.*

This was a kid willing to play his tail off for a hug, and he was facing *rejection* before he ever had a *chance.*

Robinson looked inside himself for answers, and at that moment, there were none.

What, he thought, was this guy *hoping to accomplish,* by *attacking my greatest fears?*

"Well kid," the coach explained, snorting like a skunk at a garden party, *"You're a Mormon. I'm a Roman Catholic. You Mormons just don't understand* the way life is. We Catholics have grown up in *the real world."*

"Are you kidding me?" Robinson asked. Dan had nothing against

> *"Why?" he inquired, incredulous, dumbfounded and perplexed by the sudden abandonment, which panged his giant heart, for all this quarterback had ever craved was acceptance and approval*

Fred von Appen

This is a point Robinson *will take to his grave.*

To Robinson, faith isn't a means to an end, a way to hedge his bets, to curry favor or act as a sycophant or mercenary. His faith stemmed from *true conviction* to do what is *right and what is good.*

"This coach never told me, *'The other guy we have is better than you,'*" Robinson says. "He never said, *'How are your legs?'* He never even brought up *competition.* He never even asked me about *competing.* He just told me I could never compete because I'm . . . a *Mormon?*"

To a quarterback in a bad program trying to swim parallel to shore in a riptide, this was the unkindest cut of all; the surprise in the punch-bowl, the *put-down* that you can't believe you just *heard with your own ears.*

One would think that a coach who knew anything about Mormons wouldn't pick on a kid who had spent a lifetime learning how to *persevere,* and all would soon learn that Robinson had the determination — *and strength* — of Job.

Ask any jockey, and he'll tell you — you don't throw the whole horse away just because he's banged up a little. It's not just speed — it's *heart* — and someone who won't run from a fight.

You never know who you are until you are called to rise.

"I think he just broke his coccyx."

"His what?" von Appen screamed, ripping away his headset. *"What did you say?"*

This might be an injury you would *never* hear a football trainer tell his head coach, but on this day against New Mexico, this was only one of the endless problems Dan Robinson was suffering, and trainers were doing their best to relay the facts to Fred von Appen while simultaneously keeping Robinson standing upright.

Robinson had been routinely described by coaches as "Ichabod Crane," the gangly schoolmaster featured in Washington Irving's *Legend of*

Catholics, but he'd read his Bible inside and out, and nowhere could he find a passage where *quarterbacks* are predestined, regardless of whose interpretation of the Bible you chose to believe.

This legendary tongue-thrashing would become typical of a failing program that didn't know *how* to win. From that point forward, Robinson would be repeatedly told he was nothing more than a lead pony, certainly not a racehorse, and was frequently pushed not to *win,* but to *quit.*

Sleepy Hollow, circa 1820. In case you missed the book, movie or cliff notes, Crane was killed in the novel by the *Headless Horseman.*

Each Saturday afternoon, the Hawai'i coaching staff, while taking no ownership in his fate, would wheel Robinson out again, like a sheep to the slaughter. This day, however, was even worse, as New Mexico's defense featured an up-and-rising star named Brian — *yes, that Brian* — Urlacher, now of the Chicago Bears.

In an interesting subplot, Hawai'i coaches had made a game-time decision to move a defensive end to *offensive guard,* which is like asking a man-eating lion to stop, change gears and join a Broadway play, line-dance and, oh yes, *memorize a script,* all in a single night.

Robinson alone would pay the price.

Twenty-seven times Urlacher planted Dan Robinson into the ground. Twenty-seven times Robinson would somehow struggle to his feet, eyes squinted, sweat dripping from his bloody chin, as he painfully touched his ribs, his knees, his *face,* to make sure all the essential parts were still there. Each time, he would suck in deep breaths until his broken ribs screamed, then exhale and grimace as the pain took hold. He stepped gingerly on a sprained ankle, so as not to make it worse. His tailbone burnt like fire, as if someone were searing his spine with a red-hot poker.

Then Robinson would adjust his thigh pads, his shoulder pads, duck back in the huddle, and call another play.

Robinson wouldn't find out until game's end that *both* shoulders were dislocated, but the pain had been so bad everywhere else, he didn't have time to *feel* those.

Oh, and the *broken coccyx?* That's a shattered tailbone. He had that, too.

UNIVERSITY OF HAWAII ATHLETICS

Dan Robinson

If you've ever seen Urlacher splattering quarterbacks in the NFL on television and wondered what he might do to *you* if he had a running 10-yard head start . . . well, *now you know.*

But 27 times?

It got even worse. During the school's 1998 preseason banquet, the lights dimmed for a showing of the football team's highlight reel from the previous year.

"Highlights?" drawled defensive assistant coach Don Lindsey. *"What highlights? They could fit that film in a skoal can."*

Attendance would plummet to an *average* of 29,274 over von Appen's tenure, but in the final home games of 1998, the stadium was so empty you could hear a pin drop. "They could have fielded a team of cadavers and fared *no worse* than 0-12," penned a local scribe.

Such futility mercifully reached a crescendo, and von Appen was fired.
Hugh Yoshida, von Appen's old teammate, understands how coaches think and act, and he is the first to step forward and ask that people remember the now-retired coach with both grace and mercy.

"Fred just didn't know how to be a head coach," Yoshida says, in retrospect. "He's not a bad human being, trust me.

"But from the public's viewpoint, he and his staff *were* negative. They complained about the locker rooms, they complained about the fields, they complained about our lack of financial resources that they *needed* to win. In the long run, his complaints would help pave the way for changes they enjoy today.

"But at the time, it was difficult and often made things worse."

Players always have mixed memories of their former coaches, and von Appen's are no different. Today they use words such as *eccentric* ... *eclectic* ... *hard-driving* ... and *arrogant* to describe their former boss. Some express remorse over how he will be remembered, while others could care less.

Fred von Appen himself left huffing over the circumstances that surrounded his downfall, but his way with words didn't do him any favors.

"They asked me to win the Kentucky Derby," he frequently told the press, *"but they asked me to do it with mules."*

Now *that* will motivate your quarterback to jump around on all fours *and* throw a saddle on his back.

Truth told, under von Appen, the Hawai'i offense *had* temporarily improved on his watch, albeit from 105th in the nation in 1996 to 103rd in 1997. Then, in a brilliant move, von Appen flip-flopped defensive coach Lindsey, he of the infamous *skoal-can* remark, to *offensive* coordinator, which was like putting a milk bucket under a bull.

Hawai'i fell further, to 118th in 1998; dead-last in the nation.

Honolulu ... overlooking the University of Hawai'i, towards Diamond Head, one of Hawaii's premier locations

Defensive coordinators specialize in *how not to score,* and apparently, when switched to offense, they still adhere to *what they know* — a tidbit someone should've shared with Fred von Appen.

"We never had the same game plan twice," Robinson recalls. "One week we played New Mexico, and I threw the ball *57 times.* The very next week, against Texas El Paso, I threw it *three.* Either way, we were *game-planned to lose.*"

But history is cruel, and it loves scapegoats: The blame will forever fall on the captain of the *Titanic,* not the crew or the iceberg they collectively failed to avoid.

If it's any solace to von Appen, that other aforementioned captain — James Cook — met a similar fate. In 1779, the natives — weary of Cook's excesses — attacked the man they once considered deity, beat him, and skinned him. Von Appen would be similarly thrashed, as the locals rhetorically dismembered him in coffee shops, sports bars and the media.

Hawai'i was the worst college football team in America.

"We were out of heroes," says Robinson. *"And we were out of hope."*

His voice softens, like an air-crash survivor trying to block out the sound of screeching metal, the smell of burning rubber, and the memories of the searing heat.

"I still wanted to play," he adds, sounding nothing like a quitter.

"They may have broken my legs, but they didn't break my heart."

Dan, like all his teammates, simply wanted a *chance.* There's nothing worse than being just a big chunk of talent that, like a block of marble, can't become *anything* without the artisan who is willing to chip away, chip away, chip away, until you become *art.*

▼▼▼▼▼▼▼▼▼▼▼▼▼▼

"They asked me to win the Kentucky Derby," he frequently told the press, *"but they asked me to do it with mules."*

▲▲▲▲▲▲▲▲▲▲▲▲▲▲

Locals refer to gossip as *"the coconut-wireless,"* and coaches, fans and media alike were abuzz across the state of Hawai'i. Debate had shifted from the plainly obvious — *"von Appen must go"* — to the real-life question of *"Who can they pay to stay?"*

The situation was grim. The price to buy out the remainder of von Appen's contract had cost the school an additional $260,000, meaning the University had now spent $560,000 in four years just to *get coaches to leave.*

Three problems were grossly evident, and the media was having a field day. Callers to talk shows like Bobby Curran, Perry and Price and anyone else who would listen cast doubt that school regents could even *find* enough money to *attract* a better coach. Writers such as Stephen Tsai in the *Honolulu Advertiser* and Paul Arnett of the *Star Bulletin* debated whether 0-18 was worth fixing.

Why would any successful coach risk a career to resuscitate the burnt-out Hindenberg?

Hawai'i hadn't faced such public ridicule since the Great Depression in 1949, when the Honolulu Zoo was nearly forced to shut down due to lack of money and total disrepair. The zoo's solution was to purchase a popular local elephant, which brought back crowds and enabled it to buy time and publicity while it found a way to survive.

Where would Hawai'i find another elephant?

The remaining players were wondering the same thing. "A new coach is going to come in here, and in three years, it's going to be the same thing all over again," predicted senior Eleu Kane. *"How long is it going to take for Hawai'i to figure this out?"*

Hawai'i's high school coaches weren't far behind in their opinions, and they further tightened the noose for the potential candidate. "What we need," said Wai'anae High School head coach Leo Taaca, "is a coach who *understands* our local *lifestyle* and our *kids.*"

Farrington High Coach Skippa Diaz agreed. "That 0-12 hurts," he said, "and the problem is that *it took them a long time to get in that hole, and it will take them that long to get out.*"

"There might be no better place to *live* than Hawai'i," wrote Len Pasquarelli of the *Atlanta Journal-Constitution,* "but there is no *worse* place to coach football. Turning around the Hawai'i program will require *progress* just to reach '*shambles*' status."

Pasquarelli also pointed out the budgetary problems within the athletics department and that academic standards would make recruiting — to fix a team this bad — virtually impossible.

What a mess. What a giant, giant mess.

The Hawai'i job was going to require someone bigger than life, someone who felt virtually preordained for the job, someone whose drive exceeded money or facilities or failures, someone who could embrace struggle and felt a higher calling to be there.

While University regents wondered where to find such a unique candidate, Hawai'i itself — the actual state, not the school — already had an idea.

For 30 years, the winds whispering through the thick banyan trees and palm fronds over breathtaking Kapi'olani Park, on the east end of Waikīkī, had held a special secret.

Hawai'i's pleasantly brisk and surprisingly cool trade winds were about to whisper a message to the California coast, where there lived a football coach who had prophesied he would one day coach at Hawai'i.

Now the world would see if he had the guts to chase his dream.

Chapter 3
"A DREAM IS SOMETHING NO ONE ELSE SEES . . . BUT YOU"

Grant High School of Portland, Oregon, traveled to Hawai'i in 1969 to play in a basketball tournament against host Kalani, Farrington and Radford High Schools.

In between games, Artie Wilson and June Jones, two teenage members of that squad, snuck away and found themselves at Kapi'olani Park, breathing in Hawai'i's awe-inspiring beauty, right down to the wizard stones and joggers who ran laps around the perimeter.

Cool ocean breezes speckled their freckled faces. Sitting on a slight hill, they rested their chins in their drawn-up arms; little boys whose little lives made dreaming so much *fun*.

"We sat in this one area," Artie recalls. "When we left Portland, it had been 45 degrees and raining, and when we got to Hawai'i, it was all sunshine, warm breezes and 80 degrees. I remember June just got this glassy look in his eyes, and he kind of stared off into the distance.

"He said, 'Why *would anyone want to be anywhere else?'* We were both in awe. We both agreed that we had to figure out a way to get back here. Then June said, out of nowhere: *'I'm going to coach here one day.'*

"I said, *'What?'* We were just kids. But he said, *'This is where I want to be.'*"

Kapi'olani Park

"Artie," June said, "you're the only person in my life who ever *believes me.*"

"I don't know if I *believe you,*" Artie replied. "But it's definitely OK to *dream,* my brother."

The swaying banyan trees sucked in the secret.

June Jones and Hawai'i now had a date with destiny.

Life, however, in its serendipitous twists and turns, doesn't just *allow* dreams to come true; it demands much, much more. There are always those *small* issues that only *time* can address — you know, *identity, knowledge, free will* — those philosophical wonders we all fleetingly chase, like water rushing toward an open drain.

Yet there's a magic in sports, one that's far more than just competition; more than just endurance, more than camaraderie — sometimes, even more than friendship.

It's the magic of risking everything for a dream that nobody else sees . . . but you.

Real coaches, even if they're wrong, will fight you over this simple fact. If you can beat the dream out of a boy, he becomes a dentist, a real estate broker, or a used car salesman.

If you can beat the dream out of the boy, then, well, *he was never a coach at all.*

The father of modern astronomy was born on February 19, 1473. Who would know that Nicolas Copernicus would develop the first heliocentric model of the universe in modern times? Four hundred and eighty years later, on February 19, 1953, the father of the modern Run 'n' Shoot was born.

Who could know that June Jones III would one day take the reigns of the four-wide offense from Darrel "Mouse" Davis and prove to the world that the *pass,* not the run, is really the center of the football universe?

To be honest, the world should have seen it coming.

When June Jones was a 9-year-old boy, he played only one board game, and not surprisingly, it was one where he could take *strategy* and stick it in your ass.

All-Star Baseball was the real deal.

It wasn't like the lame Strat-o-Matic, which was more simulation focused. All-Star Baseball (ASB), designed by the famous Ethan Allen, had been around for decades. Little June would passionately buy each year's player cards, collect stats, and amass thousands of box scores.

If June and his friends weren't outside flinging a baseball *for real,* they were inside playing the *game* — forming leagues, holding mock drafts and running up and down the street waving the day's results.

The game enabled you to mix and match different eras, so that current major-league stars could play against Hall of Fame players, meaning that you could actually put Pete Rose up against the famed Babe Ruth. The game board for ASB has two spinners on top of a diagram of a baseball field.

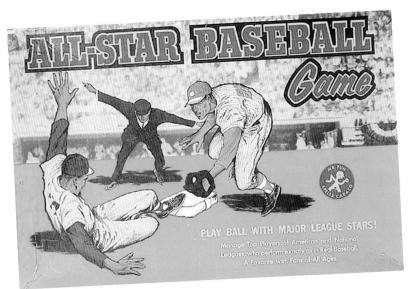

ALL-STAR BASEBALL Game

PLAY BALL WITH MAJOR LEAGUE STARS!
Manage Top Players of American and National Leagues, who perform exactly as in Real Baseball. A Favorite with Fans of All Ages.

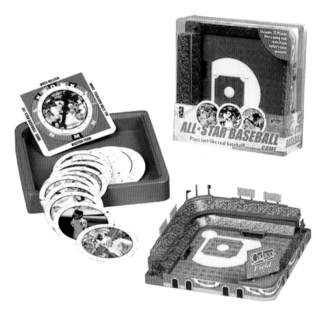

June, on the other hand, absolutely loved it.

In years to come, it would make second and 5, or third and 6, or first and 10 all just a matter-of-fact equation.

Ty Cobb once called George Sisler *"the nearest thing to a perfect ballplayer,"* but June Jones, after years of playing Sisler in All-Star Baseball, disagreed.

"I truly believed that George could've been better," June said, *"if only he had been with the right team."*

Are you kidding me?

God makes certain people to be *players* and certain people to be *coaches.*

Do you need more proof?

Holes for inserting base-runner pegs are located at each base. A cardboard back panel that is inserted into cutout slots in the board displays the key to the game cards and has cardboard wheels that can be turned to display the correct inning, the number of outs and the score.

Each circular player card has a series of lines and numbers arranged in a circle around its center. The card is placed on a spinner, which the batting player spins. Clay Severeide, June, and Artie would spin the metal pointers with rubber bands so as to avoid blisters. Once the spinner comes to rest between two lines, the number for that section defines what happens to that batter.

If one or more runners are on base, the pitching player spins the other spinner, which displays zones that define whether runners advance, score or are out on the play.

Some special plays, as well as attempted steals, require the use of two special pink situation cards that go on the pitching player's spinner and indicate the result when spun.

Confused? For those of you who hate math, you should be.

It's hard to find a sincere love for people of different colors and cultures in middle-class white suburbia, but even from childhood, June Jones III had an uncanny desire to respect and understand others who might not look, talk or necessarily *even believe* like he did. This lifelong career staple would grow to serve him well, perhaps preparing him for the day when he would become head coach of the most racially diverse team in America.

Thus it's not surprising that young June, at age 10, became fast friends with Artie Wilson, one of the black boys on his Little League baseball team. Jones and Wilson would somehow forge a lifelong friendship, in spite of their ebony-and-ivory differences.

"This was a *big deal* when we were growing up in the '60s," recalls Wilson, "because there was *extreme* racial tension. Watts occurred during those years, and there was the civil rights movement. Yet June and I were best of friends, and that didn't sit well with everybody. There are people that, to this day, will never understand our friendship."

In fact, June would attend church with Artie and his family, where he looked like a single marshmallow stuck in a half-gallon of Rocky Road.

Artie's mom insisted they sit directly behind the front row, where each week one peculiar little boy with big ears would constantly turn around and stare directly at June. One Sunday, June couldn't resist. "Haven't you ever seen a *white* boy before?" he whispered. That little boy was Terrell Brandon, who — despite never growing taller than 5-feet-9 — played 13 years in the NBA, including two All-Star seasons.

Wilson's dad, Artie Sr., had played baseball for the Negro League's Birmingham Black Barons, and the boys loved the stories, each one a history lesson within itself. June and Artie Jr. would listen for hours to stories about Piper Davis and Ed Steele. A brash young kid named Willie Mays to this day credits Artie Sr. for teaching him the game of baseball. The senior Wilson amassed 1,609 hits, and he was actually the

COURTESY OF ARTIE WILSON

1948 Negro All Stars from left to right: Verdell Mathis, Artie Wison, Sr., Piper Davis and William Powell

thanks to Artie Sr., Jones talked about talent such as *Oscar Charleston* or *Spotswood Poles* — black men who far outplayed their Caucasian counterparts.

BASEBALL

4TH ANNUAL RICKWOOD CLASSIC

BIRMINGHAM BARONS

(VS)

HUNTSVILLE STARS

SUNDAY MAY 16 2:00 PM

A TRIBUTE TO THE BIRMINGHAM BLACK BARONS

Score Card 100¢

COURTESY OF ARTIE WILSON

Artie Wilson Sr. sliding into third base

COURTESY OF ARTIE WILSON

last .400 hitter in baseball since Ted Williams, when he ended the 1948 season at .402.

"If I hit .400 in the Negro Leagues," Artie Sr. would tell the boys, *"I would have hit higher in the majors, because I would have had better pitches to hit."*

These brash comments made June and Artie giggle with glee, but the stories — oh, the stories! — would last a lifetime. There was the one about the guys who had daytime socks and nighttime socks, the only difference being *the number of holes;* or Cool Papa Bell, who was so fast that he could flip off a light switch and be in bed before the room got dark.

Names such as Ty Cobb, Joe Jackson, Rogers Hornsby . . . these names rolled off the tongues of any *white* boy who followed baseball. But

Thanks to Artie, Jones was given a gift at an early age: He never saw color, but he darn sure *understood results.* June grew up learning that more than 4,000 men had played in black leagues, and *three dozen* of those would fight through segregation, racism and stereotypes to somehow reach baseball's hallowed Hall of Fame. Subconsciously, June would wonder, *what might happen if you were on an island and — like the black leagues — you could find a way to beat the world with the island's own men?*

When Artie was selected to the National Honor Society, Jones stood up and congratulated him with a black power handshake.

"Not cool, not back then," says Artie, who, by the way, has become one of Hawai'i's wealthiest real estate developers. "But June didn't care about anything but *me*. Today, when I see him go for it on fourth down, when I see him throw out of his own end zone, it's because he believes *you should leave it all out there* and that *relationships* are everything, regardless of what color you might be."

"Fourth down on his own goal line? June will kill you. He'll stick the dagger in your heart."

It was an action-packed childhood. June and Artie spent their days playing basketball in June's backyard, baseball in the adjacent park down the street or racing to Yaw's, where they'd munch on the greatest hamburgers ever and wash them down with a Green River soda, a funky combination of 7-Up and lime syrup that pickled your palate and tickled your tongue for a lifetime.

Occasionally, they'd shag fly balls for the Portland Beavers at Civic Stadium, back in the days when there was grass, before Multnomah went modern and installed the crappy artificial turf and field-level box seats.

Jones certainly didn't come from wealth, but his family did well enough in the financial services industry to provide a nice, clean home in one of Portland's conservative, cookie-cutter, middle-class communities.

"Even still," says Wilson, "we all knew that the best future for all of us would be to get a scholarship — for baseball, for basketball, football — *something*."

Apparently, before you achieve, you must believe.

June Jones, like all boys, was far from perfect. Everybody, at least once in their lives, has done something *stupid* — like the time that June and Artie climbed up on the roof of the high school locker room and threw a *metal garbage can* into the adjacent pool at their unsuspecting friend Nick Rulli. This was funny — even *hilarious* — unless it had actually tagged Nick in the head, and June wouldn't be a famous football coach today.

He'd be doing time for involuntary manslaughter.

June was a crazy driver, too.

June's mom had a wood-grained, 1968 Ford Fairlane station wagon, and Artie could never understand how that car stayed running, because Jones rammed it into everything in Portland — especially the cars of the kids from school who delighted in bragging about their nicer rides. When

COURTESY OF ARTIE WILSON

Artie Wilson (center foreground) was an outstanding basketball player, dating back to high school … June Jones above left

Perhaps these are the crazy reasons that June would always understand and appreciate a kid like a Colt Brennan who might need a second chance.

Have you ever said, *"There but for the grace of God go I"?*

Boredom is June Jones' biggest problem. For a man of Jones' mindset, life is a Rubik's Cube, and he simply *toys* and *plays* and *resolves* each situation until it's done, and then he seeks desperately for the next greatest uphill challenge he can find.

At the Portland airport waiting on the flight to Honolulu for the Public School Tournament. Tim Meyers, Artie Wilson, Jackie Chunn, June Jones and Danny Percish

June would pull into Yaw's and see their shiny Camaros and Trans-Ams, he would bump them, just enough to remind them he was there, but not enough to leave a trace.

"If every dent and every ding could tell a story," says Artie, "June would *owe* a lot of people *a lot of money*."

On NE 33rd Boulevard in Portland, there is a street as steep as a ski slope, and driving down it full speed should be illegal. June, on the other hand, would drive as fast as possible, with everything in the beat-up Ford clanging and banging away, and he'd find *new ways* to hit the approach. On any given jump, *anything* could've happened, and June could've killed unsuspecting passers-by.

It is actually *possible* to make a Ford Fairlane *airborne,* but you have to hit it *just right.*

June Jones

1970 Grant High School Varsity Basketball team. Artie Wilson #12 front and center and June Jones #34 on the back row

At age 6, June told himself that he would one day be a professional athlete in some sport. Playing sports for June was a means to an end — something he *would have to do* in order to *coach.*

My, how other kids mocked him . . . until he *performed.*

June never *looked* like an athlete, but my God, how they were shocked when he proved he *was* one. Gangly, even goofy, and never intimidating, Jones just repeatedly — in every sport — *found a way to win.*

It's said that *every* fighter has a *plan,* until he gets a *little blood in his mouth,* and June somehow could find that blood in every opponent at every sport.

In golf, he shot a 72 at age 12 with future PGA pro Peter Jacobson at the Waverly Country Club in Portland, Ore. (This was the same course, by the way, where Hawai'i's Jackie Pung won — and lost — the 1957 U.S. Women's Open when she mistakenly signed the wrong scorecard and was disqualified. Ironically, it had been June's grandfather — June S. Jones Sr., president of the Waverly Country Club — who had handed Jackie the winning trophy before the error was discovered.) June would lay down his clubs, however, and not pick them up again until — against all odds — he would play in the NFL.

In hockey, June went to every Portland Buckaroos game at the Memorial Coliseum and learned the intricate details of the Western Hockey League. He learned to whistle a slap shot past either one of your ears.

In baseball, June could rear like a stallion on the mound and throw a fastball down your throat.

Then he met a guy named Jim Chambers, who had played at Roosevelt High School and eventually the Baltimore Orioles. Chambers admonished young June to *pitch,* not just *throw.*

Chambers explained to June the importance of *developing other pitches* and showed him how a slider could dance and sway like a goddess and make hitters absolutely guess about things like *timing* and *speed and where the ball might be.* June learned that *the mystery* of what *might happen* could hold a hitter's attention just as well as a fastball down the pipe.

Jones hated school, and he hated studying more, but he understood what was necessary enough to go through the motions, score straight A's and become Portland's *National Scholar Athlete.*

When provoked to fight, June would confound his aggressors with *logic,* never raising his voice.

The problem was that no scholarships exist for *coach.*

June Jones has *always* loved the underdog. He believes that people with heart, indeed, have a chance, but that without *coaches* to direct them, then, to be honest, the underdog is just waiting to get his or her ass whipped.

June Jones wanted the shot to coach those *underdogs.*

"What always amazed me," says Artie, "was his ability to *compute.* June could analyze any game, any situation, and figure out a way to be a *difference-maker.* He wasn't fast, he wasn't strong, he just knew how to win, and he could beat you at your own game."

COURTESY OF ARTIE WILSON

June Jones has itty-bitty hands.

"June used to say,' *Man, if only I had your hands!*'" chuckles Artie Wilson.

All mankind is guilty of uttering, *"If only!"*

But if June had *those hands,* history would have to be rewritten and we might never have been blessed with his *true calling.*

Bigger hands, for June, would have meant athletic stardom. Bigger hands would have pushed June across that finish line between athlete and coach. Funny, but had God granted June *bigger hands,* you would not be reading this book.

COURTESY OF ARTIE WILSON

1970 Grant High School Varsity Football. June Jones #10 top right

Athletes are individuals, and they work very hard to improve themselves. Coaches, on the other hand, spend a lifetime improving *others*.

How many times have you prayed for *bigger hands?*

What if God's answer to your prayers is to take your own *itty-bitty hands and find a way to win?*

John Robinson, Dan Fouts and Bobby Moore were standing outside an American Legion baseball game, waiting for a chance to talk to that night's starting pitcher — a kid by the name of June Jones. Robinson was the offensive coordinator of the University of Oregon; Fouts, of course, was the Ducks' starting quarterback, and Moore, well, he was a pretty good wide receiver, who would eventually change his name to *Ahmad Rashad*.

They took the flabbergasted young June out behind the school for a game of catch.

In years past, Jones' father had routinely taken him to Eugene to watch Bob Berry and Tom Blanchard quarterback the Ducks, but June had no idea Oregon had any interest in *him* until — bam! — they just appeared *en masse* at his baseball game. Before you knew it, Bobby Moore was running pass routes in the shadows and June was tossing him tight spirals, while Dan Fouts taught him a thing or two about how to hold the laces.

"I couldn't believe it," says June, "I mean, I had forever been an Oregon Ducks' fan, but I never dreamed they wanted *me*. I was blown away. We're talking about *Dan Fouts* and *Bobby Moore*."

"If you come to Oregon," John Robinson said, "you will be *the next Dan Fouts*."

Never mind that the workout was against NCAA rules or that Robinson had told the *very same thing* to five other quarterbacks.

Life, however, in its serendipitous twists and turns, doesn't just allow dreams to come true; it demands much, much more. There are always those small issues that only time can address – you know, identity, knowledge, free will – those philosophical wonders we all fleetingly chase, like water rushing toward an open drain.

The star-struck Jones headed to the University of Oregon and, after a year and a half of sitting on the bench, reality settled in.

With *three other quarterbacks sitting in front of him,* including future Hall of Famer Dan Fouts, Jones suddenly realized that when it comes to college football, all that glistens isn't gold, and that *coaches* and *promises* usually don't belong in the same sentence.

His best friend Artie was playing basketball on scholarship at Hawai'i.

If I'm not going to play, June reasoned, *at least I can have my friend.*

So Jones transferred to Hawai'i, his next whistle stop on a train ride of broken dreams, where he would continue to sit *for nearly another three years.* He would earn two letters in baseball, play JV basketball under a guy named Rick Pitino, but in football — *nothing: 10 plays in that entire time.*

The handwriting was on the wall.

Dave Holmes was the Hawai'i head coach, until they fired him for winning, and he was replaced by a guy named Larry Price. Price would install an offense called the *Hula-T,* tell Jones he couldn't wear white shoes like Joe Willie Namath.

Since Price had told the players they could not have facial hair, Jones, in protest, grew a Fu Manchu mustache that would stay with him in some form all the way through 2006.

This whole football thing had run its course.

June was done.

Dave Holmes

UH SPORTS MEDIA RELATIONS BY RON IHORI RKI PHOTOS

He made up his mind. He was going to follow his father into the financial services industry and be *done* with this whole football thing altogether.

June was so tired of coaches who acted like their job was not to *make* a boy but to *break* a boy, and he refused to be *their boy*.

June decided to go home, transfer to Portland State University, get his degree and move on with his life.

June Jones as a lanky, high school quarterback ...

Chapter 4

"SHOW ME A GUY WHO CAN THROW, AND I'LL SHOW YOU A GUY WHOSE HIPS WE CAN FIX"

Hips.

Hips are perceived differently by women than men. When a woman is pregnant, her *hip*s will tell her if she's carrying a boy or a girl. A woman instinctively learns from an early age to use her *hips* to measure pressure or pain. To a woman, *hips are intimate. Hips* can move an unborn child from the back to the front, like away from the *coccyx.* In art and culture, *hips* are often viewed as a symbol of fertility.

Boys and men, on the other hand, don't know how to use their hips.

But in 1964, a *high school coach in Portland, Ore.,* would build an *entire offense around hips, and the game of football would never be the same.*

▼▼▼▼▼▼▼▼▼▼▼▼▼▼

While other coaches would fall in love with the sound of their own voices, Mouse fell in love with a receiver's hips, or a quarterback's eyes. A quarterback, you see, could take full advantage of the safety by simply driving him out of the center of the field with his eyes. A slotback, then, could take full advantage of the safety's absence by driving off a linebacker with his hips and creating space down the hash.

▲▲▲▲▲▲▲▲▲▲▲▲▲▲

Mouse took Ellison's base formations and began to add more layers, based on years and years of discovery, things like field markers and hashmarks and base routes, and how a player could use his shoulders to *lean his way* into *open space.*

Spread the field: two outside wide receivers, two inside slots, space out the linemen.

If the other guys were going to be bigger, faster and stronger, then hell, make 'em defend the *entire field.*

And that's when it hit him: *hips.*

Mouse suddenly realized that in a single second, he could grasp everything about *fluidity* or *range of motion* or a player's ability to *play under control,* the way you *plant a foot* and move to the left or to the right: All of these secrets could be unlocked by simply watching *their hips.*

Out-manned and out-gunned and weary of having his boys trounced by *bigger* boys, Darrel "Mouse" Davis *had to find another way to win.* It seemed that his kids were never big enough, strong enough or fast enough to simply blow people off the ball in the offenses he'd tried, like the traditional Wing-T, the veer, or the option.

Mouse had experimented with putting kids in the slot position and using the hashes to open up the field. But the seminal moment occurred when another coach showed him a book by Glen "Tiger" Ellison entitled *The Run and Shoot,* and suddenly *it all made sense.*

Mouse, all 5 feet 8 inches of him, had *discovered a way to measure a kid's heart.*

Perhaps because he was so little himself, Mouse Davis would devise a *system* around things that would have nothing to do with traditional size, strength or speed.

Given no other choice, he began to coach football *backwards.* He went from one thought process to another, working the scenarios until he found something that *worked.*

Mouse Davis, the "Godfather" of the Run 'n' Shoot

Like boxing, sometimes the best way to deliver a punch *is to step back,* like offensive linemen who were too small to push a frog off a log — but darn sure could stand up and use their hands and *technique* to shield a quarterback for three and a half seconds while he put the bird in the air.

By *watching a boy's belly button,* Mouse Davis could determine *skill,* and football is little more than a solid game of chess.

"I decided that all this talk about size and strength was bullcrap," Mouse says. "And I was determined to *prove it.* Who said *you can't win with little kids? Who made that rule?* I believe you can take a little kid, and if you can teach him *how* to turn little plays into *big plays,* then, well, *he's not that dang little anymore.*"

And so it went. Mouse Davis developed entire *positions,* such as *slotbacks* and *S-backs,* and made it clear to these players that, unlike other coaches, he cared less about *punishment* and more about *self-discipline.*

Punishment, Mouse believed, only created *fear.* Mouse would teach generations of coaches that true coaching, true motivation, true *discipline* doesn't stem from *anger* but from *love.*

While other coaches would fall in love with the sound of their own voices, Mouse fell in love with a receiver's hips or a quarterback's *eyes.* A quarterback, you see, could *take full advantage of the safety* by simply *driving him out of the center of the field with his eyes.* A slotback, then, could take full advantage of the safety's absence by driving off a linebacker *with his hips* and *creating space down the hash.*

And so it was that Mouse began to inflict *hips* on other coaches.

For an amazing five-year period in the history of Portland high school football, *hips* would become the measure of both pressure and pain.

And then, like only a Mouse can, he would scurry to a hole on the back side, call the *Scramble Right 90 Switch* — and boom! — *big-time touchdown,* and suddenly little boys who had been put down and defeated for a lifetime were jumping up and down and celebrating in the end zone like it was Christmas.

Fun is contagious, and Mouse Davis put the *fun* back in football, into the hearts of boys who, unbeknownst to themselves, had the right *hips* to carry them to victory.

The history books now pour out the names like a rushing brook: John Buchanan . . . *really fast, great hips, could really run;* Bobby Zeigler, Gordy Gredvig, little Billy Kellar . . . a hurdler, and *wow,* do hurdlers have *great hips;* Bob Palm, John Mills, Clint Didier, John Errness, Dave Stief . . . the list goes on and on.

And make no mistake — film doesn't lie, and Mouse was never far away, watching every single step of every single play of every single boy and how he moved his *hips.*

Mouse had made a *career decision* to *build up,* not *tear down* his troops, but that would never give his kids an excuse to question *where* to place their *feet.*

To beat Goliath, David needed only confidence, a slingshot, and three smooth stones. But like David, with the Run 'n' Shoot — *if you could shoot straight* — you would need just one.

Kids that once were afraid to line up in formation suddenly *couldn't wait to play.*

And — *truth be told* — you might want to button your hat and tighten your laces, or Mouse and his little boys with *great hips* just might embarrass you, like the one night they passed and threw to perfection, giggled and hung 105 points on the board — *and didn't give up a single one.*

Are you kidding me?

Mouse Davis and his offense, along with three straight state high school titles, earned him the right to become head coach at tiny Portland State University. It was there that somebody told him about a quarterback who, fed up with football, had transferred from Hawai'i, a Division I school, to simply finish out his degree.

Mouse burrowed in, tantalized by the thought of finding a *true* quarterback.

PORTLAND STATE UNIVERSITY DEPARTMENT OF INTERCOLLIGIATE ATHLETICS

The career of Mouse Davis spans five decades

Don't get me wrong: Mouse totally believes in the underdog, and he knew that he had built a better mousetrap, but he couldn't help but ponder what might happen in his offense if you had a *thoroughbred* pulling the trigger.

So he set out to find June Jones III and convince him that returning to football might just be the best choice of his life. He was going to *hug* this kid and tell him he *loved* him — and tell him if he could put the ball in the air, he could make him the best quarterback God ever created.

And for the record, June's *hips,* back then, had more dings than his mother's old Ford Fairlane.

But show me a guy who can throw, Mouse thought, and *I'll show you a guy whose hips I can fix.*

Chapter 5

"A REVOLUTIONARY WINNER . . . AND A CULTIVATOR OF MEN"

An odyssey can be defined as a long wandering marked by many changes in fortune, and before June Jones would become a modern-day Tom Blake and Hawaiian hero, then he, too, would have to chart a similar and amazingly serendipitous course.

Just as two colliding atoms can oscillate together to create perfect *timing,* so apparently two human beings can randomly collide in a *chance* meeting and have their lives forever changed.

It's hard to imagine that the modern renaissance of today's Hawai'i football program might actually be traced to Palouse, Wash., a tiny enclave in the eastern region of the state, where in late spring the wheat is still green and ripples like water.

Yet it's true. In 1932, Palouse was a land of amber waves where warm-hearted farmers learned to thrive behind inspiration, cultivation, dedication and perspiration. How perfect, then, that in September of that year, Palouse gave birth to native son Darrel "Mouse" Davis, the fifth of five children.

Forty-three years later, Mouse, as the new head coach of Division II Portland State University, would collide with quarterback June Jones, who had been oscillating back and forth between two universities for four years and had finally quit football "for good" after playing just 10 downs in that entire span.

Mouse would nibble through a myriad of NCAA regulations to enable June an opportunity to enjoy one final year of eligibility. He invited Jones to join the team for spring practice.

Neither man could possibly understand the lifelong ramifications of the scenario that was about to unfold. Soon, very soon, Mouse and June

The irascible Darrel "Mouse" Davis

would both be teaching the world a thing or two about *timing,* and both would be joined at the *hips* for life.

Fascinated by this new coach, June did his homework and discovered that this Mouse character was willing to test the vertical and physical limitations of both players *and the field on which they played.*

Davis jokingly considered himself not to be short but *"height-challenged."* June, he of the *itty-bitty hands,* bonded further with Davis after learning his coach had been given the nickname "Mouse" by his older brother Don due to Davis' own *tiny hands.*

"You have hands like a mouse!" his brother once declared, when as boys Davis misplayed a Little League baseball.

Yet decades later, as "luck" would have it, who better to mentor *itty-bitty hands* than a man with hands *like a Mouse?*

Furthermore, Mouse was charming, witty, with bright eyes, a warming laugh and giant heart much larger than his diminutive size. He always had a quip, a quote or a chuckle, always something *positive* and a way to brighten your day.

Jones, he of the Fu Manchu mustache, Joe Willie Namath facemask and white shoes, loved both the rebel and the underdog, so he quickly became fascinated by Davis' wide-open Run 'n' Shoot philosophy, which challenged every long-held coaching theory that insisted one must be big and tall in order to win.

Speed, of course, helps *any* offense, but in the Run 'n' Shoot, you didn't necessarily *have* to be fast either.

So when Davis invited Jones to participate in spring drills, June initially was reluctant.

Mouse's challenge for him to play again was so, well, *uplifting,* as opposed to the *oppressing arrogance* of his former coaches, he actually thought he had a chance to play and found it downright difficult to resist.

June Jones at Portland State

Life is full of freeze-frame, *what-if* moments, but this one was monumental: It would have historical, record-setting *future* ramifications for the University of Hawai'i — and for the *future* of the NCAA record books.

June Jones told Davis, yes, I'll play, but with a caveat: *only in spring practice.*

That March, Jones tucked his bushy hair into a Portland State helmet, ran a hand across his mustachioed face and trotted out for practice in his trademark white cleats.

Life is about choices, options and decisions. *With that single decision, Jones — and all of football — would never be the same.*

Had he said no, June today would be a financial planner, Hawai'i would still be losing — and you wouldn't be reading this book.

The bias against the forward pass is deeply ingrained in football. It was *illegal* until 1906, and even then it was severely restricted. It wasn't until 1933 that a quarterback was allowed to throw a forward pass from anywhere behind the line of scrimmage.

Once legalized, it was disdained, in large part because it had been legalized to make the game safer, and a big point in the game's favor to those who played it was its *danger*. Right up until the mid-1940s, in a rearguard attempt to slow the spread of such perceived cowardice, roughing the passer was actually *encouraged*.

Then a small-college coach named Elmer Berry, who had used an innovative passing attack to sneak up and beat bigger schools, got so worked up about the anti-pass sentiment that in 1921 he penned a scathing book entitled *"The Forward Pass in Football."* As he wrote,

> Apparently, many regard the forward pass simply as a valuable threat, something for occasional use, something to take a chance with, something the possibility of which makes the real game still workable.

> To a large degree, this is the attitude of the larger colleges. In general, they frown upon the forward pass; opposed it, sneered at it, called it basketball, and have done what they could to retard its adoption. It has taken away from the advantage of numbers, weight and power, and made the game one of brains, speed, strategy — *even luck if you please* — and rendered the outcome of their "practice" games with smaller colleges uncertain.

Uncertain, indeed: If there's anything Mouse Davis *loves,* it's the look of an *uncertain* defense.

Succeeding with the offense, Davis decided, would come down to *a unique blend of technique.* He made Ellison's simplistic formation come to life behind his passion for perfection. Davis had mouse-model-tested his theories for 15 years at the high school level, and he was ready to prove himself right again at the collegiate level.

Mouse and all of his future protégés became sticklers over tedious repetition, repetition, repetition: For a ball and receiver to arrive together, the timing had to be perfect — and for the players, *second nature.*

Mouse exalted the virtues of precision and consistency, as well as the *predictability of defenses.*

Davis had built a better mousetrap to compensate for his team's deficiencies only to learn that it offered some surprising advantages. First, it delivered the ball into a runner's hands on the other side of the line of scrimmage, thus removing the biggest defensive beasts between the quarterback and the goal line.

One, two, three four, throw: Note June's eyes, hips and shoulders as he quarterbacks Portland State

The pass had always been viewed as a complement to the run, but it apparently could function as a substitute as well.

Next, by dividing the field into thirds and then shortening — and timing — the passing game, he had reduced the number of decisions his quarterbacks had to make. In doing so, Davis had reduced the passing game's biggest risks: *interceptions and incompletions.*

Mouse put a man in motion to hold the defense in check until the snap of the ball. "Our receivers get at least *half* their yards *after* the catch," Davis says.

By spreading the field, his teams were always one missed tackle from a touchdown; the tighter teams played him to prevent the short pass, the more it opened up the deep ball.

Do that against a Mouse Davis team, and trust me, then and now, you will pay.

"One, two, three . . . throw! One, two, three, four . . . throw!"

In the spring of 1975, June Jones could not believe his eyes.

First of all, a Mouse Davis *practice,* much less a game, is a thrilling aerial circus, with footballs heaved in long arches in every direction and receivers as quick as water bugs licking up footballs on every single open patch of grass.

Second, Jones saw, for the first time, a *head coach* actually *coaching,* with *everything* centered on the *forward pass.*

One-two-three-four . . . throw!

Mouse even coached the offensive linemen, teaching them to work off the balls of their feet, butts upright, and how to handle the assault of four or five — *even six* — guys coming with their ears pinned back.

To someone as swift of mind as June, who had been jerked around by two

▼▼▼▼▼▼▼▼▼▼▼▼▼

Just as two colliding atoms can oscillate together to create perfect timing, so, apparently two human beings can randomly collide in a chance meeting and have their lives forever changed.

▲▲▲▲▲▲▲▲▲▲▲▲▲

previous schools and countless coaches, it was as if he had been told he couldn't play a radio but was now being asked to conduct a symphony orchestra.

He also was startled at the way Mouse constantly integrated inspiration, dedication, perspiration and *cultivation,* ever so slowly rebuilding their confidence and self-esteem in a manner that would give his kids a *chance* to win.

Best of all, June couldn't believe *how wide open* his receivers were, compared to the rote offenses he'd studied and tried to quarterback before.

Learning a system based around *individual belief* and *personal discipline* was *powerful* to June Jones. He, in his two other stops, had grown accustomed to coaches just yelling, screaming and *making* a kid do something he inherently didn't believe in or couldn't comprehend.

In Mouse Davis, Jones had found something he could both *love and embrace.*

It all made perfect *sense.*

Everything was based on *timing.*

Quarterbacks weren't just throwing from the pocket, *but mostly on the run.* And — get this — *lifting their right foot on the follow-through,* absolute heresy throughout modern football history.

Mistakes were eliminated via *repetition.*

Space was created by *spreading the field.*

And June was hearing directions the likes of which he'd never witnessed:

"Quarterbacks — 'bug' your eyes! Show the safety the whites of your eyes! Use your eyes to move him one way or the other!"

"Slotbacks — keep your hips under control!"

"Receivers — catch the ball in the noose!"

There were go-routes and choice routes — Jones could actually *choose* his receiver! June was winging the ball deeper than ever before, and best of all, there were *receivers right there to catch them!*

Coaching legend Mouse Davis, circa 1975

"You seem to have a lot of faith in me," June told Mouse.

"That's what fathers *do!*" cracked Mouse. "Now, *keep throwing, kid.*" Before the deciduous trees in the daily Portland rain would have a chance to turn crimson, before the maple trees blistered red, June Jones would be a starting quarterback — *for the first time in his life.*

It's a bumpy ride through the deep orange hues of the mountainous Big Pass between Portland, Ore., and Bozeman, Mont., but it's a necessary evil when your budget is as small as your players and you have a game to play the next day against Montana State.

It was there that a young June Jones would begin to get his hips right, begin to come of age, hit the *90 Z Switch*, (as Mouse would later describe) *"right down the rail for the touch,"* and earn the starting job at Portland State for keeps.

Mouse had done what great coaches do: He gave a worthy player *hope* by reigniting his competitive fire. History could finally be made, as Jones was about to make the most of this unlikely redemption. Soon, June would emulate his new head coach, in more ways than just one. Like Mouse Davis, he would not only become a revolutionary winner, but also a cultivator of men, and he wasted very little time in doing so.

Just ask Hawai'i native Mel de Laura, who was about to be swept into the odyssey of June Jones III.

Chapter 6
IT PAYS TO BE STRONG

In September 1975, George Lucas crafted a make-believe story of what would eventually become *Star Wars Episode IV: A New Hope*, which would smash Hollywood box-office record books.

That very same year, 958 miles north of Hollywood, up the 405 and into the splendor that is Portland, Ore., a real-life story of new hope was coming soon to a stadium near you, and it too would assault the record books of the NCAA.

Never underestimate a genius with a chip on his shoulder, and Mouse Davis, who had been told countless times his rinky-dink, high school Run 'n' Shoot offense would never work at the collegiate level, was about to drive his point home with characters who, over time, would prove to be as memorable as Luke Skywalker himself.

Davis' script was all about second chances and proving to the world he could win football games with his own version of *Star Wars*. He had reignited the engines and laser arm of burned-out quarterback June Jones, who was dazzled by the Davis aura and system and had made the decision to play one more year.

And while June's story was unfolding into a pretty remarkable one, Jones himself was about to do one better when — with the permission of Mouse — he invited a troubled but talented wide receiver from Hawai'i to join him in his redemptive effort at Portland State in 1976.

Mel de Laura, who had a bit of a chip on his shoulder himself, was about

▼▼▼▼▼▼▼▼▼▼▼▼▼▼

Never underestimate a genius with a chip on his shoulder, and Mouse Davis, who had been told countless times his rinky-dink, high-school Run 'n' Shoot offense would never work at the collegiate level, was about to drive his point home with characters who, over time, would prove to be as memorable as Luke Skywalker himself.

▲▲▲▲▲▲▲▲▲▲▲▲▲▲

to become June Jones' first ironic decision that would lead, 24 years later, into helping build the University of Hawai'i into the haven of hope it is today.

Who could ever have predicted that in 2007, in what seemed like a galaxy far, far away, the NFL would draft or sign 11 players from the University of Hawai'i and that Mel de Laura would be one of their primary sources of strength?

The definition of fate is "an *inevitable event predestined*," and it was on the practice field one afternoon at the University of Hawai'i that June Jones and Mel de Laura met while tossing footballs as young quarterback and receiver during the Larry Price era.

They quickly connected over the fact that both were already married, with children either already born or on the way, and they lived next to each other in the Red Hill subdivision, on Ala Kapuna Street.

That's where the similarities ceased, making this relationship a most unlikely one.

June had been reared in upper-middle-crust Portland; not so de Laura, who grew up on the gritty streets of Pālolo, with four brothers and a sister. As kids, they played basketball on a dirt court and football on a gravel driveway. His father worked two jobs; one at the submarine base at Pearl Harbor, and the other serving as the only refrigerator-air-conditioning man in Hawai'i.

Trouble came early and often to de Laura, whose neighborhood park was populated by glue sniffers and pot smokers. He had his first fight in the third grade, when he bounced a boy off a flagpole, which, as Mel recalls, "put a big ol' lump on his head." He liked fighting, and that would lead to years of altercations. "But that first fight, that's where it all started," he says.

Though he attended Damien, a local private school, he spent as much time wasting his opportunity as his parents did trying to pay for it. His behavior was unlike that of most athletes, as he spent his free time smoking cigarettes, drinking and making poor choices of friends. He didn't even play football until his freshman year, when he promptly quit.

As a sophomore, he applied himself and became a starting defensive back and wide receiver. Coaches raved about his speed and natural ability. De Laura, however, stupidly broke into the athletics office a week before the first game, stole shirts and shoes and then was kicked out of school and banned from sports.

Frustrated, his mother enrolled him in a weight-lifting club, another of God's tiny, fragile twists for which we all can only pray. His body responded and swelled, and by his junior year he was a punter, a tight end — and then he became *lineman of the year.*

Mel de Laura worked his way to become one of the strongest wide receivers in all of football. Though he was only 5-feet-10 and 185 pounds, he would eventually bench-press 485 pounds and run like a deer. It wouldn't be long before he found himself one day on the practice field as a wide-out at the University of Hawai'i, where a young quarterback named June Jones asked him to play a little catch, and history was made.

A year later, Mel and June found themselves at Portland State, where Mouse Davis would amazingly squeeze another year of eligibility out of the NCAA for them both.

This, my friends, is just the beginning of the story.

There's a magic in football, and sometimes it's about chasing a dream no one sees but you. Mel started out fifth on the depth chart but

Before there was Davone Bess or Ashley Lelie in the Run 'n' Shoot … there was Mel de Laura …

didn't stay there long. The first chance he was given in practice, de Laura took a short pass and darted 70 yards for a touchdown.

He also spiked the ball, which promptly brought the attention of Davis. *"We don't do that here!"* Mouse said, referring to the spike.

Then, on the very next play, de Laura did it again — boom! — *70 yards down the hash,* hips heaving like Secretariat, for *another* score. He spiked it again, too, but this time Davis just *grinned,* because all coaches get a little smarter when a true racehorse shows up.

De Laura was exactly the kind of player Mouse Davis loves — undersized, hard-working, and with a heart bigger than his biceps.

"Mel was a freak of nature," says Mouse. "He simply had been overlooked and needed a second chance. *But what I liked most about Mel was that he could score."*

"Mouse was such a father figure," de Laura says. "If it hadn't been for Mouse and June, I don't know where I would be in my life. As a player, I had been good everywhere I went, but I didn't get the ball. Everywhere Mouse and June go, it feels like a family, and *they just make it fun again.* I had never really been coached before, either."

He'd also never been *so wide open.*

Not surprisingly, there would be one more critical element to this story.

"I was a split end when I got to Portland State," de Laura says. "But Mouse moved me to slotback, *because he told me I had great hips."*

Oh, and did it ever become fun again.

Davis was ready for his collegiate premiere; his team, ready for theatrical review. Jones and de Laura — and some pretty good other players with names like Dave Stief and Clint Didier — began to set the first precedent of all Mouse Davis–June Jones teams: *shatter records.*

That's when a college football team that no one cared about just a single year before would send shivers down the spines of rain-soaked fans and blow the lights out of the scoreboard at Portland's Civic Stadium. Yes, this was the same stadium where Jones had grown up shagging flies with little Artie Wilson.

Leave it to a Mouse to turn mere crumbs of a program into a gourmet meal.

"One game," says de Laura, "it was unbelievable. June threw for, like 600 yards, and the *backup* threw for like *400?* This offense is nuts, bro. I would just come back to the huddle laughing and say, June, c'mon, *throw me the ball!"*

Jones would finish the year with a Division II record of 3,518 yards, while de Laura caught more balls than any receiver in the country.

An even more amazing footnote is that Jones rewrote the NCAA record books the year before the radical rule changes that would eventually open up the passing game for all quarterbacks. The liberal rule changes the following year would actually play right into the hands of Mouse — and of course, June Jones.

Learning the offense, Jones watched and listened to every single thing Mouse Davis said and did with great detail. "I wrote down everything, and I mean *everything,*" June says today. When picking up the hardware for his 1925 Nobel Prize, George Bernard Shaw said, *"All forward progress depends on unreasonable people,"* which, therefore, makes Mouse *at least* the football equivalent of a Nobel *candidate.*

There were still coaches who laughed at Davis' theories, as if he was a little kid who thought he could fly by jumping off a roof with an umbrella — but not June Jones.

Furthermore, Davis had given Jones more than just a playbook. He had given him a game plan for *life* about how to coach *people.* All successful formulas contain strong principals and core values, and June was a *formula strategist.*

Jones, ever the quiet thinker, had already begun to take the influence of Mouse, and he was already adding wrinkles of his own, plotting the day when he would be a coach who might just *never run the ball once* during a real game.

Mel de Laura today as a Hawai'i assistant coach

The word "resurrection" means *"a coming to life again, being alive again after death,"* and both Mel and June had experienced *second chances* — and, to steal from George Lucas — *a new hope.* They found themselves on airplanes being courted by NFL teams as free agents, and both signed with the Atlanta Falcons.

Incredible.

But the story doesn't end there. Sadly, the careers of June Jones and de Laura would suddenly take separate paths. Jones' would skyrocket, while de Laura's, at times, would fall on bitterly difficult times. After injuries ended his playing career, Mel bounced around in odd jobs, small-time coaching positions, even working as a bouncer and a truck driver.

"I was the type of guy that didn't pass up *anything,*" de Laura says. "I had to work odd jobs to survive. I hung around again with some of the wrong guys. *Maybe I was the wrong guy.*"

Then, one day seven years ago, while working as a truck driver in Oregon and coaching at a tiny high school, Mel received a phone call.

It was his old friend June Jones, who offered him a chance to return home and become the strength coach at the University of Hawai'i. Mel de Laura would return to Hawai'i, where he would not only be reunited with June but also his father, whom he would get to enjoy before he passed away.

Today, de Laura runs one of the top strength programs in all of college football.

Above all else, to de Laura, June was *loyal,* a trait that meant more than anything else. "You can count on June," de Laura says. "Even when you get in some trouble, he'll be right there for you, even if you've made a mistake."

Chapter 7
FOOTSTEPS TO HAWAI'I

There's a fine line between a *mission* and a *journey,* but each requires the other.

When the Hawai'i football Warriors won 11 games in 2006, pundits called it luck, critics called it a weak schedule, and the entire nation simply didn't see it coming. But the resurgence of Hawai'i football had been 30 years in the making, and from the time June Jones stepped foot on a field in the National Football League, he had been *preparing* for the day when he would assume command of the Hawai'i program.

Hawai'i's *"surprising"* success was not the least bit so to those who knew him well.

You see, the *pioneering* of *any* enterprise contains the *soul* of it, and within *the first steps of any journey* one usually finds the whole *motive, purpose* and *plan* of the venture. Without a *beginning,* there can be no end; had one paid close attention to each of June's stops prior to his Hawai'i ordination, one would have seen this unfolding like a red-splashed Pachi Pachi flower.

All of June Jones' experience in the NFL would not only overqualify him to captain the ship at Hawai'i, but it would also demonstrate a three-decade *consistency of purpose.*

June Jones, with the Atlanta Falcons in 1978

JUNE JONES
QUARTERBACK
FALCONS

Height: 6'4" Weight: 200 College: Portland State
Drafted: No Acquired: Signed as Free Agent, 1977
Birthdate: 2-19-53 Home: Portland, Oregon

512 JUNE JONES

◆ QUARTERBACK

Passing Record					
YEAR	TEAM		ATT	COM	YDS	TDS
1977	Falcons	NFL	1	1	-1	0
1978	Falcons	NFL	79	34	394	1
Lifetime Totals			80	35	393	1

Possessed with a great arm and much potential, June was Falcons' backup quarterback in 1978. He enjoyed an outstanding career at Portland State, firing 25 touchdown passes and throwing for 3518 yards during senior campaign.

JUNE ENJOYS THE STOCKMARKET BUSINESS.

© 1979 TOPPS CHEWING GUM, INC. PRTD. IN U.S.A.

Steve Bartkowski, Bob Gagliano, Barry Sanders, Bobby Hebert: What do they have to do with the Hawai'i football program?

Before June Jones would complete his mission of seeing his footprints again on the beaches of Waikīkī, he would have to endure a journey that would take him through Atlanta *twice,* bitter winters in Canada, Denver and Detroit, hot summers in Houston *twice* and, finally, San Diego.

Through each test, June continued to glean ideas from other coaches and pad his playbooks on *both* sides of the ball. He worked with people and players of all sizes, cultures and *attitudes,* honing his own skills and *preparing* for that day when he would *shock the world.*

And for June, when he did, it wouldn't be so shocking to him — not even a little bit.

Within these pages are tiny clues that *unlock* all of the chapters to come. Soon, you will learn about the so-called *amazing* turnarounds of Hawai'i players with names like Robinson, Pisa, Ikaika, Lelie, Ulbrich, Forney — *my, the list is long!* — as well as the scores of walk-ons and rejects that are now routinely beating the best America has to offer.

And, if you read carefully, you will see a little Barry Sanders there, a little Steve Bartkowski there, a little Bobby Hebert over there, a little Junior Seau right there. Then you will start to inhale perhaps the biggest of Mouse Davis miracles.

"Everything in life," Mouse says, *"is stolen. We just package 'em up, make it all work, and make it, let's just say, pretty special."*

Mouse never lost a lesson on protégé June Jones.

Just as Papa Joe will forever be etched together with Penn State — or Tom Osborne at Nebraska or Barry Switzer at Oklahoma — so too will Jones be remembered at Hawai'i.

When such men take downtrodden programs and become *fathers of tradition and hope,* one *must* look back and *see just how they got there.*

Coaches take players to places they can never reach on their own.

Listen up, *young Colt.*

If you read carefully, you'll find advice that will keep you playing on Sundays *for a long, long time.*

Steve Bartkowski is an Iowa-born quarterback who has spent most of his NFL career in Atlanta, Ga. When he speaks, people in the Deep South refer to it as the *"God's honest truth."*

When "Bart," as he's affectionately called, answers a question about anything, words ripple off his lips like gospel, because he's not apt to exaggerate — he just *tells the doggone truth,* and that's the way it is.

COURTESY STEVE AND SANDEE BARTKOWSKI

First-round pick Steve Bartkowski with free agent June Jones

"The first time I saw June Jones," Bartkowski says, "*man,* I just couldn't believe his *confidence.* I knew he had played at *a small school* somewhere and set a bunch of records, which I didn't care too much about, but I couldn't believe *how confident he was about the passing game.*"

Forgive Bart for being a little casual about Jones' record-setting performances at tiny Portland State, for Steve himself, as you might recall, wasn't *too bad* as a collegian.

In fact, he was a consensus All-American his senior season at the University of California, a not-so-little school, and the *very first player taken* in the 1975 NFL draft by the Atlanta Falcons. Bart, the big-money, first-round pick, met June, the free-agent nobody, when Atlanta signed Jones to a free-agent contract in 1977.

"June helped me *immensely* in my own game," Bartkowski says. "I learned more from him than *anybody.* I didn't see June as a threat, I saw him as a *teammate.* He taught me how to throw the deep ball, even though he couldn't throw it himself. *"Open up your core to the target,"* he'd say. I had a good arm; I could throw it out there pretty good, but what he taught me about *my eyes,* really trusting your *eyes* to *connect* to the *rest of your motor skills.*

"He told me to watch the receiver the entire way, from the time the ball leaves my hand until he catches it. Do not follow the ball with your eyes. Follow the receiver. That takes discipline. Your brain will tell your hand what it has to do to get the ball to the receiver, and your body and hips will adjust *naturally to his* speed.

"It's funny, because June was such a proponent of the four-wide offense, and now, *everybody's* doing what he and Mouse were talking about back then. It's a shame everybody hates the name "Run 'n' Shoot," because everybody's stuck on that, but they're all doing it, *so what's the big deal?*"

The down-home Bartkowski, ever the prankster, chuckles aloud.

"Once I spent a little time learning from June, I realized how in college he could have put up such big numbers with such a marginal arm, marginal range, and even more marginal velocity."

The result?

COURTESY STEVE AND SANDEE BARTKOWSKI

Steve Bartkowski leads the Atlanta Falcons, circa 1978

Today, Bartkowski is still just one of *six* quarterbacks in *NFL history* to have achieved back-to-back 30-touchdown passing seasons; the other names, in case you're wondering, include some not-so-shabby guys, such as Brett Favre, Peyton Manning, and Y.A. Tittle.

And Colt?

"Well, the biggest thing June taught me is that when you're dropping back, *don't get too closed down on your drop,* and *keep that left shoulder open.* But Colt needs to go out there, do what June tells him and have *fun.* This time *next* year, it will be *all business,* so open up that left shoulder and *go out there, spin it and have a little fun.*"

Are you kidding me?

A beautiful mosaic is built a single, tiny tile at a time. Only the artisan can envision its future splendor, until suddenly the picture comes into focus and the whole world marvels with wonder and awe.

Everywhere June or Mouse have been, you will find those tiny tiles that today add up to an intricate, international mosaic of the impact these men have had on all of football.

And there always seems to be a recurring theme: *Worst to first.*

In the Canadian Football League, Mouse used the offense to turn around a last-place 2-14 Toronto team and put them in the championship Grey Cup *in a single year.* In Canada, you have 12 players, not 11, and — *oh, gosh!* — don't ever give Mouse an *extra* man. He took their skate motion, put four or five guys in motion at once, ran the offense, and rode it all the way to the title game.

With the Houston Gamblers in the now-defunct United States Football League (USFL), they took a rough young quarterback named Jim Kelly and shattered every single-season professional passing record. Teaching this raw talent to use his *hips* and *eyes* and *throw off the right foot,* Kelly *made rain,* throwing for 9,842 yards and 83 touchdowns over two seasons.

Kelly took what he learned from Mouse and June to Buffalo in the NFL

and made history. Four Super Bowl appearances later, you can now rub Kelly's bust at the Pro Football Hall of Fame.

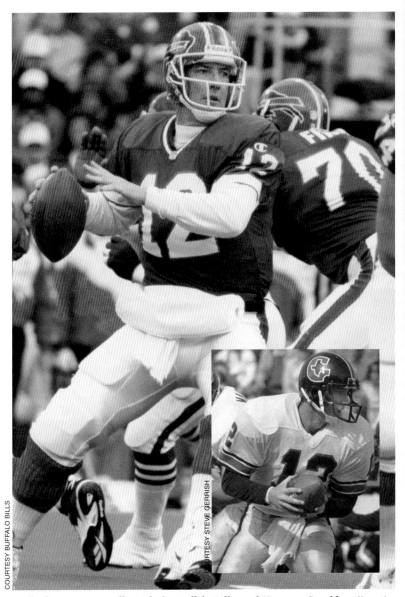

Hall-of-Famer Jim Kelly with the Buffalo Bills, and Houston Gamblers (inset), where he met June Jones

The Denver Gold: Greg McMackin, Joe Haering, Mouse Davis, June Jones, Bob Gagliano all converged to take a last-place team to the USFL playoffs ...

With the USFL's Denver Gold, Mouse and June took nondescript players — Todd Gerhart, Billy Johnson, Vincent White, Lonnie Turner, and Bob Gagliano, a rag-tag team of nobodies — and went from last to, *yep,* a division championship.

There is a critical footnote in history here that must be addressed:

Jim Kelly took 75 sacks in his rookie season under Mouse and June, a point that negative press somehow always seems to find. This would prompt an insecure Buddy Ryan to eventually refer to the offense as the *"Chuck 'n' Duck."*

June, ever etching away in his playbooks, realized the problem was twofold: First, quarterbacks new to the offense would hold the ball too long, and he would remedy that through *repetition, repetition, repetition;* second, the protections had to be corrected, so June began coaching the offensive line *himself.*

The ever-evolving Jones learned from his mistakes.

Years later, Buddy Ryan would be run out of football. Timmy Chang, however, during his freshman year at the University of Hawai'i, would throw the ball 469 times and take only 10 sacks.

"The more the quarterback understands what we do, the fewer times he gets sacked," Jones says wryly. "We have it down to a science now. Ask Colt how many times he gets sacked — *or even hit,* for that matter. Compare us now to any other offense. Let Buddy know that we're *extremely* proud of how well we keep our guys standing up."

The Kansas City Chiefs drafted Bob Gagliano in the late rounds as a little-known prospect in 1981. After failing to get productivity, the Chiefs cut him, and after bouncing around from team to team, Gagliano found himself ready to quit football, until he ended up in training camp for the USFL's Denver Gold, with — *you guessed it* — Mouse Davis and June Jones.

So obscure was Gagliano that any question regarding his pro career would be considered *"out-of-bounds"* in a game of Trivial Pursuit, eclipsed by highly paid opponents with household names like Steve Young and Doug Flutie.

And for Mouse, it was hardly love at first sight.

"I'm not Jim Kelly," Gagliano says. "They didn't think of me as a guy who could lead the Run 'n' Shoot. In fact, I felt a little bit of a cold shoulder from Mouse. You have to understand that Mouse is *just like a dad.*

"Mouse is friendly, but he's tough when it comes down to what he *requires* from you — *and those eyes, man, those eyes!* They can light you up, for better or worse.

COURTESY DETROIT LIONS

Mouse and June would later coach the Detroit Lions, taking Bob Gagliano (seen here) with them

"I just wasn't his first pick to lead the offense. So I just kept my head in the playbook. I kept studying, I kept learning. I kept throwing. But June's encouragement, behind the scenes, was incredible. He taught me defenses and *how to find the open guy. Nobody* breaks down a defense like June.

"He kept telling me, *just believe in yourself, and you'll get it done. Just believe in yourself.*

"Just believe in yourself."

"June finally went to Mouse and said, *'This guy can get it done in a game situation.'*

"So they put me in. We're down on the goal line, Mouse calls the play, the receiver got jammed, the defender played him head-up really well — and I back-shouldered him for the touchdown.

"June said, *'Wow! — that needs to be a play.'* And *he turned it into the fade-stop.*

"Today everybody in football runs the fade-stop.

"I'll go to my grave believing it started right there. I saw it in June's eyes."

Alas, the playbook added another page. Start the copy machine.

Bob Gagliano, who today works for a major California title company, would run the offense and, *of course,* lead a last-place team to the playoffs.

By the way, the ever-loyal Jones would take Gagliano with him to the NFL in Detroit and again in Atlanta.

"It was *so much fun* playing for those guys, but that's not what I take away from the whole experience," Gagliano says today. "What I got is that *June Jones believes in second chances.*

"June becomes one of those guys that just *stick* in your heart.

"For June, faith is a cornerstone," Gagliano says. For a moment he grows silent. Emotion begins to bubble forth, and you can feel it coming, so grab a Kleenex.

"I went through a couple of rough spots, and June took me aside and said, *'You're young, you're being influenced by the outside world. Just be careful.'*

You see, the pioneering of any enterprise contains the soul of it, and within the first steps of any journey one usually finds the whole motive, purpose and plan of the venture. Without a beginning, there can be no end; had one paid close attention to each of June's stops prior to his Hawaii ordination, one would have seen this unfolding like a red-splashed Pachi Pachi flower.

"June never yells. He *never* screams. He's a quiet leader who you don't want to let down.

"One time, I was going through a tough time. It was a decision I was trying to make on a personal relationship. *He told me to pray about it.* But then he said, *'Just make sure you keep your head out of the dirt.'*

"I know Mike Shanahan, Bill Walsh, Mike Holmgren, Terry Shea. *They are all great coaches,*" says Gagliano. "But *none* of them are June Jones.

"I'll never forget when June said this: *'You can't help people greatly unless they suffer greatly.'*

"That's his legacy right there."

And what about Colt Brennan?

"My definition of character is who you are when nobody's watching," Gagliano says.

"When you're in the limelight like Colt, with the best offense in the nation, touted to be a Heisman guy, well, *relax,* depend on June to be your mentor and *do those little things off the field* that your teammates respect.

"Colt is going to be tempted continually. Challenged continually. All of the things that make or break a young man. A *single football season can boil down to an entire life.* Colt is now living the microcosm of an entire life.

"As for football, nobody coaches this but June: Once you come to the trigger point, don't take your eyes off the target, *especially the long ball.*

"And tell Colt, if he *ever* gets in bad weather, like wind conditions, tell him June will go off if, in a cross-wind, if he *doesn't throw with the same motion.* This is another *June-ism,* and it's like a golf swing. Colt, don't change your throwing motion *into the wind.*

"Don't throw harder or you'll lose it.

"Most quarterbacks throw harder in the wind," Gagliano says. "June says, *'Keep it consistent. Just keep throwing the same way you've been taught.'*

"Sounds simple, but it's not. Colt will learn. Colt will learn."

"June teaches that *your built-in computer is your eyes,* and what he coaches is that trajectory, how to throw it, repetition . . . *all this other stuff works itself out.*"

You won't find a gold-plated trash can anywhere inside the NFL Hall of Fame in Canton, Ohio, but perhaps somebody should gild one and place it there.

When Warren Moon was struggling mightily with Houston in 1986, head coach Jerry Glanville made the decision to hire June Jones to rekindle his quarterback's desire to play. "At that point," Moon says, "I was disenchanted with playing in Houston. I was contemplating whether or not I should ask to be traded."

Unbeknownst to Moon, Jones was negotiating behind the scenes not only to become the new quarterback coach but also to keep Warren in Houston. "I suggested to Jerry [Glanville] that he should keep Warren until I had the opportunity for a full spring," Jones says.

For all practical purposes, Moon had been only days away from being shipped to the Raiders. "After the spring," June says, "I talked to Jerry and told him to let me keep working with him." Glanville went to GM Ladd Herzeg and pled his case, and Moon stayed in Houston.

Moon could throw a football a country mile, but he struggled with *trajectory.* "June watched a lot of my film," Moon says. "He liked what he saw, but he realized that when I threw the deep ball, I threw it in a straight line."

"I knew Warren could spin it," says former Falcons' star quarterback Steve Bartkowski. "But when June got there, he had lost his desire to play. June sat him down and remade him. The next thing you know, he

was having *fun* again. He was so excited he was playing like he was in college."

June's secrets? "Well, he worked on my *eyes* and taught me that my eyes go to my brain and my brain to my body and my body to my arm — and to keep my *eyes* on the *receiver,* not the ball," Moon explains, as if we — *phew!* — haven't heard it before. "But then we really went to work on my trajectory."

This is where Jones would go high-tech in an effort to shock the football world.

"He made me throw balls into a trash can from 45 yards away," Moon laughs. "We would start and end every practice with a drill where we threw balls into a trash can. The quarterbacks would hold contests to see who got the most. We visualized the receivers and threw the balls in the can. It didn't take long before I was throwing the ball with beautiful trajectory."

Warren Moon, with agent Leigh Steinberg, poses with his bust at the NFL Hall of Fame

"June understands talent, and he knows how to get the most out of a quarterback," Moon adds. "He knows the game, and he exudes the confidence of a guy who's won five Super Bowls and been to 10 Pro Bowls. His confidence as a coach makes you that kind of player."

Moon rewrote the Houston Oilers and NFL record books. Houston went from, well, dead-last, to a division championship and the AFC Championship game, once again debunking the theory that a team can't win with the Run 'n' Shoot offense, in spite of the name that a fearful coach refused to call it. Warren went to the Hall of Fame.

"June either *creates* a quarterback or he *rebuilds* one," says Bartkowski. "Just look at the careers this guy has affected. I was happy to hear Warren mention June when he was elected to the Hall of Fame."

That's not too bad for a guy who once had *lost his desire to play.* "I owe a lot to June," agrees Moon. "When you think about it, if Jerry hadn't hired him, who knows? I talked to Colt quite a bit last year, and I told him that he's going to be a lot better in the NFL because of June. There's no doubt about that."

But trash cans?

Are you kidding me?

"He runs scared." That was the first thing Mouse Davis noticed about Barry Sanders when he and June arrived in Detroit with the Lions. When the pair installed the Run 'n' Shoot, Mouse and June were faced with a dilemma, albeit a good one: *How do you use a future Hall-of-Fame running back half the size of the prototypical Run 'n' Shoot running back?*

In the Run 'n' Shoot, the single back is relied upon to block the playside three or defensive end *alone* or to pick up blitzes, and he is basically a

▼▼▼▼▼▼▼▼▼▼▼▼▼▼

"Barry ran scared," June says. "You could see the whites of his eyes when he'd glance over his shoulder as he danced away, and that was just beautiful. When he ran scared in our stuff, there was simply more air for him to run scared to."

▲▲▲▲▲▲▲▲▲▲▲▲▲▲

sixth offensive lineman. This requires him to be the size of a small Oklahoma work shed, enabling him to stand up to the force of men with the size and quickness of grown tigers who have ridiculously bad intentions of what to do with a quarterback if they could ever get to one.

Once the offense begins to hum, teams tend to spend more time trying to find the swirling mass of *wide open* receivers than they do finding the quarterback.

This creates gaping holes for the offense's huge running backs, who often find themselves running behind safeties whose backs are turned and are running directly in front of them, for fear of getting beat by the deep ball.

Ridiculous, you say, *and you're right.*

This is why, if you do the research, you'll find that there's always been a 1,000-yard rusher in this offense, dating all the way back to the likes of Joel Sigel at, as Bartkowski would say, *"some little school"* — Portland State University — and 15 years of high schools prior to that.

Now Mouse and June had *something* from Oklahoma, but *hardly* the size of a work shed and *quite a bit more talented* than anything they'd ever seen in their lives: world-class Barry Sanders, who, on his tiptoes, was 5-feet-8-inches and soaking wet weighed *maybe* 203 pounds.

And, *ahem*, he was the *best runner in history.*

How would Mouse and June make the offense work now?

Asking Barry Sanders to block the playside three all day would be like asking Liberace to carry the piano on his back into the concert hall before he played it.

Pencils poised, Mouse and June went to work. First of all, he *was* Barry

The results were absolutely devastating.

Forget about the fact that the Lions went from, *of course,* worst to first, or that they would eventually ride the Run 'n' Shoot and Barry Sanders running — *in open space* — to the NFC championship game.

Here's something your pals at the local pub don't know: *Barry Sanders despised contact.* He hated it so much that he confided in June Jones that he loved the offense because *"there's nobody around me when I get the ball."*

One Saturday, during walk-throughs before a game against the physical Green Bay Packers, he privately told his coaches that the only reason he played the game was *for the money* — that he didn't even *like* football.

"Barry *ran scared,*" June says. "You could see the *whites of his eyes* when he'd glance over his shoulder as he danced away, and that was just beautiful. When he *ran scared* in our stuff, there was *simply more air* for him to *run scared to.*"

While other coaches would have berated Sanders for his lack of toughness or courage, Mouse and June made the game *simple* for the football-hating Sanders, who hated practice even more.

They reduced the running game *to just three plays,* and Sanders could run them in his sleep. He was allowed to practice when *he felt like he needed it, but if his body was beat up from the week before, he might not take a single snap all week.*

In fact, under Mouse and June, *he never even donned pads until game time.*

"He is very intelligent," Jones says. "But don't ask a great player to do what he can't do or doesn't want to do. Find a way to win with the things he does best."

Now the whole world knows why Barry Sanders retired.

When Bobby Ross took over the Lions, he reinstalled two-back sets, which immediately allowed defenses to tee up with eight- and nine-man

COURTESY DETROIT LIONS

Running back Barry Sanders, the best to ever play the game. Note the whites of his eyes as he 'runs scared.'

Sanders, which is a pretty good jumping-off point. Second, the offense does *create open space,* correct?

Logically, they backed into it.

June came up with ways to utilize the smaller back, and has ever since. He took pressure off of Sanders via new protection schemes, more screens and *creative ways* to make him *a hot receiver off the end* and put him *in open space,* where his speed and quickness became a distinct disadvantage to the defense.

fronts to physically shut Sanders down. Ross also doubled practices, made them full contact and told his team it was *"my-way-or-the-high-way."*

Sanders *took the highway,* and *pro football lost its greatest running back ever.*

In fact, Sanders told the media that the only coach he would ever play for is *June Jones.*

Physically, emotionally and spiritually moved by his time with Barry Sanders, Jones took the experience and added a few new wrinkles to his ever-expanding playbook.

"Now we have stuff in there for the little guys," June says, smiling. "And now we actually *coach* them *to run scared."*

Are you kidding me?

Apparently not.

Ask "little guys" like Allen Pinkett of the Houston Oilers or Steve Broussard and Eric Pegram of the Atlanta Falcons, the latter of which still holds the record for most rushing yards against the San Francisco 49ers.

What does this mean to the University of Hawai'i?

At Hawai'i, lost in the maze of giant sledgehammers like Nate Ilaoa, were "little guys" like Mike Brewster and Mike Bass, all of whom have *Barry Sanders* to thank for it, but who squirted for first downs whenever they felt like it.

And while you're at it, look up Todd Fowler. You've never heard that name, but as a big, stiff, white rookie out of tiny Stephen F. Austin University, he rushed for more than 1,000 yards with the Houston Gamblers while *blocking the playside three for Jim Kelly.*

"It's not hard," Fowler says, *"when you're running against air."*

Coaches teaching players not to be tougher but to actually run scared?

Wow. Are you kidding me?

The Cajun Cannon only played in one Pro Bowl, and that was under a coach named June Jones during his tenure with the Atlanta Falcons. Yet Bobby Hebert's stay in Atlanta would not be without controversy, for it would be wrapped around the short-lived presence of preeminent quarterback Jeff George, he *of all God-given talent in the world.*

"If I could've had Bobby Hebert just a little earlier in his career," laments June, in regard to the 'The Cajun Cannon' (above), "I think it would've been amazing for both of us." As it was, Hebert enjoyed his only Pro Bowl season under Jones

Hebert and George would become indelibly wrapped together, like roses and thorns.

Bobby Hebert, born in Larourche Parish, La., is now a sportscaster. But in his day —*wow, in his day!* — he could sling the rock, and he would play *beyond hurt,* including those times when the tendons were excruciatingly fraying, like an unraveling rope, from his degenerative right elbow.

Bobby would *play for pride* — so much so that if his right arm failed him, this courageous Cajun would chew it off and learn how to throw left-handed and *still find a way to beat you.*

"Where I come from," Bobby said, *"if you don't play hurt, they will hang you from the highest tree."*

Hebert led the Michigan Panthers to the USFL championship in the league's inaugural 1983 season. Years later, he helped bring the Saints their first playoff appearance in franchise history and now resides in their Hall of Fame.

"June has *great communication* skills," Bobby says. "He is so good at dealing with different personalities and individuals. Out of all 15 years of pro ball I enjoyed, *he is the best coach ever.* And the reason, I think, is that because *I never had an understanding of the quarterback position* or paying attention to detail . . . he *taught me everything.*

"With June, something might look good in theory, but he helped me to *adjust, like when we went to the shotgun.* Up to that point, everything was the half-roll, and I said, *'June, let's go shotgun, my legs are shot . . .* and, *amazing,* he *listened,* and he did it. "This was totally *unbelievable,* a coach who actually *listens.* June totally understands how to *attack* defenses.

"All these records at Hawai'i, it's not a coincidence. The fact that Hawai'i runs the shotgun now is not a coincidence. This kid at Hawai'i needs to know that June will keep him in a winning position.

"My elbow was so messed up in 1994, but because of June, I *still* made the Pro Bowl. He put me in the position to have success. *"If you have a problem with June Jones, you need to look in the mirror."*

Talk specifically about the offense, however, and you will get a less-than-congenial Bobby Hebert.

"A run-and-shoot quarterback *must* be *accurate* with the football," Hebert emphatically explains, "because the defensive backs are all trying to mirror the receivers, and they have their backs to you. *June made this famous, going back to the Warren Moon days.*

"By theory, *you throw the fade-stop on the back shoulder,* and the db doesn't have a chance. It's all about ball placement, like me hitting Andre Rison in the seam. The safety's eyes would get all big — and truthfully, he couldn't have better coverage — and then *I'd show my eyes,* and when he'd make a move, I'd throw it right by his head. If *you're a db coach, how do you defend that*?

"The best pass coverage is a pass rush, but you've got about a second and a half and the ball is gone. This kid Colt is going to kill you. He's going to kill you."

Somewhere, June and Mouse are smiling: repetition repetition, repetition.

Are you kidding me?

Chapter 8

ATONEMENT ... COLT ... AND JEFF GEORGE?

"Atonement" is a word that refers to forgiveness or pardoning, which, if done genuinely from the heart, makes *reconciliation* possible. Unless one forgives or pardons, there can be no *reconciliation,* and both parties are left spinning in a universe of perpetual doubt, confusion and a lifetime of disappointment.

On September 22, 1996, during the Atlanta Falcons second regular-season game, before a national television audience of millions on Monday Night Football, an incident occurred that would forever tie June Jones and troubled quarterback Jeff George together, one that would be relived again and again on NFL Films for more than a decade to come.

George and Jones went toe-to-toe on the sidelines; cameras zoomed in from multiple angles. Time stood still as announcers and fans held their breath, wondering for several seconds if it would actually come to fisticuffs.

In a matter of hours, George would be permanently benched for Bobby Hebert and subsequently suspended and waived. Hebert would go on to lead the team with a combination of raw toughness, willingness to play hurt and a never-say-die attitude.

However, the team would never overcome the loss of the talented George. By season's end, the Falcons would lose 13 games, 10 by a touchdown or less, and Jones would be fired, closing a chapter on one of his toughest professional years.

George would *never* regain the status he once enjoyed as a Falcon under Jones. His career would take him through stops with the Raiders, Vikings, Redskins, Seahawks and Bears and the Raiders again before he disappeared altogether from pro football.

Good riddance, cried fans, content to form their own conclusions. Truth, however, *is* stranger than fiction, so you might just want to stick around for the rest of the story.

Quarterback Jeff George, arguably the most talented – and underachieving -- passer to ever play in the NFL

To this day, few realize that the argument *seen 'round the world* had *little* to do with down and distance or the few mistakes George had just made in the game. Trouble had been brewing for weeks, when George had been late coming into camp over stalled contract negotiations — *after a career season* in 1995.

The fans blamed Jeff, but he still insists he would have been there if somebody had tendered him a contract. "I didn't hold out," he says. "I was newly married. I was trying to lay down roots in Atlanta. A holdout is someone with a contract. I didn't have a contract. But I'm not making excuses. It is what it is."

That fateful Monday night, June was caught in the middle. After several frustrating series, he made the decision to go with Bobby Hebert. "I wanted to go with Bobby, and Jeff said, *'If you do, I'm out of here.'* I said, *'You do what you have to do.'*

"No player, no individual, is greater than the team."

Atonement between the pair would be 10-plus years in the making.

So impressed were Mouse and June when they worked George out after his junior year at Illinois that they took him to *Olive Garden* for dinner, a fact that still tickles Jeff George.

"All the other coaches wanted to take me to the finest steakhouses, wine me and dine me, try to impress me," George says. "Mouse and June took me to Olive Garden. I loved it. If you think about it, it says a lot about those guys. Not that they're cheap, but what impressed me wasn't the food, *it was the company*."

What *impressed June* wasn't the stuffed-cheese ravioli, but the sauce that George could put on the deep ball, which made it no surprise when he

AP PHOTO

This debacle on Monday Night Football led to Jeff George's ouster -- and a losing season for June Jones

became the first player picked in the draft by the Indianapolis Colts. It also explains why years later, after June became the head coach in Atlanta in 1995, he leapt at the chance to salvage George's flagging career.

"Nobody throws the deep ball better than Jeff George," June says. "I've never seen a player who could throw so deep and so accurate. Until Colt Brennan, he's the best pure passer I've ever seen."

Repeatedly, George would make *unbelievable* throws look *casual,* causing even veteran quarterbacks to take pause.

"Jeff threw a 50-yard ball once *in between three guys,*" marvels Bob Gagliano. "Bobby [Hebert] and June and I just looked at each other and shook our heads. None of us would have ever even *considered* throwing it, and he got it in there. The receiver was *shocked.* You simply had to *be there* to appreciate the kind of arm this guy had.

"Jeff would make throws like that, and I would look at June and yell, *'Unfair advantage!'* June would just crack up laughing."

June and Mouse knew the *arm* was there, but they immediately went to work on Jeff's *hips and feet.*

"The main thing with Mouse and June," says George, "is *they teach you the fundamentals. They really worked on my feet, my footwork.* Up to that point, I'd been doing five-step drops all my life, and they began to apply techniques I had never heard of.

"In those two years I was with them, I learned more than I had in 15 or 20 years," George says. "I could always throw it out there, even off my back foot, but they taught me how to be accurate, how to not just depend on my arm but my *eyes* and *my mind* and my *legs.*

"They did their best to make me the *entire* package."

Over the course of the 1994 and 1995 seasons, with the Run 'n' Shoot firmly in place, Jones coached George to the best seasons of his entire pro career. George completed 60 percent of his passes for 7,877 yards and 47 touchdowns.

In 1995, George earned his only Pro Bowl berth as the Falcons made the playoffs after a come-from-behind victory in the season's final game to beat the vaunted San Francisco 49ers, 28-27.

"June and I did some great things in the NFL," George says. "People tend to overlook just how well all of us ran his offense."

Jeff George wasn't alone in June Jones' second-chance saloon. The late Craig "Ironhead" Heyward rushed for more than 1,000 yards and made the Pro Bowl. Lincoln Kennedy and Bob Whitfield played as well as any offensive tackles in football. Receivers Terrance Mathis and Eric Metcalf caught more than 100 balls for more than 1,000 yards *apiece*. Bert Emmanuel, a former *quarterback* at Rice, caught almost 100 passes himself for more than 1,000 yards.

It was the ONLY time in NFL history that a team had a quarterback throw for more than 3,000 yards, three receivers go over 1,000-yards each and a running back over 1,000 yards — while THREE OTHER receivers totaled an additional 800 yards!

Are you kidding me?

"So much for the idea that June's offense can't work in the NFL," says George. "Our offense that year was maybe the best in NFL history. I'm proud of my teammates for what we accomplished."

Bobby Hebert was a capable captain in the Run 'n' Shoot. A wizard on the delay routes, he avoided sacks and used his savvy intangibles to keep the chains moving.

COURTESY JEFF GEORGE

Jeff George, considered by many scouts as the best pure passer in the history of the game ...

But make no mistake: He was no Jeff George. *Nobody in* football, perhaps before or since, had *that* arm or accuracy.

"Once against the Dolphins," says Hebert, "we were all standing there watching Jeff warm up, and Marino was just opposite of him, so we could see them both. There was no comparison. But Marino knew how to win. I told Jeff once, *'If I had your arm, I'd be in the Hall of Fame.'*

"I always wondered what Jeff was thinking that Monday night," Bobby says. "I'll probably wonder for the rest of my life."

Maybe the answer is simple: Jeff *wasn't* thinking. Maybe we all want to make something out of nothing. Maybe it was just little more than an ugly incident that, once captured on national TV, took on a life of its own. Maybe we are all judging a guy because he got into an argument with a coach. Let's face it: He didn't run a dog-fighting, gambling ring, shoot a man in a strip club, or beat his wife or drive drunk. He *argued* with his coach.

Maybe it's time to forgive Jeff and stop judging him, lest we be judged ourselves.

When the argument broke out on the sidelines that fateful night in 1996, it almost got worse before it got better. Hebert, ever the Cajun, nearly stepped into the middle of the fray. "I thought about stepping into it myself," Hebert recalls.

Boy, would NFL Films have had a lifetime of fun with that one.

If you watch the film, June isn't angry but *clearly frustrated.* Here was a man who had spent an entire career proving he could coach or communicate with *anybody,* and on national television, Jones and his *dream quarterback of all time* were trading words. After a brief exchange, June finally just pursed his lips and stared straight ahead.

"There's not a whole lot I can say about it today," Jeff says, "but things like that go on in the NFL daily. Practices, games, you name it. If you had a camera on every Hall of Fame quarterback of my time, like Steve Young, Dan Marino, Joe Montana, Brett Favre, you'd probably see the same thing. It's a shame that it had to be caught on camera."

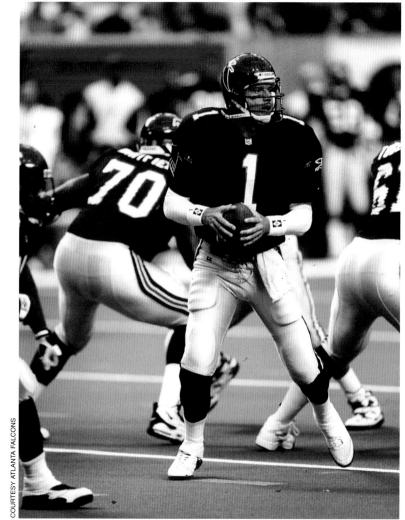

COURTESY ATLANTA FALCONS

Jeff George had his most productive years under Jones in the Run 'n' Shoot

"But that doesn't say how I feel about June Jones," George says softly. "The bottom line is that we are both competitors, and that whole thing was about a quarterback wanting to win.

"Any competitor who was about to get yanked would've reacted the same way. It's unfortunate that June and I are tied at the hip because of that incident."

Today one finds quite a different Jeff George. He is on his way home — not from the bright lights of an NFL practice but from his son's Little League baseball game. He lives quietly in Indiana with his wife, Teresa, two boys, ages 11 and 6, and their 9-year-old daughter.

Time — life — has a way of humbling us all. Unbeknownst to spiteful fans, Jeff George spends his days raising money to defeat breast cancer. His foundation pays for hundreds of mammograms and treatment in Indianapolis, where he hopes to save the life of even one individual who tests positive, as was the case with his own mother just five years ago. He has orchestrated thousands of dollars to care for the underprivileged and battered women in the cities where he once played.

Gone is the attitude of this once-famed first-round pick, whose face adorned the cover of *Sports Illustrated*. Absent completely is the *arrogance* that plagued George in each of his NFL stops. The aloof ego, the standoffish style, the *petty pride* have been replaced by an obvious and distinct *humility, reflection* and *maturity.*

Evangelist Billy Graham once taught that *atonement* must begin *inside* a person, not the *outside*. *"God looks at your character,"* he said. *"Humility . . . brokenness . . . contriteness . . . unconditional love . . . perseverance . . . patience . . . loving someone who actually hates you . . . actually* blessing *those who curse you*. This leads to a *revival* of one's heart, one's *spirit,* one's *soul,* which produces an entirely *different person* than people *thought they once knew"* (emphasis added).

This Jeff George is not the same one everyone *thinks* they know. He has endured name-calling, been labeled a head case and stamped as a has-been. Some of it is deserved and some of it isn't, and George just shrugs when confronted by the criticism and finger-pointing that has haunted his career.

"To be honest, I can't control what people choose to think about me," Jeff

▼▼▼▼▼▼▼▼▼▼▼▼▼

Atonement is a word that refers to forgiveness, or pardoning, which, if done genuinely from the heart, makes reconciliation possible. Unless one forgives, or pardons, there can be no reconciliation, and both parties are left spinning in a universe of perpetual doubt, confusion and a lifetime of disappointment.

▲▲▲▲▲▲▲▲▲▲▲▲▲

says softly. "When you get labeled or stereotyped in the NFL, you're stuck, and that's usually it.

"But of course, I'm sorry the whole thing with June happened. If I had it to do over again, I'd do it all differently. My *entire life* would have turned out different. June and I are friends now. I would do anything to rewind time and play for June Jones. Had I just listened, I could have played forever for that man.

"To play for June again would *be a dream come true,*" he adds. "Even as a backup. I still have a lot left in the tank. I can help a team, even if it's to bring along a young quarterback like Colt."

Did he mention Colt Brennan?

"Remind Colt to stay humble," George says with a whisper. "Tell him to listen to June, and he'll be the best quarterback ever. Colt's going to win every award in America, but the most important thing — *trust me* — is to be the leader of his football team, and everything else will follow."

It might behoove Colt, as well, to *always know* where the cameras are, especially if it happens to be a Monday night.

June Jones sits silent on the other end of the phone as the words of his former quarterback are read to him. So moved is he that he must hang up, reflect, gather his thoughts and call back.

"Jeff George can still throw the ball better than 25 starting NFL quarterbacks," June says, clearly touched. "I've always been in awe of his ability, and I still am today. *Who knows what the future holds?*

"Still, all things in life happen for a reason," Jones adds. "I might never have had the opportunity to coach this great Hawai'i program or enjoy these past nine years *if that single incident* had never happened. You forgive, and you move on. I have never looked back. Hawai'i is where I was

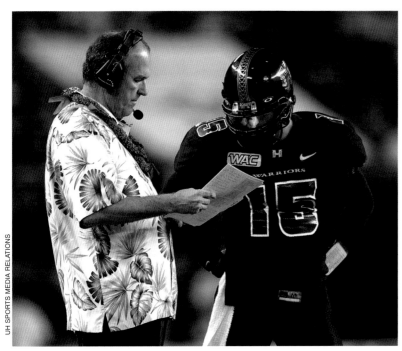

June Jones with Colt Brennan, whom Jones likens to Jeff George ... the physical comparisons are eerie

Tribulation produces perseverance; perseverance builds character. And character brings *hope. And hope, even after the bright lights of the NFL fade away, does not disappoint.*

"I'm not living with regrets," Jeff says. "God has given me the best life a man could have. I know He has a plan for my life. I have my faith, I have my family, and football is a distant third.

"Tell Colt to put my life to good use," George grins. "If he can learn something from all of this, then *hey, it's all been worth it.*"

Worth it? Jeff George? Healed and humble?

Are you kidding me?

called to be. I am doing what I love to do, in the most beautiful place in the world.

"But I love Jeffrey, and I forgive him."

There is a final amazing footnote forever overlooked by the national media, because what you are about to read doesn't sell newspapers or cause a stir on the six o'clock news. During Jeff George's first year in Atlanta, when he married his high school sweetheart, the first person who called him and talked to him about marriage was . . . *June Jones.*

"He gave me a Bible," George says. *"He taught me faith."*

Apparently, as evidenced by his powerful new demeanor, Jeff George *is reading it,* too.

Chapter 9

EDDIE WOULD GO . . . BUT HAWAI'I WOULD THROW

Professional football is a vortex of outrageous personalities whose actual *knowledge* of the game typically pales in comparison to their extreme levels of *responsibility*. There are owners and general managers and assistant GMs, scouts and personnel directors and more, all of whom have input into the final product the head coach and his staff must ultimately put on the field — and, of course, somehow *win*.

This often creates severe animosity between coaches and management, when staffs are forced to work with players whom they didn't draft or, worse yet, *didn't even want*. All the while, they are under intense scrutiny from their peers in the organization and excruciating pressure from media and fans.

"If they ask you to cook the meal," says former NFL legend Bill Parcells, *"then they should at least let you pick out the groceries."*

Alliances often form between colleagues in various departments of the organization who then team up against other *perceived* competitors, where generally they fight for either more control or more power. Many different personal factors further divide a team, such as gender, age or ethnic backgrounds.

High-ranking officials in football organizations sometimes *encourage* office politics; it costs them little but gives them *more control,* as they can play off underlings who are fighting amongst themselves. Sometimes these authority figures are themselves "players in the game," creating cliques or teams deep within the organization as they compete for power with fellow executives striving for recognition from top brass.

Then, of course, there is the constant supply of *misinformation* — both

June Jones as a quarterback at the University of Hawai'i

to the media and the staff — which creates further animosity when missteps make the morning's headlines.

If this sounds vaguely familiar, perhaps like the hierarchy of your own office politics, imagine that everyone in the cubicles around you is making millions upon millions of dollars, which significantly ups the ante. And imagine that each morning, on your way to work, radio jocks — and live callers — questions every decision you made the day before.

Sound like fun? Are you kidding me?

This explains why the days of a Vince Lombardi *fathering* a football program in Green Bay —or a Don Shula in Miami or a Chuck Noll in Pittsburgh — are a thing of the past. The NFL is a multibillion-dollar empire, one of the biggest businesses in the world, and *dozens* of jobs rest on every single bureaucratic decision.

Coaches are often the *last* to know, but they are the *first* to be held accountable.

It takes an extremely disciplined, intestinally strong man to hold the reigns of an NFL team and all that comes with it. It is a job that wrings one dry, which explains why coaches typically look like worn-out dishrags by season's end.

While most coaches see the NFL as the pinnacle of success, June Jones was marching not only to a different drummer but to an entirely different band altogether. After two-plus decades of mind-numbing mental NFL gymnastics, his thoughts were beginning to wander to the left — far left: about *2,600 miles to the left of San Diego,* to be exact.

"I always wanted to be the *father* of a program," June says. "I always knew tradition had to be *created,* and I really wanted to do it in Hawai'i. From the time I played at Hawai'i, the program had won here, won there, but it had *no tradition* of winning *year-in* and *year-out.*

"I always wondered, *'Why couldn't we be the Miami Hurricanes of the Pacific?'*

"At all the stops we'd made, we'd proven with the offense we could take over last-place teams and win, but we never stayed long enough at any stop to create a legacy.

"I was growing tired of the NFL, and it was just becoming time to go."

Steve Bartkowski saw it coming. "June told me his rookie year (1977) that he was one day going to be the head coach at the University of Hawai'i," Bart says. "I was surprised he waited as long as he did."

Sometimes, waiting isn't an option — it's a *requirement.*

Before Jones could fulfill his dream, God would place yet another test in his path. Jones, who along with Mouse Davis had engineered the greatest offense in the history of mankind, would have to prove he had other tools that had little to do with the Run 'n' Shoot, passing records, lights-out scoring or great quarterbacks.

One was *patience, patience, patience.*

No eye could see nor ear hear nor heart conceive what God had in store for June Jones.

But he would have to *wait.*

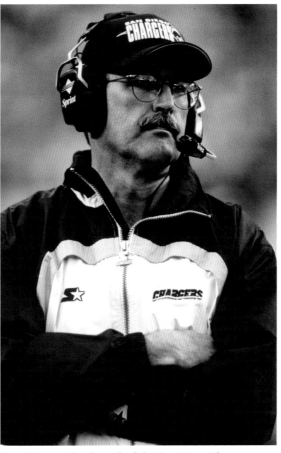
UNIVERSITY OF HAWAII ATHLETICS

June Jones as head coach of the San Diego Chargers

"Waiting on what you want can be miserable," Jones says. "But *waiting* allows you to see things you didn't see, hear things you didn't hear, understand things that you maybe didn't before. *Timing,* in any venture, is critical, and *waiting* is the hardest part."

Renowned author and philosopher Harriet Beecher Stowe once said: *"When you get into a tight place, and everything goes against you, 'til it seems as though you could not hang on a minute longer, never give up then, for that is just the place and time that the tide will turn."*

So it was in 1998 when, with the call of the Hawaiian tradewinds now howling in the ears of June Jones, he still had one last gut-wrenching, hand-wringing, brow-furrowing stop to make.

Patience, indeed.

Ryan Leaf was the second player taken in the 1998 draft by the San Diego Chargers, right behind another quarterback by the name of Peyton Manning.

June Jones had been added to the Chargers staff as quarterback coach in an effort to groom the young rookie, who had been tendered a four-year contract worth $31.25 million, $11.25 million of it *guaranteed.*

"June had gone with me to work out Ryan Leaf," says Bobby Beathard, Chargers' general manager at the time. "Everybody in football missed on that dingbat. We knew Ryan's personality was a little quirky, but I thought if anybody could make him productive, it would be June Jones."

Bobby Beathard, in case you've never heard the name, is not exactly a slouch when it comes to picking football talent. In fact, over the course of his 38 years in the NFL, he's arguably the greatest general manager in league history. His teams competed in seven Super Bowls; in 1966 with the Kansas City Chiefs, in 1972 and 1973 with the Miami Dolphins, in 1982, 1983 and 1987 with the Washington Redskins and in 1994 with the San Diego Chargers.

Four times Beathard's teams won the Super Bowl, the crown jewel of professional sports.

The relationship between Jones and Beathard dated back nearly 30 years, when Beathard, while scouting other players in the Portland area, put June through a workout to determine whether he was an NFL–caliber quarterback. Listening to him discuss Jones is like talking to your uncle as he recalls his fondest memories of a favorite son.

"I actually took him out on the roof of one of the buildings there at the university," Beathard remembers. "They had some sort of track up there, and I took him out there to time him in the 40. Wow, it was the fastest time I'd ever seen. Looking back, he reminded me of Michael Vick."

Beathard pauses for dramatic effect, then belly-laughs at his own joke.

AP PHOTO

Even June couldn't save Ryan Leaf, the biggest bust in NFL history

"Truthfully, I couldn't get my stopwatch to go that *slow*. I looked down and shook it, because I knew it couldn't be right. *Nobody* could run that slow. But somehow, June did. And he had these tiny hands, like Mickey Mouse."

Beathard grows dead-serious, however, when it comes to Jones' real skills.

"He understood offense," he says. "What he and Mouse did for football was pretty amazing. I stayed in contact with him when he was a player and then as a coach. When I got to the Chargers, we brought him in because he had one of the best *minds* in football.

"I knew it would take a special person to get along with Ryan, and June was the guy we picked to do it."

As it turned out, Beathard was right. Jones *would* be the only person who could get along with Ryan Leaf, but that proved not to be enough.

Peyton Manning would go on to NFL greatness and Super Bowl heroics, while Leaf would win only four games in his entire pro career.

Two of them were under Jones, including Leaf's only 300-yard passing performance. At one point, his passer rating dipped to 39, the lowest in league *history*. In one game, he completed only a single pass. He was equally bad off the field, attacking reporters, screaming profanities at fans and having to be restrained by teammates.

It wouldn't be long before Leaf was run out of football forever.

The chaos that ensued led to the firing of head coach Kevin Gilbride. Beathard promoted Jones to head coach, where, in spite of a losing record, he immediately brought a spiritual calm to the listing ship of the San Diego Chargers.

Leaf would go on to be considered one of the biggest disappointments in sports history. ESPN would list Leaf first on their list of the 25 Biggest Sports Flops between 1979 and 2004. "He was," says MSNBC commentator Michael Ventre, "the biggest bust in the history of professional sports."

Jones quickly won over the Chargers, all of them, especially perennial All-Pro linebacker Junior Seau, who couldn't believe how knowledgeable June was *on both sides of the ball*. Jones surprised everyone when he brought as much aggressiveness to the defense as he did the offense.

"He understands every part of the game," Seau says. "And he is a leader, a motivator. It was refreshing to play under him. He brought something to the locker room I'd never seen before. It was refreshing. It was *fun* to come to work again."

"Everything June does as a coach," says Beathard, *"just makes perfect sense."*

As for Leaf? "As it turned out," says Beathard, *"nobody on the planet could get along with Ryan Leaf, not even June, which says all you need to know."*

One can see how fatigued Jones must have been by 1998. For 20 years, he had been fighting with one hand tied behind his back. There was always the issue of the offense and *proving* the Run 'n' Shoot would work.

Winning teams don't make wholesale changes, so June and Mouse were always starting at the bottom, fixing last-place cellar dwellers, reviving the careers of aging or overmatched players, working with underdogs and fighting the egos within their own organization.

Never once had Jones enjoyed complete control. Never once was he entrusted to pick *all the groceries.*

But Bobby Beathard, never the fool and with four Super Bowl rings on his fingers, saw the swift adjustment in attitude sweep across his Charger team, and he began making big plans for June Jones in San Diego.

"June is one of those guys who has great insight with players," Beathard says. "He relates to every single player *individually,* and then he relates to the entire team as a *whole.* Few coaches can do that. He can identify the hot button for each player to make them successful. He breaks them down into what they *can do,* not what they *can't do.*

"He's approachable. He's honest. He's all the things that most coaches aren't. He is so far ahead of the game in his mind, it's ridiculous, and he's never had the opportunity to work with top talent, yet he still won games and broke records everywhere he's been. Some NFL people are scared of his style of offense, but when *hasn't* it worked?

▼▼▼▼▼▼▼▼▼▼▼▼▼▼

"Waiting on what you want can be miserable," Jones says. "But waiting allows you to see things you didn't see, hear things you didn't hear, understand things that you maybe didn't before. Timing, in any venture, is critical, and waiting is the hardest part."

▲▲▲▲▲▲▲▲▲▲▲▲▲▲

"If you could somehow get into the mind of June Jones, that's something a lot of people would pay a lot of money to do, and we were willing to do that. If you can't play hard for June Jones, you don't belong in football. We decided that we wanted him in San Diego for a long time, and we told him so.

"There was no question in our minds he was going to win for us there."

For every little boy who has held a seashell to his ear, closed his eyes and listened to the roar of the ocean, this story is for you. *It's OK to dream.*

For when June Jones closed his eyes, he could still feel the frothy surf of Makapu'u, smell its ocean breezes, and he longed for the warmth and inescapable sincerity of the Hawaiian people. His best friend Artie was already there, having settled in Honolulu after a successful basketball career at the university, and he was now a successful real estate broker and sports announcer.

June's heart was panging like pinui drums as he craved a return to the islands.

When Fred von Appen was fired as head coach at Hawai'i, it was as if the planets had aligned in a celestial beckoning for Jones to make his move.

The problem, should you choose to call it such, was the *multimillion-dollar offer* being dangled before him by Dean Spanos, owner of the Chargers.

June had always told people that money didn't matter. Here was a life-test, to literally *put the money where his mouth was.*

There are two things Jones always does in times like these: *Pray and call Artie.*

71

Jones would trade phone calls with his agent, Leigh Steinberg, then call Artie and relay the news and discuss the possibilities.

"What do I do?" Jones asked his best friend. "My heart is in Hawai'i, but they're making it tougher and tougher to go."

"Raise the bar," Artie suggested. "Ask them for everything. Just go for it. Tell them you want your son's college tuition. Ask for more money. Ask for bonuses. Then, when they turn you down, you'll have a reason to take the Hawai'i job."

In a matter of hours, in the middle of the night, Wilson's telephone abruptly jangled again.

"You're not going to believe this," Jones said. *"Leigh just called me. They've accepted everything."*

"Are you kidding me?" Artie said, incredulous. *"That's it, then. You're staying in San Diego. You can't say no. That's just too much money."*

The details of June's decision to shed his pro football skin and leave behind the red tape, formalities and stifling politics, as well as its alluring millions, may be read in Jones' own words in the foreword of this book.

Artie was waiting for the Chargers' to make their announcement when June called to tell his best friend *he was coming home* — that he had turned down millions to earn just $320,000 at the worst football school in the world.

"Shocked is an understatement," Artie says.

"I'm *not* turning my back on the NFL," Jones tried to explain to Artie, who was numb.

A breathtaking view of Hawai'i's Makapu'u shoreline

Artie Wilson shares the news: June Jones is coming to Hawai'i!

But *not all good things* come to those *who wait.* Behind his boylike glee of a dream come true, there were some hard, cold facts.

Yes, June *finally* would be able to *shop* for his own groceries — *after* he rebuilt the whole supermarket, *by hand.*

"I didn't want to tell June," Artie says, "that there just weren't many other people who even *wanted this job.*" The program was in such ruin, school administrators actually had discussed its abolishment.

It would require another *worst to first miracle:* The Rainbows had lost 18 straight games under von Appen. They traveled 2,500 miles *minimum* for every road game. The Athletic Department was fraught with budgetary problems. The academic standards made it difficult to keep top local players from enrolling in mainland schools.

One local scribe had written that the Hawai'i football program *"was absolutely impossible to rebuild."*

"It's not *impossible,*" Jones argued with Artie. "The *fun* is the *challenge.*" Artie was no longer listening; he was sitting on the other end of the phone dumbfounded, fantasizing about *just how much stuff* $4 million would have actually bought.

"I have a plan for getting things done," June said with confidence. "You'll see, Artie. *You'll see.*"

You better have a plan, Artie thought, *because this time, buddy, you've really blown it.*

Bobby Beathard was stunned.

In 38 NFL seasons, *nobody* had turned down an offer like this one; if Beathard's hearing served him right, Jones was telling him he was headed to — of all places — *the University of Hawai'i!*

Are you kidding me?

Beathard, the pro football power broker, was not accustomed to hearing "No" after all of his years in football and having learned from the likes of coaches Hank Stram, Don Shula and Joe Gibbs. But here was 45-year-old June Jones saying exactly that.

"He told me he couldn't stay," Beathard says. He sighs in disbelief, 10 years after the fact. "Incredible! He told me it was his dream to be the head coach of Hawai'i. He told me he wanted to be the *father of a football tradition.*"

Chargers' owner Dean Spanos was equally amazed. "We wanted him back because he really pulled the team together for us," Spanos says. "But any time a guy follows his heart and does what's best for his family . . . you *have* to admire that."

Beathard still recalls that day, wondering what might have been with his San Diego Chargers had Jones just said *"Yes."*

"That was a sad day for me," he says softly. "It might have been the saddest of my career, actually. I was happy to see June so happy, but frankly, I was just sad."

The waiting for June was finally over. Jones sacked up his Mouse Davis teachings, playbooks and game film, as well his lifetime of NFL experience.

With that, he embarked on the *second* most dangerous journey in Hawai'i history.

Big-wave surfing legend Eddie Aikau had joined a 1978 voyage as a volunteer crewmember on the double-hulled canoe *Hōkūle'a,* which planned to follow the ancient 2,500-mile route of the Polynesian migration between the Hawaiian and Tahitian island chains.

The *Hōkūle'a* left the Hawaiian Islands on March 16, 1978, developed a leak and soon capsized. In what is now a legendary attempt to get help, Aikau bravely paddled out into the enormous swells toward Lāna'i on his *surfboard* and was never seen or heard from again.

Now June Jones paddled toward Hawai'i on faith, knowing full well that his career would either sink or swim.

There was no turning back.

He would heed the call of the pounding waves on the shores of Waikīkī.

Just as Eddie would go, now *Hawai'i would throw.*

All of football wondered if June Jones would ever be heard from again.

Eddie Aikau

The Hōkūle'a

Chapter 10
RAINBOWS . . . TO WARRIORS

If faith is, indeed, the substance of things hoped for, the evidence of things not seen, the job as head football coach of the University of Hawai'i certainly qualified as one enormous *leap* of faith. For when June Jones walked back onto his old campus in January 1999, he was shocked by what *he didn't see* — yet he knew what everyone *was hoping for.*

Wow! June thought. *This is going to take more than just faith to hold this deal together. Prayer, and lots of it, and some scotch tape wouldn't hurt. How could they have ever hoped to win under these conditions?*

It took Jones little time to assess what he had left behind in the want-for-nothing NFL, where stadiums are built like cathedrals, treatment rooms are better than most hospitals and new equipment is a daily, not biannual occurrence.

June had made a point of telling people how, in the NFL, coaches had little control. In college, he said, *there are no excuses.*

"It's your own fault," June said, *"if you don't win at the college level."* As he took inventory of his situation, however, knots rose in his stomach.

Are you kidding me?

June strolled through the equipment room. Not only was the room itself dilapidated, the *equipment* was in terrible shape. The battered white helmets were still adorned with rainbows, which at periods throughout history Hawai'i players had worn with tremendous pride.

While rainbows have deep spiritual meaning to the indigenous people of

UNIVERSITY OF HAWAII ATHLETICS

Hawai'i, the *logo* was no longer *politically correct* for a *football team* in an era where a *rainbow* stood for an entirely *different* kind of *aloha.*

June cringed, sharpened his pencil and put that at the top of his list. He loved the Hawaiian people and the deep roots of their heritage, but this would have to change. He had to find a way to turn his current Rainbows into Warriors in a manner the culture would both embrace and understand.

That was only the *beginning.*

The third floor of the Athletic Department, which houses the football offices, was under renovation, and carpenters had framed it out on one end. The school, however, had run out of money to finish it, and now it was covered in tarps.

The filthy carpet in the coaching office hadn't been changed in nearly two decades. The desks in the meeting rooms hadn't been replaced since June had *played there* 20 years before.

Players referred to the locker room, weight room and meeting rooms as *"the ghetto."* When comparing their broken-down "amenities" to *better* schools, they referred not to the Ohio States of the world but to the pristine new facilities of Fresno State and San Jose State.

The team's "grass" practice fields were littered with rocks, lava and glass.

The turf on Cooke Field, the practice field outside the Athletic Department, was so worn it shone in the afternoon sun.

Aloha Stadium was layered with AstroTurf, a dangerous faux-grass surface that had been ripped up in every other stadium in the country due to the irreparable harm it wreaked on athletes.

Even the *footballs* were ridiculous. The departed Fred von Appen had made a deal on cheaper balls that weren't even made of leather, but a *leatherlike* rubber. "They bounced like basketballs," recalls quarterback Dan Robinson. Worse yet, against the sweaty palm of a quarterback's hand, they were slicker than snot on a doorknob.

As for personnel, it was already January; there would be little to no recruiting for the 1999 season. With few exceptions, June would have to win with the *exact same players who had lost 18 straight games.*

Jones' list grew longer and longer. He grimly realized that the wholesale changes he must make to *teach them how to win* were not going to be immediately popular among University regents, fans or media.

But the ever-steadfast June didn't care. *Winning* would change *everything,* and to win, he had to *utterly change the culture.* Nothing short of *drastic maneuvering* would make a dent in this lifeless mess he had just inherited.

As surely as you can see your reflection in a pool of water, so too could you see the character bubble forth from the heart of June Jones as he witnessed his tasks ahead.

He pursed his lips, his eyes narrowed and he set out to engage his enemies and perform the initiative for which he had been championed: *singleness of purpose.*

The players squirmed nervously in their desks in the football meeting room as they waited to hear for the first time from their new head coach. Rumors abounded. They knew he had some fancy NFL passing offense, but there were quite a few laughs at the thought of him using it *here.*

Many of them had never heard of June Jones. There were whispers that the new coach had turned down "a bunch of money" to come to Hawai'i, and the general consensus among the players was he must be certifiably nuts.

What does he want with us? What is this guy hoping to prove?

What happened next, however, stunned every person in the room. June Jones strode confidently to the front and faced his team for the first time.

"Last year," Jones told his young charges, "we were 118th of 118 schools in the country. *This year, we are going to win, and we are going to be the number-one offense in America, with the same guys that are sitting in this room right now."*

He was just warming up.

"You guys are going to be part of the biggest turnaround in NCAA history," June added.

"Trust me: This team is going to make history."

In the back of the room, several Hawai'i linemen, including Adrian Klemm, now with the New England Patriots, and Kynan Forney, now of the Atlanta Falcons, exchanged quiet smirks.

"You obviously ain't watched any tape, Coach," Forney muttered under his breath, within earshot of a few teammates. "I know you comin' in from the league and all, but you ain't got no idea *just how bad* we are."

"I've looked at the tapes on all you guys," June continued, with a wave of his hand. "You're not bad . . . you guys are just missing *technique. For example, you defensive backs . . ."* — Jones began to demonstrate, physically, himself — "when you're taught to do an inside jam, we're going to teach you how to get your hips right, get your jam right and how to take the other guy's position away from him."

Now everyone in the room was sitting at attention, including Forney and Klemm. *He's already coaching all of us, and telling us more than we knew when we got here.*

"I said, 'Man, he *did* watch the tape!'" Forney says. "And right there, first meeting, he's teaching *technique* to the whole team, doing it himself, right there at the podium. I'd *never* heard a coach talk like that in my life.

"My first start under von Appen, I was told to 'just go block the guy,'" Forney adds. "I had no idea about angles, leverage, nothing. Just go block the guy. I could see immediately with June that things were about to get better — and fast."

Quarterback Robinson, he of the broken coccyx, couldn't believe his ears.

"I could honestly say that I was ready to hang up my cleats," he says. "I was so beat up, mentally and physically. So were my teammates. We were like an abused dog that somebody kicked around every day, for no reason at all.

"That day, June breathed into us new hope and new life."

This guy's either crazy, thought the players, *or he actually knows what he's doing.*

Either way, they were ready to give him a chance.

▼▼▼▼▼▼▼▼▼▼▼▼▼▼

"Last year," Jones told his young charges, "we were 118th of 118 schools in the country. This year, we are going to win, and we are going to be the number-one offense in America, with the same guys that are sitting in this room right now."

▲▲▲▲▲▲▲▲▲▲▲▲▲▲

Robinson and running back Charles Tharp, who had been a WAC Pacific Division freshman running back of the year, were called into June's office.

"Fellas," June said, "I'm going back to San Diego. I'll be back soon. I understand you guys are the *leaders.* You've got to keep going to class, keep everybody else going to class, keep everybody working out, and we'll get this thing rolling. You *are going to have to trust me."*

Robinson brought up the touchy subject of the rubber footballs.

"Dan," June said, calming his signal-caller, "I'll get you some *real* footballs. *Just keep throwing."*

"He got me *real* footballs," Robinson says today, still laughing with boyhood jubilance at the memory. "It was amazing. *Real footballs.* Suddenly, I could throw a spiral again."

Robinson followed Jones' advice. By spring 1999, he would be in the best condition of his football career for his senior year, which was a miracle in and of itself. Blessings, he learned, often come in the midst of a storm: Had Robinson not been allowed to extend his eligibility as a medical redshirt after his brutally painful 1997 season, the strapping 6-feet-4, 219-pound gunner from American Fork, Utah, would have missed what was about to become the greatest year of his life.

Tharp, on the other hand, obviously knew little about Jones, his NFL career or his history with superstars, including Jeff George. If he had, then he *never would* have singled himself out by *ignoring* Jones' advice and participating in less-than-respectable off-field activities.

Without batting an eye, just as he had with Jeff George, June cut the WAC Pacific Division freshman running back of the year before Hawai'i ever played a single down.

But, you say, *I thought June is about second chances?*

This is *always* the case when he is dealing with the *individual,* but not when the *individual puts himself ahead of the team.* Jones has always been willing to work with individuals through individual crises; when blatant behavior, however, threatens the *entire* team, he is equally quick to remove the cancer before it spreads.

"Second chances?" asks Forney. "Shoot — *June will give you five or six chances.* If you fail, it's because you keep blowing it. Don't blame June. Trust me, it's not him. If you can't get along with June, man, you don't belong in a helmet."

A man who cannot rule his own *spirit* is like a broken-down city without walls — a risk Jones couldn't take in the rebuilding of a brand-new program.

"We were stunned," Robinson says. "You talk about opening some eyes. Everybody looked at each other in the locker room and just said, 'Wow.'

If he'll cut Charles, he'll cut *anybody.* It set a tone for our behavior, that's for sure.

"The guys began to realize how *serious* June was about winning."

It got better. Jones then declared to former Punahou standout Afatia Thompson and Avion Weaver, the backup running backs: *"You guys are going to rush for over 1,000 yards this year. I promise."*

Robinson didn't comment aloud when he heard that, but he shook his head in disbelief.

"You have to understand something," he says. "We couldn't rush for 1,000 yards when we *were trying to do nothing else but run the ball. Now, here's this guy saying we're going to lead the nation in passing* and *rush for 1,000 yards?*

"Are you kidding me?"

As spring practice approached, change was everywhere. June, knowing that he must stand and be judged for the promises he'd made, was *living up to them.*

He had informed the Athletic Department they would now be Warriors, not Rainbows, though the media would continue to refer to them — at least for this season — as the hybrid *"Rainbow Warriors."*

Jones, to anyone and everyone who would listen, would insist his players *were now Warriors.*

The practice field had been refurbished, courtesy of local booster Alec Waterhouse, who had been represented by fellow businessman Ed Wong.

New equipment began to trickle in, a fact not lost on a single player. There was new gear, shorts that were comfortable to wear, little things, seemingly irrelevant to the outside world, but justice to those who had been oppressed for so long.

Hope that is seen is *not hope.* Yet when you hope for something you can't *see,* it's perfectly fine to *eagerly wait for it* with perseverance.

A whole football team had persevered; their *hope* was now restored.

Chapter 11
"THOSE ARE OUR GUYS"

Sporting News Magazine called June Jones' new eclectic crew of coaches the *"worst staff ever assembled."*

Fortunately, June Jones reads *Sporting News* for entertainment, not self-help.

He had to win *now,* and he fell back on *loyalty* and *relationships* in order to do it. Jones, strong in his faith and belief in people, had long trusted that God will *never leave you or forsake you,* and that a *true* friend is closer than a brother.

At Hawai'i, he seized the chance to practice what he preached.

"Relationships aren't easy," he says, *"but they are the greatest asset* any person can have. If I have any gifts at all, they are *loyalty* to others and an ability to help people grow."

Relationships, like plants, must be cultivated and nurtured or they will not grow. A single wheat field, for instance, might have more than 30,000 miles of roots — greater than the circumference of the earth. The deeper the roots, the stronger the tree, and each of Jones' relationships had evolved from chance meetings, chance circumstances or chance opportunities.

Yet from such little seeds, mighty trees had grown, because June *was willing to invest the time, make that extra phone call, send a little money or go that extra mile.*

▼▼▼▼▼▼▼▼▼▼▼▼▼

Hawai'i's soon-to-be heroes would no longer be forced to lean upon their own understanding, but now had men of sound principles to direct their paths. Regardless of one's history, within the football offices players could and would find at least one coach who could identify with their needs.

▲▲▲▲▲▲▲▲▲▲▲▲▲

Who better to teach such principles to his new football team than men who *lived* them?

"Assistant coaches, historically, have no job security," Jones says. "They're scared to death every year of being fired. *It's my fault* if I'm stupid enough to hire a guy who can't do the job. *That's why I don't hire people because of what they know.*

"I hire them as people. And I never fire a coach I hire, ever, unless they are disloyal to me or someone on the staff."

June went to work building his first Hawai'i staff, and to the media, his selections ranged from the sublime to ridiculous. When it was all done, it would be a walking, talking thesis on theology, ideology, criminology and *psychology.*

If you've ever seen the movie *Armageddon,* you get the picture.

For June, it was both fun and easy; kind of like a real-life game of *All-Star Baseball.*

Unemployed George Lumpkin was Jones' first hire, which really rattled cages.

Lumpkin and Jones had known each other for almost 30 years. The pair had met in the early 1970s, when June was Hawai'i's backup quarterback and George was a graduate assistant coach. Lumpkin had been a stellar Hawai'i defensive back who had shattered school interception records.

Hawai'i Assistant Head Coach George Lumpkin

"When Fred [von Appen] got the Hawai'i job, and I was coaching in the NFL, I actually called Fred and told him, 'You need to keep George on your staff,'" June says. "Fred ignored me and fired him.

"George was *purposely* my first hire."

Before June called, Lumpkin was out of football — and out of work.

Today, Lumpkin recalls that moment with emotion. A single tear streams down his dark cheeks from behind his sunglasses. You can't see his eyes, but you most certainly can see his heart.

"June has *always* been there for me," George says. "I had some tough times. There were times when I'd be short on cash. June never asked questions. He just sent the money.

"He never preached. He just loved me. Everywhere he went, he always offered me a job. When he went to the Atlanta Falcons, my phone rang, and it was June. He offered me the opportunity to reach the goal of being a pro assistant coach.

"It just wasn't the right timing for me. That blessing wasn't for me.

"When June took the Hawai'i job, he gave me a *second chance* to be with him. This was my blessing. *"Here, at Hawai'i, this is my blessing."*

Not only did Jones hire Lumpkin, he also made him *associate head coach,* where he would assist Greg McMackin, the new defensive coordinator, in all facets: d-line, linebackers and secondary.

Try explaining *that* to the press.

Over a period of 23 years, Lumpkin worked with four different head coaches at UH and became involved in every aspect of the defense. He was a part of virtually every memorable event in modern UH football history, including the team's first game at Aloha Stadium in 1975; its entry into the Western Athletic Conference in 1979; its first postseason appearance in the 1989 Aloha Bowl; and its first conference championship and subsequent Holiday Bowl in 1992.

Two high school coaches were June's next stunning choices.

First, he hired Ron Lee away from St. Louis High School, where, along with his older brother Cal (who would join the Hawai'i staff several years later), he had won 14 Prep Bowl titles and 18 Interscholastic League of Honolulu championships with the island's own St. Louis Crusaders.

June had known the Lee brothers for decades, after the pair had shown

So bad were the beatings inflicted by the Lee brothers that a "mercy rule" was created specifically for the Crusaders, who once enjoyed a 55-game consecutive winning streak. Under the rule, when a team develops a 35-point lead on its opponent, the clock is allowed to run. It stops only for timeouts, between quarters and for injuries.

Just across the way, at Hawai'i's Punahou School, was longtime high school offensive coordinator and head coach Dan Morrison. Jones had

UNIVERSITY OF HAWAII ATHLETICS PHOTO BY LOIS MANIN

Ron Lee

up in Mouse Davis' office during the Portland State days. When Mouse and June went to the Denver Gold of the USFL, they had invited Ron to training camp to learn the offense.

With the help of Mouse and June, Ron and Cal would import the Run 'n' Shoot back to Hawai'i, where they became the most prolific high school coaches in island *history*.

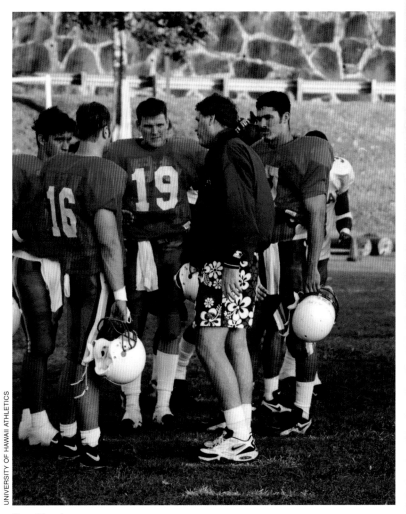

UNIVERSITY OF HAWAII ATHLETICS

Dan Morrison

known him since 1983 and had assisted Morrison with annual clinics for quarterbacks, receivers and kids. Several current players on the UH roster also had played for or against Morrison at Punahou, including right slot Craig Stutzmann, who ironically had played for Ron Lee at St. Louis High. With an accomplished background as an *educator,* as well as a thorough knowledge of the quarterback position in the Run 'n' Shoot, Morrison was a perfect fit as a mentor and tutor. June would make sure his quarterbacks, from their *first day in the system,* would not be without a soothing voice in their earhole, teaching, reinforcing, guiding, directing, uplifting and encouraging them to greatness.

The soft-spoken Morrison, a former quarterback himself at Santa Monica College, was the perfect man for the job of quarterback coach, at least to June.

Reporters shook their heads, and fans weren't far behind.

"Is he going to hire every high school coach on the island?" asked one discouraged writer to a local Internet forum.

"What's exciting about this?"

Troubled Mel de Laura was next, but due to in-house politics, the "official" announcement of his hiring would have to wait.

June then hired Wes Suan, who had spent nearly 20 years at tiny Linfield College before returning home to Honolulu to join the 1999 staff. Suan had grown up in Oʻahu's North Shore town of Waialua and had spent more than 25 years on the mainland when Jones came calling.

After coaching at Leilehua and Waialua High Schools, Suan took an assistant coaching position at Linfield in 1979, where he would not only be offensive coordinator but also assistant athletic director, equipment manager and even the tennis coach.

June assigned Suan to running backs, a critical position in the Run 'n' Shoot, for the backs are the last line of defense between onrushing blitzers and the offenses' invaluable quarterback.

"Wes is a guy who understood me and the offense pretty well, but most

UNIVERSITY OF HAWAII ATHLETICS PHOTO BY EUGENE HOPKINS

Wes Suan

importantly, he understood *the people and the culture,"* June says. "I'd been thinking about him for a long time. He started recruiting the second he got here."

On the surface, the selection of special teams coach Dennis McKnight seemed odd.

Among the quiet leaders on Jones' staff, McKnight stood out like a roaring lion among sable antelopes. With his gravelly, Jesse Ventura growl, obnoxious temperament, enormous chiseled physique and gutter-mouth philosophies, he didn't seem to be a "normal" fit with the rest of the staff.

This could be, perhaps, due to the fact that McKnight is far from anyone's definition of *"normal."*

This is until, of course, you realize that Jones had known him since 1992, when McKnight was a lineman for the Detroit Lions. McKnight had played 10-plus years in the NFL, both as a lineman and special teams

standout. But when June called him to Hawai'i, the Drake graduate was tending to his chain of car washes.

Jones would entrust McKnight to restore the meaning of *full contact* into the hearts of the players, as well as a ferocious, meat-eating instinct to Hawai'i's once-lame special teams. This fact resonated through the players the first time the hulking McKnight, all 6-feet-5, 290 pounds of him, stood up before them and declared that playing special teams for Hawai'i was now going to require "a big heart *and a scrotum full of testicles."*

Ahem.

June knew what he was doing. Just as a washing machine requires an *agitator* to produce clean laundry, so too would McKnight castigate and aggravate — *as well as preach and teach* — to help June remove the most stubborn stains from within the attitudes of the depleted Hawai'i program.

"He also predicted that come Christmas Day, we'd be playing in a bowl game," says Robinson.

"He told us that he wasn't there to be popular, he was there to win, and that he didn't care if *the whole world* hated him," jokes another player. "That was impossible, because *the whole world* hadn't met him yet. But we quickly learned that his heart was *way* bigger than his bite."

A lifelong predator himself who once delighted at deliciously hunting down the weak between NFL sidelines, McKnight quickly began to patrol the recruiting circuit with the same vigor. He intimidated invaders, marked his space and, of course, roared often. He was *personally* willing to fight if he encountered a threat to his territory, which heckling fans would soon find out.

Lost but talented kids became McKnight's specialty; he *loved* helping June redirect *floundering young lives.*

He would *prove* this to be true multiple times over in years to come, as he wrapped his thick, meaty forearms around the necks of countless wayward players. More often than not, walk-ons, misfits and troublemakers would gravitate toward the rough, tough, street-smart reasoning of Dennis McKnight.

The growling Dennis McKnight, back in the days when he had hair

In 1999, this included a talented young linebacker named Pisa Tinoisamoa, whom he and June would rescue from a courtroom and certain jail time. Though he needed another 30 points to be academically eligible on his SAT, Tinoisamoa was still the best player Hawai'i had signed in a decade. Grades would prevent him from playing his freshman year in 1999, but McKnight, Jones and the staff had sent the nation a message:

If you've screwed up — if you're running from ghosts and you're out of hope, give us a call.

Trust me: Dennis McKnight ain't 'fraid of no ghost.

The color commentator on radio broadcasts for Hawai'i football in 1998 was Rich Miano. The O'ahu native was popular, after having played locally at nearby Kaiser High School. The undersized safety walked on at Hawai'i, where he was drafted in the sixth round by the New York Jets and became a star NFL safety for 11 years.

"When I was a kid, I never thought about playing in the NFL," says Miano, who would play for the Jets, Philadelphia Eagles and Atlanta Falcons and record 16 career interceptions, including two against Hall-of-Famer Troy Aikman *in the same game.* "I only played one year at Kaiser. Walking on at the University of Hawai'i, to be honest, was pretty far-fetched.

"When I was a junior I started drawing some interest from the NFL, but even still, it was little more than a dream."

Football dreams often come true on special teams: Miano *never* wasted a single opportunity to be spectacular. Covering punts and kickoffs, he made an indelible mark as one of the most dangerous players in the NFL. It's impossible to watch Miano highlight films without learning the definition of the word *splat.*

Miano was a young, good-looking, trendy goal setter, and Jones immediately saw how the players would not only look up to him but also *respond* to him. Everything Miano does is well thought out and systematic — so much so that sometimes it's monotonous.

Secondary coach Rich Miano, who aspires to one day be the head coach of Hawai'i

However, it's reasonable, *perfect* for the shaping of impressionable 18-year-old minds.

Need proof?

"I had limited ability, limited football skill, but I kept believing and setting goals my whole career," says Miano, counting on his fingers. "When I first walked on, all I wanted to do was make the traveling squad. When I achieved that, I wanted to play special teams. Next, I wanted to make all-conference. Then I wanted to be an All-American. My next goal was to play in the NFL. That was followed by the goal of playing four years to get my pension. Then I wanted to play 10 years. By the end of my career, my goal was to retire healthy.

"If you set attainable goals, and you work hard, you can reach every one of them. I tell these kids that if I can do it, *they can do it*."

The only problem was that *coaching* didn't appear anywhere within those goals, at least until June Jones gave him a call.

"I met Rich in 1983, and I was always impressed with his work ethic," says June. "When I was in Atlanta, we brought him in, because I knew he would always be ready to play, he understood our kind of football and he would be a great teacher to the younger guys. He finished his [playing] career with us."

When Jones took the Hawai'i job, the first guy he thought of to coach his secondary was, well, a color commentator.

"I admit, he'd *never* coached before," June explains. "But he grew up here. He played here. He lived here. Yes, he was in the radio booth, but having coached him, I knew he knew football, and I knew just from his comments *on the air* that he *desperately* wanted to turn this thing around.

"Why not give him that chance?"
Heck, considering June's other hires, *why not?*

To coach the offensive line, he selected young Mike Cavanaugh, who had been an assistant with Jones in San Diego with the Chargers. He had been an o-line and strength coach at a number of small-town whistle-stops, including Murray State (Kentucky), Sacred Heart University (Connecticut) and Ferris State University (Michigan), where he helped the program win two Midwest Intercollegiate Conference titles.

In 1997 he became the assistant o-line coach and quality control coach for the Chargers, where he worked under Joe Bugel, one of the NFL's most famous line coaches. He worked inside, on the computers, break-

ing down film and soaking up every lesson Bugel offered. Jones watched carefully.

Mike Cavanaugh

"Cav learned a lot from Joe Bugel, a guy I really respect for his mentality, his attitude toward all protections, but especially ours," June says. "When I asked him to come, I also knew that I could teach him the schemes, and that he'd be a good technique guy."

"When do our guys get here?"

The question was a fair one from new defensive coordinator Greg McMackin, who was staring out the floor-to-ceiling windows in Jones' ramshackle third-floor office, which overlooks the Hawai'i practice fields. The coaching staff gathered around the windows together for the first time and took a look-see.

Down below, there appeared to be an intramural flag football game in progress. There were balls being casually tossed around, players running around in rag-tag fashion in various color shirts and shorts and socks. Coach McMackin looked out the window to see what McKnight and Jones were watching. "When are our guys coming in for camp?" he asked.

"Coach," growled Dennis McKnight, "Those *are* our guys."

McMackin blanched; then turned redder than usual. A fireplug of a man whose soft voice belies his ruddiness, McMackin had more *real coaching* experience than the rest of the 1999 staff *combined*.

His early resume included Idaho, Stanford and Utah. In 1985, while coaching the Denver Gold secondary in the USFL with Mouse and June, he so impressed Jones that June never forgot him.

From there he would become defensive coordinator of the Miami Hurricanes and, eventually, the Seattle Seahawks, where Jones plucked him from Dennis Erickson's staff.

"I was the defensive coordinator for the Seattle Seahawks, and June was coaching the Chargers, and we talked before we played each other," McMackin says. "Four games before the season was over, he told me it was his dream to coach Hawai'i. I thought, 'What a great deal, to go to Hawai'i.' So when he came over here, I joined him."

McMackin, says Jones, "always has an attacking 4-3 blitz scheme. Greg

has one of the best defenses no matter where he goes. I've always been impressed with what he's accomplished in both college and the NFL and the impact he'd had on Ray Lewis, Warren Sapp, Chad Brown, Cortez Kennedy, Shawn Springs, all those guys. I knew Mack would help us *immediately*."

Staring out Jones' office window, the usually ubiquitous McMackin was speechless.

"If you've ever seen the movie *Stripes*," says McKnight, "that's what *our guys* looked like. No standard issue of socks, or shorts or t-shirts. They looked like a dysfunctional group of guys trying to run some seven-on-seven drills. One of the quarterbacks was actually throwing *to a girl*."

McMackin sighed.

Greg McMackin, arguably the best defensive coordinator in all of football – though Jerry Glanville would argue this point …

"Well, they *are* 0-18," he reasoned. "And if they weren't, we wouldn't be here."

The glory of young men is their strength. The splendor of old men is their wisdom.

For the first time in history, the Hawai'i football program had *both*, regardless of what *Sporting News* might print.

The final tally was two high school coaches, a truck driver, an unemployed ex-coach, a radio commentator, a car-wash owner and a small college, jack-of-all-trades. Throw in two NFL assistants, one of whom had little on-the-field experience, and there you have it.

Wow.

Are you kidding me?

There was a beauty, however, to June's master plan, one that could only be seen in the eyes of the beholder. For sure, he had stayed true to his ideals of hiring *people*. He had narrowed the program's focus with men of strong character who believed in him and the system, and their *unity* and *confidence* would begin to saturate the atmosphere.

▼▼▼▼▼▼▼▼▼▼▼▼▼

Wise men listen, and increase learning. Men of understanding heed wise counsel. Only fools despise wisdom and instruction, and June, one by one, was eliminating excuses for losing.

▲▲▲▲▲▲▲▲▲▲▲▲▲

Within his staff were *teachers,* great leaders of men, chock full of character and life's wisdom, who could offer *something* far beyond football to every player, regardless of race, culture or creed.

Hawai'i's soon-to-be heroes would no longer be forced to lean upon their own understanding but now had men of sound principles to direct their paths. Regardless of one's history, within the football offices players could and would find at least one coach who could identify with their needs.

There, in separate offices, they would discover authentic men whom they could trust; someone with whom they could talk; someone with whom they could even pray — mentors who genuinely wanted them to succeed.

Wise men listen and increase learning. Men of understanding heed wise counsel. Only fools despise wisdom and instruction, and June, one by one, was eliminating excuses for losing.

"I remember," says June, "a quote from [NBA coach] Pat Riley, who said: *'If a team doesn't speak with one voice, you're beaten before you tee it up.'* Our staff spoke with a *single* voice."

If the Hawai'i players would incline their ears to wisdom and apply their hearts to understanding, 1999 had a chance to be very, very special, indeed.

Chapter 12

"NOT ONE BOY LEAVES DEFEATED"

Spring of 1999 in Hawai'i wasn't the best of times. The islands were the geographical equivalent of Anna Nicole Smith: externally beautiful, robust mountains, but internally tormented and more than a little dysfunctional.

The Honolulu Police Department was facing allegations of brutality and discrimination after three innocent men were shot and killed by officers. Trash piled up around the island when garbage collectors declared a work stoppage.

The economy was its worst in decades. Residents who lost jobs in the private sector found that traditionally secure government jobs were not readily available. In addition to private companies making workforce cuts, the city, the state and the military also announced that jobs would be eliminated.

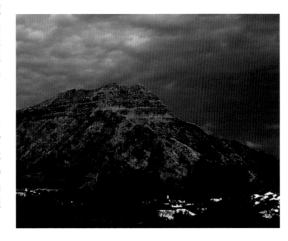

The trickle-down effects of the first Gulf War were pounding the state like the waves on the North Shore. State revenues were horrific and tourism was at its lowest point. Reading the morning paper over a steaming cup of Kona coffee was enough to deflate your spirit and send you back to bed: People were fleeing the state for jobs in Los Angeles or Las Vegas because there were no opportunities anywhere.

A published report from the University of Hawai'i Economic Research Organization was bleak. "Hawaii's economy has clearly bottomed out," it read. "Eastbound visitor arrivals are down. There is convincing evidence that the construction cycle in Hawaii has bottomed out. Labor markets tend to lag general economic conditions. Non-agricultural jobs continue to decline."

The *only* good news was that "civilian employment" had risen by a whopping .05 percent, which basically meant Burger King was now open until 2 a.m.

Scandal rocked the revered Bishop Estate — Hawai'i's largest private landowner and among the nation's richest charitable trusts — when trustees came under fire from the attorney general and a court-appointed master. Henry Peters became the first trustee criminally indicted in the estate's 114-year history. Federal prosecutors also indicted former state senator Milton Holt, an estate employee, on theft charges.

"It was *all* gloom and doom," says former Hawai'i athletic director Hugh Yoshida. "The state had no money and neither did the University. We didn't have the private entities to do what was needed. There was no funding for anything. When June got here, the mentality of everything we were dealing with couldn't have been more negative.

"For someone to turn down something perceived to be better to actually come here, that was a total change for the entire state of Hawai'i. Instead of being treated as lesser-than, somebody had chosen them ahead of something else. That's the kind of impact June Jones made on all of us. People kept asking why, and he kept saying, you'll see.

"He brought hope to the entire state."

A leader, my friends, is one who sees *more than others see*, who sees *farther than others* see and who sees *before others do.*

In spite of the national criticism surrounding his staff, June Jones quickly became a lone source of optimism among the people of Hawai'i. As spring practice approached, curiosity and excitement began to peak throughout the islands as Jones spread his brand of encouragement with evangelical fervor.

While it's admittedly difficult to balance optimism and realism, intuition and planning, faith and fact, June had little choice if he hoped to be an effective leader.

Whereas the departed Fred von Appen was a recluse, Jones was singing like a tea kettle up to its neck in hot water. He shook every hand he could grab, kissed every baby within reach and missed nary a moment to reach out to the community. His message of hope, backed by his simply likeable personality and sincerity, played well to all but the most cynical critics. Booster meetings, rotary luncheons, pork cookouts in parking lots — Jones was everywhere. The locals embraced his wit and disarming charm.

RALPH "PBASE" OMOTO

Whether it was his meek spirit, his gentle name, or his uncommon embracing of the nonfootball community, June gave the people his breath, and they in turn offered *aloha*.

As for football, anyone who could type the words "Run 'n' Shoot" into an Internet search engine suddenly realized that, on the field, the boys just might have a fighting chance.

Meanwhile, in the bowels of the football offices, June and his staff of eccentrics were toiling late into the night, discussing, arguing, plotting on just how they could take lemons and make lemonade. In the classroom, he and his staff were pushing his players' average GPA to 2.50.

One afternoon, Yoshida walked into June's office, where he was lost in thought and furiously scribbling notes in a playbook.

Yoshida, obviously, is of Asian descent, slight in stature, but with a deeply powerful spirit. He has honest, dark eyes that radiate beneath a crop of side-parted but thinning jet-black hair. His tone is soft but firm; when he speaks, one feels his genuine conviction.

Yoshida, as athletic director, didn't want to discourage his new coach, but he did realize privately that Jones had put his career in jeopardy, particularly if he had any aspirations of returning to the NFL. However, one thing Jones quickly asserted to all who would listen is that regardless of how bleak any situation might seem, he had the confidence to carry them through.

"I asked him, 'Is this what you anticipated? Is this what you thought it would be when you came back?'" Yoshida says.

Jones lifted his head but didn't look at Yoshida. He stared straight ahead, unblinking, into space.

"He didn't say a word," Yoshida says. "He knew what I was saying was true. I would've loved to know what he was thinking. But few people understand June. He thinks differently than everyone. *There is something inside him that makes him believe he can make a difference.* This is something he wanted to do, *something he personally told himself he would do.* This is what separates June Jones from the rest of his colleagues in coaching.

"In football, coaches don't take risks. They do everything possible to cast themselves in a totally positive light. Not June. He puts everything on the line, and he's not afraid to ruffle feathers. I knew this was far greater than football for him. He wanted to make a difference *on the entire state of Hawai'i, at a time when Hawai'i desperately needed it.*

"That says everything about his character, how he lives life. That, to me, is what began to motivate the kids. They saw the intangibles.

"They began to see that their coach was willing to *risk it all along with them.*"

Years on the coaching carouse had taught June a few things: Winning college football teams and traditions — Michigan, Notre Dame, Nebraska, Tennessee — do not happen by accident. They must be built — and inspired — from the ground up by people who know precisely what they are doing, not only on the field but also on the administrative level.

In the final analysis, the guiding light has to be the head coach, the man who hires the staff, decides upon the technical approach and brings together each of the vital parts: academics, motivation and personal interrelationships.

While the University of Hawai'i had lost sight of its football heritage, the same could not be said for its rich island traditions and educational acumen. A total of 616 programs are offered throughout the University of Hawai'i system, with 123 devoted to bachelor's degrees, 92 to master's degrees, 53 to doctoral degrees, 3 to first-professional degrees, 4 to post-baccalaureate degrees and 115 for associate's degrees and various other certifications.

But what about football?

For Jones and his staff, there would be, well, enough scholarships to field a team; how good a team remained to be seen. With many long nights in his immediate future, at least Jones could take solace in the island's burgeoning coffee plantations, making Hawai'i the only state to produce java commercially. With game-film videotape spinning through the late-night VCR, June and his staff would need every drop.

Many, many nights the muffled roar coming down the hallway in the football offices was the snoring of the enormous Dennis McKnight, curled in a fetal position on his tiny loveseat office sofa, where he would collapse, utterly exhausted.

When it comes to leadership, there are no shortcuts.

Unlike most mainland jobs, June had to be extremely sensitive to vast cultural diversity. The Hawaiian Islands are roughly 33 percent Caucasian, 22 percent Japanese-Americans, 15 percent Filipino-Americans, 12 percent Hawaiian and 6 percent Chinese-Americans,

RALPH "PBASE" OMOTO

Graduates of the University of Hawai'i come from a diverse culture

along with a smattering of African-Americans, Koreans, Samoans and Micronesians.

"The nicest thing about Hawai'i is that when we select a beauty queen at the university we don't have just one," says past president Dr. Thomas Hamilton. "We have a Polynesian beauty queen, a Chinese beauty queen, a Japanese beauty queen, a Filipino beauty queen, a Portuguese beauty queen, a Puerto Rico beauty queen, a Negro beauty queen, *and* a Caucasian beauty queen. Six, seven, eight beauty queens all in a row. That's what I like best about Hawai'i."

"The state is very clannish," Yoshida says, in an attempt to expound on the islands' intricate cultural tapestry. "We have all grown up in very ethnic backgrounds. However, the Hawai'i people all come together like no other if you present the proper cause."

Like, say, *Hawai'i football*, for instance.

Hatred stirs up strife, but aloha, or love, conquers all. Jones and his diverse staff began to hug their diverse players, to openly demonstrate aloha, and slowly, painstakingly, their once-divided team began to pull together as one.

"Our boys were like abused dogs down at the shelter," says McKnight. "They just hadn't been hugged and told they'd be OK in a long, long time."

June, along with Hawaiian-born Wes Suan, Ron Lee and Rich Miano, began to teach the critical importance of *aloha* and *ohana*, which is Hawaiian for "family." Family, to Jones, means *nobody* gets left behind or forgotten.

"June has the *aloha* spirit," says linebacker Kurt Gouveia, who played for Jones with the San Diego Chargers. "June always has his hand out to help somebody else."

The actual concept of *ohana* is complex. The mainland concept of family is a mother, a father and their children. In Hawai'i, however, the "other" type of family is more the norm than the exception. Many families consist of parents, grandparents and children all residing under a single roof. It's not unusual to see a child being raised by a grandparent or auntie, while the parents live and work elsewhere.

The Hawaiian family, or *ohana*, can also consist of others *not related by birth*. A valued friend can be a member of your ohana. An entire group of close friends or associates can be an *ohana*. The late Hawaiian music superstar Israel Kamakawiwo'ole often referred to his Internet friends as his cyber *ohana*.

Therefore, taught June, soul food–eating boys from Texas, Mormon quarterbacks from Utah, surfers from San Diego and Polynesian kids from the North Shore should resolve their differences, join hands and *embrace ohana*.

As surely as the sun rose each day over Hawai'i's splendor, the righteousness of *ohana* began to heal deep scars between players. Imperfect young men with imperfect *seasons* began to let go of the past. Selfishness began to dissipate in the face of harmony and growth. June displayed good tidings to the meek; he picked up his brokenhearted kids and proclaimed *liberty*.

Champions don't become champions in the ring; they are merely recognized there.

The weight room was open before sunrise. With every clang of a barbell, you could literally *hear* fat turning to muscle. Quarterbacks and receivers began to find their way to the practice field before sunup to throw on their own. Grades were improving. Players were suddenly noticeably absent at local college bars and parties.

They had yet to play a down, but June Jones couldn't help but smile.

▼▼▼▼▼▼▼▼▼▼▼▼▼▼▼

Hatred stirs up strife, but aloha, or love, conquers all. Jones and his diverse staff began to hug their diverse players, openly demonstrate aloha, and slowly, painstakingly, their once-divided team began to pull together as one.

▲▲▲▲▲▲▲▲▲▲▲▲▲▲▲

Recruiting at Hawai'i has always been a glaring issue. As a member of the Western Athletic Conference, or WAC, Hawai'i's "local" recruiting trips to the West Coast of the U.S. mainland require a five-to-seven-hour flight each way and at minimum, an overnight stay. Any place on the East Coast to scout a prospect requires that a coach stay for *days* — on a recruiting budget of only $65,000. During the season, coaches are unable to leave on Thursdays or Fridays.

Meanwhile, back at the fat-cat ranch, football powers like Florida State, Southern Cal, Miami, Auburn, UCLA — the list is endless — enjoy rich budgets, plenty of scouts and coaches and the ability to go anywhere anytime. The University of Florida, for instance, flies its coaches in *two* planes: a Cessna Citation seven-seat jet and Beechcraft King Air. Florida State coach Bobby Bowden once made 48 trips on a state-owned plane in a single season, at a cost to taxpayers of $60,000.

Not so for the Hawai'i staff, who spent more time with shoes in hand waiting in security lines than visiting recruits. Jones and his staff realized very early in his tenure that they would have to depend on locals and

walk-ons to help win games. Many future scholarship players to come would originate as walk-ons.

Open tryouts are the stuff of Hollywood lore, except that June made it reality at Hawai'i. It didn't matter if you thought a football was pumped or stuffed; if you could throw it, catch it, protect it or defend it — well, there just might be a jersey waiting for you in the Hawai'i locker room. With little time or money to travel, June and his new staff became adept

at *telemarketing*: The phone was their weapon of choice. Learning to *adapt* and *overcome*, Jones explained to his staff that they simply couldn't travel.

"That very first year," June says, "we decided to create an *atmosphere* that would make players *want to come here*. It started at the very beginning. Over time, the players would be recruiting us, we wouldn't be recruiting them, but in 1999, we had to begin with the end in mind."

Though few of the new recruits would help that season, Hawai'i still landed 14 junior college prospects, compared to eight during von Appen's first season. June's brilliance of having such local coaches as Morrison and Lee aboard panned out quickly, as a number of hometown kids reversed their choices to go elsewhere and jumped aboard the Hawai'i train, which was ever so slowly beginning to creak forward.

"Pati [Mailo] was all set to go to Utah, but the Hawai'i coaches came in and did a good job of convincing him to stay home," said Sivaki Livai, head coach of Kahuku High, of his 6-feet-2, 240-pound standout. "He was the backbone of our defense. I believe he can play right away."

Mailo topped the list of six other local stars who opted to be Warriors, including an offensive lineman named Vince Manuwai, who also changed his mind and chose Hawai'i. Little did Manuwai realize the life-changing ramifications of his choice, which, as for so many others under Jones, would one day result in NFL fame.

There is a line of demarcation on the Hawai'i campus, as the school is not so tactfully divided into two parts: Upper Campus and Lower Campus.

In the spring of 1999, the eyes of the scientific world were focused on Upper Campus, where Ryuzo Yanagimachi and other University of Hawai'i researchers announced they had cloned mice.

More than 50 mice, spanning three generations, were cloned using a process dubbed *"The Honolulu Technique."*

Meanwhile, the eyes of the football world were focused on Lower Campus, where June Jones, Dan Morrison, Ron Lee and other University of Hawai'i coaches announced that they, too, were about to clone *Mouse.*

▼▼▼▼▼▼▼▼▼▼▼▼▼▼▼

As surely as the sun rose each day over Hawaii's splendor, the righteousness of ohana began to heal deep scars between players. Imperfect young men with imperfect pasts and imperfect seasons began to let go of the past. Selfishness began to dissipate in the face of harmony and growth. June displayed good tidings to the meek; he picked up his broken-hearted kids, and proclaimed liberty.

▲▲▲▲▲▲▲▲▲▲▲▲▲▲▲

Nearly 100 boys, spanning countless generations, would be cloned using some Honolulu techniques of their own.

When Dan Robinson trotted out into the bright Hawai'i sun for his first spring practice under June Jones, he couldn't believe his eyes.

"There were fans," he says. "The practice field was lined with fans. And they were *cheering* as we came out. That was a little different. The year before, we'd had about 10 people out there for spring practice, and nine were reporters. People were up in the parking garage just to get a glimpse of us. It was crazy."

McKnight had a different reaction.

"Say what you want about [von Appen's] coaching ability, but they did know how to recruit," he says. "We took the field, for the first time, and I couldn't believe how talented the o-line really was. And these kids didn't whine, bitch or moan. They *worked hard,* day one.

"But I do remember thinking, *'How did this much talent possibly lose that many games?'*

Coaching? Could it be so simple?

Are you kidding me?

"By fall, we'd completed the best off-season program we'd ever had," says Robinson. "June and his staff had broken down every single position, and we had all begun to relearn everything we knew. I'd never seen a head coach who could stand in front of a room and coach every single position to the finest detail.

"The assistant coaches were phenomenal. I had never been around a staff where *every single coach was exactly on the same page*, on everything. Just for laughs, you could literally ask another coach a question, and you'd get the *same exact answer* you just got from your position coach."

The best executive, said former U.S. president Theodore Roosevelt, *"is the one who has sense enough to pick good men to do what he wants done, and self-restraint enough to keep from meddling with them while they do it."*

Control freaks *destroy* morale.

June believed in *singleness of purpose*, and then let your coaches coach.

One voice.

Robinson loved what he saw happening with his wide receivers, where Ron Lee told them to forget everything they *thought* they knew, to *trust him* while he *rebuilt* them from scratch.

"Every practice," Dan says, "all you heard was *'catch it in the noose, catch it in the noose.'*"

"The noose," as defined 30 years before by Mouse Davis, is achieved by opening wide the fingers of both hands and connecting the thumbs and forefingers to form a circle, or *noose*, which fits perfectly around the point of a spinning football. Should you ever want to sit through a lecture on catching the football, then insert yourself into a Mouse Davis or June Jones' practice and try catching a ball *off your pads*.

Justice will be swift.

"To this day," says June, "I'm still shocked at the number of All-Pro receivers in the NFL who *don't know how to catch*. If a ball touches your equipment, you're taking the risk of it caroming off, which could mean an interception, or worse: six points the other way. All of our guys are disciplined. They catch with their *hands*, not their *shoulder pads*."

Furthermore, Craig Stutzmann, Dwight Carter, Attrice Brooks, Ashley Lelie and the rest of the receiving corps were told, under no uncertain terms, that they would be fast, they would *never let up on a single route* and they would play the entire game at the same speed at which they started.

"You will run hard, fast and *competitively*," Jones told them.

Between the coaching of June Jones (l) and Dan Morrison (r), Dan Robinson became one of the best quarterbacks in college football

Competitively?

"We don't run plain routes," Jones says. "We *competitively* run to space."

Meanwhile, on the offensive line, Mike Cavanaugh, barely standing 5-feet-6, is a portly man with thick, round glasses. He stood in absolute contrast to the thick-chested, oak-tree stature of Dennis

McKnight. As a pair, however, they worked well in tandem, alternating between intimidation and intimacy.

The hitting was intense from the outset. Offensive line play might be the most critical aspect of the Run 'n' Shoot, for every opposing coach thinks he is the first to come up with the "brilliant" idea of multiple blitzes to pressure the quarterback into mistakes, a trap set by Mouse years before.

"It all begins up front," McKnight growled, and they listened, for he could physically still take any *two of them* to the ground if he so chose.

"You know the whole world says you guys can't play," Cavanaugh barked in his unforgettable raspy voice. "Have any of you boys ever been to Missouri? Do you know what is says on the license plate? It says, *'The Show Me State.'* Well, if you think you can play, then you *better start showing me!"*

The *crack* of pads echoed across the field, sending chills down the spines of Hawai'i faithful who gathered to watch the new Warriors butt horns like rams, sweat dripping through their facemasks. Hopes were soaring higher than Hawai'i's gasoline prices.

This did not look, sound or act like any Hawai'i football team they'd seen before.

Linemen who had never been taught *technique* were being instructed to *drop their butts*, set at *angles*, use *leverage*, have *fast hands*, get *their head around*, use *proper set and proper punch*, keep their *hands inside the defender's body* — and they were mesmerized.

It was like the day in algebra class when, suddenly, *it all just makes sense.*

McKnight would walk behind the troops, firing salvos of encouragement, until he caught a mistake. *"You look like Tarzan,"* he roared, *"but you play like Jane!"* Of course, Cavanaugh would then quietly follow behind McKnight and rebuild that player's confidence. And — surprise — they'd do it all over again.

Build up, tear down, build up, tear down — but always leave them built up.

Offensive line coach Mike Cavanaugh

"June told us in meetings," McKnight says, "that we were not to be just yellers and screamers. Now, we would yell for emphasis, but if we tore into their butts, we made sure we *immediately went right behind 'em and loved 'em up.*

"June *insisted* that *not one boy — whether he was a starter or a redshirt who would never play — ever leave our field feeling defeated. June said there would not be one kid left behind."*

Repetition, repetition, repetition.

During an afternoon film session, when Cavanaugh overheard a player snort that 6-feet-5, 322-pound Adrian Klemm and the more svelte 6-feet-5, 317-pound Kanalau Noa had become his "favorites," he exploded. "Let me tell you guys something," he said. "If you want to be my favorite, then be the best, and *you'll be my favorite.*"

Cavanaugh and McKnight would frequently repeat that *"the eye in the sky don't lie,"* in reference to the video cameras that captured their every move, which later would be broken down together in team meetings. In one such meeting, Cavanaugh grabbed a videotape and held it high above his head.

"Every practice, every game, every day, this is your *signature*," he said. "When somebody from the NFL pops this in, they aren't going to ask if it was hot or cold, or if you were sick or tired, or whether you were hurt or not. *This is your signature*. You need to put your *signature* on this tape *every single time you put on a helmet*."

For fun, the starting defense occasionally would be invited over to give the offense a "look," with players blitzing from all angles. Days, then weeks passed, and with every blitz pickup, every protection covered, confidence began to swell, and — well, *practice* was *fun again*.

Running backs Avion Weaver and Afatia Thompson took pride in their new roles and would grow to love splattering defensive ends and blitzing safeties. "But we told them, when you do get the ball, the holes are going to be so big you won't believe it," says McKnight. "June reminded them that [the late] Craig "Ironhead" Heyward rushed for over 1,000 yards and went to the Pro Bowl in Atlanta in this offense."

Avion was more of a pure runner than Afatia, but neither fought against each other; rather, they *collaborated* to perfectly complement one another.

"Keep your heads up, boys!" McKnight would shout each day, to anyone who would listen. "Keep your heads up! We're going to be playing at Christmas. If you don't believe it, leave now. *But I'm telling you — we're going to a bowl game, and when we get there, we're gonna kick somebody's butt!*"

Hawai'i? Bowl game?

Are you kidding me?

UNIVERSITY OF HAWAII ATHLETICS

Chapter 13

THE LOVE AND PATIENCE OF A KUPUNA KANE

Digging deep into Hawaiian customs, June grasped how the people instinctively embraced a duty of love, respect and obedience to their elders, who in return lovingly provided *direction* to meet the needs of the people.

In Hawaiian tradition, there is a great respect for elders, or *kupuna,* which surpasses any feelings of individuality. In old Hawai'i, *kupuna* are respected as keepers of Hawai'i's wisdom and knowledge. Still today, younger Hawaiians are told *nānā i ke kumu,* or to *"look to the source."*

A *kupuna kāne* is a wise *grandfather,* and June gave his defense one in the form of defensive coordinator Greg McMackin. With the patience of Job, McMackin was given the arduous task of resuscitating the worst defense in all of college football.

McMackin entered the meeting room with his defensive troops, who were noticeably nervous.

At first blush, the 5-feet-10-inch Greg McMackin doesn't seem intimidating. His grandfatherly nature is evident from the moment he speaks: He is articulate, soft-spoken and steady. It's hard to believe this gentle man mentored the likes of Ray Lewis, Cortez Kennedy and an array of other NFL defensive superstars. Harder still is to imagine this polite little Irishman unleashing the hounds of hell on an offense.

Believe it. It's always the quiet ones that kill you.

"The first thing I'd like to do," he told them, "is apologize to you. Since I don't have any film of us, I have to use our film from Seattle to show you what it is we're going to do."

Greg McMackin

UNIVERSITY OF HAWAII ATHLETICS PHOTO BY RICHARD WOOD

Linebacker Jeff Ulbrich, now of the San Francisco 49ers, had to pinch himself to believe what he had just heard.

"I thought, 'He is *apologizing to us for using NFL game film?*'" Ulbrich says, incredulous. "We're the last-place team in the *world,* and he's *apologizing* to us for showing us what he had just done to make the Seattle Seahawks one of the best defenses in the NFL?

"We couldn't believe it. Usually, when a new coaching staff comes in, they have to 'sell' you on their concepts. Here, there was no selling at all. This was like, 'Here's what we did at the highest level of football, and, uh, it works.' The Seahawks had just led the NFL in forcing turnovers. He could've said, 'You guys are dead last, I'm an NFL coach, and we're going to do this my way.' No, he *apologized.*

"Their *humility* made a *huge* statement to me right there, from the very beginning."

There's an old joke about two campers in the woods who spot a salivating, hungry grizzly running toward them at full speed, clearly with bad intentions.

One quickly begins to lace up his sneakers.

"You can't outrun that bear," says his frightened friend.

"I don't have to," the other replies. "I only have to outrun *you.*"

Such was the "it's-all-about-me" mentality of the horrific Hawai'i defense, which, in 1998, had long ago ceased to play as a team but as individuals with personal agendas.

The DNA of a defensive football player should be congruent with that of pack-hunting carnivores, but Hawai'i's players were so downtrodden that the blood had curdled in their veins. Nobody cared, because regardless of how they'd been coached, the result always had been the same.

"This game is hard work, regardless of your record," Ulbrich says. "When you consistently lose, you don't get the payoff, the reward. Eventually, you just go numb."

McMackin's boys needed a blood transfusion to melt their hearts of stone. It would take more than just consistency to take away their brokenness, to fill their emptiness. They needed encouragement. They needed to see that *something they were told to do* actually would *work* once they stepped foot on the playing field.

They needed a father's love.

Long before McMackin's pressure defenses dazzled Division-I schools and embarrassed NFL offenses, he was just a boy growing up in Springfield, Ore., only a stone's throw from Eugene. His career goal was to be a physical education teacher, thanks to the impression made upon him by one of his own PE teachers.

The lineage of McMackin's work ethic can be traced back through both his father and grandfather. His grandfather built houses and worked odd jobs during brutal economic hardship; occasionally he would let little Greg pound nails alongside him, while simultaneously driving home the lessons of life.

His father, a former boxer who was raised on the streets in Sacramento and fought in World War II, would rise at 5 a.m. and work his *two jobs* until after midnight each day.

This kept the family warm and fed, until the Christmas season when he sheared off three fingers in a wood mill accident.

> *McMackin's boys needed a blood transfusion to melt their hearts of stone. It would take more than just consistency to take away their brokenness, to fill their emptiness. They needed encouragement. They needed to see that something they were told to do actually would work once they stepped foot on the playing field.*

"That Christmas," McMackin remembers, "he was out of work after his fingers were cut off. *But family always came first.* We had walnut trees in the backyard. So, for extra money, he and I sat at the table cracking walnuts and listening to the Oregon game on the radio together . . . we later sold [the walnuts] to get money for Christmas."

When McMackin seriously hurt a bully in a high school fistfight, he fully expected to face his father's wrath. What he got, instead, would have long-reaching ramifications on his life, his coaching career and ultimately the 1999 University of Hawai'i defense.

"He just listened," McMackin says. "He *never yelled.* Basically, he did the *opposite* of what I expected. He said, 'You can *never* lose control of yourself like that again.' And that was it. He basically gave me a pass. That made an impression on me, something I think about every day I'm on the field with these young men.

"Just because somebody uses bad judgment once doesn't make them a bad person."

Fate tipped its hand when the 24-year-old McMackin landed his first coaching job at no other than *Aloha High School* in Beaverton, Ore. There, the one-time little *nutcracker* was introduced to the business end of the wily mind of none other than the King of Mice, Mouse Davis himself, who was coaching crosstown at Hillsboro High and already owned two state championships.

"Mouse took me under his wing," McMackin says. "I was the new guy in the Metro League. He had beaten everybody else in the state so badly, I think he just needed a friend. From there, I went to coach for Mouse's brother at Oregon College. Mouse basically made me a family member."

The pieces all fit. When the ever-loyal Mouse took control of the USFL's Denver Gold, of course he offered McMackin his first pro job, all the while teaching him how to hone character, relationships, knowledge, intuition, experience, past success and ability.

His way to the top hadn't been easy. McMackin, when he was still a small-college coach, vividly recalls the day at a coaching clinic when the speaker told the audience, "You guys will never be more than 1-AA coaches." "That didn't sit well with me," McMackin says. "My grandfather told me since I was a boy that I could be anything I ever wanted to be if I worked hard enough."

Now, decades later, what would *this* grandfather tell his boys at Hawai'i, who hadn't won a *road game* in seven years and hadn't won a *single game* in nearly two?

Hear now, children, the instruction of a true *kupuna*.

"The first thing we did in 1999," McMackin explains, "is get the bad-attitude guys *away* from the good-attitude guys. If a guy kept missing workouts, June would cut him, and he didn't care who the guy was. He probably cut 12 to15 guys who had scholarships just because of their attitudes. He told them they could keep their scholarships and get their education, just get off the field.

"We didn't come in and try to get rid of everybody. We actually tried to *save everybody.*

"June and Mouse care less about your talent and more about your attitude. If your attitude stinks and you refuse help again and again, then there's nothing we can do for you. That was a big part of our message, part of *ohana.* We had to become a *family,* and *everybody had to learn to sacrifice* for the team.

"*Nobody* is greater than the team."

Sacrifice to June Jones is an ongoing process, not a one-time payment.

It only took a quick glance around the Hawai'i practice field to realize there was nary a Ray Lewis or Cortez Kennedy *anywhere*. It's easy to be a great coach with great players, but when your players are average, *real coaches* emerge.

Not to mention grandfathers, who *always* have a trick or two up their

Secondary coach Rich Miano and defensive coordinator Greg McMackin

sleeve. McMackin was about to pull a wooden nickel out of thin air — *poof!* —right behind your ear.

"We need as much speed as we can get on the field," McMackin told June.

After discussions with the other defensive assistants, George Lumpkin and Rich Miano, McMackin's diagnosis was that *speed* would be their only chance.

Together, the red-eyed staff reviewed film, laboring over the defense and formations and strategies the way an emergency room surgeon gets elbow deep in a bloody rib cage to massage a failing heart.

"We have to pressure people into mistakes," McMackin said. "We need to rethink everything and everybody. I think we need to move safeties to linebackers and linebackers to ends and move the ends inside to tackle."

Parameters were suggested: If a linebacker weighed 250 and could run a 4.8-second 40, he would be moved to the defensive line. If a safety weighed 210 and ran a 4.6 or less, he'd be moved to linebacker.

UNIVERSITY OF HAWAII ATHLETICS PHOTO BY LOIS MANIN

Rich Miano – love the shorts! – coaches the secondary

June and the other coaches agreed, and thus began the biggest defensive overhaul in the history of college football. Scribbling on a grease board, they began moving players laterally, sideways, vertically, proposing various combinations, matchups and schemes.

"How do you guys feel about moving Anthony Smith from safety to linebacker?" McMackin asked. Miano and Lumpkin agreed. "He's a slow safety," said Lumpkin, "but at 210 [pounds], he'll be a *fast* linebacker."

"We got a kid on offense that you guys could use," June piped in. "Robert Kemfort. We've been looking at him as either a running back or a receiver, but he can definitely run and he's pretty physical."

"Sounds like a linebacker to me," Miano grinned.

"While you guys are stealing my skill players, you may as well take a look at [receiver] Yaphet Warren, too," June said.

The coaches chuckled, and Yaphet Warren and Robert Kemfort became Division I linebackers, just like that.

"Nate Jackson's really young," McMackin said, "and he's only 151 pounds. But pound-for-pound, he's the toughest kid I've got out there."

"Free safety," said Miano. They all nodded in agreement.

"What about Shawndel Tucker and Quincy LeJay?"

"Well," Miano said, "They're both good athletes. I think Shawndel can cover, he can run in space, but Quincy can't. We'll get him killed if we stick him out there by himself."

"Well," McMackin said, scribbling, "if we're playing field-corner, boundary corner . . ."

Scribble, scribble, scribble . . .

". . . then when we get on a hash, we'll move Shawndel to the wide side; Quincy, we'll roll to the short side, and not let him ever get in any one-on-one mismatches."

"Perfect," said June.

"Now the junior college kid from Northwest Mississippi . . ."

"Dee Miller," said Miano. "I like him at strong safety. He's got good hips and good eyes."

Scribble, scribble, scribble . . .

"I think we need to put Joe Correia at defensive end," Lumpkin said.

"The baseball player?" June asked. Correia had been a former quarterback and minor-league baseball player but had grown to enormous size.

"If that's the case," McMackin said, "we'll move Mike Iosua and Matt Elam inside, to the tackles."

"What about the other end?" June asked.

"Well, this might surprise you," McMackin said, "but the Ulbrich kid — he was hurt and didn't play in the spring, but he's totally outplaying [middle linebacker] Matt Paul. I've got a feeling that Ulbrich has a chance to be pretty special.

"I say we build around him. I'm thinking we move Ulbrich to Mac [middle linebacker] and turn him loose and move Matt Paul to the other defensive end. That will let us run a lot of zone blitz, and our ends can drop, kind of like playing with five linebackers and two guys inside. And Matt's speed *as an end* is going to cause people some problems."

Scribble, scribble, scribble . . .

And so it went, into the night, until they had drafted an entirely new defense.

"We're going to have some problems with really good inside running

teams," McMackin predicted. "We just don't have the personnel, but we'll be fast to the ball, we'll force turnovers and hopefully, we'll make our own luck."

"You guys having fun yet?" June asked.

Are you kidding me?

▼▼▼▼▼▼▼▼▼▼▼▼▼▼

"The first thing you do is gain the players' confidence. The second thing you do is praise them for whatever they do right, however small it might be. Take the smallest thing, and build, build, build. Don't yell, don't scream. Let them know when you're upset, but if you yell all the time, they'll tune you out. Correct the bad things while you're building on the good things."

▲▲▲▲▲▲▲▲▲▲▲▲▲▲

The next step was installing the new defense.

"It's critical, in the beginning, to be very, very patient," McMackin says. "You cannot get frustrated. You have to display unwavering confidence in the staff, the plan and the players and what they are doing."

"The first thing you do is gain the players' confidence. The second thing you do is praise them for whatever they do right, however small it might be. Take the smallest thing and build, build, build. Don't yell, don't scream. Let them know when you're upset, but if you yell all the time, they'll tune you out. Correct the bad things while you're building on the good things."

"Then you teach. That's the biggest thing. Become a teacher. Once they understand your system is sound, you're less of a coach and more of a teacher."

Repetition, repetition, repetition.

Throughout the 1999 Hawai'i fall training camp, Mouse Davis watched from the sidelines as a *very* interested observer. Not once in 30 years had he neglected June Jones, and he wasn't about to fail his old quarterback, especially now, when June needed him the most for encouragement and support.

"No big deal," Mouse said. He didn't interfere, it was no longer his place

or his team. He let his coaches coach. He watched from a distance, arms crossed, gum cracking away behind his always beaming, radiant smile. Next to Mouse was Heather McMackin, Greg's wife. Other frequent visitors to practice included McMackin's children and grandchildren.

"Mouse always said to make football a family deal," McMackin explains. "Heather's been my partner in this whole thing since I started."

Who better to teach *ohana* than men who *live by it?*

It's impossible to know how much energy that Jones and McMackin, two of Mouse's favorite protégés, pulled from the old coach that fall as they set out on a mission deemed impossible.

But don't kid yourself: After all these years, McMackin and June, just like the boys they were now teaching, were warmed by Mouse's *acceptance* and *approval.*
Mouse, too, was emotional, for *true* teachers don't do this for money.

There is only one Mouse Davis

True teachers understand that *teaching never ends.* That's why Mouse, a grandfather himself many times over, was there *in person,* leading *by example.* A true teacher's lessons live for eternity, imparted from generation to generation.

It hadn't been too long since Beverly, Davis' best friend and lifetime partner in marriage, whom he always called his *'lil girl,* had passed away from cancer. On this day, his football ohana was one person short, and he missed her dearly.

If only the 'lil girl could see these boys now, he thought.

Footballs filled the blue Hawaiian sky amid the cheering of the optimistic fans who ringed the sidelines. Coaches barked instructions of "In the *noose!*" . . . "*Pop the eyes!*" . . . "*Open your hips!*" . . . "*Run to space!*"

Mouse Davis turned away, looked toward the heavens and wiped away a tear.

Chapter 14

THE MONSTER IN THE MIDDLE FROM MORGAN HILL

It's true: Pressure *really* does make diamonds.

When Connecticut-based Apollo Diamond, Inc., shocked the world by announcing that its scientists can now grow *diamonds* in a laboratory setting using pressure and carbon gas, *wow,* did the traditional, billion-dollar diamond mining industry ever go ballistic.

Apollo didn't make *fake* diamonds, such as cubic zirconium. They made *real* diamonds, chemically and structurally identical to a mined diamond. So good were they, in fact, that when the *Wall Street Journal* sought independent experts to do comparative reviews, the "grown" diamonds were declared more perfect than ones that came out of the ground.

Apollo scientists, interestingly enough, begin with a "seed" of a diamond, roughly the size of a shirt button. They place the seeds into a "growth" chamber, where carbon is then "rained" onto the diamond seeds, thus "growing" a new diamond one crystal at a time on top of the seed. The diamonds are then cut and polished into perfect, *authentic* diamonds.

June Jones was growing diamonds on the football field long before anyone ever grew one in a lab. The process was eerily similar: Start with a seed of talent, put them in the growth chamber that is his "system" and then let pressure run its course.

"We were blessed, to be honest," says Greg McMackin. "In 1999, we really had two diamonds on both sides of the ball: Jeff Ulbrich and Dan Robinson. These were two young men who really just needed direction. They both wanted to be coached. They were willing to do anything to win."

Such amazing discoveries capture the vivid imagination of June Jones. If you want to bore June, try to hold his attention for more than 15 seconds with a story that begins, "Now, this is the way we've always done it before." He'll excuse himself and find the quickest exit. He's not interested in how it's always been done.

However, start talking innovation, such as growing a diamond from scratch, and the two of you might be there for a while. This is how Mouse hooked June 30 years ago, when he taught him entirely new theories and methods to teach the game of football differently than it had ever been done before.

"When you hire June," says Bobby Beathard, "you don't just get a coach. You get an innovator. You will get a guy who will *discover new ways* to win football games."

Today, literally thousands of high school, college and pro coaches enjoy the fruits of their labor, but it's thrilling to explore the Mouse Davis–June Jones anthropology. It's akin to tracing physicist Stephen Hawking's modern advances back to Albert Einstein, Einstein to Isaac Newton and Newton to Galileo.

The miracle is that, by 1999, both Robinson and Ulbrich had long ceased to dream about becoming diamonds. Once proud athletes, they no longer

> *The miracle is that, by 1999, both Robinson and Ulbrich had long ceased to dream about becoming diamonds. Once proud athletes, they no longer considered football fun, and the real-four-letter word – quit – had actually crossed their minds. Like their teammates, they had been beat-down, put-down, kicked-down to the point that, forget their bite, their bark no longer worked, and it wasn't even worth the effort if it did.*

considered football fun, and the real four-letter word — *quit* — had actually crossed their minds. Like their teammates, they had been beaten down, put down, kicked down to the point that, forget their bite, their *bark* no longer worked, and it wasn't even worth the effort if it did.

Ulbrich's shoulder and knee were shot, and he was forced to undergo surgery for both. As for Robinson, there wasn't a single part of his body that didn't hurt. He had suffered broken legs, shoulder separations, broken ribs, fingers — you name it — and of course, the now-famous broken coccyx.

This was the situation until June and his staff showed up with a process that could cut away years of defeat and polish them to brilliance.

Of course, the traditional football industry went ballistic and said it couldn't be done *in Hawai'i*, not realizing that the louder it protested, the more pressure it applied; all the better for the diamond-manufacturing Jones and his crew.

But nobody said it would be easy.

Ironically, the übertough Jeff Ulbrich wouldn't have wanted it any other way.

A leisurely drive through Morgan Hill, Calif., will give you a deeper look into the psyche of Jeff Ulbrich. Located in the southern part of California's Santa Clara County, this tiny bedroom community was founded in the early 1900s and named after Hiram Morgan Hill, who had retreated to the deep country back in 1884. Originally a community of ranchers, farmers and orchardists, Morgan Hill today is a thriving metropolis of roughly 42,500 people, give or take the mailman.

Ulbrich grew up with two older sisters but frolicked in a neighborhood full of rough-and-tumble boys, most of whom were older than he. Jeff wrestled and played soccer. "All of us were old-school farm kids," he says. "My friends and family all worked in the farming industry. These were all legitimate tough guys, products of the land. It was a great starting point for me. Morgan Hill was my foundation."

During his sophomore year at Live Oak High School, Ulbrich tried out for football when teasing members of the school varsity dared the young champion wrestler to try his hand on the gridiron. "You can't hang," they bet him, which proved to be a big, big mistake: From the day Jeff snapped the chinstrap on his very first helmet, he fell in love with the sport. More than one heckler found himself on the receiving end of his vicious tackling; being hit by Ulbrich was like standing in front of a cannon holding a lighter.

"In later years, the X's and O's of football had little to do with what was in my mind or what was ingrained in my heart," says the intense Ulbrich, who rocketed to first-team All-League as a safety and became his team's Most Valuable Player. "It was a great starting point."

Morgan Hill

He was a walk-on at San Jose State, where he redshirted a year before he was sent packing, a move the school would later deeply regret. "They didn't even give me a chance," Ulbrich says. "I never even got in the rotation." So he followed the footsteps of other local boys to Gavilan (Junior) College in south Santa Clara County. In his lone season, he earned first-team All-Conference and became his team's MVP, which attracted the attention of Hawai'i coaches, who offered him a scholarship.

Ulbrich played in only seven games his junior year, starting three at strong inside linebacker. His knee injury in the season's fifth week against hated Brigham Young was career threatening; yet against better judgment, he limped through the pain to finish the year. The result was about what you would expect from a one-legged linebacker: 41 tackles, one sack and a fumble recovery.

By the end of the 1998 season, the Hawai'i football team was little more than a group of really frustrated individuals. The words *"Hawai'i"* and *"team"* didn't even belong in the same sentence. A few players who might have had pro potential weren't playing for the *team* but for the *highlight reels,* in the hopes of somehow getting a one-way ticket out of hell.

"It was absolutely the most frustrating time of my life," says Ulbrich. "As for *ohana,* it didn't exist, not on this football team. From my perspective, away from the team, I was questioning whether I was going to play anymore. I had the really bad knee injury and I was really struggling in rehab.

"My shoulder wasn't so bad, but with the knee I was missing school and I just didn't want to be there anymore. Everything had fallen apart. Anyone who has enough talent to actually be a Division I athlete anywhere can only imagine what it's like to be 0-18. Consistent failure, after a while, just wears down everything inside you."

Sick of losing, fed up with the attitudes in the locker room, his football dreams dashed, Ulbrich resigned himself to thoughts of life in the real world.

UNIVERSITY OF HAWAII ATHLETICS PHOTO BY FRANCES CAMERA

Hawai'i "Monster" Jeff Ulbrich

That is to say, until the morning guys were pounding on his dorm room door, yelling and screaming that the NFL's June Jones was the new head coach at the University of Hawai'i.

Ulbrich grabbed his crutches and, as fast he could, hobbled straight to the football office.

They are going to know who I am, he said to himself.

All I want is a chance to prove it.

June wasn't there that day, but Dennis McKnight sure was. "I sat with Dennis McKnight for 15 minutes," Jeff remembers. "It took him about 15 minutes to get my fire burning again, to make me forget about everything from the past . . . it literally all just disappeared. Coach McKnight is so focused, so intense, and he started telling me about June and talking about winning a *bowl game.*

"I knew if I could get healthy, these NFL guys would be a great barometer of where I stood as an athlete, because they knew what NFL talent looks like. Coach McKnight told me about June's offense, all of his success in the past, and he guaranteed me that June was going to make this a winning program."

Ulbrich, however, was still on crutches, his knee still heavily braced. He missed all of spring drills, but he was there on the sidelines for every practice — and in meetings, on the front row, playbook open and pencil sharpened. His fire rekindled, he hit the books in the classroom and pushed his grades back to respectability. He spent hours watching film with the other assistants and prepared for fall, vowing that, if given the opportunity, the people of Hawai'i would never forget him.

"Ulbrich reminds me of Rocky Balboa," says McKnight. "He attacked the game of football like he attacked life. Whether it was school, his girlfriend or football, you didn't joke around with Jeff Ulbrich, because to him, this was no joke. He's a throwback to Dick Butkus or Ray Nitschke. One look in that kid's eyes and all of the coaches just went, *wow,* there's the heart and soul of our football team, right there."

Pressure can be toxic or intoxicating, depending on the mental makeup of the individual under fire. From the time Hawai'i's camp opened in fall of 1999, it quickly became evident that farm boys from Morgan Hill simply don't break; instead, they dare you to turn up the heat in the crucible.

"It didn't take long," says McMackin. "Jeff really started flying around and showing us what he was all about. To that point, he hadn't played a lot because he'd been hurt. Matt Paul was our starting middle linebacker, but I noticed Jeff right away. His heart and his instincts were amazing. To be honest, Jeff was still hurt, he wasn't 100 percent, but there was no denying his toughness.

"Part of coaching is recognizing the *desire* in a young man. June is all about *hunger.* He's after the hungriest guys, not always the most talented guys. Hungry guys make plays, and Jeff made plays."

Not to say Matt Paul wasn't a sound football player, as well as Ulbrich's best friend. "When we made the decision to make Jeff the heart of the defense, we moved Matt to defensive end," McMackin says. "He didn't like it at first, but he accepted it when I carefully taught him how our defensive ends are really outside linebackers with their hand on the ground." Paul was a nasty, temperamental player, and he would grow to excel at defensive end.

The only way to eat an elephant is a bite at a time. McMackin patiently installed the Seattle defense — one package, one blitz, one coverage at a time. "We built around Jeff, built up everybody's confidence and slowly kept throwing more and more stuff at them," he says. "The biggest task was keeping their confidence intact." None of the coaches told Ulbrich that, privately, they all realized he would have to play the game with superhuman strength for Hawai'i to even have a chance to win.

Jeff Ulbrich never told his coaches that he simply needed to be *appreciated* for them to extract what they needed. Adversity hadn't killed his spirit; it had *galvanized* him.

UNIVERSITY OF HAWAII ATHLETICS PHOTO BY RICHARD WOOD

The very sight of "44" put fear in the hearts of many Hawai'i opponents

"Coach Mack has a fire in him," Ulbrich says. "He *cares* about you, on and off the field. I wasn't used to coaches asking me personal questions, about my life, my family or my friends. He was like a father or a grandfather. When you develop that kind of rapport with your players, guys like me will lay *everything* in our hearts on the line for you. We hadn't played a game yet, but I was having the most *fun* I'd ever had in football."

Repetition, repetition, repetition.

"The best part of that fall camp," recalls Ulbrich, "is when all of us, as players, could believe 100 percent in the staff. June really surrounded himself with guys that didn't just speak, but men who *delivered it*. From Mack to Lumpkin to Miano, they took all the adversity, all the junk, and turned us into something. They rebuilt our confidence. My odds of *ever* playing in the NFL, without June, without those guys, were *zero*. Our team was so thirsty for success that these guys touched our souls."

The *smell* now wafting through the locker room, the meeting rooms and the practice fields wasn't sweat, or tape, or dirty carpets, or aging desks or even old attitudes.

It was the smell of life.

Poppy jasper isn't quite a diamond but a rare precious stone formed by the unique combination of volcanic and seismic activity in the El Toro mountain region of what is now known as Morgan Hill.

In folklore, the orbicular poppy jasper is thought to function like adrenaline, waking up and energizing areas of the body that appear to be sleeping. It inspires a positive, joyful attitude and provides the motivation to take creative action. Native American Indians believed it healed brokenness and heartache and enhanced strength and willpower.

It was also used to make rain — so much so, in fact, that among certain tribes the word *"jasper"* means *"rain-bringer."*

June Jones and Greg McMackin had uncovered a gem of their own from Morgan Hill, who, once polished, would inspire all the same traits as his native poppy jasper.

When Greg McMackin finally unleashed Jeff Ulbrich on the Western Athletic Conference, number 44 did what he did best:

He made rain.

Chapter 15
A DONKEY IN THE DERBY?

The now-burgeoning Hawai'i football history books hold a treasure every fan should find. Before Colt Brennan could rocket to the moon, somebody had to orbit the earth.

Almost forgotten under the weight of Brennan's torrential downpour of touchdowns, Timmy Chang's outrageous 17,000 yards, Nick Rolovich's thrilling comebacks and stunning BYU victory, on pages now yellow from time, you will discover photos of a kid with really bad legs and a megawatt smile:

Dan Robinson.

Arguably the toughest quarterback to ever lace up a flak jacket in the Hawai'i locker room, Robinson is the de facto godfather of what has become Quarterback University. If they kept records for grittiness and guts, his name would appear above all others.

Jones didn't recruit Dan Robinson. He *inherited* him in the wake of a catastrophic event, which is a little like rearing somebody else's kids after their real parents are swept away in a hurricane.

Before June Jones could achieve his heady goals as a father of tradition or a purveyor of hope, he had to begin somewhere, and that somewhere was *someone* named Dan Robinson, who would have to relearn everything he knew just to play a single season.

Tradition is defined as a continuum of change through time, representing the unbroken development of a *culture.*

Robinson was ground zero of the Hawai'i quarterback culture — the very

Captain Comeback – Quarterback Dan Robinson

first Thanksgiving turkey or Christmas tree, depending on your point of view.

Dan Robinson's major college career began auspiciously, in a bizarre tale of *Death, Lies and Videotape.*

Boise State head coach Pokey Allen visited Dan Robinson and his wife in Rexburg, Idaho, to offer the quarterback a scholarship just as he was finishing a record-setting junior college career. Devout Mormons, the Robinsons prayed about their decision and were set to commit to Allen the next day.

Only it happened that Allen, who had battled cancer, would succumb to the illness the *day after* visiting the Robinsons.

Then there was the offer from Danny Ford and the University of Arkansas. Again the Robinsons prayed, accepting that Arkansas and the Deep South must be God's will, and Dan prepared to become a Razorback.

It might have been, except that the letter-of-intent Ford had promised never came.

"It was minus 30 degrees in Rexburg," Robinson says. "I had seen Hawai'i play against Brigham Young, and I knew I could play there. I told my wife, 'I bet it's warm and sunny in Hawai'i.' So I sent them my tapes, and I ended up in Hawai'i."

At minus 30 degrees, common motor oil congeals to the consistency of a hockey puck; hydraulic fluids freeze; hot water instantly turns to ice; and pretty darn good junior college quarterbacks from Utah hallucinate about single-handedly lifting a failing program from the mire.

Even Robinson's unbending faith couldn't heal Hawai'i, and each Saturday afternoon, when bones cracked throughout his body as he was buried beneath waves of thousands of pounds of sweaty flesh, one must wonder what Robinson was thinking.

When June Jones arrived, the coach sat in stunned silence when he first popped in the tapes of Robinson. He did his best to glean something from the game film of his quarterback, but within a matter of moments he realized it was futile. In fact, he couldn't bear to watch.

"The only thing you could tell on film," June says, "is that he was one of the toughest human beings you've ever seen in your life. The film was a joke. I could tell he had a good arm, but man, he was getting killed, every snap.

"That's about all the film was worth. I never looked at it again."

▼▼▼▼▼▼▼▼▼▼▼▼▼▼

In 1999, Seabiscuit literally would be resurrected in the human metaphor of one Dan Robinson. The similarities are eerie; from the long string of consecutive losses, to the rejection and abuse of his former coaches, to his crooked legs and ungainly gait and history of injuries.

▲▲▲▲▲▲▲▲▲▲▲▲▲▲

power. In Red Pollard, Seabiscuit found a jockey who *understood* him, in spite of the fact that Pollard had never ridden on a grand stage.

If you've seen the movie — or read the more amazing book by fascinating storyteller Laura Hillenbrand — then you know the rest of the story. Often, however, what gets lost in the translation is the unique trinity of the colliding forces that created the outcome: the horse, the trainer and the jockey. Each one was useless without the others.

Seabiscuit, once rejected and alone, would catapult to greatness, whipping stronger, bigger horses with known pedigrees to become the best racehorse America had ever seen. Seabiscuit was a hero for a country trapped in the grim reality of the 1930s Depression.

"For a brief moment," says Hillenbrand, "a little brown racehorse wasn't just a little brown racehorse. He was the proxy for a nation."

If you think the last seven paragraphs are just about a horse, keep reading.

In 1938, columnist Walter Winchell published his annual list of the year's top 10 newsmakers. Franklin Delano Roosevelt was among those mentioned. So was British prime minister Neville Chamberlain and Nazi leader Adolf Hitler.

The tenth spot, however, went to a horse.

Seabiscuit was tough but not pretty. He had boxy, stumpy legs that wouldn't straighten and an ungainly gait. He was overworked and underachieving, and after he struggled in horse racing's minor leagues for the first three years of his life, equestrian aficionados considered him all but finished.

That is, until the horse fell under the tutelage of Tom Smith, a trainer whose communication and methods of teaching were *opposite* of what all believed to be true. He instantly realized Seabiscuit's raw, untapped

In 1999, Seabiscuit would literally be resurrected in the human metaphor of one Dan Robinson. The similarities are eerie: from the long string of consecutive losses to the rejection and abuse of his former coaches to his crooked legs and ungainly gait and history of injuries.

"They asked me to win the Kentucky Derby," blasted Fred von Appen, Robinson's previous coach, "but they asked me to do it with *mules.*"

The media wasn't far behind.

"It's great seeing new head coach June Jones being hands-on," wrote a local columnist, *"but I'd sure feel better if the Rainbows could recruit a couple more quarterbacks in time for this fall."*

The butt of countless donkey jokes, Dan Robinson had learned to not even glance at a newspaper stand — or worse, turn on a radio or TV —

Seabiscuit, like Robinson, resurrected his career to become one of the winningest horses in history

for his fragile psyche hurt worse than his body and honestly could take no more.

Robinson had fallen harder and farther than Humpty-Dumpty. The challenge of putting him back together again, says Richard Gerson, Ph.D., a renowned sports psychologist and founder and president of the HEADcoaching Institute, is that one must be very delicate in unraveling damage that has already been done.

In fact, like Seabiscuit, Dan Robinson had *learned to lose..*

"Frustration is a subset of self-fulfilling prophecy," teaches Gerson, who has counseled countless top-flight athletes and whose 23 books have been printed in 10 languages and countries. "Hawai'i football in 1999, if you analyze it, was *programmed* to fail."

Gerson, like many other sports psychologists, was more than just a passive observer when June Jones took over the program. He and other clinicians like him quickly realized they were witnessing a textbook dissertation on how to heal a broken-down athlete.

But Jones didn't have the luxury of a sequestered classroom or laboratory setting. His 0-18 football team was on public display for the world to witness, his every move scrutinized and analyzed.

"Before June arrived, you had the frequent changes of offensive and defensive strategies," Gerson explains. "You had the negative atmosphere created by the coaches. There was yelling, screaming, in-fighting and confusion. There was an overall lack of leadership.

"Athletes are just like racehorses," he says. "If the athlete doesn't believe in himself, if he doesn't believe in the coaching staff, the self-fulfilling prophecy comes into play. The result is frustration, loss of self-confidence, loss of self-esteem. Eventually, athletes like Dan Robinson and his teammates find themselves just going through the motions week after week, and the result is they get their butts kicked, and they have no clue how to make it stop."

Gerson's matter-of-fact diagnosis is akin to listening to your dentist as he nonchalantly clatters around in your mouth while discussing the root canal he's performing. It doesn't matter how wide your eyes get or how tightly you squeeze the arms of the chair; the drill keeps grinding.

"The mind tries not to accept the negative event," he says. "The mind, instinctively, tries to turn it into something positive. If we say, 'We're probably going to lose' or 'Here we go again,' the mind works to give you what you want. This is why when teams quit playing to win but start playing 'not-to-lose,' they lose. How many times have you seen a team with a big lead go to the 'prevent' defense and give up the winning score? They are playing not to lose, and you end up losing.

"Because the mind works to give you what you want the most, the Hawai'i players were actually sabotaging themselves. The unique thing here is that you can't break the cycle by exhortation. Slogans don't work, yelling louder, playing harder, running faster — none of that breaks the negative mental cycle like they had.

"June came in, and like Mouse years before him, flexed his system to *match the skills of the players,* not the other way around. Players' minds are like buckets. You will get what you fill them up with. Give them tasks they can do, and they'll succeed.

"In the case of Robinson, it was *critical* for June to give him somebody to coddle him a little, tell him he's OK, let him get a little success and ever so slowly build him back."

Now, before you roll your eyes and chalk all this up to psychobabble, you need to meet Dan *Morrison,* one of the *high school* coaches Jones was mocked for hiring. If you stood in line at the bank behind Morrison, you would never even think to ask for his autograph or suspect that he has nurtured every single quarterback in the last decade of Hawai'i football.

He looks *exactly* like a middle-aged *psychology* and history teacher, which is what he was when he was an administrator at Punahou School, one of the top independent schools in the nation. There Morrison tutored some of America's most brilliant minds, including the founder of AOL Steve Case and future presidential hopeful Barack Obama. He also was

▼ ▼ ▼ ▼ ▼ ▼ ▼ ▼ ▼ ▼ ▼ ▼ ▼

"Athletes are just like racehorses," he says. "If the athlete doesn't believe in himself, if he doesn't believe in the coaching staff, the self-fulfilling prophecy comes into play. The result is frustration, loss of self-confidence, loss of self-esteem. Eventually, athletes like Dan Robinson and his teammates find themselves just going through the motions week after week, and the result is they get their butts kicked, and they have no clue how to make it stop."

▲ ▲ ▲ ▲ ▲ ▲ ▲ ▲ ▲ ▲ ▲ ▲ ▲

head coach and offensive coordinator of the school's football program, where he discovered that studying the strengths and tendencies of quarterbacks was his life's calling.

In 1984, he traveled to Houston to watch Mouse Davis and June Jones turn Jim Kelly into the most prolific pro quarterback in history. Morrison developed an intuitive understanding of the position and devoted himself to quarterbacks so wholeheartedly that his life was incomplete without them.

"I always believed," says Morrison, "that creative people are those who seek the *second* right answer. There are always the *conventional* answers, but there's *another* right answer out there. I'm fascinated by people like that in football history. Mouse and June were doing things nobody in football had ever done before. When I went to see June, he had an infectious personality, and it was interesting to hear his thoughts conceptually. June sees the world — and football — through different lenses. He offers far more than the first conventional answer."

Believe it or not, Morrison was reluctant to leave Punahou. He did so, however, because June asked him to coach his quarterbacks, which is the Holy Grail for a Jones-coached team. "To be asked to specialize in what the head coach actually does best himself, that was the highest compliment he could pay me," Morrison says.

"I never believed that punitive teaching is effective in any way, shape or form," he adds. "The only way you can succeed for long periods of time is to allow 'free flow' to exist. I believe that players need to be confident and happy with what they are doing. I took this job because June believed in building relationships *around* the player and that the staff and program transcended the offense itself.

"We believe that you touch the human spirit first and let the quarterback come later."

Huh?

Are you kidding me?

Together, Jones and Morrison wrote the curriculum for a cognitive teaching model that today sets the standard for all past, current and future Hawai'i quarterbacks.

First, they begin on the grease board, drawing plays, explaining drops, routes, reads, progressions and coverages.

Second, they show their students plenty of film — teaching, reinforcing and building a relationship of trust. There's no argument when the film includes the likes of Jim Kelly, Warren Moon, Bobby Hebert or Jeff George.

Third, they take them outside and have them throw against air, carefully correcting footwork, hips, eyes, shoulders and throwing motion.

Fourth, they ease them into seven-on-seven drills.

Fifth, they introduce live scrimmages, carefully building in complexity by showing them multiple looks, blitzes and formations.

Sixth, they take them into Aloha Stadium, where they throw until the environment becomes natural and the offense second nature.

"Every progressive step," says Morrison, "the player, one, must be aware of it, and two, you cannot bypass any stage. You have to be careful in your teaching. You cannot coach quickly. The quarterback's comprehension and understanding, on both sides of the ball, is the most important thing.

"Homer Smith [former UCLA offensive coordinator] told me once that 'It doesn't matter what *you know*, the only thing that matters is what the *player knows*, because they have to play the game. You can have the most advanced mind in the history of football, but if you don't *teach* it properly, you're begging to get beat."

Seabiscuit had Tom Smith and Red Pollard; Robinson had

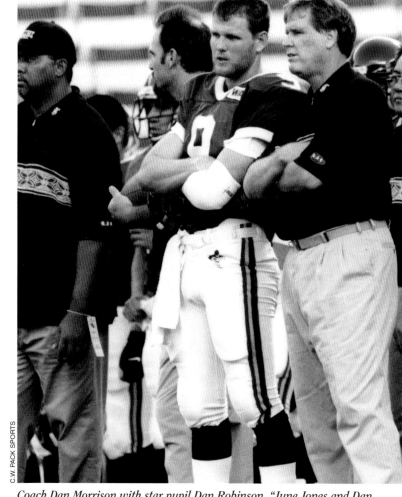

C.W. PACK SPORTS

Coach Dan Morrison with star pupil Dan Robinson. "June Jones and Dan Morrison are the best quarterback coaches in America," says Robinson, sentiments that would be echoed by Nick Rolovich and of course, Colt Brennan.

June Jones and Dan Morrison. As a trinity, each equally dependent on the other, they set out to win the Derby.

Upon meeting Robinson in person, Morrison was surprised at his maturity, until he discovered that his Mormon quarterback already had completed a two-year mission to Hong Kong and was a married family man.

"Some of the things Dan experienced were really unfortunate, but at the same time, they made him *unique*," Morrison says. "We got a chance to see his character, his inner strength. June and I realized this kid had something centered deep, deep inside him.

"He had a burning desire to win. Our job was just to put him in a position *where he could."*

Slowly, Morrison and Jones began to hand Robinson the reigns of the offense.

"The uniqueness about most quarterbacks is they really want to learn," Morrison says. "You have a captive audience. There's a point where the depth of it comes into play. We carefully begin to ask him, 'What do *you* see? Where do *you think* your eyes should go?' If Dan only did what we *told* him to do, we had failed. Dan had to slowly, instinctively, inherently, *grow into knowing* what to do, in *all* situations."

People who meet Morrison often think he's an introvert. He is an utterly selfless man. In fact, only his quarterbacks seem to know him well. He's seldom quoted in the press; on the rare occasion that he is, you will never hear him credit himself, not once. In fact, he shuns public attention.

In the presence of quarterbacks, however, he is gracefully at ease.

"June and Coach Morrison kept telling me, over and over, *'Just trust in it, and this is going to encompass everything that needs to be done,'"* Robinson says.

"It was amazing. For me, as a quarterback, June could tell me exactly how the defense was going to play us, on every look, on every snap, and what each of my responsibilities were in each situation.

"Coach Morrison never left my side. He was in my ear, constantly reassuring me. If there was something I physically couldn't do, they would *adjust to me,* not yell at me."

In practice, Jones saw Robinson severely struggling with the half-roll, a mainstay of the Run 'n' Shoot. After a quick conference with

Morrison, just as he had done many years before with Bobby Hebert, Jones approached Robinson with a solution.

"The half-roll is really giving you fits, huh?" Jones quizzed.

"Coach, my legs are a mess, but I'll get it done somehow," Robinson insisted.

"Would you be more comfortable out of the shotgun?" June asked.

Robinson was shocked. His eyes lit up:*"Absolutely, Coach!"*

From that day forward, Dan Robinson would only take snaps under center in short- yardage situations: problem solved.

As the 1999 season drew nigh, even the players on the *defensive side* of the ball couldn't believe the new and improved Dan Robinson.

"He didn't look like the same quarterback," says linebacker Jeff Ulbrich. "He'd make throws and we'd turn to each other and say, *'Did you see that?'"*

Dan Robinson, once rejected and alone, was about to catapult to greatness, whipping stronger, bigger horses with known pedigrees, to become the best quarterback Hawai'i had ever seen and a hero in the hearts of its people.

Who's the donkey now?

"Yah! Yah! Ride the rail! C'mon boy!"

Are you kidding me?

Chapter 16
FROM PRETENDERS TO CONTENDERS

Looming in the distance was none other than the top-20-ranked University of Southern California, the 1999 home opener for Hawai'i. A sellout crowd of 50,000 was eagerly anticipating the debut of June Jones, the newly christened *Warriors* and the Run 'n' Shoot offense.

Like an invading army, USC and the mighty Trojans would soon pour onto the shores of Honolulu, flexing their awesome college football power with a roar of indignation.

For eight months, Jones had been preaching *tradition, tradition, tradition.* He taught his players to saturate themselves with the pride and patriotism of their program, to the point that Saturday's battles would take on cause far greater than football, offering hope to an island nation.

Now, in their very first game, his boys would see what *tradition* looks like, up close and personal. USC, forever a PAC-10 powerhouse and one of the nation's greatest college football traditions, had produced nine national championships and six Heisman Trophy winners in its storied history, and the team viewed Hawai'i as little more than a speed bump en route to another title.

June had a right to be *gravely* concerned. He and his staff had worked diligently and prayed without ceasing as they rebuilt the psyche, character and confidence of his fragile Warriors, even to the point of digging up the old University of Hawai'i alma mater, which Jones now insisted his players would sing following every game.

▼▼▼▼▼▼▼▼▼▼▼▼▼▼

"Tonight is the night that we learn how to win," June predicted. "Winning is not just a will to survive. If you are to be Warriors, winning, not surviving, has to be our culture. Tonight you must learn how to win. We are not going to go through the motions in the second half. What we've shown you in practice is much harder than anything you'll see in the second half.
Let's go find a way to win."

▲▲▲▲▲▲▲▲▲▲▲▲▲▲

While he didn't have time to completely overhaul the team's logo and uniforms, Jones did away with the controversial rainbow and the white helmets, unveiling sleek black helmets with a new logo that featured a Menehune warrior. It gained instant, unanimous approval among the players.

While USC trained in glistening, multimillion-dollar, state-of-the-art facilities, June was getting results with, uh, more *primitive* resources. He had his quarterbacks — *especially* the rigid Robinson — tap-dancing back and forth around wooden two-by-fours to improve flexibility and footwork. "I'd never had anybody *coach my feet — or my hips,*" Robinson says. "It was the cheapest workout ever, but wow, did I ever start to have flexibility in my hips."

June also had his quarterbacks doing medicine-ball drills, as they learned to use their abdomens in the throwing motion. "That really helped my throwing motion, my overall strength, my velocity and my accuracy," Robinson adds. "Everything was starting to work in sync. At the snap of the ball, I could preset my feet, adjust my hips, make my read, show my eyes, drop my shoulder and zip the ball out."

Like the mythical Hans Brinker, Jones was putting a finger in every leaking hole of the Hawai'i dike, but he knew the damage the floodwaters could wreak if they broke free. He also knew that if a leader can't navigate his people through rough waters, he *alone* is responsible when the ship sinks, and June is not one to make excuses.

The mind of a head coach is a lonely place. This is why June Jones chooses to *lean not on his own understanding.* Many nights, after another long film session, the exhausted June could be found in his office — not just poring over game plans, but *praying.*

He was not praying for victory, for the God of the entire universe could care less about who wins or loses a football game. June prayed for *leadership,* for *wisdom,* for he believes that God most certainly cares about *people* and the lessons one learns in the face of adversity when confronted with an unstoppable force — like, say, the fighting USC Trojans, for instance.

In a matter of days, he would lead his young boys, heads no longer bowed, down a dark tunnel and into the light of the greatest battle of their young lives. It was his job to ensure they left with their dignity intact, regardless of the score, and to continue to see growth and progress within their hearts, their lives and their upstart football program.

The media was calling it David versus Goliath, which, technically, wasn't fair or true.

According to history, Goliath was a hulking, heavily armored, 10-foot-tall Philistine soldier, who mocked the tribe of Israel and dared any man to fight him. All who tried were summarily killed. Then David, a shepherd boy, accepted his offer and, with slingshot in hand, felled Goliath with a single devastating shot to the forehead.

The part of the story that is often overlooked, however, is that long before David ever faced Goliath, he twice engaged in hand-to-hand combat against animals of the wild who sought to devour his sheep. Therefore, David had spent a lifetime battling stronger opponents and his own fears, enabling him to face the giant with overwhelming confidence.

Thus David technically had two preseason games under his belt — the Lions and the Bears — long before he had to play the Giants.

Not so the Hawai'i football Warriors, who would be facing the giants from the opening whistle.

In the midst of a late-night prayer session, June was struck with an inspiration: *Divide the season into four quarters. Take the focus away*

from USC and put it elsewhere. Give the kids an attainable goal; instead of USC being the end-all, make them a stepping-stone en route to that goal.*

The next day, he stood before his troops and followed his extraordinary insight.

"Men," he said, "we're going to divide our season into four quarters. The first quarter is the month of September. We've got USC coming up, then Eastern Illinois, Boise State and SMU. *I don't care which games we win,* but we must win at least three games in the month of September."

This didn't sit well with linebacker Jeff Ulbrich. "I'd been taught my whole life that you set out each week to win every single game," he said. "I didn't understand, at the time, the brilliance of what he was doing. But I do remember thinking, hey, we're 0-18, and this guy is talking about winning *at least* three out of four, so let's go do it. Looking back, what June did was turn USC into just another game."

And, you should know, it was not a minute too soon.

USC 62, Hawai'i 7

In their most lopsided season-opening win since 1929, the Trojans scored on eight of their first nine possessions, forced five turnovers, and whipped Hawai'i, 62-7.

The Warriors' losing streak went to 0-19, the longest of any school in history.

The "new-and-improved" Dan Robinson had been unsteady. Unsure of his reads, he held the ball too long and went down beneath waves of white jerseys four times. Nervous against one of the nation's top-ranked defenses, he fumbled a snap, which was recovered by USC and led to another Trojan touchdown. He blew a read on a tight coverage and threw a costly interception. Robinson completed less than 50 percent of his passes — 16 of 39 — for just 169 yards.

Meanwhile, USC's buzz saw of future NFL stars played like, well, NFL stars.

PHOTO BY GEORGE F. LEE

Dan Robinson steps and fires … note the protection of tackle Adriann Klemm (63) whose near-perfect play at Hawai'i would lead to an equally impressive NFL career …

Future Cincinnati Bengals Carson Palmer and Maefou MacKenzie were responsible for five touchdowns. Future New York Jet Windrell Hayes caught a 32-yard touchdown. Future Cleveland Brown David Gibson recovered two fumbles. Running back Chad Morton, who would play for four NFL teams, rushed for 95 yards and a touchdown.

As soon as the game ended, as promised, June Jones sent his team to midfield. Fans headed up the stadium steps to leave were stunned to suddenly hear . . . *singing.*

In Green Mānoa Valley
Our Alma Mater stands
Where mountain winds and showers
Refresh her fertile lands

The flag of freedom beckons
Above her shining walls
To larger truth and service
Our Alma Mater calls.

They retreated to the locker room and waited for Coach Jones.

"You have to imagine us, sitting in the locker room, sweaty and deject-ed, waiting for June to come in," says Robinson. "We were scared to death. In the past, this would have meant more yelling, more screaming. We had no idea what to expect. The year before, if we had played so bad, they would've changed the whole offense. I would've been running the option the next week."

Jones burst into the locker room *smiling*.

"Wow!" he said, shaking his head. *"Man, those guys were fast, huh?"*

Players toweled sweat from their faces and raised their heads. This was unlike any postgame speech they'd ever heard — par-ticularly after a devastating loss.

"We're OK," Jones insisted. "Dan, we had a touchdown on the first play of the game, but we missed the read. We hit it all week in practice, but in a hostile environment, we just missed it. O-line, d-line, we did pretty well. We just have to get the game to slow down a little. We did OK in the secondary except for a couple of coverages that got away from us. We're going to be fine . . . that's the best team in the country you just played."

Robinson remembers this like yesterday. "June didn't say *you* missed it," he says. "He said, '*We* missed it.' He kept saying, 'we blew this coverage,' or 'we blew the protection,' right on down the line. It was *we, we, we,* never once 'you guys are idiots, you guys are terrible athletes.'"

This theme continued in subsequent meetings following the loss.

Not one coach raised his voice in the aftermath. It was business as usual. Not a single thing changed. The attention immediately turned to review-

▼▼▼▼▼▼▼▼▼▼▼▼▼▼▼

"You have to imagine us, sitting in the locker room, sweaty and dejected, waiting for June to come in," says Robinson. "We were scared to death. In the past, this would have meant more yelling, more screaming. We had no idea what to expect. The year before, if we had played so bad, they would've changed the whole offense. I would've been running the option the next week." Jones burst into the locker room smiling.

▲▲▲▲▲▲▲▲▲▲▲▲▲▲▲

ing the USC film while getting ready for Eastern Illinois. The players walked on eggshells for a day or so, waiting for the axe to fall. Instead, the exact opposite occurred. Time and again, June and the staff kept empha-sizing what they *had done right*.

Sure enough, the "eye in the sky don't lie."

True Hawai'i freshman Pati Mailo had deliv-ered a mind-numbing, special-teams *splat* on the opening kickoff. The ferocity of the hit, and his attitude as he stood over his fallen opponent, was enough to make Dennis McKnight play it over and over while the players cheered and stomped their feet.

On offense, receivers were running wide open. Center Dustin Owens, nicknamed "Snickers" for his 20-plus-a-day candy bar habit, had made decent line calls. Robinson hadn't been horrible, he just needed more reps.

"Dan, we need to step up in the pocket," June explained, freezing the film. "See, see? Right there! We've got guys open down the hash, we just have to step up and see it. Dan, remember to move that safety *with your eyes* . . . we'll *own* the center of the field if we *just learn to use our eyes.*"

On running plays, Afatia Thompson had ripped off more than 7 yards a carry for 55 yards. "I told you the holes would be huge," smiled McKnight, slapping Thompson on the back.

Ulbrich had been a sideline-to-sideline phenom at his new middle line-backer position, racking up 17 tackles, which led the entire WAC.

The best part was the warning USC running back Chad Morton had sent to future Hawai'i opponents. "All I know," Morton told the media, "is every time I carried the ball, I was looking for number 44. That man can play the game."

In a defensive film meeting, the players watched with awe when Ulbrich viciously stopped Morton head-to-head for no gain in what coaches call the "A" gap, or the space between the center and guard. As Morton struggled to his feet, Ulbrich grabbed him by his shoulder pads, pulled him facemask-to-facemask, and whispered in his ear.

Coach McMackin grinned. "What'd you say to him, Jeff?"

"I told him to get used to seeing me," snarled Ulbrich. His teammates clapped and roared their approval.

McMackin knew he had found a live wire in Ulbrich, who had the intensity and power of Thor and the speed to roam sideline-to-sideline. Knowing his defense severely lacked depth and talent, McMackin realized Ulbrich could be the difference in making the zone-blitz work.

"We're gonna give you more and more freedom, Jeff," he instructed. "We're not going to make you stick with gap or to a side; we want you to just be a football player and run to the ball, OK?"

To a middle linebacker, such direction is akin to a winning lottery ticket.

"What happened after USC was twofold," says coach Dan Morrison. "Our staff was acutely aware of what these guys had been through. June had been in the NFL long enough to know how to take a bad loss and turn it into next week's win. The players were looking for leadership and watching carefully to see how we'd respond.

"When we didn't change a thing, they realized how much belief we had in the system. We didn't blame anything on the kids. We just kept reassuring them that everyone would be fine. As a staff, we stayed disciplined, we maintained our routine and we built atop their small successes. Players know true leadership — they could see it for themselves on the film, and they were drawn into it."

The fear, ignorance, uncertainty and lack of imagination that had once foiled the Warriors clearly belonged to the past.

PHOTO BY GEORGE F. LEE

Yaphet Warren reaches deep inside for inspiration ...

Watching the film was the key, says Robinson. "Looking back, that game was huge. After we sat down and looked at the film, you could see we had a system, and the system worked. The lights went on for the entire team. It was a matter of execution. We actually were more sold after *losing* to USC. I know how that sounds, but it's absolutely true."

Hawai'i 31, Eastern Illinois 27

Jamal Garland stared upward into the balmy Hawai'i heavens, waiting for the Eastern Illinois Panthers' opening kickoff to tumble down into his awaiting arms. He was oblivious to the footsteps of the herd that thundered toward him as the ball thumped into his arms, and behind two beautiful blocks he was off to the races — until he was hit and fumbled at the 38-yard line.

On the very next play, EIU quarterback Anthony Buich caught Hawai'i napping with a daring flea-flicker on first down and threw a perfect strike to split end Phil Taylor for a lightning-fast score before most fans had even found their seats.

Eight seconds into the game, Hawai'i already trailed, 7-0. Twenty-five thousand fans groaned as one, for they had seen this all too many times before. They stopped the Warriors on their first possession, and moments later, Chad Larner hit an 18-yard field goal to cap a 13-play, 79-yard drive. Hawai'i now faced a *10-point* deficit.

While boos began to emanate from the stands, there was no sign of panic on the Hawai'i sidelines, where players were remarkably relaxed, calm and poised. The Warriors managed a field goal but still trailed when the "ring-down" phone on the bench jangled.

Robinson answered. "Dan, just relax," Coach Morrison said calmly from the coach's box high atop the stadium. "You need to know that Attrice can run right past their guy. June is thinking 60 Z Go, so be sure to put enough on the ball that Attrice can run away from them. Let's go have some fun."

Moments later, Robinson entered the huddle and clicked his chinstrap and looked into the eyes of his teammates.

"We're gonna go *Trips Right, 60 Z Go, Trips Right, 60 Z Go. . . .*"

He glanced at Attrice Brooks.

"Alright, Brooksie, we need this one. I'm gonna lay it out there, so be fast, OK? On two, on two. . . ."

As they broke the huddle, Robinson shouted after Brooks, who was notorious for forgetting his routes.

"You remember the play, right Attrice?"

"I'm going *deep, dawg!*" he hollered back, as he trotted out toward the right sideline.

With slightly more than two minutes left in the half, Robinson dropped the ball perfectly beyond the outreached arms of two defenders and into the outstretched hands of Brooks, who took the ball in full stride and raced 80 yards for his first Division-I touchdown, which tied the game.

The Warrior bench erupted like fireworks in celebration of the very first offensive touchdown of the June Jones era of Hawai'i football.

The jubilation was short lived, however, as Buich answered less than a minute later with a 10-yard touchdown, and Hawai'i went in at halftime trailing 17-10.

"Personally, the best thing that could've happened to us was to be trailing at half-time," says Morrison. "I think, for our entire season, it was critically important that we actually fell behind early. We had a chance as a team, as coaches, as players, to come together at halftime, review our opportunities, stay the course and put the pieces back together. That brought us together like nothing else."

▼▼▼▼▼▼▼▼▼▼▼▼▼▼

"A warrior is many things," June said. "A warrior is a brother. The faces in this room will be what you remember for a lifetime. Look around. You must learn to count on the person next to you, the person in front of you; the person behind you. We are warriors now."

▲▲▲▲▲▲▲▲▲▲▲▲▲▲

June's words to the team at the half were succinct.

"Tonight is the night that *we learn how to win*," June predicted. "Winning is not just a will to survive. If you are to be Warriors, winning, not surviving, has to be our culture. Tonight you must *learn how to win*. We are not going to go through the motions in the second half. What we've shown you in practice is much harder than anything you'll see in the second half. Let's *go find a way to win*."

The second half was a shootout. Eastern Illinois didn't want to be the first team to lose to Hawai'i in two years, but the stubborn Warriors suddenly were refusing to cooperate.

Phil Austin made a one-handed interception at the Eastern Illinois 29 with just 1:47 gone in the second half. Two plays later, Robinson hit Dwight Carter on an out, who then extended the ball as far as he could and hurled himself — as he was being hit — into the end zone for the tying touchdown.

When safety Daniel Ho-Ching stopped the Panthers' next drive by recovering a fumble at the Hawai'i 36, Robinson needed only three plays and 1:37 to score again, this time to former local prep star Craig Stutzmann, and the Warriors led, 24-17.

Five plays later, Eastern Illinois counterpunched with running back Wayne Brown, who sprinted down the left sideline to tie the game again.

Meanwhile, on the Hawai'i sideline, something mystical was happening.

"I had to keep calming Dan down on the phone," says Morrison. "He was excited. The offense was clicking, and he was starting to see it. He couldn't wait to get back on the field."

No kidding. On the next Hawai'i possession, Robinson moved the Warriors 79 yards on 10 plays. If *who you are* dictates *what you see*, then Robinson was becoming a real quarterback.

"We started completing passes like we did in practice," marvels Robinson. "I was like, oh my, this really works. I was *seeing it*. I remember throwing a deep ball to Channon Harris up the left sideline. It was in traffic, and I just stuck it on him. Right there, everything just slowed down for me, just like June and Dan said it would. I wasn't watching my receivers at all. I was watching the defense. After that, it was lights out, a whole new dimension."

So excited was Robinson that he was blurting out the plays as fast as he could in the huddle in an effort to get back to the business of throwing. This in turn created high-class problems for the offensive line — *too many* first downs *too quickly*.

"Calm down, Danny," smiled Big Red Phillips, his heaving left guard. "We're exhausted. Remember we've got to protect your butt, then run 40 yards when you *complete a pass* just to get back to the huddle. Just call the plays a little slower and give us a chance to catch our breath."

Out of breath or not, tackle Adrian Klemm could be seen, time and again, racing downfield to help a receiver get to his feet after a catch or to congratulate Robinson with a tap on the butt. There was a magic in the huddle never felt before.

Robinson finished the drive with a picture-perfect, 14-yard scoring pass to Brooks that gave Hawai'i a 31-24 lead.

EIU fought back gamely, until Robert Kemfort, the wide receiver-turned-linebacker, made the initial hit to stop fullback Andre Jones short of a first down on fourth and 1 at the Hawai'i 20-yard line, with 7:20 left.

Eastern Illinois would only manage another field goal to close out the scoring. As the final seconds ticked off the stadium scoreboard, bottled-up emotion exploded like shaken champagne, and the Hawai'i players splashed like boys in a river of unbridled joy.

"You would have thought we just beat Notre Dame," said McMackin, who watched the postgame celebration with awe. Some players high-fived; some dropped to their knees, pounded the turf and wept with joy; everyone was hugging anyone who would hug back. "They celebrated," agrees Morrison, "like they'd won a bowl game."

The drought was over. "It wouldn't have mattered if we beat a high school team that night," says Robinson. "For the *first time, we walked off the field winners.*"

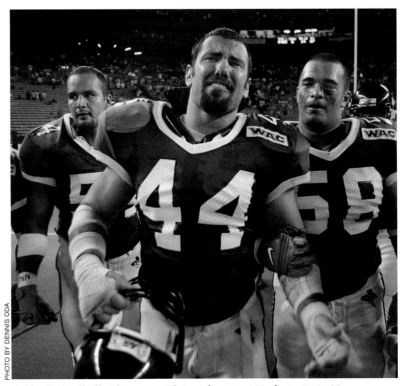

PHOTO BY DENNIS ODA

A bloodied Jeff Ulbrich weeps with joy after Hawaii's first win in 20 games

Postgame celebrations rocked the Hawai'i campus into the morning hours.

When the once-harassed Robinson returned to his house, his neighbors had erected a giant sign of congratulations. It included a picture of a blasting rocket leaving its launchpad. "I was speechless," he says.

Watching the Eastern Illinois film was like watching prophecy unfold before their eyes.

The mental toughness of the defense and the scheme was beginning to materialize. Eastern Illinois converted only four out of 15 third downs.

Hawai'i forced a fumble and an interception and held them for no gain on two fourth-down attempts. Ulbrich and Quincy LeJay had nine tackles apiece to lead the team, which finished with four sacks. Ho-Ching had eight tackles. Joe Correia, the former baseball player, played in spite of a broken hand. End Mike Iosua played with stingers (pinched nerves) in his neck. Tackle Tony Tuioti played with a bad back.

On offense, the Run 'n' Shoot was beginning to click.

Attrice Brooks caught only two passes, but both were for touchdowns. "We startin' something," Brooks whooped.

"It's called *winning.*"

Senior Dwight Carter, meanwhile, broke a 14-year-old, single-game school record with nine catches for 220 yards and a touchdown, eclipsing Walter Murray's 153 yards against Colorado State back in 1985.

And *Seabiscuit?* Dan Robinson broke his first Hawai'i record, passing for a single-game school record of 452 yards. He completed 24 of 40 with no interceptions and four touchdowns, breaking the old mark set by Garrett Gabriel in 1989.

"The best stat," says Robinson, "was I was *never* sacked. Not once. Big Red [Phillips], Snickers [Dustin Owen], Adrian [Klemm], [Kaulana] Noa, Manley [Kanoa] — they were perfect."

And June? "Let's not get too high over a win or too low over a loss," he warned. "We have to do this again Saturday night. Boise State isn't going to come in here and play dead just because we won a game. Trust me, fellas, they *don't care.*"

It was back to work. The players recognized the pattern: business as usual, but *business was good.*

Repetition, repetition, repetition.

"But don't you doubt for a second," smiles McKnight, "we were happy to get that doggone monkey off our backs. We were winners. And there is no feeling like *winning.*"

Hawai'i 34, Boise State 19

An *epiphany* is a sudden, intuitive realization through an ordinary, daily occurrence or circumstance. Through the medium of *repetition, repetition, repetition,* June Jones–coached players — *specifically* quarterbacks — enjoy many epiphanies through the course of a single season.

When a Bobby Beathard says that "everything June does makes sense," it's because Jones is constantly applying cognitive psychology in a way seldom seen in football. Long before June ever stepped foot on a practice field, famous American psychologist Jerome S. Bruner created a learning process called "instructional scaffolding," wherein young adults were capable of absorbing ridiculously intense amounts of information when given to them in bite-sized pieces, or layers, which he likened to *scaffolds.*

Bruner's handiwork reads like a Jones' coaching clinic and, at the very least, validates June's methods:

Make the tasks interesting and fun

Simplify the tasks into attainable portions

Allow the student to manage the process and recognize when they achieve a goal

Maintain pursuit of the goal through motivation and direction

Control frustration and risk in problem solving through personal interaction

Demonstrate daily an ideal version of the act you want performed.

The result, writes Bruner, is that "where before there *was* a spectator, you now have a *participant.*"

Evidence of this theory was Robinson, who by the season's third week was "seeing things" he hadn't seen before. June repeatedly had told him how the "deep ball" would suddenly materialize before his eyes as he immersed himself deeper and deeper into the system. Robinson was still surprised, however, when it actually *happened.*

"June kept saying, *'When you throw the deep ball, keep your eye on the target at all times.* The week of Boise State, I just couldn't believe how accurate I was becoming! In practice, I was getting so accurate I could put it on a *specific spot* on the receiver."

Infants don't get steak; solids come at the same pace as the development of their ability to digest them. Robinson's appetite now was craving more than baby-food routes like the bubble, the X or Z screens or the slide.

He wanted the deep ball, the filet mignon of the Run 'n' Shoot. So June fed him a fat, aged Angus: the fade-stop, vintage Bob Gagliano, circa 1985.

"June said, 'Listen, if they're fronting your guy, hit him in the back shoulder,'" Robinson says. "If he's running to the side of the receiver, don't throw it *past* him, throw it short; *back-shoulder him,* so the receiver can stop, adjust, come back and catch it."

Continuing to build a *scaffold* at a time, June taught Robinson how to open his left shoulder, just as he had instructed teammate Steve Bartkowski years and years before.

"June and Coach Morrison kept telling me that when I set my feet, *open my left shoulder* and stay positioned on my follow-through," Robinson says. "Show the eyes, adjust your hips; open your shoulder, set and fire."

"By the time we played Boise, I knew exactly where I could take the ball, and I could do it quickly and accurately."

Are you kidding me?

PHOTO BY GEORGE F. LEE

Craig Stutzmann (22) accepts congratulations from Manley Kanoa (76)

Epiphanies were everywhere against Boise State.

The Warriors fought back — again — from certain defeat for the second week in a row. After trailing 19-7 at halftime, Dan Robinson engineered three touchdowns in less than 12 minutes to rally his team to a stunning 34-19 victory, giving Hawai'i back-to-back victories for the first time in several years.

The patchwork defense continued to gel, in spite of the Broncos using a maximum-protect scheme that neutralized the Warriors normal blitz package. McMackin shifted the defense back to a standard 4-3, which opened the floodgates.

On Boise State's *first possession,* Quincy LeJay jumped a late throw by Bart Hendricks and returned the interception for a touchdown, his second on the year. Ulbrich had three drive-killing sacks and 17 more tackles, giving him 43 already in the young season.

Hawai'i sealed the victory when junior wide-receiver-turned-linebacker Robert Kemfort made a game-changing play for the second time in two weeks, sacking Hendricks on *another* fourth and 1 at his own 26.

Midway through the game, right defensive end Joe Correia's excruciating broken left hand was giving him fits.

"Switch him to the other side!" barked McMackin. They did, enabling him to put his broken hand down in a three-point stance and still grab with his good right hand. Correia finished with six tackles and a quarterback sack as the defense held the Broncos to just 70 total yards in the second half.

The most fun, however, was watching Dan Robinson move the Broncos entire secondary strictly *with his eyes,* just as June and Morrison had coached him to do.

Avion Weaver stiff-arms a Boise State defender ... the Run 'n' Shoot spreads the field, often leaving enormous holes for its huge running backs ...

"June worked and worked and worked," he says, "to teach me how to move the safety completely to the opposite side of the field with just my eyes. I had their db's running all over the place. It was amazing to see the frustration on their faces, to see them looking at their coaches saying, 'What do we do?'"

After Robinson punched it in on a 1-yard quarterback keeper with 11:09 remaining, the defense stiffened. Moments later, Robinson hit Channon Harris with a perfect 43-yard, over-the-shoulder strike, and on the next play he found Dwight Carter in the end zone for a 5-yard touchdown.

When Kemfort held the Broncos on fourth down, Robinson, now playing at a different level than he ever had before, went right back to the deep ball, hitting slotback Craig Stutzmann straight down the center of the field for a 26-yard score.

"On that play, if you look at the film, you can't even see the free safety," laughs Robinson. "I think he followed my eyes all the way to the bench. Craig ran right down the very hash the safety just vacated. I threw it, and Craig caught it.

"It was beautiful."

Dan Morrison agreed. "When we won that game," he says, "the whole season just began to really take on a life of its own. That's when I began to think something special just might happen."

Hawai'i 20, SMU 0

In 1999, the "Road Warriors" were a popular professional wrestling tag team, famously comprised of Michael "Hawk" Hegstrand and Joseph "Animal" Laurianaitas, two imposing muscle-bound wrestlers garbed in face paint.

As the Hawai'i players opened practice in preparation for their first road trip of the year, Coach Dennis McKnight, who bears an eerie resemblance to "Animal," came crawling out on the field. His massive physique was shirtless; his face painted. Amidst the laughter, whooping and hollering of the players and other coaches, McKnight growled, in pro-wrestler shtick, that Hawai'i would now be known as the "Road Warriors."

McKnight's silliness broke the ice and distracted the players from the obvious: Hawai'i hadn't won a road game in seven years. In fact, they had lost 24 consecutive *conference* road games, dating back to a Halloween afternoon in 1992 at the Sun Bowl against Texas–El Paso.

The trip to Dallas to face Southern Methodist University was another giant test in a season of firsts. It would not only be the first road game under the Jones' regime but also the first conference game. Many questions remained to be answered.

It's undeniable, however, that fans in both states would have paid to see a cage match between McKnight and Peruna VII, SMU's jet-black Shetland pony mascot. Peruna, like McKnight, had a flair for the dramatic: Against Texas Tech, Peruna had attempted to mount Misty, Tech's own equine mascot. Against Texas, Peruna had sent longhorn Bevo to the ground with a powerful kick to the ribs. Against Texas Christian, the same week TCU had unveiled the school's brand new field turf, Peruna ordained it by defecating at midfield.

Even the outrageous McKnight didn't dare attempt to top that one.

The Warriors enjoyed spirited practices, including one in which receivers recall not dropping a single pass. Just as he had in every other facet of the program, Jones quickly introduced new protocol for road games: The team would leave on *Wednesday* for a Saturday game, giving the players several days to become acclimated to the long flight, the five-hour time change and mainland weather.

The players were elated, and energy was high. In years past, Hawai'i would take red-eye flights, often arriving hours before game time, then fly home immediately after the contest. Upon arriving in Dallas, game preparation remained exactly the same: calm, steady and consistent. The only distraction, says Ulbrich, was "being asked 200 times about the seven-year losing streak on the road. If one more guy had asked me, I swear, I was about to kill somebody."

Anyone who knows Jeff Ulbrich realizes he probably *meant* that.

The night before the game, June brought the team together for what would become a pregame road ritual. He told them about the Cherokee Indians, who had been a band of warriors, and the brotherhood that had been felt between them. He explained how throughout centuries, the Cherokees balanced old and new, adapting to change while preserving the essence of what makes them Cherokee, such as respect for each other, treating each day as a gift, preserving harmony through humor and prayer, speaking the language, singing the songs and dancing to honor the Creator.

"A warrior is many things," June said. "A warrior is a brother. The faces in this room will be what you remember for a lifetime. Look around. You must learn to count on the person next to you, the person in front of you, the person behind you.

"We are warriors now."

A wave of energy follow Jeff Ulbrich everywhere he goes; his intensity will raise the hair on your arms simply by walking past him. Teammates had grown so accustomed to his frequent raging tantrums that they not only *relied* on them for motivation and inspiration, they even *videotaped them* as sort of a future reference, adrenaline-on-demand injection.

Prior to the SMU game, Ulbrich exploded, raging about past, present and future. He lashed out at the critics, the harassment, the frustration. "I think guys were more afraid of Jeff than anything out on the field," laughs McKnight. "Let's just say Jeff is — for lack of a better word — *unique* in the intimidation department."

The defense got the message: Led by the monster in the middle, the Warriors shut out the Mustangs, 20-0, winning on the road after 24 consecutive conference defeats. It was the first shutout by Hawai'i since blanking Southeast Missouri 34-0 in 1994 and the sixth consecutive quarter in which they had not allowed a team to score.

The offense, on the other hand, severely struggled: Nobody knew that both Robinson and his backup Mike Harrison had suffered from stomach flu the night before the game — to the point that coaches wondered if *either* would be able to play.

The dirt-tough Robinson, as he had throughout his career, fought through pain, vomiting, fever and dizzy spells to play. On the fourth play of the first quarter, he threw a deep, 64-yard spiral to Channon Harris for a certain touchdown, only to have Harris — who hadn't mishandled a ball in practice all week — drop the pass. Robinson came back to Ashley Lelie on a deep 43-yard post, which set up a redemptive 38-yard touchdown to Harris. In the fourth quarter, he struck again on a 13-yard lob to Craig Stutzmann.

Kicker Eric Hannun hit two field goals, including a booming 50-yarder, to round out the scoring.

The first-term report card was promising.

Hawai'i had dictated, for the most part, the style and tempo of play in its games. The USC score reflected failed execution more than sloppy play. The defense was playing far above its head. The team was no longer committing the deadly penalties that plagued its efforts in years past.

The Warriors had played hurt, even poorly in spurts, and still found ways to win. It was a far, far cry from the memories of the past. September had come and gone, and the "worst team in America" was now unbeaten in conference play, 1-0 on the road, and 3-1 overall headed into October.

"The way June divided up the season," says Morrison, in hindsight, "made the loss to USC a success. We were 3-1 going into October. We were right where he said we had to be. Something that Mouse and June believe in is called *one-snap-and-clear.* You drop a ball, you throw an interception, you make a mistake, you lose a game, one-snap, and it's over and gone. Move on. Give yourself a chance to line up again."

How about one *month,* and clear: Hawai'i was no longer a pretender but a contender, and the best was yet to come. USC was now a distant memory, fading from view now in the rearview mirror.

The Trojans were gone — but not *forgotten.*

PHOTO BY GEORGE F. LEE

Kick-returner extraordinaire Jamal Garland

Chapter 17

"HE KAU AUANE'I I KA LAE 'A'?": THE ROCKY REEFS OF REALITY

Homecoming at Hawai'i had become a running joke.

"I called the box office to see if I could get tickets for the homecoming game," wisecracked a local disc jockey in 1998, the year prior to Jones' arrival. "They said yes. I said, 'What time does the game start?' And the guy said, '*What time can you be here?*'"

At the University of Hawai'i, what is designed to be every school's traditional annual festival had become a fiscal fiasco. Homecoming had turned into a tragic Shakespeare's *Tempest:* a week full of dramatic action, special effects, music, magic, monsters, dancing, storms, even drunken humor — but no victory at the end.

In fact, just as it did in Shakespeare's play, each year that Hawai'i attempted to dine from the feast at its table, it magically just disappeared. The school had lost six homecoming games *in a row*. In 1998, San Jose State had embarrassed them 45-17, which is like a little boy being spanked publicly in front of his friends during his own birthday party at Chuck E. Cheese's.

If ever there was a time for this oppressed college football team to become defiant, *homecoming* would be a great place to start. The people of Hawai'i desperately wanted to reclaim this football holiday; they were overdue this celebration, this massive gathering of *ohana,* the chance to be filled with spirit, hope and rejoicing.

If you can't win your own homecoming game in front of family and

friends, then how can you possibly learn to win a championship or a bowl game in a hostile environment?

The first week of October ushered in the start of the season's "second quarter," according to Jones' instructions to break the season into four parts; i.e., September, October, November, December.

▼▼▼▼▼▼▼▼▼▼▼▼▼▼

In fact, just as it did in Shakespeare's play, each year that Hawaii attempted to dine from the feast at its table, it magically just disappeared. The school had lost six homecoming games in a row. In 1998, San Jose State embarrassed them, 45-17, which is like a little boy being spanked publicly in front of his friends during his own birthday party at Chuck E. Cheese.

▲▲▲▲▲▲▲▲▲▲▲▲▲▲

Privately, however, he was preaching a different sermon to the staff as they prepared for the University of Texas–El Paso.

"We're *not* losing homecoming," June told them, as they reviewed the UTEP game film. "No way. We will not be conservative. We need to hit to the whistle, jump right on these guys, pin them down, put our foot on their throat and put them away. They're coming off a big win. Just like us, they're starting to believe in themselves. They've already played at Oregon and Kansas State, so they know what to expect on the road.

"This game is going to define who we are. This is a must-win game."

His coaches responded to his call to action — particularly the NFL–bred Miano, who instinctively perks up when he merely gets a whiff of a playoff atmosphere.

It's not as if June Jones had cornered the market on armchair psychology or motivational philosophy. It's not as if Texas–El Paso was clueless that Hawai'i was attempting to turn a very important corner in the rebuilding of its program.

Furthermore, UTEP coach Ronnie Bailey had been a linebacker coach under former Philadelphia Eagles head coach Buddy Ryan, who had infamously mocked the Run 'n' Shoot as the "Chuck 'n' Duck," a fact of which Jones made his staff aware. "Bailey is a good coach. He understands the principles of the Run 'n' Shoot," June made clear. "He has seen it, he has practiced against it and he had a boss who didn't believe in it."

Furthermore, UTEP had just whipped previously unbeaten New Mexico State 54-23 just a week after New Mexico State had beaten number 22–ranked Arizona State. Texas–El Paso was the top-ranked team in the WAC, followed by Fresno State, Rice and — shockingly — Hawai'i.

"I don't know anything about odds and polls," Jones told reporters, "but this is the best team we've faced since USC."

With safety Daniel Ho-Ching out with his shoulder injury, Joe Correia still suffering from a broken hand and sore knee and Attrice Brooks nursing a sprained thumb, June was more than a little cautious.

"We need to mature this week," he said. "Playing hurt is part of the game."

PHOTO BY GEORGE F. LEE

People would pay a lot of money," says former NFL GM Bobby Beathard, "to know what goes on in the mind of June Jones."

"I cannot stress how important this game is for our fans, for *ohana*," June said.

In moments, his Warriors would take the field to face first-place Texas–El Paso before a boisterous, near-capacity crowd that desperately wanted its island heroes to reciprocate their *aloha* with a homecoming victory.

All around him was a sea of green and white, Warriors securely tucked away behind thick padding, miles of prewrap and athletic tape and fresh,

clean uniforms. The smell of a cold pregame locker room is reminiscent of Lysol, antiseptic, tape, gauze and liniment. Players are conditioned to this smell. It means combat is imminent.

"Hear that crowd?" Jones asked. He paused for effect. Penetrating the concrete from the rocking stadium above them were the muffled sounds of stomping feet, thumping drums and screaming trumpets.

"They are all here *for you*. They believe in *you*. *This is about school pride*. For many of you seniors, you will never get the chance to feel this again. What will this game say about us when we're done?"

Jones raised his right arm high and forward, and swiftly, dozens followed. Bodies packed in tightly. White hands held black hands. Brown hands held white hands. Even Jeff Ulbrich, his RPMs already screaming inside his chest, reverently closed his eyes.

Heads bowed. For some, tears began to drip onto the concrete floor.

"Father," June prayed, "let each man here play to his potential for Your glory."

"Alright guys . . . win on three . . . *one . . . two . . . three — WIN!*"

Like a green and white bird they soared as one, down the tunnel and into the night sky.

The stands erupted, reverberating with a roar like they had never heard before.

Robinson leaned his head forward, jammed his right thumb up under the top of his helmet and wiped the sweat from his brow. He stuck his forefinger in the towel and dabbed the sweat beading under his eyes.

He simply couldn't believe this crowd.

Let's give 'em what they came to see, he grinned.

Hawai'i 33, Texas El-Paso 3

The words "team victory" typically are among the most well worn of coaching clichés. But on this night, it was unmistakable, as the Warriors gave the fans the blowout victory they so desperately craved.

Afatia Thompson and Avion Weaver rushed for a combined 180 yards. The offensive line shut out feared UTEP defensive tackle Brian Young, who would go on to a stellar NFL career. "I never even saw him," says Robinson, "until I shook hands with him after the game."

So complete was the win that punter Chad Shrout was called upon only *once*.

The defense didn't allow a touchdown, stretching their streak to 10 quarters. After scoring 54 points the week before against New Mexico State, UTEP could only squeak out 173 yards and three points. "They whipped us," Bailey told reporters. "We got whipped on the offensive side of the football."

Matt Paul, the linebacker-turned-defensive-end, batted down a pass, which was intercepted by Joe Correia, broken hand and all. Shawndel Tucker and Ulbrich had two more interceptions.

"What was important about UTEP," says Ulbrich, "is that in the beginning of the season, we had hoped to win. Then after we won a game, we thought we could win. Against UTEP, we *expected to win, and we did.* You could just feel the energy turning."

June stayed true to his word, allowing his coaches to pin back their ears and be aggressive, which culminated in a fake punt for a first down by Bronson Liana.

Robinson torched the UTEP defense but refused to take credit. "All I do is drop back and throw the ball," he said. "The scary thing is that we can actually be a lot better than we are right now."

"Robinson," said a disbelieving Bailey, "doesn't even look like the same quarterback we saw last year. We were physically and emotionally beat up tonight."

The coaching staff had challenged the troops to play hurt, and they did. Defensive end Matt Elam continued to play even after breaking his ribs in the fourth quarter. Jacob Espiau was lost with a horrific hamstring pull, but others stepped up in his place.

After the game, the fans had waited while the team gathered at midfield and sang the alma mater at the tops of their lungs.

When the dust settled, wide receiver Dwight Carter was ranked *eighth in the nation* in yards per game, and Robinson was ranked *tenth* in total passing yards, with an amazing passer efficiency rating of 125.7.

Athletic director Hugh Yoshida had been absolutely giddy in the Aloha Stadium press box during halftime. When he spotted Lenny Klompus, the CEO of Bowl Games of Hawai'i, he looked at him and deadpanned, "We accept."

"I haven't made you an offer yet," Klompus answered.

"No," said Yoshida, "but you will."

As fans opened their Sunday newspapers, they were hit with shocking news:

"Hawai'i needs just three more wins to receive a bid for either the Aloha or Oahu bowls. [Lenny] Klompus has said that if the Rainbows win seven games, he guarantees they will be sent an invitation."

Hawai'i?

Are you kidding me?

Rice 38, Hawai'i 19

June did his best to shut down all talk of bowl games, lest his team's humility become false and their focus be directed toward that which had yet to be attained. Vanity only serves to pump up worldly young minds, a risk that could defraud the Warriors of the very reward for which they were fighting.

Defensive coordinator Greg McMackin was nervous about Rice's running game -- and the Owls ran wild.

"We've been doing just fine focusing on one week at a time," he said. "We need to focus on Rice and forget all this talk of bowl games, or there won't be a bowl."

In Hawai'i, elders warn *"He kau auane'i i ka lae 'a'?,"* or "Watch out, lest your canoe land on a rocky reef." This, in essence, means what your mother always told you: *Don't count your chickens before they hatch.*

With his team basking in the inebriation of the homecoming win, Jones

for the first time had to caution against *overconfidence,* and the upcoming Rice University Owls were no laughing matter. For starters, the Hawai'i defense, while doing a bang-up job, was severely banged up themselves. Everywhere you looked, somebody was sporting an icepack or ACE bandage, and several starters would be unable to play.

Second, Rice had the most powerful option running attack in the Western Athletic Conference. In the week prior to facing Hawai'i, they had run the ball 62 times against Tulsa. As McMackin broke down their

Hawai'i wasn't all offense under June Jones: Even in defeat, thundering hits on defense became another trademark.

film against the likes of Michigan and Texas, he wasn't thrilled with what he saw. Before the season, he had forewarned that Hawai'i would be mismatched against strong, inside running teams.

There is no elixir for pride like reality. Rice, behind quarterback Chad Richardson, ran the option to perfection, rolling to a convincing 38-19 conference win. Richardson alone had 169 yards and three touchdowns, including a 60-yard burst directly up the middle on the first play of the second half. The quarterback ran right past a frustrated and confused Ulbrich, who mistakenly had chased the fullback on the play.

"That killed us," Ulbrich admits with disgust. "We're a zone-blitz team, and against a good option team, if you guess wrong, you're going to have big problems. They had small, annoying little linemen and tight ends and fullbacks that could pull and run. They guessed right a lot and caught us in a lot of bad calls. They knocked us on our heels. It was humbling."

One game and clear.

Nobody moves to Hawai'i to experience a change of seasons. Autumn and winter in Hawai'i are measured not by falling leaves or temperatures but by the growing size of the big surf at the North Shore.

Yet colors were, in fact, *changing* all over the Hawai'i campus in the shape of the athletes and characters that made up the shimmering fabric of June Jones' football club. From the start of fall training camp, June had set his eyes on fostering *ohana,* purposely separating friends and forcing them to share rooms with teammates whom they didn't know. Defensive linemen had ended up with quarterbacks, safeties with receivers, linebackers with running backs. All color and cultural lines were crossed.

It's difficult to understand the loving plan of a father, who plants tiny seeds of hope that often cannot be seen or understood until they begin to sprout. A true father realizes that the real work isn't in the harvest but in the cultivation. Long before the fig tree blossoms, before fruit appears on the vines, before the fields yield food, a father rejoices in the *seeding and nurturing* of his crops.

Now, at the crucial time of midseason, when former Hawai'i teams had fallen flat, those precious seedlings were pushing through in the forms of happiness, cohesion, care and respect. Coaches call this *character.*

There was the joyful heart of hulking defensive end Tony Tuoiti, who wore nothing but shorts and flip-flops and daily could be seen walking to class or from meetings happily strumming his tiny ukulele. Robinson's two-year-old daughter could be seen eating rice or ribs for breakfast with the offensive linemen, who cheerfully babysat while Dan and his wife attended classes. Academically ineligible Pisa Tinoisamoa was being herded by other players into the weight room and every classroom in order to build his physique and his GPA.

Then there was the remarkable change of attitude of Adrian Klemm, the former high school Santa Monica Athlete of the Year. Klemm had firmed into a menacing beast. He had virtually disappeared from the club scene and the take-out line at McDonald's, instead choosing to feast on opponents, whom he frequently taunted.

"Offensive linemen are taught to turn around and go back to the huddle," says Coach McKnight. "If you're kicking a guy's butt, you just keep doing it. We tell them not to wake a sleeping dog. But not Klemm. He was nasty. He would stand over you after he pancaked you and tell you how bad you suck — and then dare you to get up."

Teammates were finding him little fun to be around anymore.

"He completely changed," says Kynan Forney. "He stopped eating Big Macs. He was the first guy in the weight room. He was cocky. I said, 'What's your deal, man?' He said, 'June said I'm good enough to play in the league [NFL], I just need to work *harder* and be a *leader*. So I'm gonna work, dog, and that's it.' Adrian lit a fire under *everybody*.'"

A college football season is a six-month microcosm of life. By October, the unabated thrill of the start of the season has worn away. Coaches must be cautious not to push their athletes too hard in an effort to preserve their minds and bodies for the intensity of November and, hopefully, a bowl game in December. Yet the midseason games are critically important to a successful season.

This is when character must kick in. Coaches take all of the intangibles and turn them into measurable statistics and manageable risk. Players must trust their coaches; fight through the doldrums of injury, class work and monotony; remain focused and motivated on the ultimate goal; and dig deep within their storehouses to find what they need to win.

It's up to the coaches to keep those storehouses replenished, which is no simple task. The environment can become unstable overnight; this is why great leaders like June Jones articulate their vision clearly, explicitly and often. He and his coaches never reacted to dips in attitude, performance or media scrutiny. They stayed constant in their standards, values and progress.

At Hawai'i, this was made more difficult by the expectations of the student-athlete. College football players don't live like rock stars in Hawai'i — not even close. "The facilities," says McKnight, "are almost third world. You're there to get an education, play football and enjoy the scenery. That's about it."

Players squeeze their mighty frames into the same tiny desks as other students, at the same early morning hours as anybody else. The differ-

ence, however, is usually that by then they have already endured a practice or a weight room workout. The injured or sore were given no exceptions; try sitting in a cramped wooden desk listening to a lecture on *volcanology*, while the only thing erupting is the blinding white-hot pain in your neck or back, as was the case with ends Mike Iosua or Tuioti, who never complained.

The sweat of summer had become the fragrance of fall, and great tests of character awaited to determine if these Warriors had the guts to rise to greatness.

Hawai'i 35, Tulsa 21

Pep talks don't win football games. The tedious ebb and flow of a football season sees to that. So when the Warriors traded the lushness of Hawai'i for the parched oil fields of Oklahoma, there was an unspoken understanding that this was a must-win conference game, long before June Jones gathered the team the night before the contest.

However, from his very first day on the job, June had told his players that what they would take away from football would mean more to them than "anything you will learn on Upper Campus," and he never wasted a moment to make good on his promise and further their education.

That night's lesson included the story of the Flying Tigers, who were credited for destroying almost 300 aircraft, with a loss of only 12 of their own in combat. The shark-faced fighters remain among the most recognizable of any individual combat unit of World War II, and Jones was quick to draw similarities to their innovations, their tactical accomplishments, *their camaraderie* and how what seemed like meaningless victories resulted in enormous, long-term dividends.

Unbeknownst to his young players, Jones did not have fond memories of Tulsa. Fifteen years earlier, June and Mouse had coached in the same stadium with the USFL's Houston Gamblers. Behind future Hall-of-Fame quarterback Jim Kelly, they were enjoying a 28-13 lead when disaster struck: Oklahoma Outlaws' quarterback and future Super Bowl MVP Doug Williams heaved a pair of late touchdowns, and Houston lost 31-28.

Just 18 hours after the Hawai'i players learned about the Flying Tigers, bombs were falling from the skies at Skelly Field at H.A. Champan Stadium. On this day, Jones made certain that, this time, he would leave Oklahoma with a smile.

Daytime television's infamous Dr. Phil had been a middle linebacker for Tulsa in 1968, when the team had suffered a debilitating 100-6 loss to Houston. This game might have been a good time to bring him out of retirement — not to play defense, but for crisis counseling.

Everywhere you looked, it seemed, you saw wide receiver Ashley Lelie, with a streaking football not too far behind his back shoulder. Craig Stutzmann continued his downfield dominance, catching another 34-yard bomb for a score, one of his two touchdowns on the day. Dwight Carter padded his WAC-leading numbers with 41 yards and a touchdown.

Afatia Thompson lumbered for 73 yards and a touchdown. The Hawai'i defense intercepted three passes. Robinson fired on all cylinders, evidenced by his 283 yards.

"Not only was I moving the secondary with my eyes," he gleefully told Coach Morrison, *"but the linebackers were moving, too!"* Morrison couldn't help but shrug, as if he had no idea this day would ever occur.

The Warriors' five victories on the year matched their total *for the last five years.*

No sooner did the game end than June merely wanted out of Oklahoma, as fast as they could get the plane off the ground. Not to take anything away from Tulsa, but to an NFL coach, this was little more than a live scrimmage, especially when Texas Christian and a young man named LaDainian Tomlinson, who was averaging 170.4 yards per game, were en route to Honolulu for *next* Saturday's game.

The conference race and bowl game talk were interesting distractions for Jones and his staff. To some degree, it was a double-edged sword. On the one hand, it kept the pontificators busy with something to talk about on TV and radio and in newspaper columns, while giving Jones motivational fodder for the task at hand.

"The minute we start believing in anybody other than the guy next to us in the trenches is when we can start getting ourselves into trouble," Jones told them. "We've been successful with the one-game-at-a-time approach and there's no reason we should stop that now."

On the other hand, it was difficult to ignore. Last year's critics were now bandwagon catalysts, and players who were once largely ignored could no longer walk down the street without being recognized. Family members were already bugging them about bowl tickets and hotel reservations for Christmas.

▼▼▼▼▼▼▼▼▼▼▼▼▼▼▼▼▼

"The minute we start believing in anybody other than the guy next to us in the trenches, is when we can start getting ourselves into trouble," Jones told them. "We've been successful with the one-game-at-a-time approach and there's no reason we should stop that now."

▲▲▲▲▲▲▲▲▲▲▲▲▲▲▲▲▲

"Barring some unseen malady," screamed the local paper, *"the Rainbows will take part in the postseason parade for the first time since their WAC championship season of 1992."*

Jones and his coaching staff, particularly Greg McMackin, were hardly exchanging high fives. They were busy watching film of TCU, whose running back seemed strong enough to carry the entire state of Texas through four tireless quarters.

"This team is dangerous," McMackin kept telling the other coaches. "They're still a very dangerous football team. Just like Rice, they're great at the option, and the Tomlinson kid can run through anybody."

When a radio announcer asked Jones whether he would prefer to play in the Aloha Bowl on ABC or the O'ahu Bowl on ESPN, he bristled.

"I know this sounds like a cliché, but all I'm worried about right now is TCU," he said. There was no denying the frustration in his voice. "If we keep taking each game one at a time, the rest of this stuff takes care of itself."

Some people never listen until it's too late.

Coaches switched Robert Kemfort (26) from offense to defense, where he became a hard-hitting linebacker

Texas Christian 34, Hawai'i 14

Blunt-force trauma to the chest typically results in a broken rib — or in this case, two — when Dan Robinson stepped up into the pocket against the talented Texas Christian front seven and learned just how pointed a Horned Frog can be.

"When I heard them snap early in the first quarter," Robinson says, "I knew it was going to be a long day. Two plays later, I was picked up and slammed on my back so hard I thought I would die. The good news, I guess, is that my back hurt so bad, I forgot about my ribs."

Jeff Ulbrich, however, quickly returned the favor moments later. With

PHOTO BY GEORGE F. LEE

TCU facing a third and 1, Ulbrich crushed Tomlinson with a clean but vicious tackle that resulted in a high ankle sprain. "It was somewhere in the first quarter," Ulbrich says. "I hit him with everything I had. I heard something pop, he grunted underneath my weight, and he was done."

That was with 4:42 to play in the first quarter. Tomlinson would return to see limited action in the second half but was limping so badly he was finally removed altogether.

Robinson wasn't so lucky. He was sacked three times. He was hurried 10 times. He was knocked down 17 times. "That is one tough kid," said Dennis Franchione, TCU's head coach. "We kept knocking him down, and he kept getting back up. He's going to be sore tomorrow."

Hawai'i, for lack of a better word, imploded against the smaller, quicker, trapping and pulling TCU offensive line. As frustration grew along the defensive front, it spread throughout the sidelines, killing confidence. The Warriors missed field goals and extra points, suffered momentum-killing penalties and played miserably before their hometown crowd. Worse, injuries continued to mount.

The trouncing couldn't have ended soon enough for Robinson. His excruciating, shallow breaths left him panting to breathe; by game's end, he had to loosen his flak jacket just to do so.

As he limped to the tunnel, a group of drunken fans leaned over the railing and poured pint-size cups of beer upon the fallen Warrior. For a Mormon who never before had tasted alcohol, who had stood heroically in the face of all adversity in the name of Hawai'i, it was a lesson of a lifetime of just how cruel the world can be.

As he wiped the stinging beer from his burning eyes, Robinson fought back tears.

If they spit on Jesus . . . he thought . . . *I can take this. . . .*

How long, thought Robinson, *must the righteous suffer?*

Afatia Thompson was the other half of Hawaii's one-two punch with Avion Weaver

Chapter 18
DO YOU BELIEVE IN MIRACLES?

At the encouragement of Dan Morrison, Dan Robinson agreed to attend the weekly Quarterback Club luncheon the Monday following the humiliating defeat to Texas Christian.

The season was at a crossroad. The next two games were conference contests: first San Jose State, then Fresno State, which ranked among the WAC's elite. This was no time for summer soldiers or sunshine patriots; it was an opportunity to stand up and be counted or to simply fade away.

Yet when setbacks strike, as they often will, when the journey, as the poet said, seems all uphill . . . these are not the times to shrink silently away into the shadows. Morrison, June and the other coaches knew this all too well. These are the times when you get up, get dressed and get out. You *face* your demons, not *hide* from them.

As always, their gutsy, Utah-bred quarterback could be counted upon for leadership; Robinson, a true cowboy, likened it to "getting back on the horse that threw you."

He was uncertain, though, how he would be received by the public after being showered with beer just two nights before. They arrived at the hotel and made their way to the luncheon room. Coach Morrison put a gentle hand on Robinson's sore shoulder.

"You ready, Dan?" he said, smiling softly.

"Let's go, Coach," Robinson replied. "Let's get it over with."

They opened the door. The doctors and lawyers and preachers and politicians and business people who made up this lunchtime crowd wheeled to see Morrison and his hobbled quarterback.

As Robinson walked down the aisle, his integrity intact, the people began to stand, one by one. One clap, then two, pierced the silence, then suddenly burst into a sea of thundering applause. The searing pain in Robinson's back and ribs vanished. The *true* people of Hawai'i could not be judged by the actions of but a few intoxicated drunks.

These are the people we play for, he thought. *This is what real* ohana *is all about.*

Morrison spoke that day, but Robinson doesn't remember a word he said. His mind was someplace else — like, say, *the secondary of San Jose State* for instance.

> ▼▼▼▼▼▼▼▼▼▼▼▼
>
> *These are the people we play for,*
> *he thought. This is what*
> *real ohana is all about.*
>
> ▲▲▲▲▲▲▲▲▲▲▲▲

Hawai'i 62, San Jose State 41

San Jose, Calif., is only 21 miles north of Morgan Hill.

Morgan Hill you will remember, was the home of man-eater Jeff Ulbrich, who had been — ahem — *rejected* by San Jose State. Men like Ulbrich need little motivation, but this is the worst kind for an opposing coach. Not only had San Jose State sent him packing years before, but now Ulbrich was back, full of vengeance and leading the WAC in sacks and tackles.

This is not to mention that half of Morgan Hill was claiming to be related to Ulbrich and clamoring for tickets. From the opening series, Ulbrich made it clear that he would not be blocked, and he played a major role in San Jose State's four fumbles and three interceptions. "He played like a madman," says Dennis McKnight. "You have never seen an individual so possessed in your life, so determined to prove a point. He put an exclamation point on every single tackle he made that night."

In the first half, San Jose State rushed for *minus 28 yards.*

Robinson started red-hot, throwing his first touchdown four plays into the game on a 42-yard post to a streaking Channon Harris. Then, disaster struck, though no one would ever know its severity. Looking deep, Robinson never saw the missed block or the defensive tackle racing untouched toward him — until, that is, he was lifted off his feet and driven into the turf with his right arm crooked above his head like a question mark.

"I knew it was bad," Robinson says. "I knew it was separated, because my arm went limp immediately. When I came to the sideline, I knew I needed to keep throwing to keep it from inflaming. There was no way I was coming out, though. Not after the week before. I was going to prove to the people of Hawai'i that I was tough, and that I could play."

Robinson went back into the game, and the Warriors scored 27 consecutive points, including an 18-yard touchdown to Ashley Lelie, his career first. Craig Stutzmann caught *two* 26-yard scores, the latter in which he broke 10 tackles to get into the end zone.

The season had been one of *firsts,* and the game against San Jose State would be no different: It was the first time Hawai'i had ever enjoyed a 33-7 *halftime* lead.

"We started taking people out," says Ulbrich, "and all of a sudden, they went down and scored a couple of times. You've got to remember, we didn't know what it was like to play with a lead."

Robinson couldn't even feel the football in his throwing hand, but when you're playing on sheer will, apparently it doesn't matter. By game's end, Robinson had thrown for 371 yards and four touchdowns to set Hawai'i's school record with 2,801 passing yards, breaking the mark set by Garrett Gabriel in 1990.

"Dan was slower than Moses," says Klemm, "but he was tougher than nails."

He also led the WAC in passing, *with three games to play.*

The Warriors broke 60 points for the first time ever. "They were lucky," says Robinson. "Had I been healthy, we could've scored a lot more."

Hee-Haw!

Are you kidding me?

The championship talk could no longer be stifled. Coffee shops, newsstands and talk shows were abuzz with the reality that *this weekend* the once also-ran Warriors would be playing for at least a part of the WAC championship. At that time, few encapsulated these thoughts of Honolulu better than *Star-Bulletin* sports editor Paul Arnett, who wrote:

> For those of you who stuck your head in a cold bucket of water just to make sure you weren't California dreaming last Saturday afternoon, go get a 10-pound bag of ice because you're going to need it.
>
> Not only did Hawai'i receive two points in this week's Associated Press Top 25, the Rainbows nailed down five points in the ESPN/USA Today coaches poll as well.
>
> At the beginning of the season, the only people allowed to think such nonsense were the players and coaches on the Rainbows' football team. Spouses and girlfriends don't count. The rest of you who actually thought in the light of day with people all about that such a turnaround was indeed possible, go to the medicine cabinet. Just because it happened doesn't make you sane.
>
> Reality says this Saturday night at Aloha Stadium Hawai'i is playing for a share of the Western Athletic Conference title and a bid from Bowl Games Hawai'i to take part in the Christmas Day doubleheader. It's true. Even Rainbows' head coach June Jones is willing to articulate the popular rage. Well, sort of.

"I'm not going to change my philosophy until we get that seventh win," Jones said. "We're just going to worry about Fresno State. Our season goal was to be 6-3 at this point. We wanted a shot at it with three home games left."

"I'm not talking about too much of anything except Fresno State. All those championships and all those bowls take care of themselves if you just keep winning. We probably have a shot to be in a bowl game and we have a shot to win the title, so, we'll see how it goes."

If there was a defining moment for last year's downtrodden Rainbows, it was the brutal loss at Fresno State.

There, at fog-shrouded Bulldog Stadium, Fresno State took the last bite of the Fred vonAppen era and spit it out on the grass in the form of a 51-12 beating. Anybody who saw that game won't soon forget the carnage or the shocked silence in the dressing room.

Now, nearly a year later, the teams meet again on the artificial surface of Aloha Stadium. San Jose State can tell its hated rival that payback, island-style, isn't pretty.

The Godfather's Michael Corleone described it this way, "Today, I settle all family business."

Or as senior offensive tackle Adrian Klemm said after Hawai'i secured the bizarre 62-41 victory over San Jose State, "At the beginning of the year, nobody believed we would be playing for the conference championship this weekend. But tell Fresno State they'd better believe it."

You won't have to tell the Bulldogs anything. Fresno State head coach Pat Hill will do it for you during this week's practice. As unlikely as it was for Hawai'i to be in this position, many preseason magazines tabbed the Bulldogs as the team to beat.

Now, the WAC title will very likely be decided Saturday night. The last time a Rainbow game held this much importance was seven years ago against Wyoming. That night, Hawai'i clinched it first conference co-championship.

That title wasn't nearly as improbable as this possibility. Oh, like this year's team, that one was picked to finish eighth. But in 1992, Bob Wagner's eventual seven-win about-face began at the end of 1991. Hawai'i nearly stunned Notre Dame the last game of that season and it carried over into the 1992 campaign.

This year's team entered 1999 with the nation's longest losing streak and extended it to 19 games after being blown out in the season opener with Southern California. But instead of pushing the panic button, Jones told them it was only one game. Think about it tonight, put it behind you tomorrow.

Now, eight games and six victories later, the Rainbows stand on the threshold of one of the nation's greatest swings since Bob Wills and the Texas Playboys. Even Jones conceded the Rainbows are where they want to be.

"I'm feeling great about being 6-3 and proud of the guys winning three on the road," Jones said.

Not even the championship team of 1992 turned that trick. The last time it happened was 1988. Jones was in his final year with the Houston Oilers back then. But he's here now and has the Rainbows closing in on possibly the greatest turnaround in NCAA history.

It's time for the bucket. And throw in a little ice while you're at it.

College football fans caught wind of it that afternoon on ESPN's College Gameday, and the reaction across the mainland was about what one would expect:

Hawai'i?

Are you kidding me?

Shrouded behind the smokescreen of bowl hype and headlines was the spaghetti-like throwing arm that was connected to the seized-up shoulder of Dan Robinson. Immediately following the San Jose State game, Jones had shut down all talk of his quarterback's mangled shoulder. There was zero mention of it among the players or in the press.

Privately, Jones knew the score. Just as he had in years past with Barry Sanders, June would limit Robinson in practice.

"Don't throw *any more* this week," Jones instructed. "You're not throwing a ball again until Saturday in warm-ups. In practice, go out with the first team. We'll go through the running game first, so the media sees you out there. Then we'll put the other quarterbacks in there for the passing reps."

It worked. Not one paper reported his injury. "Technically," says McKnight, "he should've been finished for the year. Monday, Tuesday, Wednesday, he couldn't even hold a football or throw a 5-yard out. Come Saturday, we were going to ask him to win us a championship. It shows you the kind of guy he is."

June wasn't done with just Robinson, however.

He pulled Ulbrich and several other starters out of practice as well. "At first, I was a little upset," Ulbrich recalls. "I took pride in my conditioning and in taking all the reps. But when I look back on it. . . ."

Ulbrich pauses in thought. "Looking back, if he hadn't done that, who knows? June always knew where we were, mentally, emotionally, spiritually and physically. That's just one of the things that makes him the coach that he is today."

Hawai'i 31, Fresno State 24

On a night perfect for football, with the temperature hovering around 72 degrees, a thundering crowd packed itself into Aloha Stadium to witness history. Under the magic of the stadium's glowing lights, Dan Robinson spun a football in the palm of his right hand and prayed for strength. He realized it was now or never.

True competitors hurt before — even after — a play. Snap to whistle, however, *they have to go.*

"*Dan . . . get ready to go!*" yelled Jones. "*Hum it out there Dan-O, just like you did last week!*"

This is it, Robinson thought. He gripped the laces, and pain sizzled up his arm like electricity. He flicked the ball forward with such great pain that tears welled in his eyes. His first throw took off like a duck and nearly landed in the front row of the stands. With each toss, his shoulder popped like the opening of a soda can. His broken ribs were wrapped tighter than a roasted pig in banana leaves.

Every throw was like tugging a string on a ball of yarn; instead of loosening, it just grew tighter. Robinson approached Ulbrich. "Jeff," he said, "you guys are gonna have to carry us until I get my arm and shoulder going." Ulbrich, eyes wide, nodded. Moments later, in the locker room, he exploded into another vintage Ulbrich tantrum.

"*This is an unbelievable opportunity!*" he screamed at his teammates, gripping the facemask of his helmet so tightly that his fingers burned white. "*There is not one guy here who has been close to this in your whole career! We're in a position to win this thing tonight! This is something I've wanted my whole life! I will not let anyone ruin this for me, or for any other member of this football team!*"

Ulbrich laughs today at the memory. "I was a bit out of control," he says. "I probably didn't make a lot of friends at that moment. It was very, um, *tense.* But it was *necessary.*"

As Robinson predicted, the Warriors went three and out on their first series. Fresno State quickly scored on an eight-play drive when Paris Gaines plunged in from 3 yards out. Again Robinson could muster no offense, and Hawai'i punted. Safety Dee Miller then picked up a fumble from Bulldog fullback Derrick Ward at the Hawai'i 48.

"Settle down, Danny," June said. Robinson's natural adrenaline was slowly lubricating the shoulder, and he was feeling less and less pain.

The medical name for adrenaline is epinephrine. It is produced in the adrenal glands above the kidneys, where it circulates in the bloodstream and is therefore considered a hormone. It has effects on parts of the body far remote from where it is produced. When faced with a dangerous or frightening situation, adrenaline is the key factor in a human's flight-or-fight response mechanism.

Inside of Dan Robinson, adrenaline had slowed his body's release of insulin to a mere trickle. With his blood sugar rising, the quarterback dealt with the most stressful situation of his life by stepping up into the pocket and firing a 5-yard touchdown to Dwight Carter to tie the game.

Just three plays later, defensive end Mike Iosua drilled his helmet directly into the football, which again was being carried by Ward. The ball squirted free and again was recovered by Miller. Robinson calmed his teammates and led a time-consuming drive, capped by his own 1-yard, feet-first slide into the end zone.

At the half, Hawai'i led 13-7. Ulbrich and the defense had been stellar, stopping the Bulldogs three times on third downs and holding future NFL quarterback Billy Volek to just 69 yards passing.

After a scoreless third quarter, Hawai'i seemed to have the game in hand with 14:13 left in regulation, when Robinson hit Ashley Lelie with a 15-yard touchdown. But Fresno State stormed back on a 13-play, 77-yard drive, capped by Volek's sneak into the end zone with just under 10 minutes remaining.

Robinson did his best to run out the clock on the next Hawai'i drive, but kicker Eric Hannum missed a 29-yard chip shot with four minutes to play. Five plays later, Fresno State appeared to be stopped on a third and 2 at their own 47 at the two-minute warning, until safety Nate Jackson was called for roughing the passer. Volek then threw a 28-yard touchdown.

▼▼▼▼▼▼▼▼▼▼▼▼▼

"This is an unbelievable opportunity!" he screamed at his teammates, gripping the facemask of his helmet so tightly that his fingers burned white. "There is not one guy here who has been close to this in your whole career! We're in a position to win this thing tonight! This is something I've wanted my whole life! I will not let anyone ruin this for me, or for any other member of this football team!"

▲▲▲▲▲▲▲▲▲▲▲▲▲

With little time left in the fourth, Robinson rolled left against his body and spotted Dwight Carter racing away from the defense. "I let it rip," says Robinson. "But my hand wasn't normal; it slipped out, and they picked it off with 30 seconds left. I couldn't believe I had just given them the ball back.

"Ulbrich ran over to me and grabbed my pads. He screamed at me, *'Don't worry! I gotcha! I will get you the ball back!'* I went over to the bench and put my head in my hands and just started praying for the defense to hold them."

When Ulbrich set the defensive huddle, he loved the salacious, raw energy glaring back at him. "Every single guy in that huddle had the same eyes," he recalls. "I could see it in their eyes. Trust me, I was going to go off, but I realized I didn't need to. I can remember it vividly. Every guy in that huddle was in the right place. It was a beautiful thing. It was one of the purest moments of my life."

The defense held. A long Fresno State field goal attempt sailed wide, and the season of firsts continued.

Overtime.

Are you kidding me?

Fresno State scored first in overtime on a field goal. Now all the pressure in the world fell squarely on the broken shoulder of Robinson, who responded in kind with a labrum-searing rifle shot to Dwight Carter near the goal line. What happened next surprised even Jones: *Twice* Robinson changed June's play-call — both passes — and attempted quarterback sneaks, only to be stuffed both times short of the goal line. Jones couldn't believe Robinson: Fresno State was excellent against the run, and there was no way the Hawai'i offensive line was going to blow them off the ball from their standard two-point stance.

"I've never heard a stadium, even in the NFL, that loud," recalls McMackin.

"It may as well have been a dome," agrees Ulbrich.

"I thought the stadium was going to collapse," says Robinson.

Fresno tied the game again with a field goal of its own. When Hawai'i reclaimed the ball, Jones turned immediately to his field general. His eyes pierced Robinson like lasers.

"Dan, listen, if we're going to win this thing, *you've got to trust me* on these goal line calls! *Stick with your reads! Stop changing the play, OK? We've been here before! You have got to trust me!*"

"Stutzmann is running a corner route, OK? They are doubling him to the outside! One guy outside, one guy inside . . . now listen Danny . . . here's the deal . . . take your eyes backside, because the guy with the leverage is going to let him go . . . you turn and throw it to the cone . . . YOU HAVE TO TRUST ME! This is a touchdown, OK?"

Robinson nodded, and Jones continued.

"Everything you've learned for eight months comes down to right here, right now! We come out first this next OT . . . let's go 90 Streak Z Delay, and this time, stay with what I tell you!"

Jones slapped his quarterback on the butt. With the crowd so deafening he could barely hear, Robinson grabbed a chinstrap in either hand, buttoned his hat and trotted back out across the turf in the first — and last — double-overtime game of his football career.

Hawai'i faced third and 6 from the Fresno State 9-yard line when Robinson stepped into the huddle. He looked at Craig Stutzmann and was forced to yell to be heard above the din.

"Stutz," he rasped, *"we're gonna go 90 Streak Z Delay, 90 Streak Z Delay . . . I'm gonna take my eyes backside, and the guy with the leverage is gonna let you loose. I'm gonna roll a step or two, move him out of there*

UNIVERSITY OF HAWAII ATHLETICS

Coach Dennis McKnight – the 1999 version, with hair – leads the celebration on the Hawaii bench

Hawai'i was forced to tie the game on a 22-yard field goal by Hannum, who hadn't exactly been automatic; he'd already missed an extra point and a field goal. The Hawai'i sideline held its collective breath. Hannum's kick whisked into the night sky, then cleanly arced between the uprights. The stadium exploded into bedlam.

140

and throw to the cone. Alright? Just like practice, now. Pitch and catch. Big men, gimme time to get it off, OK?"

"First sound . . . first sound. . . ."

At the snap, Robinson took two steps to his right, opened his eyes wide down the hash, pulled the under guy like a puppeteer, then wheeled right and threw to the corner. Just as June predicted, the inside guy followed Robinson's eyes; when he saw Robinson turn back, he did his best to recover, but it was too late. Caught in a squat, you could almost hear the safety's groin pop as he fell to the turf. The ball whistled past his earhole and into a perfect noose formed by the soft, waiting hands of Craig Stutzmann.

Touchdown!

Now it was Ulbrich's turn, as Fresno State would get one last opportunity.

Billy Volek quickly moved the Bulldogs to the Hawai'i 12. On third down, however, defensive end Joe Correia — *yes, the baseball player!* — sacked Volek all the way back at the Hawai'i 22, which brought up fourth down.

Everyone was on their feet — every man, woman and child in the stadium — screaming at the top of their lungs as Volek went under center for fourth down.

Every player on the Hawai'i bench stood at the edge of the sidelines; several were holding hands.

Volek dropped to throw. Fresno State receiver Charles Smith darted past Shawndell Tucker and broke to the right corner of the end zone. Volek fired. Tucker recovered; now he and Smith were running side by side in pursuit of the ball.

Time stood still. Jones checked the backfield: no flags.

Both players leaped.

Incomplete!

PHOTO BY GEORGE F. LEE

Oh what a feeling! Jonathon Kauka (43) celebrates ...

The final score remained *Hawai'i 31, Fresno State 24.*

Smith fell into the north end zone wall as hundreds of fans poured onto the field. Aloha Stadium exploded into chaos, disorder, euphoria. Confetti rained from the sky. Fans mobbed the goalposts in an attempt to bring them down. Players rejoiced as they hugged fans, cried on their knees and dove into piles like little boys diving into presents at Christmas time.

Do you believe in miracles?

"I was numb," says Jones. "The feeling at midfield, right at that moment, was awesome. That's what we play for. The emotions of the kids . . . even the coaches . . . it's what makes college football so unique. It was breathtaking. It will live with me as long as I live — forever and ever."

The Warriors had officially earned an invitation to the Oʻahu Bowl on Christmas Day. *"Earned"* was the key word.

Robinson had become Hawaiʻi's all-time leading career passer, with 5,254 yards. His 2,992 yards of total offense bettered the 1988 record (2,937) of Warren Jones. He had 493 total plays on offense, topping Rafael Cherry's 1984 mark of 463.

With the win, Robinson now had nine straight 200-yard games.

Yaphet Warren — the other wide-receiver-turned-linebacker — had 17 tackles.

Jeff Ulbrich had 16.

Robinson, just two weeks removed from his first and last beer, walked selflessly through the Aloha Stadium parking lot with his wife Jill. Together they stopped at each tailgate party to shake hands with the fans and *thanked them* for Dan's opportunity to serve them as their quarterback.

"The food was great," he says. "But most of all, I realized how special these people were. They had waited so long to just be called winners. I was nothing more than an instrument to deliver what they had prayed for. I thank God for that. It was an honor. The guys that threw the beer on me — that wasn't Hawaiʻi, not at all.

"The people of Hawaiʻi are the real warriors. I was fortunate — they just let me wear the badge."

Bear Bryant used to say there were three types of quarterbacks in the world. Funny, he never once described *the first two,* but he always jumped to the third.

"The quarterback that every coach is seeking directs his team with maximum results," the Bear said. "He is a student of the game. He is logical in his thinking. He is bold in his action. He does whatever necessary to win a football game. He is confident, which in turn gives his team confidence in both him and the offense. He is a winner through preparation. *He listens when coached.* Now *that* is a quarterback who will give you winners through action and leadership."

Dan Robinson, take a bow.

No one was more dedicated than Dan Robinson, who spent hours jumping back and forth over a two-by-four to improve his footwork

Avion Weaver sinks Navy with a huge blast up the middle

Hawai'i 48, Navy 41

Had you asked any Hawai'i player in 1999 the significance of playing Navy, they most certainly would have said the following:

Can we stop an option team?

Big losses to Rice and TCU suggested the answer was *no*. Hours of film revealed gaping holes — not in the team, but in coaches June Jones and Greg McMackin. Blocking down on the knees in the NFL is forbidden and

something Jones and McMackin literally forgot to coach. So when Rice did it, they were surprised; when TCU did it, they were disappointed . . . in themselves.

"The four years I was in the NFL," admits McMackin, "they [college teams] have really brought this kind of blocking scheme a long way, and I'm not sure that it's good for the game."

Jones wasn't nearly as nice: "It's harmful to the players and should be illegal, exactly as it is in the NFL, and I don't care who thinks I should or shouldn't say that."

Channon Harris – June Jones' first slotback recruit from Los Angeles

Fool me once, shame on you. Fool me twice, shame on you.

Fool me . . . *oh, never mind — you get the point.* Navy had the misfortune of being third in the gauntlet. Based on the film, they just assumed they would do to Hawai'i what the two prior option running teams had done.

According to the film, if that's your yardstick, the midline option should have gutted Hawai'i like a roadside possum.

Think again.

There is a saying among the Hawaiian people: *"He lawai'a no ke kai papa'u, he pākole ke aho; he lawai'a no ke kai hohonu he loa ke aho."* The literal translation is, "A fisherman of the shallow sea uses only a short line; a fisherman of the deep sea has a long line."

When interpreted, it can mean that a person whose knowledge is shallow does not have much, but he whose knowledge is deep does.

Now, the application of this Hawaiian proverb to football is simple: You tell Jeff Ulbrich, when facing an option team, to no longer worry about *who might* get the football but to instead hold a staff meeting on the head of the quarterback. Suddenly, Greg McMackin's troops had the depth of experience to do so.

"We watched the film," says Ulbrich, "and Navy had played some pretty good teams. They had just as much success with the option as Rice or TCU. Coach Mack was fed up, though, with the blocking schemes. He told me to just destroy the quarterback. So I did."

Somebody forgot to tell Ulbrich and the defense that Hawai'i was a three-point underdog.

In perhaps the most surreal moment in Hawai'i football history, June Jones accepted the WAC Championship trophy from league commissioner Karl Benson prior to kickoff.

Then the fun began. Receiver-turned-linebacker Yaphet Warren blocked a field goal. Ulbrich killed the quarterback. Dan Robinson *broke 11 more records* and threw for 530 yards. Dwight Carter caught 10 passes, including two touchdowns.

In another first, Hawai'i finally whipped an option team, exorcising yet another demon.

"I can't explain to you how it feels," said Tony Tuioti. "It's like being on a roller coaster. You can't get off. You can only enjoy the ride."

"Who would have thought Hawai'i would pull off something like this?" Benson said after the game. "Watching this team this year and the one that didn't win a game last year, it's hard to believe it's the same team."

Washington State 22, Hawai'i 14

Emotionally drained: That's how players describe the loss to Washington State. If you run down the statistics, nothing jumps out. Washington State didn't do anything special. Hawai'i didn't get whipped, nor did Washington State play great football.

"I've always played the game with a kind of 'no-regrets' attitude," says Ulbrich. "But that's a game I regret, because we could have won. We should have won. We were just emotionally drained. We played them well defensively. It was heartbreaking."

Coach Morrison smiles at Ulbrich's comments. "There's nothing beautiful about a loss," he says, "but there is something beautiful about a game that, just a year before, would have been *just another loss*. That shows you how far these kids had come. They had grown to the point that they expected to win, no matter who the opponent was, and hated losing. That's a classic example of the change in their paradigm from just a year before."

Ulbrich, of course, led the team with 18 tackles. Tony Tuioti had two sacks. Nate Jackson had a sack and Quincy LeJay had another interception.

Here's something, however, that was never printed in the paper or broadcast on TV: Robinson, again, didn't practice the entire week. He never wore pads until game time.

A Washington State runner finds himself in the crosshairs of wild-man Jeff Ulbrich

PHOTO BY GEORGE F. LEE

"In spite of everything, we were still champions. We didn't have the depth, or the talent or the facilities of any other team we played. But *we had the guts,* and we had a coaching staff that made us believe we could win — and we did."

Hawai'i's 19 seniors, including 11 starters and 6 fifth-year players, participated in the "Senior Walk" that game. The packed stadium stood for several minutes as they roared with appreciation for this most unlikely team.

"This season was dedicated to our seniors," Jones told the crowd. "These guys have been through so much. This has been a great tribute to them." For the first time in nearly a decade, however, the final regular-season game wouldn't be the fans' last chance to see their Hawai'i stars. In just three weeks, Oregon State would make the five-and-a-half-hour flight to the islands to face the Warriors in the O'ahu Bowl.

In a final twist of fate, Oregon State, like mighty USC, was another PAC-10 team that had whipped UCLA, 55-7.

Who's writing this script?

Hawai'i would get one last chance to slay the giant — a fitting end to a storybook season.

Goliath who?

Are you kidding me?

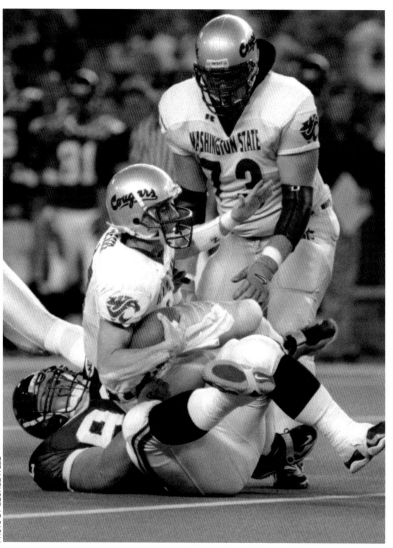

Lui Fuga unceremoniously spanks former Hawaii high school standout Jason Gesser

"My arm was shot," he says. "It was completely numb against Washington State. I played the game because I was the leader. I did my best, but I couldn't even feel the football. We had so many injuries on the sidelines that it looked like a hospital. But nobody made excuses and nobody complained.

Seniors of 1999
Phil Austin, Dwight Carter, Matt Elam, Victor Fonoimoana, Ryan Gray, Daniel Ho-Ching, John Kirby, Adrian Klemm, Quinay LeJay, Kaulana Noa, Dustin Owen, Matt Paul, Andy Phillips, Daniel Reed, Dan Robinson, Chad Shrout, Josh Skinner, Tony Tuioti, Jeff Ulbrich, Yaphet Warren

Chapter 19
WHEN IT RAINS, IT POURS

Facing the Giants is a popular family movie that has enjoyed enormous success. Its storyline is surprisingly familiar: A football coach who stands up to the seemingly unconquerable giants in his life and relies on faith to move mountains.

One of the most poignant moments in the film occurs when the coach is told a story of two farmers whose crops and fields had suffered from drought. Both farmers prayed for rain. One farmer, however, took action: After praying, he went out and began to plow his field. When asked why he was doing so, he replied:

"I'm preparing my fields for rain."

Hence the difference, the viewer surmises, between *passive* and *active* faith.

Preparing for rain requires risk taking, trust and a personal strength of character that extends far beyond human measure. Years before the

A birds-eye view at the Jeep Oʻahu Bowl

UNIVERSITY OF HAWAII ATHLETICS PHOTO BY FRANCES CAMERA

movie's release, June Jones was already living the script in real life: His actions have always been a direct result of core principles and values that make up his powerful system of belief.

When June accepted the position at Hawaiʻi, he knowingly stepped up to a platform where no one before him had succeeded against such immeasurable odds. Jones absorbed ridicule, risked defeat and subjected himself

to the potential of public humiliation. He sold his vision by exciting the imagination and capturing the hearts of the people of Hawaiʻi.

Only *faith* affords one such superhuman strength. Ironically, Jones has tutored more great quarterbacks than just about anyone in history. One of the first things he teaches a quarterback is that his *eyes* must always be downfield. The second a quarterback "looks down" or lowers his eyes in fear at the onrushing assault of the defense, the play is over and disaster is imminent.

How fitting that Jones never *looks down* but keeps his own eyes poised downfield; he knows the prize that awaits the man with the *faith* to endure life's challenges.

Jones wanted to be more than just a football coach. He wanted to deliver the Hawaiʻi people from the bondage of failure, to deliver a program that could compete with anyone on any stage. While the rest of the world saw a miracle in 1999, June Jones was merely creating a *template* that would enable the program to enjoy tremendous success for years and years to come. Such leadership is not for the faint of heart.

"To me, victory always begins with surrender," Jones says. "You have to let go. You must have faith — in God, in others, in yourself. This allows the system, if you want to call it that, a chance to work."

Victory begins with surrender? Isn't that an oxymoron?

Are you kidding me?

When faced with insurmountable odds, men and women of faith rise up and sing. They are strongest when they should be weak. In the face of brokenness, they are instead complete, for they understand the healing power of truth and love.

The 1999 Warriors had bought into each of these principles; it was evident in the way they *believed* and *behaved.* Far more than football was occurring in the locker room, dorm rooms, hearts and lives of every player on the team.

There was but one challenge left.

If you're the pilot of a loaded 747 passenger jet, nobody remembers the smooth takeoff or the uneventful flight if you miss the landing by a few hundred feet. It's one thing to *say* you're going to produce the biggest turnaround in the history of college football. It's quite another to *go do it* when there are giants in the land — like, say, Oregon State for instance?

Facing the giants, indeed.

Only June Jones wouldn't have the option of yelling *'Cut!'* if things went awry.

CNN, *USA Today*, ESPN . . . all predicted Oregon State would handily beat Hawai'i. "The only people who really believed we were going to win," says Jones, "were in our locker room."

This was not without good reason. Hawai'i had lost to USC and Washington State, other PAC-10 teams, by a combined score of 84-21. Oregon State had just completed a miracle year of its own. The school's

▼▼▼▼▼▼▼▼▼▼▼▼▼▼

Preparing for rain requires risk-taking; trust, and a personal strength of character that extends far beyond human measure. Years before the movie's release, June Jones was already living the script in real life: His actions have always been a direct result of core principles and values that make up his powerful system of belief.

▲▲▲▲▲▲▲▲▲▲▲▲▲▲

first winning season since 1970 had been highlighted by a 55-7 pasting of UCLA and victories over both Arizona State and Cal.

Twisting subplots were churning in every direction.

The O'ahu Bowl would be OSU's first postseason competition since the 1965 Rose Bowl, and their new head coach was none other than Dennis Erickson — Greg McMackin's former boss with the Seattle Seahawks.

Running back Ken Simonton had rushed for 1,329 yards and 17 touchdowns on the year, while quarterback Jonathon Smith had thrown for 303 yards against Sun Bowl–bound Oregon and 469 yards against Holiday Bowl–bound Washington.

"I know Hawai'i had a good year," says Dennis Erickson. "But our story matched theirs."

On paper, Hawai'i didn't have a chance. The so-called power rankings had Oregon State winning in a rout. Several favored Oregon State by as much as two touchdowns. One CNN broadcaster consoled the Warriors, offering that "It's unfortunate the Hawai'i fairy tale must come to such an abrupt end."

When the Hawai'i coaches first watched the Oregon State game film, the consensus was pretty unanimous. "They had some great athletes," says McMackin. "We were going to need a perfect game just to have a chance."

Like a pair of gunfighters on a dusty street, Jones and Erickson — two coaches one year removed from the NFL — would duel for NCAA bragging rights on Christmas Day.

Grab the popcorn. This was going to be better than a John Wayne Western.

The Warriors had three weeks between games — time their broken bodies desperately needed to heal. Jones, as always, urged his players to spend ample time regenerating their hearts and minds as well.

One can only wonder what the Hawai'i players must have been thinking — Dan Robinson in particular. Throughout the season, he and his family had often enjoyed barbecues at Magic Island, where he would stand with his wife Jill, arm in arm, quietly absorbing spectacular sunsets that made the seas glimmer like brilliant emeralds and sapphires.

Magic Island

"After all he had been through," Jill says, "he wanted desperately to give Hawai'i a championship. There was something burning deep inside Dan that words cannot explain."

There was something else burning inside Robinson, however, that *could be explained.* With Robinson's right arm now in near-critical condition, June ordered his quarterback not to throw a football again. Robinson had so seriously overcompensated for his bum shoulder that now his elbow, too, was frayed.

The week before the O'ahu Bowl, a specialist flew in from Atlanta to give Robinson intravenous DMSO (dimethyl sulfoxide) treatments to enable him to play.

DMSO "sweats" through the skin, emitting a powerful odor similar to that of burnt garlic. In player meetings, Robinson smelled so bad from the treatment that he sat alone, on the opposite side of the room from his teammates. Racked with pain, Dan would not throw a football for five straight weeks, until the Warriors took the field for warm-ups.

Ulbrich and many others were more fortunate. "I needed the three weeks off," says the defensive captain. "By the week of practice, I felt better than I had all year."

The jungles outside Bangalore, India, are home to numerous elephant camps. There, enormous elephants are chained to simple stakes that the behemoths could easily pull from the ground if they so chose. They don't, however, because from birth they are tied to those same stakes, and as calves they are not strong enough to do so. As they grow bigger and stronger, the elephants remain mentally and emotionally tied to those stakes and therefore make no effort to break free.

The real miracle in Hawai'i could not be measured in wins or losses. Dozens of young men had broken free of the chains that once bound them — fully devoted, fully surrendered, fully victorious. All season long they had pushed through invisible barriers in a spirit-lifting mission full of vision and insight that would have lifelong implications.

Who, then, were CNN or ESPN or any other news acronym to predict their human potential?

For three weeks, the Warriors would wait patiently, quietly renewing their strength.

Soon, they would mount up with wings like eagles; they would run and not faint.

Insult to injury: That's how the Hawai'i players felt soon after Oregon State rolled into town. "It was as if everything we'd sacrificed for an entire season didn't mean anything," says Ulbrich, the *last* Warrior anyone should irritate. "They talked like they were just here to have a fun week of partying, come in, pummel us, get their trophy and go home.

"I think I had multiple tantrums that week."

To a man, all the Hawai'i players and coaches still remember the pregame banquet, just days before the contest. "It was not a healthy environment," deadpans McMackin, in classic Irish understatement.

"When you coach team sports," says Coach Morrison, "you really get a sense of when other teams have little regard for you. That night, you could just see that Oregon State wasn't taking us seriously — at all. I could look at our guys and realize they could see it, too. It hurt, it stung, and it was very much felt throughout the team. I could see the pride in our guys just well up. Guys like Ulbrich were just glaring, shaking their heads.

"June saw it . . . I credit him for not belaboring the issue verbally, because he didn't have to," Morrison adds. "He just let the emotion run its course and told us coaches to stay on track."

"Lift up your head above your enemies," wrote the Psalmist, and this was no exception. "I devoted the time," says Ulbrich, "to bring the team together and pray."

Jeff Ulbrich *praying?*

Are you kidding me?

The opening Oregon State drive gave Ulbrich major cause for concern. Something was horribly wrong. OSU running back Ken Simonton had made it look easy, darting through the defensive line and into the secondary several times before finally scoring easily on the game's first touchdown with 8:08 to play in the first quarter.

"I remember coming to the sideline," says Ulbrich, "and thinking, *Uh-oh, we have to turn this around.* You could tell it was a just a different level of talent than what we were accustomed. They were like USC talentwise, and after that first series, I told Coach Mack, 'We've got to fix this in a hurry.' I didn't say a word to my teammates, but I thought we might be in trouble."

Ulbrich's tantrums had reached tantric proportions. There had been one that week in practice and another just prior to kickoff. Now, with Hawai'i already trailing, there was no time like the present.

"We cannot let these guys do this to us!" Ulbrich screamed. *"Wake up! Either wake up, or cry tomorrow!"*

McMackin, however, was taking a more cerebral approach. Having coached with Erickson for several years, he knew his opponent's tendencies well and quietly began to make adjustments. Robinson, meanwhile, led the Warriors to two first-half scores, including an 80-yard drive that was capped by a 9-yard touchdown to Channon Harris.

At halftime, the teams were deadlocked at 10-10.

"They're a lot better than us physically," McMackin confided to Jones. "But we can keep them off balance if we keep blitzing."

"Then let's get after them," June suggested. "We have nothing to lose. Go for it."

60 Z Go is among the base routes in the Run 'n' Shoot. It floods zones and confuses safeties, more often than not leaving a man running free. Jones is apt to run the play until you find a way to stop it, and this day would be no different.

PHOTO BY GEORGE F. LEE

Ulbrich goes head-first against Oregon State's Ken Simonton

When June asked Robinson "how much do you have left in your arm?" the quarterback responded with a one-word answer: "Enough."

Morrison, upstairs, was in agreement with June to keep calling it. "The seam is wide open," he told Jones on the headset.

"How much you got left in the arm?" June asked Robinson, as he headed out with a little more than nine minutes to play in the third.

"Enough," Robinson answered through his gritted teeth.

"Let's run the 60 Z Go again . . . hit Channon for the touch."

With 9:30 gone in the third quarter, Robinson followed directions.

"Dan had already hit Channon down the seam for some huge plays," says

Morrison. "We ran it again, and they had two guys go after one. Dan caught their mistake this time, saw Channon break free, and he hit him in stride."

As he raced toward the end zone, Harris went airborne for the last 5 yards, bouncing off a diving Oregon State defender for the 30-yard touchdown as the stadium reacted with an ear-piercing roar.

On the other side of the ball, McMackin was giving his former boss a hair-pulling migraine. "Coach Mack's adjustments in the second half were unbelievable," says Ulbrich. "His adjustments were less with players and more with *play-calls.* It was like he was wearing Erickson's head set.

151

He was calling blitzes right into their runs, right into their quarterback for sacks. That game is a perfect example of how a single coach can turn a game around by himself, just by knowing the game and which plays to call. It was incredible."

OSU offensive lineman Aaron Koch remembers the confusion. "They were mixing up their schemes," he says, "and they were getting penetration with a variety of blitzes. We were expecting a lot of inside stuff, but they were coming from the outside, from everywhere. We couldn't figure it out."

Robinson thanked the defense by patiently milking the clock with a nine-play, 54-yard drive that ended with an Eric Hannum field goal and a 20-10 lead. "Avion [Weaver] was running his heart out," Robinson says. "Oregon State had said we couldn't control the clock or run the ball, and we did both on that drive."

In the fourth quarter, the defense held again, and now the frustration was beginning to mount on the OSU sidelines. Robinson obliged by keeping another long drive alive with a deep-in to Ashley Lelie on a critical third down. "You could see them begin to deflate on that pass," Robinson recalls. "That was a tough catch and a huge play."

Hannum kicked a 35-yard field goal with 4:31 to play, and Hawai'i led, 23-10.

In years gone by, Hawai'i might have folded under Oregon State's final assault. Despite being ferociously sacked six times on the day, OSU quarterback Jonathon Smith quickly marched his team downfield, and Ken Simonton, ever the workhorse, burst off tackle for a 13-yard touchdown with 1:27 to play.

The entire season now rested on OSU's ensuing onside kick.

Hawai'i recovered.

Robinson could do nothing but smile as he went under center for the final few snaps of his career. Covered in wart-sized goosebumps, with tears of joy welling in his deep hazel eyes, he took a knee and watched the final seconds of his football playing life drip off the clock. The Oregon State players could only stare, hands high on their hips, in disappointment and shock.

Hawai'i 23, Oregon State 17

June Jones had prepared Hawai'i's fields for rain; the heavens had burst wide open.

The field erupted, as did all of Honolulu. Fireworks exploded. Confetti again rained down. Households all over the island were turned upside down in raucous celebration. The Hawai'i people poured from their homes and taverns and into the streets.

Worst to first. O'ahu Bowl champs.

The biggest turnaround in the history of college football, bar none.

And the second-best offense in all of America.

The tree-trunk-size arms of Kaulana Noa, replete with tribal tattoos, held the O'ahu Bowl trophy high above his head in an image that is now seared in Hawai'i football history. The stadium was a sea of rocking emotion — in the stands, on the field, in the end zones, on the sidelines — as far as the eye could see.

Robinson raced toward June Jones. The player and coach embraced for several long seconds.

"Thank you for just believing in me," Robinson cried. *"You believed in me, you believed in us, when nobody in the world ever did. Thank you, thank you, thank you!"*

Jones gripped his quarterback's sweat-soaked head, held him close to his chest and squeezed.

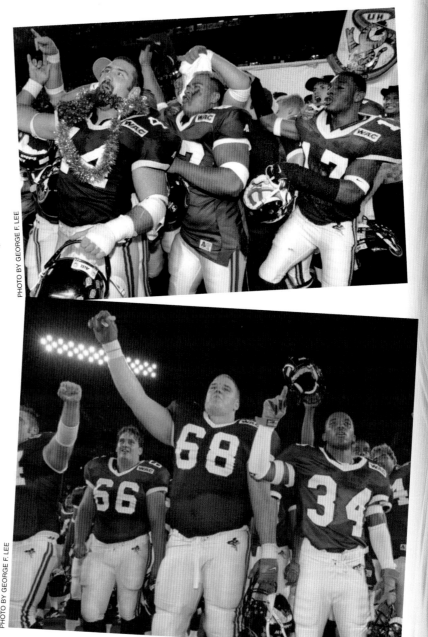

PHOTO BY GEORGE F. LEE

UNIVERSITY OF HAWAII ATHLETICS PHOTO BY RICHARD WOOD

"You're worth it, Dan," Jones whispered in his ear. *"All of you guys are worth it."*

Robinson went limp, sobbing in jubilation.

Goliath was dead. Only this was no movie.

Blessed are those who weep, for now, they shall laugh.

Blessed is the man who has suffered, for he has found life.

Broadcasters stumbled trying to say the words together in the same sentence:

Hawai'i . . . Champions. Hawai'i . . . Champions.

Are you kidding me?

PHOTO BY GEORGE F. LEE

Chapter 20
THE SHRINE OF '99

The early morning of December 26, 1999, was not unlike any other for the Robinsons, except for the incredible stench that permeated the residence. If attitude is the aroma of one's heart, then DMSO is the undeniable odor of determination.

Two-year-old Malia awoke first. Like her daddy, she began calling audibles from her crib, changing the play from sleep to *breakfast*. Dan Robinson rolled over and looked at the digital clock blinking on the wooden nightstand: *7:00 a.m.*

Jill stirred from the *opposite* side of the bed. She was curled up deep within the sheets, her head buried below the protection of the thick comforter. She had learned to sleep this way as a means of self-defense; this way, she didn't have to *breathe* her husband, who at the moment smelled like a cross between dirty diapers and a very burnt Indian curry dish.

Dan rubbed his eyes.

It wasn't a dream. The donkey had won the Derby.

We are champions, he thought. *We made history.* He grinned — giggled even — and poked playfully at Jill, who popped up from under the covers. She ran a hand through her dark, tousled hair, held her nose and, laughing, kissed her husband.

"We did it, Dan," she said. Jill, too, was exhausted. Classes had ended on December 19. She had raced to the airport to fly out for her sister's wed-

PHOTO BY GEORGE F. LEE
Dan Robinson waves goodbye to the appreciative fans of Hawai'i

ding, then flew home barely in time for the biggest game of Dan's life. She also was seven months pregnant with their second child, so there would be little time to celebrate.

Robinson swung his legs to the floor. His body ached, but not nearly as badly as he had feared. The DMSO was still coursing through his veins and, hours after the fact, apparently *still* doing its job. So well had the chemicals performed during the O'ahu Bowl that, unbeknownst to Dan, he had torn his groin muscle from his mid-thigh all the way to his belly button. He had never even felt it tear. That little surprise would come later in the week, when the DMSO would finally wear off.

"That's the difference between baseball and football," George Carlin once joked. *"Football is all about shotgun formations, bombs and blitzes and aerial assaults. In baseball, you just want to be safe and go home."*

There was nothing safe about the way Robinson felt as he stumbled to the bathroom sink to brush his teeth. Looking in the mirror, reality suddenly slapped him across his stubbled face.

It's over.

Like some twenty-plus other Hawai'i seniors, Dan Robinson would be saying goodbye to football — their mistress of so many years. For

O'ahu Bowl MVP Avion Weaver, and Head Coach June Jones

many years, Robinson had spent at least six hours every day on football, dating back to the first time he strapped on a helmet and the number 9 with the sixth-grade Highland Bears outside of American Fork, Utah. Now there were no more practices, training rituals and pregame meals. No more "voluntary" mandatory workouts.

The finality is exactly like the sudden breakup of any other long-term relationship: It hurts. Days, even weeks, flit past in a blur, as players — so regimented in their routines — don't know what to do with themselves or face the sudden influx of free time without full-time responsibility.

In the days following the O'ahu Bowl, the full impact of what these Hawai'i Warriors really accomplished slowly rippled throughout the islands, across the sea and around the rest of the sporting world. Few realized that the vision of June Jones far, far exceeded the accomplishments of the 1999 season.

"The best part of 1999," says June Jones, "was *seeing the faces* of the players, especially those seniors. They had suffered so much. It was so satisfying to see them prove to the world that they had what it takes to be conquerors."

No task is too big
When done together by all . . . (Hawaiian Proverb)

The braggadocio that typically accompanies any football championship was noticeably absent from the Warriors of 1999, and it remains so today. There is instead a reverent *ha'aha'a,* or humility, regarding what they achieved, evidenced by the accolades they earned.

June Jones, for his part, was named WAC Coach of the Year.

Dwight Carter, Jeff Ulbrich, Quincy LeJay, Dan Robinson, Adrian Klemm, Kaulana Noa, Matt Paul, Chad Shrout and Jamal Garland were recognized as either first- or second-team All-Conference. Big Red Phillips was an honorable mention.

Several Warriors would be fortunate enough to see their careers extend into professional football, early pioneers in what is now an annual pipeline of players that June Jones sends to the pro ranks.

Ulbrich, who led Hawai'i and the WAC with a jaw-dropping 169 tackles, would be drafted by the San Francisco 49ers. Klemm was picked by the New England Patriots. Noa, who had started 48 consecutive games, signed with the St. Louis Rams, while Dustin Owens would raid convenience stores for candy bars during a brief stint with the 49ers before becoming a Hitman, literally, for the New York/New Jersey franchise of the now-defunct XFL (who called themselves "Hitmen").

How good was the offensive line? Robinson had thrown the ball 566 times, yet he was sacked only 24 times, which is two times less than he'd been knocked to the ground *in a single game the year before* against Brian Urlacher and New Mexico.

Quincy LeJay, Shawndel Tucker and Dwight Carter would ply their wares via the indoor wars of Arena Football. "We were the start of a new beginning," says LeJay, who finished the season with seven interceptions and

briefly held the NCAA record for returning three for touchdowns. "Nobody did what we did, before or since. That's something special, and it's a moment I cherish."

Carter, who rewrote Hawai'i's receiving record book with 77 catches for 1,253 yards and nine touchdowns, would also play briefly for the San Francisco 49ers and NFL Europe.

Matt Elam spent a year in Canada with the Winnipeg Blue Bombers and several in Arena Football before becoming a specialist in Olympic weightlifting and a Hawai'i state record holder.

Afatia Thompson overcame the death of his brother and later became a Hawai'i Hip-Hop and R&B Artist of the Year, frequently offering heavenly thanks in the form of songs like *I Worship You, Almighty God.*

Daniel Ho-Ching fought cancer — and also beat death.

Big Red Phillips, sadly, did not.

Life comes and life goes
But what a man stood for
Lives forever. . . (Unknown)

The final days of Andy Phillips were happy ones for the strapping, jovial ex-lineman.

After failed NFL tryouts left him craving for a job that would satiate his competitive spirit, Phillips — nicknamed "Ulaulanui" by the Hawaiian people, or "Big Red" — had landed on the crew of NASCAR Busch Series rookie Spencer Clark.

Clark had finished in the top 10 of all three NASCAR West races that season, including capturing his first pole position in the season opener at Phoenix.

On May 21, 2006, the pair was returning together to Las Vegas from a

Imagine each player touching a life-size bronze statue of yesterday's heroes, replete with WAC trophy held high and the proud colors of the Hawaii flag fluttering in the background. What a testament, both then and now, that indeed, all things are possible.

156

"Big Red" Phillips celebrates the O'ahu Bowl victory

race in North Carolina. Phillips was driving the truck that towed Clark's AutoZone NASCAR Grand National West series car. Clark was a passenger.

Traveling westbound on winding I-40, just 40 miles east of Albuquerque, N.M., they inexplicably lost control of the vehicle. The truck and trailer rolled in a horrific accident. Thousands of pounds of burning, gnarled metal engulfed Phillips and Clark, snuffing out both of their young lives.

It was Big Red's 30th birthday. Clark was just 19 years old.

The tragic news devastated his wife Christine and stunned his former teammates.

"He was definitely instrumental to our success," Jones says. "Big Red was one of five guys who lined up every single game in 1999. He competed as hard as anybody. He helped bring pride back to this football team."

"I can close my eyes," says Dan Robinson, "and still see his face."

Opponents probably only remember the number 68, which typically was

the last thing they saw before the lights went out, like a big boulder tumbling down a hill.

> *O CAPTAIN! my captain! our fearful trip is done!*
> *The ship has weather'd every rack, the prize we sought is won . . .*
> (Walt Whitman)

Winning was exactly what Jones needed to continue his sweeping reforms of the program; it ensured that the legacy of 1999 would affect generations of Hawai'i football to come. Had June finished 0-12, his articulate vision and efforts would have gone the way of the Laysan Rail, a tiny Hawaiian seabird that became extinct in 1944 after rats from U.S. Navy vessels ate their way through its fragile habitat.

Jones was facing quite a few rats of his own. In months to come, he would take on every sacred cow and exorcise every demon that stood in his path. Exacting permanent and lasting change in a perennially losing program would require not a facelift, not an overhaul, but an outright extraction of *any* reminder of the past.

For some set-in-their-way islanders, the idea of such change didn't sit well. For these outspoken few, *thinking outside the box* was about as easy as changing the physical shape of their heads. They were methodical; Jones was mercurial. June was hoping that if they couldn't think outside the box, hopefully they could at least see the advantage of *growing the box they were in.*

But strong leaders take an organization in the right direction, even when it's not the popular choice to do so. Former NFL commissioner Pete Rozelle once said that "choosing a head coach is like choosing a wife." The reason, he explained, "is because it's a very personal relationship. The personalities all have to fit just right. The fans and the organization and the players are all in the same bed together. A true head coach must be strong enough to lead them all."

How apropos that Hawai'i had selected June Jones, who was about to fight for his marriage. With all eyes on the new WAC champions, the powers that be had no choice *but* to listen. Thanks to the tenacious efforts of his staff and his players, Jones was now the tail wagging the dog. Thus in the months immediately following the O'ahu Bowl, June did not rest on his laurels or bask in the glow of his team's success: He went right back to work on his checklist of change, which had been on hold during the 1999 season.

He wouldn't hesitate to enlist much-needed firepower from former friends and colleagues to aid in his efforts. Among the first was superagent Leigh Steinberg in Orange County, Calif.

Jones booked a mainland appointment.

Hawai'i football, in his mind, was no longer just a team or an opponent or a fun place to play. Hawai'i football was *an experience of a lifetime.*

Experience of a lifetime? Hawai'i?

Are you kidding me?

> The stone which the builders rejected has become the chief cornerstone. This is the Lord's doing; it is marvelous in our eyes.
>
> (Psalm 118:22–23)

A *cornerstone,* or capstone, isn't simply a decorative stone used to finish off the corners of a building with a bit of architectural flair. It is, in fact, the *fundamental stone;* if you remove it, you risk the implosion of the entire piece of work. Yet it was often rejected by inexperienced builders because it wasn't the same size or shape or consistency of the other stones.

If you inspect an old Roman archway, you'll see why. The two columns are built with perfectly carved stones. At the top, however, in the center, you will discover a triangular stone that sits perfectly in the middle and balances the two sides that arch together against one another.

That is a capstone, which June likened to his 1999 Warriors.

"That team changed the course of Hawai'i football history," says Jones. "There will never be another team like it. Today, we are *expected* to win.

Then, no one gave us a chance. That team will be remembered as the cornerstone of the tradition we enjoy today."

Forevermore, the 1999 team — the very stone rejected by the football fraternity — had become a standard of sacrifice, a tale of triumph, a harbinger of hope . . . for every future Warrior who would walk Hawai'i's hallowed halls.

Notre Dame has the Golden Dome. USC has Tommy the Trojan. Clemson has Death Valley and the Rock.

Hawai'i needs the Shrine of '99.

▼▼▼▼▼▼▼▼▼▼▼▼▼

"The best part of 1999," says June Jones, "was seeing the faces of the players, especially those seniors. They had suffered so much. It was so satisfying to see them prove to the world that they had what it takes to be conquerors."

▲▲▲▲▲▲▲▲▲▲▲▲▲

Just outside Aloha Stadium, artisans should erect an Iwo Jima–style memorial in honor of the 1999 Warriors, who ensured that Hawai'i would never be forgotten in the history of NCAA football. What Hawai'i accomplished hadn't been done in 50 years, and arguably it will never be done again. It very well could be an achievement that stands forever.

Can you imagine the mighty roar of fans if players, when filing into the stadium prior to each Saturday's contest, were given the opportunity to walk past such a monument? Imagine each player touching a life-size bronze statue of yesterday's heroes, replete with WAC trophy held high and the proud colors of the Hawai'i flag fluttering in the background.

What a testament — both then and now — that indeed, all things are possible! Such an entrance would rival the Tiger Walk at LSU or the Ramblin' Wreck at Georgia Tech.

Coaches and players alike agree that it is a tribute long overdue.

"It's been many years now," says Jeff Ulbrich, "and yet, even today, when times are tough, I still fall back on that experience. It's given me a life-long direction. As bad as things might ever get, I know there's always

PHOTO BY KIMBERLY CARROLL

Aloha Stadium

The relief he'd enjoyed from the DMSO was over, and so was his career. Yet he harbors no regrets.

"The whole season was a miracle for Jill and I," Dan says. "A guy in our church had given us a blessing. He told us that I would come to Hawai'i and become a champion. I was thrilled to see my blessing come true. We felt truly blessed by our Heavenly Father that all of our prayers had been answered."

Dan and Jill would eventually parent five children and, ironically, he would become a dentist, an *expert* in pain management. Still today, when roping horses on his ranch, if Dan Robinson plants his feet just so, pain shoots a not-so-gentle reminder through his groin of the price he paid for gridiron glory.

While some might cringe, he just smiles, for it triggers a memory of something that June Jones promised him nearly a decade ago.

"Memories will fade away, and touchdowns will be forgotten, but the faces in this room, and the sacrifices we've made, will live forever."

hope. Every man who played on that football team knows that, inside them, they have the ability to step back and turn the situation around like we did in 1999."

"Who knows where I'd be today without June Jones and his staff?" Ulbrich says quietly. "I know one thing for sure: I wouldn't be in the NFL. That season changed my whole life. I'm a better husband. I'm a better dad. I deal with people and pressure better. I'm a better person. It's just an amazing story, when you really think about it."

"It should never be forgotten."

Hanauma Bay is one of Hawai'i's most popular snorkeling spots — the real O'ahu "bowl" — where one finds scintillating colors of coral and splendid bouquets of exotic fish. It was there, a week after his final game, that Dan Robinson first felt the pain shoot like lightning through his groin. Snorkeling offshore with his family, he suddenly realized he couldn't move his left leg. The ordeal that followed was harrowing, to say the least.

Robinson and his teammates had taught Hawai'i a thing or two as well:

It's not the horse.

It's the *heart.*

Are you kidding me?

Chapter 21
ON A ROLL

Kamehameha Highway north, on the windward side of the island of Oʻahu, is a brilliantly scenic drive. To your right, pounding surf exhales along the coast as far as the eye can see. To your left are lush lowlands and captivating mountains that reach up into the low-lying clouds.

Winding up the coast, toward Oʻahu's North Shore, you pass Chinaman's Hat, a cone-shaped outcropping of lava off Kualoa Point, which resembles the peasant's chapeau worn by rural Chinese.

Then there's Kualoa Ranch, a 4,000-acre working ranch located in the breathtaking valley of Kaʻaʻawa. The ranch is popular for horseback riding and hiking and has been family owned since 1850. It is also a favorite location for Hollywood filmmakers; one quickly recognizes the stunning backdrops of *Jurassic Park, Godzilla, Pearl Harbor* and *Lost.*

Continue another half-hour north, and you arrive at Hawaiʻi's top attraction — the Polynesian Cultural Center, or PCC — where visitors enjoy seven different villages and participate in the daily adventures of Hawaiian and other South Pacific cultures.

You can study the beauty of the Samoan culture and even make fire or crack open coconuts. You can learn the *tititorea*, the Maori stick game, receive a Marquesan tattoo, toss a Tongan spear or play Fijian bamboo —

Chinaman's Hat … the distinctive cone-shaped outcropping of lava off Kualoa Point

derua — instruments. Finally, you can witness the mesmerizing fireknife dance — *'ailao afi* — a Samoan warrior tradition where participants spin multiple flaming knives in a ritual ceremony.

Fire-knife Dancing is among the biggest draws of the Polynesian Cultural Center

For most visitors, these are the memories of a lifetime — but not Nick Rolovich. All he remembers is a long discussion about football — and the smell. He'll never forget *that* smell.

Marshall, Cal and Minnesota were in hot pursuit of Rolovich, a gritty quarterback who had been a two-time All-American at City (Junior) College of San Francisco.

It was December 1999.

During his visit to Marshall, he was escorted into the stadium. Upon his entrance, the powerful lights suddenly flickered on and — *poof!* — there he was, larger than life, on the JumboTron. At Minnesota, he toured the locker room, where — *poof!* — his jersey, with his name stitched on the back, was already hanging in a locker with his name over it.

Rolovich, however, was intrigued by a chance meeting he'd had with a

guy named Greg McMackin, who had strolled into the athletic department at City College to visit — not him, but the coaching staff. It was then that Nick learned about the amazing turnaround of the Hawai'i football program, behind an NFL coach named June Jones and a powerful offense called the Run 'n' Shoot.

McMackin put the aptly nicknamed Rolo in touch with Dan Morrison, the quarterback coach.

"After my first conversation with Coach Morrison," Rolovich says, "I put the phone down and asked myself, 'Is this guy *for real? Is he just putting on a show for me?*' I'd never talked to a nicer guy in my life."

It's fair to say that Rolovich is suspicious by nature, which goes with the territory when your dad is a fireman and your aunt is the fire *chief.* Everybody he knew in his hometown of Daly City, Calif., and San Francisco was either a cop or a firefighter; Rolovich had learned to ask lots of questions and generally not to believe the first thing you hear.

But it doesn't take a firefighter to know that where there's smoke, *there might be fire,* so he decided to visit Hawai'i and see firsthand what the hubbub was all about. This idea didn't sit well with the coaches at Minnesota.

AP PHOTO

Hilarious quarterback Nick Rolovich would become known as much for his pranks as his passing

"If you visit Hawai'i," they told him, "then our scholarship's off the table. Take it or leave it."

Rolovich needed little time to think. He would have to leave that Jersey at Minnesota. Intrigued by the mystery of Hawai'i, he packed his bags for O'ahu. The Hawai'i coaches, with little to sell but themselves and the islands, had convinced a top quarterback prospect to visit with little more than a phone call.

"If a kid is smart," June says with a grin, inserting more than a dab of reverse psychology, "then he should want at least one of his five [legal] school visits to be Hawai'i, just for the sake of seeing Hawai'i. And if he's not smart, well, we couldn't use him anyway."

Granted, Hawai'i had an academic curriculum that mainland schools simply couldn't duplicate. Unique course listings include *volcanology* and *tropical agriculture.* Marine biology classes are held at the Hawai'i Undersea Research Laboratory on Moku o Lo'e (Coconut Island), modern molecular biology laboratories with immediate access to Kāne'ohe Bay and deep ocean waters.

Let's face it — Michigan or Ohio State certainly can't claim protected harbors, a pelagic fish laboratory, or a 64-acre coral reef . . . not to mention a 25-cent trolley ride to Waikīkī's legendary 6-foot surf.

Rolovich readily admits he was looking forward to seeing some coconuts, but biology labs and pelagic fish were the last thing on his mind.

I can't wait to bask on the beach and meet some Hawaiian hotties, he thought.

Rolo considered himself to be pretty smart, indeed.

He tossed some sunscreen in his bag, just in case.

▼▼▼▼▼▼▼▼▼▼▼▼▼▼▼

"The respect June received without ever raising his voice -- man, leaders yearn for that kind of ability. I was like, wow, here's a coach who doesn't just talk to hear himself talk. The rest of the team was having a blast. Nobody was putting on a show for me; in fact, most guys didn't even know who I was or that I was even there. I was amazed at how real everybody was."

▲▲▲▲▲▲▲▲▲▲▲▲▲▲▲

The rain fell in buckets; Nick Rolovich had never seen clouds this close to the ground. Hawai'i was breathtaking all right — rain was falling in golf ball–size drops, and it was difficult to breathe without drinking. There was nary a hottie in sight, unless you count 300-pound Kynan Forney in a wet t-shirt.

It was Rolovich's official visit to Hawai'i, and the Warriors were practicing on Cooke Field in preparation for the O'ahu Bowl. A trainer came over and handed Rolovich an old rain jacket. "You might want to put this on," he said. "It can come down pretty good here."

From the day he arrived on campus, Rolovich noticed straightaway that it was business as usual. He had only seen June Jones in the hallways of the football office; he had paused briefly to say hello, but nothing formal; no big deal. Everyone just went about their business: no stadium lights, no pressed jersey hanging in the locker room. Now here he was, watching practice, wearing an old rain jacket on a muddy field in the middle of an island deluge. But there was something *magic* occurring on the field that Rolovich just couldn't put his finger on.

The key moment in any relationship is the *first* moment, and Rolovich embraced the warmth and sincerity of the Hawai'i coaches over the phoniness he'd experienced everywhere else.

"The facilities were the worst I'd ever seen," he recalls. "But all the guys were having fun, laughing, and on the same page. Everybody knew what to do, how to do it and when to do it. Watching June communicate was pretty incredible.

"The respect June received without ever raising his voice — man, leaders *yearn* for that kind of ability. I was like, wow, here's a coach who doesn't just talk to hear himself talk. The rest of the team was having a blast. Nobody was putting on a show for me; in fact, most guys didn't even know who I was or that I was even there. I was amazed at how *real* everybody was."

'Rolo' consults with teammates on the sidelines

Coach Morrison, however, most *certainly* knew who he was. From day one, he was in Rolovich's head, slowly unraveling the mysteries of the Run 'n' Shoot. "We need to watch some film . . . and then I want you to talk to our quarterback," Morrison said. "But I'll warn you ahead of time . . . *he stinks*."

That's why they're recruiting me, Rolovich smirked.

"Don't get me wrong," Morrison added, laughing. "Dan's a *great* quarterback. I mean, he *literally stinks*."

Sitting next to Dan Robinson on the bus for the trip north up the coast to the PCC, Rolovich kept waiting for the laughter. He crinkled his nose, tried to keep a straight face, thinking that one or all of the players around him were in on the practical joke.

Only nobody laughed. *Man, he really* does *stink*, Rolovich thought. That's when Robinson began to explain the Run 'n' Shoot, June Jones, and the magical season of '99, right down to the acrid DMSO.

Rolovich was spellbound, oblivious to the passing panoramic blur of palm trees, ocean and mountains outside. "I was touched by how much passion Dan had for the offense," Rolovich says. "He had done great things, and he knew it, but he was totally humble. There was sadness in his voice. He had just begun to realize the potential of what he had been a part of, and you could tell he was wishing he had another year."

The next night, Nick Rolovich called his dad from his hotel room. The rain had long since passed, and the sun was setting over Waikīkī outside his balcony window.

"Dad," he said, "I'm going to play quarterback for the University of Hawai'i."

When Rolovich arrived on campus in January of 2000, it took little time for the coaching staff to realize they had the polar opposite of the stay-at-home Mormon Dan Robinson on their hands; progidal son was more like it. Wine is a mocker, beer is a brawler and whoever is led astray by them is not wise, as Rolovich would soon learn.

"I'm not proud of this," Rolovich says, "but I have to tell the truth. I'm the reason why June had a losing season that year. My priorities were so out of whack. I had never been away from home. For that whole first spring semester, I partied hard, I enjoyed myself. I didn't work hard in the weight room or the film room.

"Coach Morrison kept warning me about the fall," he continues. "He kept saying, 'You're not seeing it right now, but once we start playing games, you won't believe how much football means to this state.'"

"I was too busy having parties to care. I got kicked out of my dorm for having keg parties. We got caught . . . when you choose to party, there's a lot more trouble that comes with it. I enabled other guys to make bad choices by getting players together in situations where I wasn't responsible, they were less responsible and crazy things resulted."

"It wasn't pretty. I was living with six other players and got kicked out. That just enabled me to have more freedom to do what I had been doing. At my new place, I had a big backyard. Sure, we had fun, but I wasn't focused, and I paid the price."

AP PHOTO

Nick Rolovich could get a laugh out of anybody – even June Jones

More correctly, the *team* would pay the price.

Leaders must work harder than the people they're trying to motivate, a fact not lost on June Jones. The free-spirited Nick Rolovich and the rest of the incoming recruiting class would be just one of the countless issues he'd face in 2000. Like a patient father, June lined them all up and dealt with them one at a time, in order of priority.

Fathers see everything through a wide-angle lens. The present is usually a direct result of whatever you've done in the past; the future will improve only if you're willing to do something about it today.

Thus, that spring, the new recruits were the least of June's worries. The staff had done their God's-honest best, all things considered; lest you forget, there was the small issue of winning football games. Granted, it takes a confident quarterback such as Nick Rolovich to freely admit his own mistakes and do it publicly — which later would set an example for others to take responsibility. But June knew that many other things had

to be addressed before they could consistently recruit the level of talent it would take to compete in America's Top 20.

The 1999 season had been wonderful, yes — record setting, historical, all that *stuff* — but Jones had his mind set on far greater things. In his mind, he had done little more than merely stop the hemorrhaging. His aspirations — a *tradition of winning* — were much, much higher, and to achieve them he had to get rid of anything and everything that had contributed to Hawai'i's recent history of losing. This meant rooting out the cancer at *every single source,* in every crack, every crevice and every corner.

If you fashion yourself as a leader, here's where it gets fun. This is the part where popularity ceases and practicality, responsibility and accountability kick in.

If we're tired of being treated second-class, June thought, *we must stop acting second-class.* For every issue he checked off his list, he seemed to add one more. But now that he had an entire spring with which to operate, he moved these up to *urgent*.

☑ For starters, he was putting his foot down on the name. They were now *Warriors*. Period. There would be no more tap-dancing around the issue of Rainbows, or even Rainbow Warriors; not in the media, not in the hallways, not in a press release. His football team would live and die as Warriors, and that was that.

☑ Second, the uniforms looked like they had come out of a Hutch box from the sporting goods department at K-mart. Every *little* boy dreams of wearing one of those at Christmas time, but *big boys* most certainly do not. The Warriors June envisioned would be fierce to behold; they would represent the strength and dignity of an entire island nation.

Ask any Marine, and he'll tell you bravery and honor begin with the uniform. June needed a logo, a brand that distinguished Hawai'i above all others; uniforms that would command respect from opponents and make his players swell with pride.

☑ Third, every college football team June respected also had a *tradition of music*. The best Hawai'i could offer was the playing of "Hawaii 5-0," the theme song from the long-since-cancelled television series that was so ancient, his players hadn't been *born* when it aired.

The worst thing you can do to a football team, June thought, *is dress them like rainbows and call up the 5-0. Can you imagine USC playing the theme from Spartacus every touchdown? Navy playing the theme to JAG? Or, better yet, Oregon State playing the theme from Leave it to Beaver?*

☑ Fourth, there was the enormous issue of racial diversity — not the lack of it but the *need for more and more and more of it*. Upon June's arrival, only 24 kids of Hawaiian, Polynesian or Samoan descent were represented on the roster.

This would have to change. June knew that Polynesian kids, from birth, were taught that *hana,* or hard work, was respected; laziness was shameful. Elders passed down the old saying of

"*e ho'ohuli ka lima i lalo,*" meaning the palms of the hands should be turned down. Upturned palms were considered idle; most tasks were done with grasping fingers and downward palms — *such as ripping a tightly thrown football out of midair in full stride or beating down an offensive lineman in pursuit of a hostile quarterback.*

This paradigm shift instantly turned a half-empty glass to half full: Within five years, June's rosters would be 75-percent homegrown, and soon he would be sending Polynesian players to the NFL at an alarming rate.

☑ Fifth, June had no issues pursuing good kids in bad situations. Broken home? No problem. That just meant fewer strings attached back home, which made the island a more attractive option. Scofflaws? Those with repentant hearts would be offered a second chance via redemption and forgiveness through the currency of honesty and hard work.

☑ Sixth, the AstroTurf in Aloha Stadium had to go. Former Hawai'i Governor John Burns had built the stadium *specifically* for the University. Jones was *shocked* to learn that the school was paying the state of Hawai'i $1 million *a year* to play in its own stadium.

The state was also gorging itself on the concessions, parking and in-stadium merchandising. Abraham Lincoln once chastised his congressmen for damaging morale and undermining authority, saying they should "be arrested, exiled or hanged." When June discovered this little government hula, he and Abe were sharing similar thoughts.

Such drastic problems require innovative minds that don't flinch when drastic measures are required to solve them.

If ever God created such a mind, it can be found in Newport Beach, Calif., behind the desk and in the cerebral cortex of one Leigh Steinberg. The superman of sports agents and sports marketing, Steinberg had a long track record of leaping tall problems in a single quantum bound.

Chapter 22
HAWAI'I GOES HOLLYWOOD: MEET JERRY MAGUIRE AND FORREST GUMP

"Show me the money!"

If you've ever heard or used that phrase, you may thank Leigh Steinberg, the famed agent whose real-life clients and career became a silver-screen script for the 1996 larger-than-life blockbuster film, *Jerry Maguire,* by famed writer/director Cameron Crowe.

Art *doesn't* imitate life, because Steinberg puts the fictional *Maguire* to shame. Widely regarded as the most prolific sports management executive in history, Steinberg has negotiated more than $2 *billion* in deals for his clients and pioneered the convergence of the sports and entertainment industries.

Thus it's not surprising that Leigh also developed original television and film content for Fox, Warner Brothers Studios, ABC Entertainment and

HBO. He also capitalized on the burgeoning Internet industry by strategically aligning his firm with ESPN's Sports Zone. He consulted on Kevin Costner's *For the Love of the Game,* the HBO original series *Arli$$* and Oliver Stone's *Any Given Sunday.*

Still, most people hate agents, generally because it's perceived that they simply get rich helping rich athletes get richer. This just doesn't sit well with the guy paying $40 to park to see a Bengals' game with his 6-year-old son in minus-20 degrees in Cincinnati — *after* paying $400 for his tickets.

"I guess if the movies can make a hero out of Larry Flynt," surmised Bengals' owner and GM Mike Brown of *Maguire,* "they can make a hero out of an agent."

Everyone, however, has a place in this world. When you're in excruciating pain, you don't ask your proctologist how much he's getting paid to get his hands dirty.

Which is why, when Hawai'i football's multitude of marketing problems swelled to painful proportions in the posterior of June Jones, it's no surprise where he went to find immediate relief: Leigh Steinberg.

Sun-splashed Newport Beach, Calif., isn't *anything* like your hometown.

Take the 55 freeway west until it runs out onto Pacific Coast Highway; hang a left, drive slowly, and you'll instantly understand. The sun sits on the harbor like a fat peach, just adjacent to the Pacific. There's Balboa Island and Lido Isle, where a million dollars won't even start a conversation, much less buy you a house.

The only two gas stations in this several-mile stretch of excess are full of

Cuba Gooding Jr., Leigh Steinberg and Tom Cruise during the making of Jerry Maguire

multicolored Escalades and Hummers, most with single drivers, filling up.

Everywhere you look there are perfect-bodied people with perfect tans and perfect hair; talking, walking, jogging, trotting, but *never* sweating. All within walking distance of a block or two, you can get a scintillating sausage-and-egg skillet and a $5 strawberry shake at Ruby's Diner; buy a $20 million *used* yacht; drop 100 g's on one of the new Ferrari's at the local dealership; or learn to tack at the elite Orange Coast College Sailing School.

The sign outside the local church on Balboa Island says, *"If God brought you this far, your life can't be that bad."* So *this* is where 400-pound gorillas choose to sit when, as the saying goes, they can sit *anywhere they want.*

Then, just as you see Dennis Rodman — *yes, Dennis Rodman!* — jogging down the street in fully pierced regalia, you realize that this is the last place on God's green earth you'd envision as a creative think-tank for modern Hawai'i football.

Are you kidding me?

Steinberg used to be a founding partner of Steinberg & Moorad, a law firm that represented more than 150 clients, including the likes of Troy Aikman, Steve Young, Drew Bledsoe, Warren Moon, and practically every major professional athlete in the world. In 1999 he sold his firm to Assante Corp., a multibillion-dollar wealth management firm with clients such as Tom Cruise (the *other* Jerry Maguire) and David Letterman. Steinberg has since bought his practice back and, as Leigh Steinberg Sports and Entertainment, the firm is undertaking a massive fundraising effort.

On a typical day, Leigh doesn't sit in a palatial mansion or soak in a ridiculously oversized bathtub smoking cigars – an erroneous perception. "I've never smoked a cigar in my life," Leigh says, "and I don't own

a hot-tub." Usually, he can be found here, in his Newport Beach office, negotiating deals with more zeroes than you have on your office calculator. The creativity he writes into each deal makes his heart sing, like a baker whose life's pleasure is the wafting smell of each morning's bread.

Steinberg orchestrates contracts the way a world-class violinist zips through the Luciano Berio sequenza. Overhauling a losing college football program, however, just isn't something Steinberg enjoys. It's too political, too time consuming and frankly — to be honest — *there's just not enough money in it.*

▼▼▼▼▼▼▼▼▼▼▼▼▼

Don't let Steinberg fool you. The rich and the poor have one thing in common – the Lord is the maker of us all. At the very root of Leigh Steinberg is one, single thing – one thing that true Hawaiians appreciate above all else, and even what football fans in the coldest outposts of Buffalo, can, too. Loyalty.

▲▲▲▲▲▲▲▲▲▲▲▲▲

But underneath all Steinberg's pomp and circumstance, just when you might think that he personifies all that you hate about professional sports — fame and fortune, luxury and leisure, trappings that the average American and native Hawaiian will *never* enjoy — well, wait just a minute.

Don't let Steinberg fool you. The rich and the poor have one thing in common: The Lord is the maker of us all. At the very root of Leigh Steinberg is one single thing — one thing that true Hawaiians appreciate above all else, and even what football fans in the coldest outposts of Buffalo can appreciate, too: *loyalty.*

And this single thread illustrates that the *humility* of June Jones means more than every dollar Leigh Steinberg ever earned.

Atlanta was football crazy in 1975. Discos were *Jive Talkin',* the economy was *Staying Alive* and quarterback Steve Bartkowski was the first player taken overall in the NFL draft. A young Leigh Steinberg – who had graduated from law school prior to representing Bart – negotiated the largest rookie contract in league history up to that time.

"I had been Steve's dorm counselor at Berkeley," says Steinberg. "I had graduated from law school and was choosing between legal jobs when, *brimming* with legal experience, I represented Steve in the draft — and thus began my career."

Overnight, the blue-eyed Bartkowski became "Peachtree Bart," named after downtown Atlanta's most popular thoroughfare. When their plane landed at Hartsfield International Airport in Atlanta, Steinberg was told that the *Johnny Carson Show* had been interrupted to announce their arrival. "Steve and I looked at each other the way Dorothy must have looked at Toto in the *Wizard of Oz*," Steinberg says. "I couldn't believe the fervor of Atlanta's football fans. That's when I *knew* this is what I wanted to do."

Steinberg started an agency, determined to model it around family, respect and relationship development. All of his clients would be *required* to give huge sums of their income to the schools — high school and college — from which they came, including other charities and foundations within their new professional community.

"We believe that one person can make a difference in the world and that *relationships* are the key," says Steinberg. "One single relationship, when nurtured, can make a difference."

Relationships, indeed; little did Steinberg know that he was foretelling the future of Hawai'i football.

In 1977, an unheralded free agent named June Jones wound up as Bartkowski's roommate. When Jones and Steinberg met, there was instant chemistry.

"June is my type of guy," says Steinberg. "He is a Leonardo-type man of all seasons. He reads books and newspapers. He had theories on economics and religion, sports and theology. He followed the stock market. He put *me* into investments, like the plastic eggs that hold prizes in vending machines, and we made a killing. He had a probing, intellectual mind. It could be opal mines in Brazil, plastic eggs, DMSO, which smelled godawful . . . he is just a completely intriguing character."

Follow carefully — and at least *pretend* you haven't read it before.

"Through June, I met Mouse, and through Mouse I met Neil Lomax," Steinberg says. Lomax, it should be noted, followed June at Portland State, where, under Davis, he too would become the next — *shocker* — most decorated quarterback in NCAA history and — *shocker* — another

Steinberg client. He would be drafted by the St. Louis Cardinals, where he too became an All-Pro.

"June introduced Bart to Artie Wilson over in Hawai'i," Leigh continues. "Bart bought a house, and I would go stay with Bart in Hawai'i. That's how this whole connection was born. Everything that's happening with Hawai'i today, June was really at the epicenter some 30 years ago."

Then Leigh began to see not-so-subtle changes in the flamboyant Bartkowski.

"June and Bart became close friends," he says. "June was very strong in his faith, and he had a powerful impact on Steve. Then Steve became strong in *his* faith, and he completely changed."

June Jones as the best man at Steve Bartkowski's wedding

"June was always at real variance with newspaper clippings or success, as defined by statistics or money," Leigh says. "June was about spiritual beliefs, friendship and above all else, *loyalty.*"

"My father taught me to value relationships," Steinberg says. "You only have a certain amount of close relationships in the world. For me, June is one of those."

Their loyalty was unwavering, through June's NFL hardships and Leigh's business breakups, in both good times and bad. If ever they were asked about friendship, they told the media that *loyalty* is something in your *heart;* something you *do,* not something you *say.*

So when June turned to Leigh to help him with Hawai'i football, he wasn't knocking on the door of a superagent, he was merely seeking wisdom and counsel from a long-trusted *friend.*

With pencils poised and legal pads at the ready, June and Leigh went to work.

Every marketing recipe requires similar key ingredients: *people, product and process.* If Hawai'i football was going to be mainstream on the mainland within five years, it would need to simmer with all three.

To change Hawai'i's athletic culture, he and June would begin with its *people.* The entire state would become a selling point and the island's culture would be its battle cry.

"Hawai'i is a special place," Steinberg says. "The scent of the flowers, the spirituality, the magic and the warmth you can instantly feel. These *people* are some of the most loving on the face of the earth. There are no strangers. It's unlike anywhere else. The ocean, the birds, the land — the *inner peace* — this football team had to stand for all of those things."

Next up was *product,* where the image had to change.

"We had to reenvision what the *product* could be," Steinberg continues. "Any time you bring about change to the product, there's always some resistance. But we were less concerned with stepping on toes and more concerned with what the football program and athletic program could be from a marketing standpoint.

"How could we reenergize the revenue sources? How could the Athletic Department become competitive with mainland programs in the 21st century? How could it pull major corporate sponsors?"

Finally, they decided on the *process.*

"A sporting experience has a process," Leigh explains. "Watching a game live — how could we attract more fans in the stands? How could we improve the game experience? The process of watching it on TV — how can we make that a better experience for the television viewer or for the potential recruit? How can we take advantage of the positioning in the Pacific Rim? How can we bring in athletes from Japan and China to broaden our demographics? Can we have later start times that would enable us to have a mainland TV package?"

▼▼▼▼▼▼▼▼▼▼▼▼▼▼▼

"Forrest Gump was far from stupid," Bartkowski surmises. "In fact, if you watch the movie, he's way, way ahead of all of us. I've observed June for a long, long time. He's never worn a watch, but he's never late for a meeting. He doesn't own a pair of socks, but you can't fill his shoes."

▲▲▲▲▲▲▲▲▲▲▲▲▲▲▲

June and Leigh sketched out a plan.

No longer would Hawaiian, Samoan and Polynesian players be the exception — they would become the rule. You play Hawai'i, *you play Hawai'i.*

They pitched ESPN on a late-night TV package. ESPN loved the idea.

June started lobbing political footballs to reduce or eliminate his million-dollar overhead at Aloha Stadium. Due to bureaucracy, that one would take some time.

To develop a new brand, they enlisted the help of Athletic Director Hugh Yoshida, who in turn hired Kaua'i native and Kapa'a High School graduate Kurt Osaki. An award-winning designer with offices in Oakland and Honolulu, Osaki's signature works included new logos and uniforms for the San Francisco 49ers, Miami Dolphins, Tampa Bay Buccaneers and Baltimore Ravens.

"When I asked June what his goals were for the program and the brand, he said, 'To win a national championship at the University of Hawai'i,'" Osaki says. "I'll never forget it."

Other designs that were considered before the selection committee overwhelmingly chose the popular "H" that distinguishes modern Hawaii football

Everyone agreed the new brand should *pupukahi i holomua* — or unite and move forward. Over an eight-month period, Osaki's firm interviewed more than 200 people who represented a cross-section of the University and the local community. First, they arrived at the "tapa," where the three triangles represent "body, mind and spirit," as well as teamwork. In Hawaiian culture, *three* symbolizes teamwork; if one stumbles, two remain to support a fallen comrade in the true spirit of *"ohana."*

Second, they settled on the "H," which immediately embraced the entire state — outer islands included — as well as the program. Like the Tennessee "T" or the Michigan "M," the "H" would be the traditional Hawai'i monogram.

Third, they selected green as a color of growth and hope, in the same shade as the lush green valley of Mānoa. Silver was taken from the shimmering reflections of the daily rainfall. Black was added for accent and contrast, and the package was complete.

Next on the agenda was *music*. June had met five-time Grammy and Emmy award-winning composer Mike Post on the golf course, and he didn't hesitate to call his friend. Post had owned property in Hawai'i for nearly three decades, and he leapt at the opportunity to do something for the University. He produced theme songs for starting lineups, kickoffs, and goal-line stands. The unmistakable beating of drums and warrior chants would now resonate through Aloha Stadium like thunder in support of the new Warriors.

Post donated his award-winning compositions (all of which can be heard on **www.warriorsrespond.com**) to the University *at no charge.*

Yoshida, meanwhile, did a masterful job of navigating the new logo, the new colors and the new look through a labyrinth of committee meetings before all was finally unveiled during a Board of Regents ceremony at the Stan Sheriff Arena.

Jones received unanimous approval, which prompted a spike in merchandise sales that continues to this day. June would later add silver helmets for the road, *further* extending the Hawai'i brand. "Recruits *get off the plane* wearing our stuff when they visit us," Jones says. "Overnight, we became one of the hottest properties in college sports." Other universities called Osaki to request that he help them with something "as powerful and recognizable" as what he had done for Hawai'i.

"It's my proudest accomplishment," Osaki says.

Ironically, for all of the efforts of Yoshida, Jones, Steinberg, Post and a myriad of other minds, the university's powers that be would route all of the UH merchandise and logo revenue to its Auxiliary Service Department. Little would go to fund the countless shortcomings within the Athletic Department.

Not everyone instantly agreed. Purists blasted Jones for discarding the once-beloved Rainbow. Local news anchor Joe Moore, livid after June scrapped "Hawaii 5-0," would chastise Jones early and often *on the air,* which temporarily created an outcry not seen since 1939, when MGM Studios tried to take "Over the Rainbow" out of the *Wizard of Oz.*

The definition of a pioneer, however, is a man with arrows in his back; Jones ignored his detractors and simply forged ahead. "If you're going to make a loser into a winner," Bill Parcells once said, "then you can't worry about the labor pains — when you show them the baby, everybody eventually stops bitching."

Admiring his team's newborn image, Jones was one pretty proud papa.

Steinberg merely smiles when he reflects on his client's accomplishments.

"When he took the job, people simply *overlooked* the considerable resources June has," he says. "If we trace all the way back through this story, you have all of the people that June has worked with, like me, or coached, like Warren Moon, as part of the Hawai'i package. They not only got a great coach, but they got the biggest names and marketing people in sports. We beat the drums. We changed the logo. We reshaped the literature. We rebranded the program.

"Who in their right mind would turn down the golden ring of the NFL, return to his love and passion and make the statement he's made in every facet of this program? The answer is *a man who can.* That statement alone says it all. He cannot walk down the street in Hawai'i without being recognized or engaged in uplifting conversation. The fans adore him. He epitomizes the pride of Hawai'i. He took risks. He took criticism. But don't forget — he made the *right* decisions, not necessarily the popular ones at those times."

Film critic Frederic Brussat once wrote that
"there is a long and fascinating tradition of the 'holy fool' in spiritual literature."

COURTESY KURT OSAKI

™

Rest assured; he wasn't reviewing *Jerry McGuire.* He was writing about *Forrest Gump.*

"Holy fools," Brussat defined, are people like Forrest Gump, who follow the dictates of the heart and are often able to effect great works of mercy and compassion.

Likewise, Jones relied on Steinberg to "show him the money," and the result was a multimillion-dollar marketing plan that turned around the biggest battleship in college football. The real beauty, however, was watching June swivel-hip his way through the political, social and cultural land mines while he *executed* the plan.

Just like Forrest Gump, Jones escaped the bullies, produced All-

American talent, remained *loyal* to his friends and became a champion as a by-product of *who he is,* not what *he did.* There one finds a tribute to sheer resilience, resourcefulness and determination, where *relationships* are indeed life's *box of chocolates.*

"June doesn't waste a relationship," says Bartkowski. "Not a single one. Every person he meets, everywhere he goes — June collects facts, information and friendships. Normal people pretty much enter into relationships to make their personal or professional lives better in some way. But that's not June.

"People often overlook the fact that June was loyal to Leigh through some difficult times," Bart says. "Leigh had some partners who tried to discredit him, and he had some clients leave him. June stayed loyal, and now you see where that got him.

"See, if June likes you, that's pretty much it. He doesn't care what anybody else thinks. He's such a free spirit. He's not bound by all the things that burden the rest of us. He doesn't care. He's selfless; he's not looking for anything from you. He's always playing on a bigger field."

How pure is the *holy fool,* whose debonair soul demonstrates to the rest of us the power of love, devotion and the simple delights of life.

"Forrest Gump was far from stupid," Bartkowski surmises. "In fact, if you watch the movie, he's way, way ahead of all of us. I've observed June for a long, long time. He's never worn a watch, but he's never late for a meeting. He doesn't own a pair of socks, but you can't fill his shoes."

Might we all be so inspired to seek out the *holy fool* inside our own hearts?

Run Forrest — run!

Are you kidding me?

Chapter 23
A MOTHER'S PRAYERS

Winning seasons play tricks on the mind, like the rising of a full moon on a cloudless night. For instance, when you *think* you're *seeing the moon,* you're just looking at the reflection of the sun that recently went overhead. If someone were to ask you how many craters you counted, you probably couldn't answer.

The brand-new recruits in 2000 were acting like 1999 was *their* championship; in fact, they were just a mere reflection of the departed senior leadership: Ulbrich, Klemm, Miller, Owens, Warren, Robinson, LeJay and the rest. Now rumor had it that some of the new guys were skipping classes, smoking pot and acting in general like the WAC had already conceded the championship without them having to play a single game.

Just as a lion sees the unseen, Dennis McKnight's muscles involuntarily twitch and his nose itches at any sense of fear or overconfidence in a football team. Apparently, this all comes natural after a decade or so in the National Football League, where he routinely had witnessed teams reel off five or six wins in a row, only to choke on their own arrogance and miss the playoffs.

PHOTO BY KIMBERLY CARROLL

Some of these guys are clowns, McKnight thought; *after all June's done, here they are with their pretty new uniforms, their new look, their new image . . . and they don't realize they have to go* defend *this championship!*

McKnight left his third-floor office, stepped onto the elevator and punched the ground-floor button. The more he thought about it, the more he burned inside. He didn't like the circumstances he saw hidden in the tall, thick grass of certitude and cockiness.

How do I get their attention? McKnight wondered, as he headed to his special-teams meeting.

The elevator doors opened. He stepped out, walked down the concrete walkway and hung a left into the team's lecture hall meeting room. The auditorium seats and floor are staggered, theater-style. His feet pounded down the steps as he ignored the playful laughter behind him, as players purposely made fun of his ever-growing bald spot just loud enough for him to hear.

He reached the floor and turned and looked upward at his troops, who were fanned out among the blue-green cloth seats.

"There are guys in this room who are doing stuff that is detrimental to this football team," he said, his booming voice ricocheting off the auditorium's back wall. "Do you guys just think you're going to show up and play this fall? Do you think teams are just going to lay down for us because of what we accomplished last year?"

Then, for some divine reason, McKnight just felt compelled to tell them about Pisa Tinoisamoa.

"There's a Prop 48 guy up there in the dorms who can't even practice or meet with us," McKnight said of Tinoisamoa.

Prop 48, or *Proposition 48,* is an NCAA mandate that demands student-athletes reach certain academic requirements to be eligible, which even includes team meetings.

"His name is Pisa Tinoisamoa," McKnight said. "He's not partying. He's studying right now. And he's hurting; his Polynesian pride is wounded. He's made some stupid choices; he's been through hell, and now he's paying for it. He'd do anything to be down here with you.

"I think you guys need to look at Pisa's life and realize how fortunate you are to be here. Take a minute to knock on Pisa's door; love him up, and tell him that it's going to be OK. If we can keep him on track, he's going to make everybody on this team a better football player."

Nick Rolovich, sitting in the back row next to special-teams standout Joaquin Avila, had heard the name before but didn't know much about him.

"Who's Pizza Tonto-what's-his-name?" he whispered. "Is this the guy from *jail?*"

"He's a linebacker," shot back Avila. "He's supposed to be pretty good."

Pretty good?

Are you kidding me?

There were still people in San Diego who believed that the 6-feet-2, 225-pound Pisa Tinoisamoa was the best football player to ever hail from the region, including Hall-of-Famers Marcus Allen and Terrell Davis, a couple of other guys who were — ahem — *pretty good* themselves. Pisa was the only guy in history to be named the *offensive player of the year* (in 1997) and the *defensive player of the year* (in 1998).

In his senior year, he rushed for 1,600 yards and scored 23 touchdowns. On defense, he led the team with 75 tackles, six sacks and three fumble recoveries, including one he returned for a touchdown. He had been a three-time, all-league, all-state selection.

Nobody doubted his ability *on the field*. It was the other issues — the

gang fights, the cross-town, spray-paint tagging sprees, and — *oh, almost forgot* — the two counts of felony assault that had left his victim hospitalized — that had made Arizona, USC, Colorado and every other school in the nation turn tail and run the other way.

It had only been a year before that Pisa was facing six years and eight months in prison.

For all practical purposes, he'd thrown his life away — until June Jones dispatched Dennis McKnight to San Diego to plead with the judge to give this kid a second chance.

COURTESY TINOISAMOA FAMILY

In high school, Pisa earned MVP honors on offense and defense

"Your honor, my name is Dennis McKnight I'm an assistant coach at the University of Hawai'i. I'm here in court today on behalf of the university and head coach June Jones."

It was February 5, 1999.

The judge looked down from his bench at McKnight and glanced across the packed courtroom. At the defendant's table was the muscled, handsome Pisa Tinoisamoa, flanked by his attorney. In the gallery behind him, family members huddled, including Ruta Aunese, his mother, who clutched a Kleenex so tightly you could see the whites of her knuckles as she dabbed at her reddened eyes.

"Your honor," McKnight said, "if you'll put him in our custody, we'll change his life."

McKnight, who for the record can make the most expensive suit look ridiculously small, held up Pisa's scholarship in his right hand.

UH SPORTS MEDIA RELATIONS PHOTO BY JAY METZGER

Dennis McKnight and June Jones. "If it weren't for those guys," says Pisa, "I don't know where I would be today."

"Judge, I have his scholarship right here, if the court would like to see it."

Time stood still. The judge reviewed the paperwork presented before him by the attorneys and McKnight. "Two hundred seventy-eight days," the judge said, breaking the silence.

Ruta let out a cry. Her boy was going to get a second chance.

"With good time served," the judge continued, "you can be out by August. I never want to see you in my courtroom again. Good luck, son. Make the most of your opportunity. Mr. McKnight, I never want to see this young man, under these circumstances, ever again, and I'm trusting you on that."

"You gotta deal, Your Honor," McKnight replied.

With a single clack of the gavel, Pisa Tinoisamoa was a convicted felon in the California penal system, as well as the best recruit in the history of Hawai'i football. Pisa turned and hugged his sobbing mother, who kissed his cheeks before the bailiffs took him away.

The rest would be up to him in 278 days, beginning right now.

Now, before you start ranting about how college football programs will do anything to win football games and that athletes are given special treatment and should be forced to pay like everybody else in society, hold on to your shorts for a second, because *special treatment* was a far cry from what really happened.

Because McKnight, who is from San Diego, will tell you that when he first approached Jones with the idea of salvaging this kid that he'd read about in the newspapers, the idea of Pisa winning football games for Hawai'i *wasn't even the topic of discussion*.

"When June and I first talked about Pisa, June said, 'We're not here to profit from somebody else's losses or some kid's mistake,'" McKnight says. "He said, 'Let's just see what we can do to help this kid as a *person*. If he ends up helping us on the field, *great*, but let's start with *his life* and go from there.'"

June's first meeting with Pisa was hardly the stuff of Hollywood lore. There was no gut-wrenching, Al Pacino-style rally to redemption. June laid it on the line.

"This is your last chance," June told him in no uncertain terms. *"You need to grow up. You are either going to do what it takes, right now, or you can forget it. It's up to you."*

Pisa grows silent as he relives the moment. He clears his throat, noticeably processing the "what-ifs" of his young life.

"Nobody had ever spoken with me straight-up like that before," he says. "In the past, I knew how to work people to get my way. June and Coach McKnight just spoke the truth. It was simple, but it was exactly what I needed to be told."

Damage control was going to be tough; the media had already shaped most people's opinions, irrelevant of the truth that McKnight had dug up from police reports and his own background investigation. The more McKnight learned, the more he believed in the true character of Pisa.

McKnight discovered a mother with the faith of Abraham, who had held together a family unit ripped apart by divorce and poverty. He believed that Pisa merely needed guidance; he was determined to become a Pisa deliverer.

The felonies, McKnight argues, stemmed from a "wrong-place-wrong-time incident," where three other men jumped Pisa's brother at the Del Mar State Fair.

"Pisa was a physical specimen at 18," McKnight says. "He was a man-child. He was fast, he was strong, and he knew how to use his leverage. Any other kid fights three guys, he gets his butt kicked. Not Pisa. He whips all three of them and sends two to the hospital.

"Any other place or time, he might have been applauded for protecting his brother," the coach continues. "But because he'd made bad choices in the past, hung out with the wrong people, ignored the advice of his praying mother, this is what happens. The cops show up, and you're on the other side of the law, and you're lucky if you ever get another chance in life, ever again."

McKnight pauses. "When you make a bad choice, it doesn't matter how many times you've been picked All-State or how many yards or tackles you have," he says. "If the other guys had had guns, we wouldn't be having this conversation right now. Every kid should hear this story, because that's just how close Pisa came to a life of nothing.

"Somebody was listening to his mother's prayers."

Somebody?

Are you kidding me?

The athletic bloodlines of Pisa Tinoisamoa are rich. "Even when he was little," says his mother, *"nobody* could catch him." Pisa is the middle boy of three sons born to Ruta Aunese, the sister of Sal Aunese, the former University of Colorado quarterback who died of stomach cancer in the middle of the 1989 season.

COURTESY TINOISAMOA FAMILY

The Tinoisamoa family in 1987

understands. She raised her sons in the church, believing that if she trained them up in the way they should go, they would not depart from it when they grew older.

True to the Samoan culture, her boys understood and respected their elders. Pisa, for one, was a sensitive, quiet and confident momma's boy. He obeyed and protected his mother, loved strawberry shortcake and raced his bicycle up and down his neighborhood streets.

"We had no idea we were underprivileged," Ruta says with an adorable laugh. "Someone forgot to tell us."

His sophomore year, Pisa survived a near-fatal car accident while riding home with a friend from a party on the Fourth of July. "God spared Pisa's life," Ruta says. "My son nearly died from loss of blood." Miraculously, the brain damage forecast by doctors never occurred. Externally, Pisa bears the scars to this day.

Pisa's popularity was growing on the gridiron, and so was his trouble off of it — usually in direct proportion to his poor choice of friends. "Bad character always corrupts good morals," Ruta says. "You have to be wise about the friends you choose. Children are supposed to be a blessing from the Lord, but there were times when I didn't feel so blessed."

Without a man in the house to maintain order, her strapping sons ran wild.

"My mother is what I call a prayer warrior," Pisa says. "She never stopped praying for me or loving me. I'm embarrassed, really, by the pain I put her through. She didn't deserve it."

Ruta would wait for her rebellious boys to fall asleep, then slip inside their rooms and kneel at their beds, where she would pray for God's mercy on their souls.

"Every time you trust God's wisdom," says Ruta, "even when you don't understand it, you deepen your friendship with God. We don't normally think of obedience as a characteristic of friendship. That's reserved for relationships with a parent or the boss — not a *friend*. But *obedience* is a condition of intimacy, even if you have to go to jail to learn it."

COURTESY TINOISAMOA FAMILY

Ruta Aunese raised her three sons on her own ... and on her knees, where she frequently prayed for God's guidance. "When I pray, I don't need FBI clearance," she says. "When I call on God, my call goes straight through to Him."

Pisa's father is American Samoan and a former U.S. Marine. The oldest child of his other siblings, he split from Ruta when the boys were young to return to his native Samoa to help support his family. "It was a cultural thing," Ruta says simply, content to leave it at that.

Left to support three rambunctious, precocious boys, Ruta spent most of her time at one of her many jobs. When she wasn't working, she was cooking their meals or cleaning up behind them, as every single mother

Jail really sucks, especially when you're the *San Diego Union-Tribune* High School Player of the Year and everybody already knows who you are before the doors even clang shut. "Hey, boy, I'm talkin' to you!" yelled a laughing inmate, described by Pisa as a "large Mexican dude."

"I know who you are!" the man roared. "You're dat hotshot high school kid who teenks he's going to play in da NFL."

Embarrassing is an understatement.

"I didn't know what to expect, and honestly, that was the scariest part," Pisa says, recalling his jail *ohana.* "Everybody was from different races, different backgrounds, but we were tied together by force. Sitting in there with those other guys, man, it really sank in what I had done.

"But, just looking around, at least I could see that I still had *hope.* Most of these guys wouldn't get another chance."

Pisa hated his loss of freedom; the days dripped by. He did push-ups. He did sit-ups. He stared at the clock on the wall; half the time, it didn't even appear to be moving. He was like a caged animal. *How did I put myself here?* Pisa thought, looking at the plight of those around him. He began to retrace everything he'd ever done in his life, especially those nights when he'd found his mother on her knees, begging God to protect her baby boy.

In the stillness of the night, with his mother's prayers ringing in his ears, Pisa Tinoisamoa cried out to God.

I give myself up to you, he prayed. *Help me. Watch out for me, God. I accept you, and I accept why I'm here. Please deliver me.*

With little else to do, Pisa began to flip through a thick Bible his mom had left him. Whenever he was scared or lonely, confused or angry, he would pick it up in frustration and simply begin to read. It wouldn't be

long before this fierce football player — the same guy who had beaten another man unconscious — would read half of the entire Bible, including the part about his sins being cast into the deepest sea.

The ocean between here and Hawai'i, Pisa thought, *is pretty deep.*

So Pisa got religion, got out of jail and everyone lived happily ever after.

Are you kidding me?

> ▼▼▼▼▼▼▼▼▼▼▼▼▼▼
>
> *"I didn't know what to expect, and honestly, that was the scariest part," Pisa says, recalling his jail ohana. "Everybody was from different races, different backgrounds, but we were tied together by force. Sitting in there with those other guys, man, it really sank in what I had done."*
>
> ▲▲▲▲▲▲▲▲▲▲▲▲▲▲

He struggled mightily in school his freshman year and could only watch while the Warriors won the WAC Championship.

"Moving Pisa 3,000 miles from home, surrounding him with football and then telling him he couldn't play — that's like putting a heroin addict in a room full of loaded syringes and telling him he can't have any," McKnight says.

"People tried to push his buttons. By spring, more than once, I had to go hunt him down and find him and tell him in my own 'special' way to stay focused. He was hurting. He was alone. But June and the rest of us had made a commitment to this young man, and together we walked him through the fire."

Running back Afatia Thompson, a fire-knife dancer himself in the off-season, taught Pisa how to survive the flames. "Pisa was a character, he was a clown," smiles Thompson. "He was a Samoan kid from the mainland, and I became close to him. We understood each other. There was a bunch of us Polynesian kids who would talk to him in our own 'special,' loving way, if you know what I mean.

"I told him, 'Don't let all this stuff get to you,'" Afatia says. "Don't throw your whole life away because you're discouraged. We all did exactly what Coach McKnight said. We helped wake him up."

In the late summer practices of 2000, Pisa's grades finally caught up with his potential. In the Hawai'i coaches he had discovered father figures whom he could trust. Within himself, he'd discovered a purpose like he'd never understood before.

Ruta's midnight prayers were answered the day #10 proudly donned a helmet and trotted out to join his teammates for the first time, to the relief of the Hawai'i defensive coaches.

They would be calling on Pisa to answer a few prayers of their own.

Ruta and Pisa are all smiles … "our family is proof of God's love," she says today.

Pisa became one of the most ferocious hitters in Hawaii history

Chapter 24
MY FATHER'S EYES

Duke's Waikīkī is an open-air, oceanfront restaurant at the Outrigger Waikiki Hotel, aptly named in honor of surfing legend Duke Kahanamoku. A virtual museum, Duke's is adorned with surfing memorabilia, a *koa* outrigger canoe and surfboards. The palm-thatched roofs and umbrellas, rich *koa*-wood paneling and bamboo — not to mention the saltwater aquarium — only add to the ambience.

Throw in a couple of Hawaiian hotties at the bar, and you've got a picture-perfect *distraction* in which to tell a junior-college transfer from the piney woods country of Nacogdoches, Texas, that he's going to be the next Guy McIntyre, who was one of the better guards ever to play in the NFL.

At least that's what former Hawai'i coach Fred von Appen told 6-feet-3, 300-pound Kynan Forney. It's important to note that, in 1998, Forney wore glasses thicker than a Coke bottle, had no real understanding of major college offensive line play and — up to this point — had seen football only as a means to an education.

"The sun was setting," says Forney, laughing at the memory. "They had those fire thingies going in the sand. The wind was blowing through the palm trees. They were feeding me very well. [Von Appen] started talking to me about my athleticism, and I admit, when he told me I could be Guy McIntyre, he got me. I'd never even thought about the NFL. I said, 'Really?'"

When Kynan called home talking more about the NFL and less about his education, his father Errol cringed. "I said, 'Son, if you take the emphasis off *education,* you are going to lose your focus.'"

Herein is the story of one of the best linemen in Hawai'i football history — and how he almost never came to be.

The wisdom and instruction of a father is the beginning of understanding; by design, it is *supposed* to work something like the operating system of a personal computer. It runs silently and efficiently in the background of your consciousness. If you override it, you risk crashing and becoming little more than a blank screen. If applied properly, it will provide robust performance for all the days of your life.

Errol Forney could have been picked for the cover of author Ken Canfield's *The Seven Habits of Highly Effective Fathers.* Errol was as consistent as the smell of his barbecue grill on a muggy Saturday afternoon. He governed his own behavior. He was home when *he was supposed to be home.* He loved his wife. When he told his family, *"I'll be right back,"* he came right back. He kept his promises. He wasn't quick to anger. He was *moral.* He was his family's reference point for security, direction and confidence.

Errol ran the Forney household with the efficiency of a design engineer, which is exactly what he was throughout a long career with Southwestern Bell. His wife Andre worked in the finishing department of a local printing company, where she turned 12-hour days.

There were only three bedrooms in the whole Forney household, which Errol deemed plenty big enough for a family of five. The two used cars got the family where they needed to go. "I could have a brand-new truck this afternoon," Errol told Kynan one day, after his son asked why they never had a new car, "but I'd rather you boys have a nice Christmas and keep a roof over your heads."

COURTESY FORNEY FAMILY

The Forney Family: Father Errol, mother Andre, Kynan, and little brother Erik

Errol and Andre communicated with precision. "I never heard them fight," says Kynan. "They were together on everything. They were the first real team I ever played on." Kynan's brother Patrick was seven years his senior; his brother Erik, six years his junior. The boys were never without at least one — and usually both — of their parents.

"Our boys didn't have to depend on anybody," says Andre. "Either my husband or I were always there to pick up, drop off, take them here or there. It didn't matter if we had to go in three different directions in one night. My husband and I figured it out."

With Errol's office directly across the street from the school, the ever-mischievous Kynan always had to look around to see if his father was watching. "He never did bad things," says Andre, "because his dad would be right there to straighten him out. And if his daddy didn't catch him, then Erik, our youngest, would make sure we found out."

There was the time that Kynan — who at age 12 weighed 150 pounds and had a head the size of a bubble-gum machine — bounced on his parents'

bed and accidentally catapulted into the glass globe that protected the light fixture above the bed, which exploded.

"Kynan had a long-winded story for that one," Errol says. "We finally just looked over at Erik."

Erik, for the record, sang like a bird.

In junior high school, when Kynan came home with a bad report card, his father didn't say a word. He waited until nightfall, loaded his overgrown son into the car and took him into the slums of Nacogdoches. Errol slowed the car to a crawl.

"Look around son," he said, "because with grades like yours, this is where you're going to be living. Go ahead and pick out which house you want. You'll be using your stove to heat your house; that is, if you don't get your power cut off. Grades like that, you'll always be renting to stay. You'll never own anything."

COURTESY FORNEY FAMILY

A Chip off the Old Block: Kynan with his proud father, Errol

Once, when Kynan insisted on a pair of $110 Air Jordans, Errol calmly said no, and his mother supported her husband. "Kynan had to learn the value of a dollar," Andre says. "We made the boys earn their money. We would lay out things for them to do, then see how *well* they did it and then determine how much money they'd make. But we were not about $100 shoes."

Determined to have them, Kynan worked for months to earn the money to buy them himself. He wore them every single day for an entire school year, right up until the afternoon at the city pool when, in the words of his mother, "somebody finally stole those raggedy shoes."

Kynan wasn't highly recruited as a senior at Nacogdoches High School. However, Errol told his son, who then weighed 285 pounds, to work out *whenever scouts came to look at his teammates.* "With your size, son, if you're out there working your butt off, *somebody's bound to notice you,*" Errol said. "Sometimes, you just got to make it happen on your own."

Once again dad was right, and three different major colleges offered him a scholarship. But again, dad was right: Kynan's grades were too low to be accepted. Forced to attend a junior college, his father — yet again — seized the moment. "This is another second chance, son," Errol told him. "Make a plan, get your grades up, and stick to your plan." Kynan found himself drive-blocking at tiny Trinity Valley Community College, all the way to a junior college national championship.

His 4.9 time in the 40-yard dash raised a few eyebrows among major-college scouts, including Hawai'i's Tom Williams, and before he knew it he was sitting at Duke's in Honolulu, with visions of NFL stardom swimming in his head like it was a fishbowl.

Like a prodigal son, Kynan — prideful, strong — headed off to the faraway, mysterious land of Hawai'i, where he was certain fame and fortune awaited him. Away from his junior college coaches, who had lived in his dorm, and out from under the tutelage and constant presence of his father, Kynan did what any prodigal son would do.

"My first semester, I was placed on academic probation with a .05 GPA," Forney says. "At Hawai'i, I had no curfew, the campus was big and there were no room checks. My first year, I was staying up until two or three in the morning, hanging out with any teammates that would hang out and hitting the clubs. I was going to class *maybe* twice a week."

He pauses. "*Class* at eight in the mornin'? Ooooh, not happen'," he chuckles.

Meanwhile, on the field, the "next Guy McIntyre" was looking more like just another guy. "I remember pleading with the coaches, '*Please help me, tell me something, I'm getting killed.*' They even played me at left tackle, and told me to just '*be an athlete, go block the end.*' I didn't know *how*. People were running around me like I wasn't even there. The offense changed every week. We weren't just losing, we were losing *big.*"

By the end of 1998, the inmates were running the prison. "The kids from Cali or Texas kind of split off from the local kids," Kynan says. "The local Hawaiian and Polynesian kids wouldn't speak to us; we wouldn't speak to them, and for the longest time, it seemed like nobody liked anybody."

Hawai'i, for Kynan, slowly disintegrated from a wild life of adventure into failure and despair. He was lonely, homesick and often outright hungry. "I remember times when I had to knock on a neighbor's door just to get something to eat," he says. "I struggled. I didn't have a car. I had to beg people to take me someplace to eat."

Kynan recalls the day when he blew out his shoulder, which he feared might end his career. Jeff Ulbrich, his teammate, had blown out his knee.

The wisdom and instruction of a father is the beginning of understanding; by design, it is supposed to work something like the operating system of a personal computer. It runs silently and efficiently in the background of your consciousness. If you override it, you risk crashing and becoming little more than a blank screen. If applied properly, it will provide robust performance for all the days of your life.

"Jeff was one tough dude," Forney says softly. "I remember seeing him sitting on the training table, and he was *crying*. I was just like, *man*, if Ulbrich is crying, *crap*, this *has to be* the *lowest* point of my life."

When Kynan returned home for Christmas 1998, he felt helpless and hopeless. His father embraced his broken son with open arms.

Dad's barbecue never tasted so sweet. Kynan, between helpings of his mom's famous macaroni and cheese and giant mouthfuls of tantalizing ribs and chicken, told his folks he was through with football and through with Hawai'i.

Errol just listened patiently, like good fathers do, and waited for the Lord to renew his son's strength.

"That was a tough one," Errol reflects. "He was ready to stay home. We prayed a little bit. I told him, 'Son, life's not about the NFL. Life's about work ethic. Work ethic isn't anything more than *perseverence*. You need that *degree*.' I believe success is bred on real tough times, and *that* was a tough time. He was hurting, but I was looking down the road.

"It was *good* for him to struggle."

Now, only a *true father* can *see* that or dare say that.

He insisted that Kynan go back and finish what he started. The newspapers were buzzing that June Jones might leave the NFL to become the Hawai'i head coach.

"I said, 'Dad, they're not going to have the money to get him,'" Kynan says. "They're losing money, they're bankrupt. Trust me, he ain't coming to Hawai'i.'"

Other coaches who had heard of Fred von Appen's firing were calling the Forney household in an effort to lure the lineman to another school.

"God has a plan for everybody," Kynan says. "Sometimes you can't see it, but you've got to keep showing up to find out what it is."

Errol had a hunch, though. "A man like Coach Jones isn't going to be talking about something like that if he didn't plan on doing it," he says. "I had a good feeling when we sent Kynan back out there."

The first thing June Jones told Kynan Forney was that he wanted to make him a medical redshirt in 1999, which meant he wouldn't play until the 2000 season. "Let's get you healthy," June told him, "and bring you back strong for your senior year."

In front of the entire team, June declared that Kynan Forney had NFL potential, if he was willing to pay the price. "He said it in front of everybody," Kynan says. "That moment changed my whole life."

Errol remembers his son's transformation.

"June didn't recruit him," he says. "He could have treated him like a deadhead senior and just let him finish out his scholarship. It would have been very easy for them to go with their younger guys. But June promised to give Kynan a second chance if he'd work hard. He told him he had the potential to be a pro. I said, 'Son, the man is doing what you asked for.

"'Now go out there and do it.'"

Do it he did. Kynan disappeared altogether from the nightclubs. To flee temptation, he changed lifestyles and dorm rooms. He made a private statement of faith, telling himself that Adrian Klemm and Kaulana Noa were no better than he was, and he would prove it. Salads and supplements took the place of burgers and soul food. The weight room became his second home. And at every turn, he would bug coaches for extra instruction, either after practice or in the film room.

Kynan was making discoveries in the classroom, too. "Through God's great plan," says Errol, "we discovered that Kynan's learning problems were due to a form of dyslexia. Hawai'i, as it turns out, has one of the best programs in the nation for dyslexia. Within one semester, he made the coach's list for his work in class."

Hawai'i Warriors' 2000 Seniors

Allowed to practice but not play, Kynan's remarkable turnaround got the attention of the Hawai'i coaches. The night before the O'ahu Bowl, he knocked on the door of Dennis McKnight at 10 o'clock. Though he wouldn't be playing, he insisted the coach watch film with him into the morning's wee hours.

"Right then," says McKnight, "I knew this kid was going to make it. You could just see the *work ethic* bubbling forth in this kid. He put away childish things. We had the pleasure of watching him blossom into a full-grown man."

Back in Nacogdoches, Texas, Errol slept soundly at night, with the confidence of a father who had done his job — and done it quite well.

Kynan Forney started 11 games at right tackle in 2000, collecting a whopping 94 knockdown blocks. The offensive line allowed only 10 sacks *on the year*. Despite his team's 3-9 record, Kynan earned All-Western Athletic Conference honors. In fact, he and future NFL Hall-of-Famer LaDainian Tomlinson were the only first-team *unanimous* selections.

He was drafted by the Atlanta Falcons. He asked his dad to accompany him on the 12-hour drive from Nacogdoches to Suwanee, Ga., for his first training camp.

"That was the best drive, the best talk, we ever had," says Errol. "Halfway there, he said, 'Well, I hope I make the team.' I said, 'Son, if you're just hoping, then let's just turn the car around and go home.' He decided right then he was going to play like a starter from the day he got there."

Kynan *did* become the starter — a role he has never relinquished to this day. That, however, isn't the end of this feel-good tale.

"When I got to Atlanta," he says, "one of the trainers pulled me aside and told me a story. He told me that Dan Reeves [then coach of the Falcons] had called June during the NFL draft and asked him if he thought he could get me as a free agent. They told me June said, 'You better draft him right now, because he's better than anybody you've got.'

"God has a plan for everybody," Kynan says. "Sometimes you can't see it, but you've got to keep showing up to find out what it is."

It's a long journey from Nacogdoches to the shores of Hawai'i, to the bright lights of the NFL, where Kynan now earns millions of dollars to do what he loves and what he used to do for free. A wise son makes a father glad, indeed.

No one can imagine how proud the Forneys were the day they stood in

COURTESY KYNAN FORNEY

the crowd at the University of Hawai'i and Kynan walked across the stage to accept his four-year degree. "That was my proudest moment," says Errol. "I had always told him, the guy on your left or your right might be a little faster than you. But don't look to your left. Don't look to your right. Don't look for the pasture that might be a little greener than yours. You just keep running, and you'll finish the race. My son had finished the race."

Errol Forney, by the way, is unchanged by his middle son's money or fame. On Saturdays,

Kynan Forney and Travis Campbell

you can find him in east Texas, firing up the barbecue and extolling young Erik to *stay in school, get your degree, don't lose your focus.*

"How did I get here?" once penned songwriter Eric Clapton. *"Where did all my hopes arise?"*

The answer is so simple:

"My father's eyes."

184

Chapter 25
FENDO

"One scoop or two?"

The guy behind the counter at the Baskin-Robbins was James Fenderson, who between scoops of *Maui Madness* and *Chocolate Mousse Royale* had a dream far bigger than the eyes of the giggling children who snatched their ice cream cones from his giant hands.

It was a fantasy, really; something he'd thought about during his two years of high school on the island of O'ahu — and for yet another a year after high school, while working at Baskin-Robbins.

James Fenderson wanted to play football at the University of Hawai'i.

Those who quit their desires begin to die; James Fenderson wasn't one to quit. So he moved back to his hometown of Long Beach, Calif., where he walked on with Long Beach City Junior College.

His chances were about as small as the pink tasting spoons you'll find on the counters at your local B-R. But somebody who's hungry enough could eat an entire 5-gallon drum of ice cream with one of those tiny spoons, if he did it one bite at a time.

COURTESY JAMES FENDERSON

The incomparable James Fenderson ... the heart of a Saint, the blood of a Warrior

The overused saying, *"all good things come to those who wait,"* can be traced back to the poet Henry Wadsworth Longfellow, who stole it from the French, where it dates back to the 1500s. Waiting, in France, seems to be popular, whether it's for the right amount of air in a soufflé or for the American infantry to spare you from a lifetime of speaking German.

In the United States, however, people are so impatient they can't wait two seconds for the ketchup to inch its way out of the bottle before they dollop it on their fast-food cheeseburgers. The concept of *waiting for anything* is foreign to a society of youth that spends its time absorbed in the fantasy world of video games, where, with a two-minute tutorial, you can strong-arm androids, battle roving bands of mandogs, play in a rock band or start a major world war.

The idea of *fighting* for something or *working toward something,* other than today's high score, seems to be a lost art.

It was not so with James Fenderson. He had delivered the goods at strong safety and running back for Long Beach City College and even earned his two-year degree. But after seven months of delivering packages for United Parcel Service, Fenderson still wanted more for his life.

He looked up the phone number of the University of Hawai'i Athletic Department, and on more than one occasion, he would dial it. Time and again, whenever he could get through to an actual voicemail, he would leave message after message. He called friends who had friends who had friends who knew coaches or players at the university. Time and again, the answer was the same: *nothing.*

Finally, Fenderson's uncle called to tell him that Hawai'i assistant coach George Lumpkin was a friend of his at church, no less. He had blurted out to Lumpkin that he knew a *football player* who had worked his way through Baskin-Robbins and UPS and junior college but was a pretty good running back, a good guy and somebody Hawai'i should definitely take a look at.

"When you're a football coach," says Lumpkin, smiling, "you hear that every day: the *'I have a friend or nephew you guys should take a look at'* story. I told him what I tell everybody: 'Tell *your nephew* to try out and I promise — we'll be fair. We don't say no to anybody if you can play.' But usually, we seldom hear from those people again."

"Usually," however, doesn't apply to James Fenderson, who upon hearing the "news" from his uncle, packed his bags for Honolulu.

Assistant coaches Dennis McKnight and Rich Miano were at the Honolulu airport, eagerly anticipating the arrival of their newest recruit. When James Fenderson walked off the plane, McKnight whistled under his breath.

"Do you see that kid?" he asked Miano. Rich nodded, admiring Fenderson the way a jockey looks at a horse. Fenderson was in a cutoff t-shirt, displaying his rippling abs. His neck and shoulders looked like a block of granite stuck between a pair of two-by-fours.

The *real* Hawai'i prospect followed Fenderson off the same plane from California.

"Our guy comes walking off the plane wearing sunglasses, headphones, doo-rag, pants down to his ankles, head bopping," recalls McKnight. "I looked at Rich and pointed to [Fenderson] and said, *'Too bad we're not here to pick up* that *guy.'"*

By the time the unsuspecting parties reached baggage claim, the street-smart Fenderson had surmised that Miano and McKnight were Hawai'i coaches. He approached them, and they confirmed his thoughts.

"Hi, my name's James Fenderson, and I'm going to be walking on to your football team," he said. The coaches were shocked.

Are you kidding me? McKnight remembers thinking.

In the team van on the way back to the school, Miano and McKnight sat in stunned silence. The "real recruit" sat in the backseat, probably wondering why nobody was talking.

The journey for Fenderson grew longer. First, his units didn't transfer from Long Beach, and June Jones was forced to kick him off the field after two weeks of preseason training camp. "I was upset, it hurt," recalls Fendo, as his teammates now referred to him. "So I said, *'This is just one more thing I've got to clear up.'* So I got that cleared up, and I came right back out there and told June I wasn't leaving."

Off the field, he spent every waking minute working out and preparing for the next day. "It was funny, because during camp, I actually made the team, so I thought I'd be sleeping in the dorms. I was so naïve back then that I didn't realize the dorms were only for the scholarship guys. I was just a walk-on nobody. I had everything I owned in a single suitcase. So I unpacked all my stuff, because I thought I was staying. As soon as camp ended, though, they told me to leave *again,* even though I had made the team. I remember packing my stuff and thinking, *OK, now what do I do?"*

Fenderson did what *anyone* would do, right? He lived out of a borrowed, beat-up, 15-year-old truck, which he parked outside of McDonalds.

Are you kidding me?

He showered and brushed his teeth in the locker room after practice. He used the bathroom at Mickey Dees. He studied in his truck, where he also slept when he couldn't find room on the sofas of guys like big Doug Sims or John Kauka, who occasionally accommodated him. Food was a challenge, because only scholarship athletes were allowed to eat from the training table. "I was begging for food," Fenderson says.

"Once people realized what was going on," says receiver Ashley Lelie, "guys started sneaking out plates of food so he could at least eat." The ever-resourceful Fenderson also found he could subsist on supplements and protein bars and shakes, which were in plentiful supply in the training room.

His tenacity made him a cult hero along the sidelines among his peers. Players typically use special teams — for kickoffs and punts — to sit down and catch a breath, but this soon changed each time Fendo took the field. Soon, he was drawing even Jones' attention as he weaved his way through waves of blockers to make tackle after tackle. *"Did you see that?"* was becoming a standard sideline question as Fenderson continued to make spectacular plays.

When he wasn't practicing, studying or in class, Fendo could be found running up the steep hill outside the stadium with Mel de Laura, the strength coach, pushing his body to get even faster and stronger still.

The summer before his senior year in 2000, Fenderson was at a crossroad. He had taken out a number of student loans. He had successfully transferred enough units to play football but not enough to get a degree from Hawai'i. What it boiled down to was this: He was *paying* to play football. Mentally and emotionally exhausted after a year of living out of his car, Fenderson went to the office of June Jones.

"Coach," he said, "I literally can't *afford* to play anymore. Because of my transfer situation, I don't think I can get my degree."

June looked at his transcript. "If I asked you to, would you be willing to go to summer school?"

"Of course, Coach, but . . ."

"You *have* to pass," June interrupted. "You pass summer school, and let me see what I can do on my end."

That summer, Fendo made straight A's. When he didn't hear from June, quitting crossed his mind for the first time. "I was broke," he says. "I had done all I could do. I was at the end of the line. My hope was running out."

A special meeting had been called by the coaches, and players scrambled to get their playbooks and be on time. Amidst the chatter and small talk of his teammates, Fendo was despondent as he took a seat in the auditorium. Just looking around the room, he couldn't believe how much he loved this game, how much he loved *this camaraderie,* and how horrible it was going to be to end this way.

June walked in and strode to the front. He began talking about a scholarship that had become available and that the coaches had met to discuss

▼▼▼▼▼▼▼▼▼▼▼▼▼▼

"I believe that if you do positive things, positive things come back to you," he says. "Sometimes people don't want to make the sacrifices, but if you want something bad enough, you'll do what you need to get it. Fear can keep you from that, but you have to trust that God will be there to help you along the way."

▲▲▲▲▲▲▲▲▲▲▲▲▲▲

who most deserved to receive it, an honor usually reserved for a freshman walk-on.

"It's with great pride," June said, "that we offer this scholarship to *James Fenderson.*"

His teammates responded with a roar of applause; they stood, clapping and whistling.
"There were guys with tears in their eyes," recalls Miano. "Everyone had so much respect for Fendo. Nobody on this team had worked harder or deserved it more than James Fenderson."

"It was a bombshell," Fenderson says. "I still can't believe they used a scholarship on a senior. I realized I had to do whatever it took to show everyone how much I appreciated what they had done for me. I wouldn't have to borrow money anymore or beg for food anymore or find a place to sleep anymore.

"I was truly *one of them now.* It's a great feeling when you know you *belong.*"

Despite the scholarship Fenderson still found himself third on the depth chart at running back, until injuries to Avion Weaver and Afatia Thompson gave him a chance to start during the third week of the 2000 season. "We were struggling," Fendo says, "but I took it on my shoulders to lead by example. God had blessed me to even be in that situation, and I wasn't about to let anybody down."

He didn't. Fenderson led the Warriors with 651 yards rushing and seven touchdowns; he caught 30 passes for 216 yards and a touchdown and was named the team's Most Valuable Player.

When the season ended, June picked up the phone and began calling his friends throughout the National Football League.

"June called and said, 'You might want to take a look at this kid we've got on special teams . . . I think he can help you,'" says Randy Mueller, then the director of pro personnel for the New Orleans' Saints. "I said, *'Who?'* It's not too often a guy slips through the cracks, but James Fenderson did."

It wasn't for long. Fendo signed with the Saints and went on to play four seasons in the NFL, where never once did he have to borrow money or ask for food, and he was able to put away enough money to *buy a dozen* Baskin-Robbins.

The legend grew when *NFL Films* documented his story on ESPN, and Fenderson became a cause celeb of sorts. "People would approach me in the mall," James says. "They wouldn't know my name, but they'd say, *'You're the guy who slept in his car and made it to the NFL!'*"

Yet he remained humble — even shy — whenever a fan asked for an autograph.

"I remember the time," says McKnight, "when he called to tell me that, in the NFL, he could have a new pair of socks or a new t-shirt *every single day* if he wanted them. He was still the true, genuine Fendo, right to the end."

James and LaToya Fenderson on their wedding day, July 7, 2007

Today, James Fenderson is happily married. He is a certified trainer in Buford, Georgia, where he lives quietly and content, without a single regret in his life.

"I *believe* that if you do positive things, positive things come back to you," he says. "Sometimes people don't want to make the sacrifices, but if you want something bad enough, you'll do what you need to get it. Fear can keep you from that, but you have to trust that God will be there to help you along the way.'

When asked to recall his favorite game or favorite play of his entire career, either at Hawai'i or in the NFL, he pauses.

"It's funny, because I can't remember any of the games and don't care, really," he says. "I miss my teammates. I miss the coaches. I miss the people of Hawai'i. The people in that locker room, man, they were worth everything I went through to get there."

Does that include scooping ice cream at Baskin-Robbins?

"*Especially* scooping ice cream," Fendo grins. "Everybody has to start somewhere, and it makes the victory that much sweeter. I was just an average person who, by the grace of God, was *allowed* to do great things."

Are you kidding me?

James Fenderson runs for daylight in New Orleans; he hopes for a comeback

Chapter 26
FLAMES OF DESIRE

The emergence of James Fenderson in 2000 was not without a series of horrific happenstance that allowed him to play. One man's loss is another's gain; overlooked in the disappointment of Hawai'i's miserable 3-9 record was the unfortunate demise of Avion Weaver and Afatia Thompson, two of the mainstays in the Warriors' miracle season only a year before.

Weaver, who was on crutches after tearing knee ligaments just a few weeks into the season, was lost for the year. Likewise, Thompson tore ankle ligaments at the same time . . . and *should have been lost for the season.* But he could still walk, and, as a team captain, he made a career decision — one that effectively ended any chance he would have of ever playing football again after that year.

"I decided that if I could tape it up and play, I needed to do that," Afatia says. "Avion *couldn't* play. I was a captain. To me, it was just a huge cop-out for me if I didn't *try.* We had just won a championship the year before. I couldn't produce big numbers, but I was not going to use the injury as an excuse. I wanted my teammates to see that I was an example of the strength of the Polynesian spirit."

Furthermore, Afatia was a man of many talents, and he was not afraid to risk just one.

It was the second devastating career injury for Thompson, and the second time he'd made the decision to *"play through it."* As a senior at Punahou High School, he had blown out a knee, only to somehow finish

▼▼▼▼▼▼▼▼▼▼▼▼▼

"I decided that if I could tape it up and play, I needed to do that," Afatia says. "Avion couldn't play. I was a captain. To me, it was just a huge cop-out for me if I didn't try. We had just won a championship the year before. I couldn't produce big numbers, but I was not going to use the injury as an excuse. I wanted my teammates to see that I was an example of the strength of the Polynesian spirit."

▲▲▲▲▲▲▲▲▲▲▲▲▲

the year as the team's rushing leader. He sat out 1997, played sparingly as a freshman at Hawai'i in 1998 and then, under Jones, had a breakout season in 1999.

"When June arrived, he used all of our anger and hunger to change the philosophy to create that magical season," Afatia says. "Being a local boy, that was part of the reason I kept playing in 2000. When Coach stressed *team,* I believed it. The team's goals were always more important than my own."

This was a lesson Afatia had learned at home; long ago his parents had taught their children to use their *talents* to pursue their dreams. They encouraged their children to utilize not just one but *all* of their talents; to never bury or repress their skills due to fear; to take chances and, in doing so, watch their talents *grow.*

"If you do this," Afatia's father told him, *"you will never go hungry."*

Tihati Productions is the longest-running Polynesian show in Waikīkī, spanning nearly four decades. It is the product of Afatia's parents — Jack Eli Thompson and his wife, the former Charlene Ortiz, who built their multimillion-dollar business on an empty stomach. Raised in Kalihi, Jack and Charlene — or Cha as she's affectionately known in Hawai'i — were high school sweethearts at Farrington High School before they married in 1966.

Born on Swain's Island, roughly 200 miles from American Samoa, Jack is a combination of Samoan, Tokelauan, Spanish, Portuguese and

English. Charlene is a mix of Filipino, Spanish, Chinese, Scottish and Irish and grew up in poverty in the Kalihi Valley housing projects.

The couple was so poor at one point that they were forced to live with Alene Eleneke-Pa, Charlene's auntie, at Pālolo Housing. Eleneke-Pa had five children. One night, all that was left to feed everyone was *two cans of sardines, a heaping ball of rice and watercress with mayonnaise.*

That same night, Charlene and Jack drove their beat-up Volkswagen to a local drive-in, where they scraped up $2 in loose change — enough to buy one hamburger, an order of fries and a Coke. The couple split their "feast," and hours later, Charlene gave birth to Ruana, the first of their four children. Such were the humble roots of what would become the greatest show business family in the history of Hawai'i.

What sustained them through the bitter times was *their dream to be in show business.* They would talk about it at night, when they returned home from their day jobs: Jack as a Hawaiian Airlines' baggage boy and ramp agent and Charlene as a paper-pusher in the medical records department of Queen's Hospital. "Experiencing what it's like to be poor," says the elder Thompson, "is what taught us how to be successful."

They pursued their dreams by staging acts and networking with local promoters and entertainers, and all the while praying for the break that would change not only their lives but also the lives of many others within their extended family, or *ohana.*

The Thompsons lived life always believing "the best was yet to come." They consistently thought beyond the "urgency of the moment" to find

Nothing is more breathtaking than the ever-popular and stunning fire-knife dances

creative reserves they never knew existed, always believing in *tomorrow: tomorrow* could be the most electrifying day in their lives.

After all, it's only a day away.

Prayers were answered in 1968, when the couple was asked to replace a guy by the name of Don Ho, who was on a mainland tour. Seizing the moment, Cha and Jack had a brainstorm: They would take the most exciting native dances indigenous to the various Pacific islands and combine them into a one-hour show. The result would be something different than just an all-Tahitian or all-Hawaiian show.

Their Polynesian revue format was a smashing success. Within a year, the Thompsons began a 14-year run at the Beachcomber Hotel, and by the early 1980s they were staging shows at the Moana. Today the family business employs 1,000 people, including Afatia's sisters, Ruana and Misty, while producing eight shows *statewide:* three on Oʻahu, three on the Big Island and two on Maui.

The Thompson family grew at the same rate as its financial success. It is customary in Polynesian culture to take in the children of other relatives who may be struggling; over time, Cha and Jack would be raising 15 kids in addition to their own. "I can pretty much go anywhere on the islands," laughs Afatia, "and point to someone and say, 'That's my brother over there.' Everywhere I go, I've got a relative somewhere."

Jack and Cha were hard on the kids "to make sure we don't act like spoiled brats," Afatia says. "They taught us not to take anything for granted. I'm grateful for the way I've been raised, and I know that all we have is because God blessed us. After God, the most important thing is a strong family."

When his brother died in a home accident, the family looked inward for strength. "That was our roughest time," he says. "Everything happens for a reason, though, and my family never questioned God's plan for our lives, because His plan is perfect. I know I will see my brother again, in a place where there is no pain, no death, no fear of darkness."

Growing up, all of the Thompson kids sang, danced and performed

their many talents. Afatia grew up mesmerized by the fire-knife dancers; in May of 1998, he finally asked his father if he could participate. "I tried to explain to him," says Jack, "that it takes years, not *months,* to perfect the technique."

COURTESY AFATIA THOMPSON

The imposing physique of Afatia Thompson

191

"Half of it is getting over the fear of the fire burning you," he says. "The fire heats up the blade so you feel it, but adrenalin keeps you going. One time I was dancing and the wind blew the fire back and it burned my eyebrows. I couldn't see through one eye, but I just kept smiling and dancing."

It's no surprise that life after football finds Afatia Thompson *in the entertainment business* — as the Hawaiian Music Awards' "2007 Hip-Hop Artist of the Year" (online at **www.afatia.com**). Who could have guessed that Afatia could *lose one talent — football* — only to allow his others to emerge in a way that today reaches millions? His combined life experience of character, talent and personality has allowed him to crystallize his vision for what his talents can become.

"I'm so blessed," he says. "I was just raised to believe in my dreams, and they have not come to fruition by accident. There is always a price."

To test his son's mettle, Jack declined when Afatia asked his father to sponsor his entry fee at the Polynesian Cultural Center's World Fire Dance Competition. Showing the resolve his father had hoped to elicit, Afatia came up with the $100 himself — then shocked the world by advancing to the second round.

Afatia's dazzling smile and showmanship — featuring a blend of technique and speed — quickly elevated him to the top ranks of fire-knife dancing. There, he displayed the same dogged determination and courage that simultaneously led him to gridiron glory. When a football player talks about *fearlessness,* usually they're not referring to the potential of third-degree burns to their *face;* Afatia never once performed with "oils," which dancers often use to protect them from flames.

Thompson has been a fire-knife dancer (above left), a football star, and now a hip-hop sensation

Afatia was the Hawai'i Hip-Hop Artist of the Year in 2007

Whether the competition was fire-knife dancing, football or now a major recording career, Afatia has always been willing to surrender the concepts of safety, security and comfort for a higher reward of living in the hope of leaving *his mark* on the world.

"We had to go out and make our mark for not only our families, but also *our people* in general," Afatia explains. "You must understand that there is a pride in Polynesian people that cannot be taught.

"When Coach Jones said, *'This is battle,'* it validated the football program, it validated me, it validated Hawai'i," Afatia says. "June taught all of us that you commit *unconditionally*. That's when the plan, the resources emerge. I learned a lot from him, especially his spiritual walk with God.

"He also taught me that when retreating is not an option — *that's when your talents can become an unstoppable force.* But if you never use your talents, you will never know, and *spend the rest of your life wondering what might have happened if you had only tried.*"

The Thompson family

Chapter 27
O DEATH, WHERE IS THY VICTORY?

It's hard to know for sure what was on the mind of June Jones when he climbed into his Lincoln Town Car and wheeled out of the Athletic Department parking lot early on Thursday morning, February 22, 2001.

For weeks, however, his mind had been a blur; he had been puzzled by his team's frustrating 3-9 season of 2000. *How could a team with 23 seniors lose nine games?* Turnovers on offense, an ineffective run defense and shaky special teams had plagued the entire season.

His high hopes for Nick Rolovich had disappeared faster than the last foamy beer at one of Rolo's infamous parties. Timmy Chang replaced him and finished with 3,041 yards and 19 touchdowns, en route to eight school records, including a fifth-place finish in the nation in total offense. Still, Chang, only the second true freshman to reach 3,000 yards, had also thrown 19 picks, and June was concerned about his ability to *lead* a major college team.

To ease the loss of all the senior leadership, Jones had three former local prep standouts transferring in from other Division I programs. Travis Laboy of Utah and Wayne Hunter from Cal would shore up the defensive line. Stanford wideout Tafiti Uso would give Ashley Lelie some help in the receiving corps. At least he knew he could count on the leadership of safety Nate Jackson, one of the last holdovers from 1999, as well as offensive lineman Vince Manuwai and defensive tackle Lui Fuga.

Meanwhile, the person in the car behind June on that clear spring morning said the coach appeared to be reaching for something — a roster, a schedule, perhaps his cell phone. We'll never know. What we *do* know is that moments later, at 10:41 a.m., Jones' four-door Ford suddenly and inexplicably veered off the asphalt and roared into the concrete pillar of the Hickam off-ramp — without braking — at 60 miles per hour.

The car behind Jones slammed on its brakes and pulled to the shoulder.

Its driver frantically called 911. Judging from the horrific crash, the smoke and molten metal, he told the operator to please hurry, for he feared the person trapped inside was most certainly dead.

Artie Wilson almost didn't take the call. When you're showing real estate, it's not good etiquette. Even still, he tried to keep it short. *"Give me just one minute,"* he told his clients with a smile, as he flipped open his cellphone and lowered his voice.

"This is Artie. . . . What? . . . Why do you need June's license plate number? . . . It's 4567864. . . . Oh, dear God! . . . Queen's Hospital. . . . OK. . . . They're en route, right? . . . Will he make the hospital? . . . Omigod! . . . I'm on my way. . . ."

They had asked Artie for the tag number because they couldn't recognize the smashed humanity inside the vehicle. Just the night before, June had eaten dinner with the Wilsons, even napping briefly on their loveseat before going home stone-cold sober at 9 p.m.

"See ya tomorrow, big guy," Artie had told him.

Typically, the most lethal automobile accidents are those in which a car hits an immovable concrete wall and the g-forces felt by the human body are not survivable. The crashes you see when a car goes somersaulting down a NASCAR race track tend not to kill a driver, because at no time does the driver decelerate too fast. While the car is somersaulting, it actually loses kinetic energy over a relatively long period of time. This is usually seconds compared to milliseconds when you hit a concrete wall.

Just four days earlier at the Daytona 500, Dale Earnhardt's Chevy Monte Carlo had tapped into a car driven by Sterling Marlin, then veered right,

The mangled car of June Jones

PHOTO BY FL MORIS

slammed into the wall, bounced back slightly and then was broadsided by Kenny Schrader. Earnhardt's famous #3 drove back into the wall at an angle of 55 degrees, which is 31 degrees shy of what highway patrol investigators refer to as a "head-on" collision. The image of Earnhardt's death played over and over again on ESPN. Scientists determined that the actual *impact speed* of Earnhardt's car, calculated from the angle at which it hit, was "just" 42 miles per hour.

This, in the world of NASCAR, sounds like a love tap. But if you have a 3,400-pound projectile traveling 42 miles per hour, reduced to *zero* in a single *foot,* the force of impact is 100.3 *tons* — or the same weight as having 200,600 pounds sitting on your face and chest. NASCAR rescue workers who arrived first on the scene said that Earnhardt had died of a "severe injury at the base of his skull." This meant, in layman's terms, that his body stopped moving — thanks to his helmet, harness and safety apparatus — but his spine didn't, driving straight into the back of his skull at full speed.

June Jones, on the other hand, had driven a 4,015-pound Lincoln Town Car into an immovable concrete pillar by the Hickam off-ramp at 60 miles per hour. The impact took 1/15th of a second and required exactly 3 feet and 1 inch to dead-stop the vehicle. Jones' face had hurtled into the windshield, while his body wrapped like a wet bedsheet around the steering column and dashboard. The severity of the collision was like jumping spread-eagle off a 12-story building into an oddly shaped piece of steel.

195

You can live without a lung; you can live without an eye; you can live without a kidney. You cannot live without a liver. Though it serves a variety of functions, the most crucial is its role in the body's metabolism, much like the heart is to the circulation of blood. The liver plays a critical role in four key areas: fuel management, nitrogen excretion, the regulation of water distribution between the blood and tissues and the detoxification of foreign substances.

The liver *is not* an airbag; however, unlike with Earnhardt, the force of impact had spread exponentially through Jones' *unbelted* body. He had an open head wound to the right side of his skull. The engine had been pushed back to the dashboard, leaving his knees jammed under the steering wheel. Such a grade 5 injury to the liver is usually instantly fatal, which is why Captain Moke Haunio of the Mokulele Fire Station said that rescue workers fought to keep Jones awake while he was rushed to Queen's Medical Center.

"Queens ER . . . this is Medic two en route emergency traffic . . . 47-year-old male . . . unrestrained driver . . . single-vehicle head-on MVA [motor vehicle accident] . . . altered level of consciousness . . . airbag did deploy . . . however, patient's right-temporal went through windshield . . . massive bleeding, multisystem trauma . . . completely immobilized . . . c-collar with long sideboard . . . patient is intubated on 100 percent O$_2$ . . . mast trousers in place . . . bilateral IV line . . . lactated ringers . . . cardiac monitor showing sinus tachycardia with multifocal PVC [premature ventricular contractions] . . . blood pressure palpable 60 . . . pupils dilated and slow to respond . . . extensive swelling and deformity in one arm . . . arm is immobilized. . . ."

"Copy that, Medic 2. Bring patient to trauma room 3."

Just keep fighting, Coach! Captain Haunio prayed.

Just keep fighting!

Artie was unprepared for what he saw when he ran inside the hospital; it was a scene straight out of ER. June, unconscious and unrecognizable, laid on a gurney beneath a swirling mass of tubes and beeping machines. He had life-threatening injuries to his head, liver and abdomen. He was suffering from massive internal bleeding; Artie watched while the blood inside June's chest and stomach literally inflated him to grotesque proportions.

Nobody really thinks about death until they actually *are looking at it.* Artie had never once even considered life without his best friend. June, to him, represented love, trust, security and safety. Artie's stomach felt like someone had pulled a trapdoor out from under him. Emergency room trauma surgeon Dr. Neil Fergusson was calmly barking directions to assistants and nurses in a two-minute drill.

"I could see my best friend dying right before my eyes," says Artie. *"At that point, I thought he was gone. I simply couldn't believe it was going to end like this. I was frantic. I was desperate. But there was nothing — absolutely nothing — I could do but watch."*

He rode with June up the elevator to surgery, where hospital personnel forced him to turn back. As they wheeled June away, Artie wondered if that might be the last time he'd ever see his friend alive.

The television in Nick Rolovich's apartment was blaring; a sportscaster was ridiculing the New York Yankees for signing former Mets all-star pitcher Sid Fernandez, who hadn't played since 1997. Rolovich was late for school and hardly paying attention as he crammed books in his backpack and grabbed some other stuff he needed for class. The phone rang. He was so late, he almost didn't answer it.

"Bro, get down here!" Rolovich was caught off guard by the urgency in the voice of Brian Smith, his roommate and the team's starting center. *"It's Coach Jones. He's been in an accident. It's pretty bad.* I don't even know what hospital he's at, but the camera crews are already down here and stuff. I don't know anything else. Just get here."

Rolovich jumped on his moped and screamed up King Street, where he cut into the back gate of Lower Campus. The entire drive took maybe a minute and a half. He pushed his way past the cameras that were gathered around the Athletic Department. Reporters were yelling questions, including one who blurted out that June had just been given a 9 percent chance to live.

Nick felt as if he was about to puke. The players walked around in a daze.

It was pandemonium. Then somebody said Coach George Lumpkin was calling a meeting in the auditorium and to get their butts down there, on a hop.

"We all knew they were going to tell us he was dead," Rolo says. "I was sitting there, disgusted with myself. Here was a guy who had given me the chance to start just a year ago. I had let him down. Literally, just a year before, on February 22, I was celebrating my 21st birthday, partying like a rock star. Now here I am, praying, *'God, just let him live. Give me a chance to prove to him that he wasn't wrong when he put his faith in me.'*

"You don't miss something until it's gone," Nick says. "I know this may sound selfish, but I didn't know how to pray or what to pray. Maybe I should have only been praying for June. I don't know. But I just *kept* praying that if God would please let him live, I would never waste another opportunity in my life."

Local stations interrupted daytime programming with the news; ESPN interrupted Sportscenter. Word of Jones' crash began to travel back to the mainland and around the globe. Everywhere, it seemed, everyone was praying the same thing:

"*People all around the world* were praying," says Ruta Aunese. "We may come from different places, different lands, but the spirit of God is *one*. We all were praying with one voice to spare June's life."

Artie paced for three hours, from the waiting room to the parking lot, where he updated players and coaches, friends and family, with . . . *nothing*. After what seemed like an eternity, Dr. Neil Fergusson came down to tell him that the bleeding in June's face, head, abdomen and liver had been reasonably stabilized. They were going back in for another look at the chest and neck.

If the first miracle of the day was that June didn't die on impact, then the

▼▼▼▼▼▼▼▼▼▼▼▼▼▼

"You don't miss something until it's gone," Nick says. "I know this may sound selfish, but I didn't know how to pray or what to pray. Maybe I should have only been praying for June. I don't know. But I just kept praying that if God would please let him live, I would never waste another opportunity in my life."

▲▲▲▲▲▲▲▲▲▲▲▲▲▲▲

second occurred only moments later, when Fergusson realized that June's aorta had suffered a 75 percent tear, the same injury that instantly kills 10,000 people a year in the United States (and would later kill actor John Ritter). The *third* miracle occurred when it was discovered that Dr. Michael Dang, the best thoracic and cardiovascular surgeon in all of Hawai'i, just "happened" to be *in the hospital* and had raced to the surgery room to assist Fergusson.

Still, the news was grim — shocking, actually, when Dr. Dang first spoke to Artie. The procedure, the doctor explained, would be similar to splicing and repairing a torn water hose during the medical version of a two-minute drill.

"We're going to cut the aorta," Dr. Dang said. "I'm going to clamp it, then put in a stint-graft, then sew it back together. The trick is timing. It has to be quick. If I'm successful, then there's a chance that June won't lose feeling in his lower extremities and he'll be able to walk again. Once I cut the aorta, his lower extremities won't have blood circulation, so at that point, we're in a race against time."

Dr. Dang went back to surgery; Artie found a place to pray.

"Lord, please," he begged. "We need June worse than you do. Please, let him live!"

By the time they finished the surgery, only Drs. Dang, Fergusson and the trauma team had seen the actual size of June's heart, but one can only imagine from the life he led that it must have been huge.
Fittingly, it would now have laces, too.

George Lumpkin and the other coaches gathered the players and filed into the auditorium. Athletic director Hugh Yoshida walked to the front. Some players leaned forward and listened in disbelief. Others merely lowered their heads into their hands in shock. A few of the holdovers from 1999 wiped tears from their eyes.

"We're faced with a very serious situation," Yoshida told them. "We must live through it, we must hope for the best. This is a critical situation for June, but don't lose hope. Together, we will all pray for a miracle."

Just as Hawaiian spirituality draws *mana,* or power, from Kane in the clouds, from Kanaloa in the ocean and from Ku in the trees, June Jones was drawing on faith of his own as he drew labored breaths through a respirator. No sooner had Dr. Dang declared surgery successful, listing Jones as "guarded" in the intensive care unit, than the people of Hawai'i, from the governor on down, shared the same sentiment:

E komo mai: We wait for you.

Governor Ben Cayetano issued a statement claiming Jones as a "close personal friend" who "has had such a positive influence on our student athletes, our people and our state. Our prayers are with June and his family."

Yoshida told the media that "we are all praying, just like you, that he comes to full recovery. We all understand what June means to our community, and all the good things he has done, not only for the university, but also the entire state of Hawai'i."

Across the state, thousands of well-wishers acknowledged the fallen coach with cards and letters and inundated call-in radio programs. Fans descended on the State Capitol to sign a 24-foot-long "get-well" banner: *"Best wishes, June,"* scribbled one fan. *"You are our warrior. You are an example of not only a great coach, but a great leader. Aloha!"*

Slowly, June's prognosis improved. First, doctors said he *would* walk again, though with a limp. He *would* coach again, too; all CAT scans were normal, except for a few random X's and O's. His beloved golf game would never be the same, but who cares about golf when you've skirted a date with death?

O Death, where is thy victory?

Jones could barely speak and when he did, it was usually drug-induced jibberish. He would wake up in the middle of the night and call

THE WHITE HOUSE
WASHINGTON

March 15, 2001

Coach June Jones
University of Hawaii
Honolulu, Hawaii

Dear Coach Jones:

I was sorry to learn about your car accident, and I hope you are feeling better. My prayers are with you during this difficult time.

I hope the outpouring of support from football fans and friends in Hawaii and across the country has helped speed your recovery. Their concern speaks volumes about who you are as a football coach and as a person.

Laura and I send our best wishes.

Sincerely,

George W. Bush

out a play or a player's name, before nodding off again. Artie, amused, started writing down his abstract comments, including the one when June — staring at all the machines, tubes and hoses — seriously asked if he actually was hooked up to the television set in his room.

About a week into his recovery, June pulled Artie close, then closer. Artie braced for what he thought would be the proverbial hospital-bedside

NATIONAL FOOTBALL LEAGUE

Paul Tagliabue
Commissioner

April 6, 2001

Mr. June Jones
Head Football Coach
University of Hawaii
Football Office
1337 Lower Campus Road
Honolulu, HI 96822

Dear June:

Although today's AP report quotes you as saying that "I'm not back," I was very pleased to see that you are headed in the right direction. Keep up the good work on the physical therapy, and we look forward to your return to the coaching this season. You represent too much that's positive about the game to be missing for too long.

Everyone here sends their best to you and your family.

Sincerely,

PAUL TAGLIABUE

Support for Jones came from the NFL, Minister Robert Schuller, even the White House

ROBERT SCHULLER

July 31, 2001

Dear Coach Jones,

You are a walking miracle!

When I first learned of your tragic accident, I, like millions of others, prayed that God would bless you and hold you in His arms until you had fully recovered. How thrilled I am to now read of your return to the university -- eagerly looking forward to the coming season!

You are a dynamic "possibility thinker" and -- with God's help! -- you have turned your "scars into stars"! Through your health challenge, you have become a splendid example of a victorious person who will now bring hope and inspiration into the lives of many others experiencing a similar challenge.

To God be the glory – great things He has done!

Keep on keeping on, my friend! I love your spirit! Tough times never last – but tough people do!

May God continue to bless you and guide and guard your every step...

He certainly loves you and so do I!

Robert H. Schuller

Coach June Jones, Head Coach
University of Hawaii at Manoa
2444 Dole Street
Honolulu, HI 96822

RHS/ew

THE CRYSTAL CATHEDRAL
12141 LEWIS STREET, GARDEN GROVE, CALIFORNIA 92840

revelation. "Find my car," June rasped, "then get the key to my Harley out of the driver-side console."

"I was waiting on something profound," Artie chuckles. "Instead, he turns me into his personal valet. He never tipped me, either." Artie's first sight of the vehicle, however, was no laughing matter. Cold chills raced up and down his arms. *The front seat was gone. Dried blood and tissue were stuck to the windshield and dash.* Broken CDs were strewn everywhere. The vehicle smelled of death. Artie quickly retrieved the key and left, content to never relive that scene again. "All I could think," Artie says, "is June cheated death. It was nothing but a miracle to have him back."

The impact on the players was profound. "He's like a dad to all of us," said senior wide receiver Craig Stutzmann. "We're just trying to stay optimistic. It's hard but we're keeping him in our prayers. We're a close-knit family and whatever happens, we will get through this."

Rolovich took it a step further. "There is no question," says the quarterback, "that June's accident started me down a different path for my life. I settled down. I made the commitment to take school and football seriously. I made a decision not to take anything in life for granted, ever again."

Weeks later, Artie Wilson's plane had just landed in Las Vegas for a real estate convention when his wife called. *Oh no!* Artie blanched, fearing the worst. He had gone by the hospital on his way to the airport, and *June had been recovering just fine.*

"Honey," said Lissa, Artie's wife, "you better get back here. He's trying to leave the hospital on his own." Wilson never left the airport, literally catching the *next flight* back to Hawai'i. "June's will to live — and to leave the hospital — was incredible," Artie says. "I got back there and said, *'Man, what are you doing?'*

"June explained that he was 'fine,' and he no longer wanted to 'be a burden' on the doctors and nurses who should be caring for 'people who

are really sick,'" Artie says. "I told him, 'June, you've got stitches all over your body. You can't walk.' He didn't listen. He made up his mind — he was leaving. He didn't want the media to know, either. So I did what any good friend would do: I went down to my car, brought up *my own clothes,* got the man dressed and rolled him out."

Jones' weight had dropped to 160 pounds. His skin was the color of iodine. Yet he was thrilled to be leaving the hospital, albeit in a wheelchair. Knowing the media might stake out his own home, June insisted they go to Artie's. "It was 10:30 at night," Artie recalls. "June opened the sunroof to my BMW, looked out at the sky, and said, 'Wow, can you believe how *good* the air *smells?*'"

The lights from passing streetlights probed inside the vehicle. June flicked open the vanity mirror, where he simply stared at his scarred, gaunt visage for a long, long time.

▼▼▼▼▼▼▼▼▼▼▼▼▼▼

"People all around the world were praying," says Ruta Aunese. "We may come from different places, different lands, but the spirit of God is one. We all were praying with one voice to spare June's life."

▲▲▲▲▲▲▲▲▲▲▲▲▲▲

Artie's house was better suited for June's rehabilitation. Jones had set the goal of returning in time for spring practice. "We all thought that was crazy," Wilson says, "but you know June." Each day, doctors, therapists and masseuses would come over to work on the coach, who would find a way to muster the strength to call his other coaches and prepare for the season. Only minutes of work would leave him exhausted; he would nap for an hour, then start the whole process over again.

One evening, in tremendous pain, June asked Artie if he could use the giant Jacuzzi in Wilson's master bedroom. Artie helped him get in the tub, then went downstairs and joined his family for dinner.

"About an hour later, Lissa says, 'Where's June?'" Artie smiles. "I ran upstairs to check on him. He was stuck in the tub and couldn't get out. I hadn't thought about that. Now, I couldn't just *lift* him out — he'd had his chest cut open, his back cut open, he had a rod in his arm, he couldn't lift his legs. I couldn't ask Lissa to help — he was naked. I knew what I had to do. I said, 'Oh, *brother. . . .*'"

Artie stepped into the tub fully clothed and, in his own words, "lifted his skinny, naked butt out of that Jacuzzi. I told him, 'If only the media could get a shot of me holding you naked in my arms . . . now *that* would sell some newspapers.'"

"I wasn't threatened," says Lissa today, grinning. "I love June, but he can't have my husband."

As he fought his way back June frequently broke into public tears, endearing fans with his determination. Letters poured in from around the NFL, Robert Schuller — even the White House.

"None of us really realized how many people he'd coached, *who he was,* until the outpouring our program received from everywhere," says Rolovich. "It was surreal. I remember being in the weight room one day, and the guys were just like, 'Wow, June's touched a lot of lives, huh?' He became larger than life to us. It was absolutely mind-boggling, and to this day, I've never seen anything like it."

The coaches went through spring practice without their fallen leader. On the field, it wasn't discussed; the coaches did exactly as June had instructed them — business as usual. He wanted the boys to look forward, not backward, and he had specifically directed the coaches to keep the players focused on academics and football, not him.

"Still," says receiver Ashley Lelie, "not having Coach there, things just weren't the same."

Word of mouth had it that June might be in his office for the spring game. The players were disappointed to look up from the practice field and not see the light in his third-floor office. Then, on a hunch, Dennis McKnight went up to see for himself.

"It was incredible," says McKnight. "I turned the corner, and he was sitting there in his office, in the dark, watching practice with Artie Wilson. It was a very powerful, very moving moment. He could barely move, but ever so slightly, he turned and looked at me. Nobody said a word. But I knew right then everything — June, the program, our kids, our season — was going to be OK."

George Lumpkin has a theory — one that he's not bashful to share.

"A torn aorta and the man is still alive?" Lumpkin asks. "No *permanent* disabilities? God worked a miracle for June. It's God's plan for June to be here. It's as simple as that. You're crazy if you *don't* believe that."

Are you kidding me?

When you're the son of a fireman, you don't get weepy-eyed over a chick flick with your fiancé, snuggle kittens in your spare time or cry in public when your head coach nearly dies in a car accident. Privately, however, a spirit was stirring deep inside of Nick Rolovich that he just could no longer explain.

When June had benched him for Timmy Chang, he hadn't even fought for his job. Some nights found Rolovich alone on his couch, staring blankly at the TV, which flickered blue-gray in the darkness. It was then that tears would sometimes well in his eyes when he thought about the opportunities he'd wasted.

I let down the entire State of Hawai'i, he thought.

I let down my teammates. I let down June.

If I ever get a second chance . . . his mind trailed.

Grabbing a piece of paper and a pen, he began to write:

Coach Jones . . .

I hope you're feeling better. I know I let you down, and I'm sorry. I don't know when you'll be back, but I want you to know I'll be here every day watching film. I just want to do whatever I can to help this program be better than it was when I got here. I owe you that. I'm really, really sorry. . . .

Rolo

The next day, when no one was looking, Rolo slipped the note underneath June's office door.

Chapter 28
REVIVAL AND REDEMPTION

Walk into the University of Hawai'i football office, hang a left down the hallway and you'll find June Jones' office immediately to your right. Just past it and to the left is a long, windowless conference room, where players and coaches spend an inordinate amount of their lives watching game film.

So this is what the film room looks like this early in the morning, Rolovich joked to himself, when he first began to keep his 7:30 a.m. daily date with the overhead projector. He was no longer bothered by the fact that Timmy Chang had already been named the starting quarterback, or that the bulk of Dan Morrison's time was going into preparing Timmy for the upcoming 2001 season. Rolo realized this was quite possibly the last time he'd ever play football, and he was dead-set on contributing. Watching more and more film — even if it was by himself — was the least he could do. He wasn't battling Timmy Chang, he was battling *himself.*

So it was just another early morning – *real early, by Rolo standards* — when Nick grabbed a muffin and a cup of coffee and popped in a tape of the Run 'n' Shoot 60 series. When it came to the Z Go, one of Hawai'i's bread-and-butter plays, he backed it up and replayed it several times. The coaches were always preaching "separation," and he could really see it on this particular film. He was surprised when a weak, raspy voice from directly behind him almost made him spill his coffee down his HAWAI'I FOOTBALL t-shirt.

It was June, who had quietly taken a seat behind him.

UNIVERSITY OF HAWAII ATHLETICS

Nick Rolovich says he was forever changed by his Hawai'i experience

"See that corner, right there, Rolo? He's going to try to get a little wider there . . . freeze it . . . right there . . . there's your shot right there."

"When he showed up to help me," says Rolo, "that was his way of testing my commitment. It felt great. June is like a father. He never said a word, but good fathers don't have to. I couldn't stop smiling."

Young Timmy Chang had played his high school ball for coach Cal Lee at local Saint Louis High School, just down Dole Street and less than a mile south of the university. There Lee, long an understudy of Mouse Davis and June Jones, had employed the Run 'n' Shoot, albeit a simpler version. During his senior year alone, Chang had fired 64 touchdown passes, one shy of the national record. Though undersized, his physical gifts and basic understanding of the offense seemed to make him the shoo-in for the university's football poster boy.

Cal Lee had even resigned his longtime post at Saint Louis to accept June's offer to join the Warriors' staff. Timmy's WAC Freshman-of-the-Year honors in 2000 seemed to solidify these thoughts, but under the surface, questions lingered. For one, Chang was hesitant to become the savior of the island nation overnight. He had won so many games and accolades over so many years at Saint Louis that by the time he got to Hawai'i, he seemed almost — for lack of a better word — *reluctant,* as if he almost wished Rolovich hadn't forced him into a leadership role so quickly.

"Timmy was forced to mature," says Afatia Thompson. "Nick was struggling

Timmy Chang was forced to start as a freshman when Rolovich faltered

Tenacity was what Jones was expecting to see in 2001. Whenever June would occasionally remove his shirt after practice to jog, revealing his scar-ridden body, it left little doubt as to how *Jones* defined the word. *"Holy criminy!"* Rolovich exclaims, when he recalls seeing his coach's body for the first time. *"They carved him up like Braveheart."*

Jones and his staff shuffled players at virtually every position in an effort to prove that 1999 had not been an anomaly. When receivers coach Ron Lee suffered a mild heart attack in the days prior to the season opener against Montana, it further galvanized the players' resolve, as some wondered if the season might be cursed from the outset.

Timmy Chang threw for 435 yards in the 30-12 win over the Grizzlies, but it was wide receiver Ashley Lelie who stole the show with eight catches for 163 yards. Lelie, like all great Run 'n' Shoot receivers before him, had mastered the use of his hips and eyes to run to space in almost any situation; but better yet, he had enough pure speed to run by anyone. With Ashley stretching defenses deep and wide and Justin Colbert and Craig Stutzmann ripping them apart underneath and inside, the Montana game was an optimistic sign of potentially great things to come.

The intensity of the defense was spectacular. Pisa Tinoisamoa had dropped 40 pounds to play at 215, and it paid immediate dividends, with three huge sacks and 13 tackles. It was a fitting way to start the season, and all looked forward to the first conference game against Nevada the following week.

Terrorists, however, had other plans, and the World Trade Center bombing would be yet another devastating interruption to the complicated 2001 season.

[in 2000] — we were struggling — and Coach Jones went with Timmy to spark everybody. The consensus on the team was that if Coach says you're the guy, then we'll support you. But 95 percent of us in the locker room thought Timmy wasn't ready to be the guy, that he wasn't capable yet. He was too young to be in that situation."

The fans hadn't been bashful in their vocal harassment of *both* quarterbacks. "The fans here in Hawai'i are *tough,*" says Thompson. "They love to cheer you when you're great, but they want to kill you if you're bad." This meant, at times, that both quarterbacks were fortunate to have escaped with their lives — Rolo's mother, in fact, once had left Aloha Stadium in tears.

The nation sat in stunned silence for a little more than a week following the New York bombings. When the season resumed September 22 against Nevada, Nick Rolovich had pretty much made up his mind to ask June Jones to allow him to redshirt, or sit out, the season, rejoin his firefighting family and go do his part to fight the war on terror.

College rules allow for a player to retain their eligibility and come back for another season as long as they play in no more than two games in a single year.

Sudden injuries to Timmy Chang, however, threw a wrench in Nick's plans.

Hawai'i lost to Nevada–Reno 28-20, and Chang was sacked six times. In that game, Rolovich had been called upon for a single play when Chang was shaken up, and he threw a long incomplete fade to Ashley Lelie. That single play counted toward his eligibility. The next week, at home against Rice, Hawai'i blew a 21-7 halftime lead before eventually losing 27-24. Chang hurt his right throwing wrist again late in the game, and this time Rolovich didn't take the field. Third-string quarterback Jared Flint finished the game with two unsuccessful drives.

At game's end, Rolovich — guilt-ridden for not playing — sat at the end of the bench with his head in his hands. June snapped him out of it and ordered him to midfield to sing the alma mater with the rest of the team. When Jones announced that Chang would probably miss two weeks with a sprained wrist, Rolovich faced a crossroad.

"If I played and Timmy came back, that would be the end of my college career," he says. "If I didn't play, I could come back in 2002 and play another year."

Selfishness had cost Rolo the previous season. He knew what he had to do. Nick Rolovich bit his lip, took a deep breath, and made his decision: He would throw caution to the wind and start living up to the note he had stuck under June's door several months before. In Timmy's absence, June declared Rolo the starter against SMU.

Anybody can write a note, put it under a door and pray for redemption. Life, unfortunately, doesn't allow us to *talk* our way out of what we *behave* ourselves into. You have to *behave* your way back out of the problem, which poses a degree of difficulty in the game of football, because unlike pro wrestling, the other guys don't just follow your script.

Had this been a movie, Rolovich would have ridden into the stadium at Southern Methodist University on a mighty white steed to rescue the season from the clutches of chaos and stalled offensive drives. Instead, Rolovich threw two picks in the first half. Running back Mike Bass went down with an ankle sprain. SMU came out in real life behind some Mustangs of its own and blasted out to a 17-3 lead.

At halftime, June as usual was brief, unemotional and matter-of-fact. "He said pretty much what he says every week at halftime," says defensive end Travis Laboy. "He told us they weren't beating us, we were beating ourselves, and if we execute in the second half, we'll find a way to win."

Alone at his locker except for a cup of Gatorade in one hand and a white towel in the other, Nick Rolovich dabbed sweat from his face. Halftime is only 12 minutes, but it may as well have been his whole life. He was hearing voices, too, and they weren't human.

Demons of *guilt,* doubt, fear and insecurity had climbed up his back and perched on *both* of his shoulders, where they were filling his ears with every reason why he'd ever failed in his entire life. *You went to junior college for a reason — nobody wanted you! You suck! You blew it last year, and you're blowing it now! You lost your job to a freshman! Your teammates don't respect you! June doesn't respect you! You can't lead them! Who's the life of the party now? Why don't you just go get drunk?*

Nick's heart was trembling. His dream had started years ago, when as a boy he would play football alone, imagining himself as Joe Montana. With no one to see or appreciate, he would fire perfect 35-yard arcs to a bush, a tree — whatever he imagined the receiver to be. Such desire had fueled him all the way to this point in his life, right up to halftime in a strange stadium far away from home, against a crowd that wanted him dead.

No sooner did Rolovich close his eyes and pray for the voices to stop than linebacker Chris Brown grabbed him by his shoulder pads just beneath his chin and jarred him from his thoughts. Earlier in the month, Brown — a relative of Akebono, the towering Hawaiian sumo wrestler — had just bench-pressed 225 pounds 42 times, a team record. He shook Rolovich like a dishrag.

"Listen! Every guy on this team is with you!" insisted Brown. *"Look me in the eyes, Rolo! This is your time! Forget everything and go be you! We're with you, bro!"*

Life often boils down to such moments. Do I stay, or do I go? Hide, or step up? Run, or fight? Rolovich grabbed his helmet. Enough was enough. It was time to wrestle the demons down. He wasn't seeking peace or comfort, but *truth*. He was a football player and it was time to stop sabotaging his own life and become the man, the person, the *player* he knew he could be.

For some reason, Rolovich had always felt intimidated by June Jones. Perhaps it was June's larger-than-life NFL legacy, or his own guilt-ridden conscience for his late-night escapades or a little of both. Regardless,

when the student is ready, the teacher appears, and as they stood on the sidelines awaiting the second half, June could see in his quarterback's eyes that such a time had come.

"Now listen to me, Rolo: They're playing with your eyes," June said calmly. "That's *our* game, you hear me? Those two corners are real aggressive, and they're jumping your routes because you're not moving them with your eyes. You need to start controlling *them*, not the other way around.

Once Rolo regained the starting role, he would never relinquish it again … at one point, he threw for 1,500 yards in just three games and is the only quarterback of the June Jones era to whip arch-rival BYU …

You were OK in the first half, but we need to settle down and get on these guys."

Rolovich nodded. June turned away and smiled. He had seen that look many times before — in the eyes of guys like Jim Kelly, Warren Moon, Chris Miller and Dan Robinson.

June couldn't wait to see Nick Rolovich take his turn at the trigger of the greatest offense in the history of football.

Entire seasons can turn on a dime.
Rolovich changed his attitude, and the team changed with him. Thero Mitchell capped a five-minute drive with a 2-yard touchdown, only to have SMU answer with a 90-yard touchdown pass of its own. A minute later, Rolovich, who was starting to *have fun,* hit Tafiti Uso for a 45-yard score.

During a TV timeout, Rolovich approached Jones. "C'mon Coach, you're not still feeling that car crash are you?" Rolo asked, smiling. Suddenly, he began feinting body shots at Jones' upper body and mid-section. June cringed instinctively, and the sidelines erupted in laughter, particularly little-used backup Mark Tate, whose eyes popped to the size of silver dollars at the sight of the crazy quarterback-turned-Tasmanian devil.

"You're *crazy,*" Jones said, smirking at the hysterical Rolovich.

"Everybody loosened up," chuckles Travis Laboy. "And then everybody stepped up — Tafiti, Rolo, Abe Elimimian, Thero — unbelievable."

Let's not forget Robert Grant, a former running back now playing defense, who blocked his second punt of the day with 11 seconds left in the third quarter. Teammate Keith Bhonopha picked up the loose ball and raced in for the touchdown, tying the score at 24.

With SMU settling into deep zones to thwart the pass, Jones masterfully used the running game to protect his quarterback's growing confidence. Mitchell, playing more than usual due to the injury to Mike

UNIVERSITY OF HAWAII ATHLETICS
Rolo barks signals from the shotgun

Bass, battered through defenders for 42 yards on eight carries before scoring on an 8-yard run with only three minutes remaining in the game. When SMU returned the kickoff 92 yards for a tying touchdown, it forced overtime.

With Jones yelling, *"Use your eyes! Use your eyes!"* Rolovich did just that. On a critical third and 11, he popped his eyes, moved the safety out of the middle of the field and hit Ashley Lelie on a 15-yard square-in, which Lelie turned into a 22-yard gain. Two plays later, he hit Uso again for what would prove to be the game-winning touchdown.

SMU still had a chance to tie on their last possession. When Jones waved Rolo to his side, Nick thought for sure he was about to get his first profound sideline lesson from the great June Jones. "Listen," June said, "you're the leader out here now." Rolo's eyes beamed, and his chest swelled with pride. "Now, as the leader," June continued, "you can't let any of these guys throw Gatorade on me, because I'm still hurting from that car crash. No icewater, no Gatorade. Now, go be a leader."

Rolovich looked at his coach. June burst out laughing. The gun sounded; Hawai'i had won 38-31, in overtime, on the road. Another June Jones' quarterback had come of age. And it was the best birthday present ever for Analea Donovan, who would one day become the wife of the now-retired playboy Nick Rolovich.

Newspaper headlines were screaming that Timmy Chang's right wrist would be good enough to play the following week against Texas–El Paso, but that's not what Rolovich was hearing in the locker room. "Timmy's not ready," June told him, "and you're going to play." June stayed true to his word, and Rolovich responded with three touchdowns, including two more to Ashley Lelie. But it was linebacker Matt Wright who broke the game wide open when he returned an interception 90 yards for a touchdown just moments into the game.

To the relief of defensive coach Kevin Lempa, the defense led the way in a resounding 66-7 victory, the most lopsided of June Jones' coaching career. It would be the largest margin of victory 59 points ever by a Hawai'i team. Chris Brown and Pisa Tinoisamoa led waves of Hawai'i tacklers to the football. Hawai'i had seven tackles for losses, defended 14 passes and had 10 quarterback hurries. Kevin Millhouse picked off a second pass for a 39-yard touchdown; then Robert Grant nabbed yet a third interception for a 26-yard score.

Just like that, the Warriors were suddenly 3-2, but the Chang-Rolovich saga continued. Jones — ever the psychologist — wouldn't publicly give Rolovich the permanent nod. "Timmy is our best quarterback," June told the press, but he also said that Chang had "aggravated" his wrist in practice and would not play the next week when the team traveled to Tulsa, Okla.

"Timmy was extremely talented, but you have to remember he was just 19 years old," says Rolovich. "We weren't far apart in talent, but in life, we were way apart. He used to look at me the way a little brother looks at you. He was so popular, but I think he enjoyed the time off while he was hurt."

June knew *exactly* what he was doing. Timmy's alleged "injury" was giving both quarterbacks a chance to grow and heal, in more ways than one. Rolovich, with only seven games left in his college career, was having the time of his life.

"Rolo is a leader but he has his own style," says Lelie. "He's funny, he keeps everybody laughing and loose and before you know it, everybody's making plays." This was fast becoming apparent, even to his opponents. When the obnoxious 10-man Tulsa band wouldn't stop interrupting the Hawai'i offense during warm-ups, Rolo took matters into his own hands. "I got this one, Coach," he grinned, ducking into the huddle.

"Let's go 80-Z Choice . . . Ashley, no matter what, run the out."

Ashley looked up and started to protest — *the band is on the . . . oh, I get it.* The team broke the huddle, Ashley ran a deep out to the corner and Rolovich dropped a perfect, tight spiral — *DONG!* — right off the tuba. The tuba player dropped like he'd been shot, as did numerous Hawai'i players, who couldn't stop laughing.

What mattered most, of course, was what Nick did *after* warm-ups, which was to lead Hawai'i to a 36-15 victory and its third consecutive conference win. Rolo completed 25 of 34 passes for 324 yards and three touchdowns, including two more to Ashley Lelie. At one point Rolovich completed nine consecutive passes, and he finished the game with no interceptions.

The Warriors were beginning to play with rhythm — on offense, defense *and special teams.* Pisa had 14 more tackles, safety Jacob Espiau had six. Abraham Elimimian and Keith Bhonapha tackled the Tulsa punter for a safety. Kicker Justin Ayat banged a 55-yard field goal and Matt McBriar crushed a 69-yard punt. They were playing as a team.

When the Warriors learned that Boise State had upset Fresno State, their next opponent, it sunk in: Hawai'i *was back in the race for the conference championship.* Rolovich and his teammates returned to O'ahu full of optimism and hope.

That's when Rolovich was summoned to June's office.

No way, he thought. In a matter of seconds, his demons returned. *You knew it was too good to be true! See? You wasted your eligibility! He's going with Timmy! You're done! It's over!*

This time, however, Rolo shook off his fears. This time, he would not cave. *There's no way he's going to pull me now for Timmy Chang,* he thought. Rolo summoned his courage, for *this time,* he would go down fighting.

"Hey Coach," Nick said, taking a seat in front of June's massive desk. The walls in Jones' office tell a unique story. Rolovich couldn't help but check out the autographed photos from Deion Sanders, Marvin Hagler and Junior Seau, or the framed personal letter from George Bush, or the Atlanta Falcons helmet June wore in the NFL.

Frankly, though, on this day, he didn't care where June had been or who he knew. All he cared about was starting against Fresno State and whipping the Bulldogs. He took a deep breath to muster his courage, but before he could lay it on the line, June cut him off.

"Listen, I want you stop reading the newspapers," June said. "Here's the

What it's like to sit across the desk from head coach June Jones

deal: Keep doing what you're doing, and you're going to play. You're the starter for the rest of the season."

Huh? Nick couldn't believe it. Yes, he could believe it! He must believe it! Get thee behind me, demons! From the day he arrived on campus, June always had said that he would never hesitate to play the guy who gave the team the best chance to win. With few words, June had just spoken volumes.

A year ago, this might have been good cause for a kegger. *Not this time.* Rolo grabbed his playbook, singled out Coach Morrison and began to prepare for Fresno State, the 18th-ranked team in the nation.

Something special was happening up in the dorms, but it could no longer be classified as a *party*. Channon Harris, Justin Colbert, Pisa, Ashley, Rolo — heck, *all the players* — were getting together to sit and talk for hours about *football, life, even classes.* "The communication was getting better and better," Rolo says. "Guys would talk about plays, routes, defenses, offenses. We'd go over everything the coaches were giving us."

Pisa, too, was blossoming before everyone's eyes — not just by leading the conference in tackles but in the classroom. "I learned to lead by *example,*" Pisa says, a fact with which Rolovich readily agrees.

"Pisa was just amazing," Rolo says. "He made our offense so much better by talking about defenses. He taught us how great players make great plays."

"Coach Jones talks all about relationships," says defensive end Laanui Correa. "He's always talking about *the guys in this room next to you.* That's what started happening, big-time. Nobody wanted to be without each other. We all hung out together. Not just partying. Being *together.* That's what builds a team. Up in those dorms, just communicating with one another — that's where our team came together."

"I know this sounds funny," says Rolovich, "but often, I'd tell my girl-friend, 'I love you, but I need to go be with the guys.'"

"Doesn't surprise me a bit," kids the mischievious Pisa. "You know Rolo's from San Francisco, right?"

With only four minutes to play, future NFL first-round draft pick David Carr tossed a perfect 35-yard spiral into the waiting hands of Rodney Wright for his fourth touchdown of the night to give Fresno State a 34-31 lead over Hawai'i.

For much of the game, the Bulldogs had lived up to their Top-20 billing in front of a packed crowd at Aloha Stadium and a national television audience. Early in the fourth quarter they had led 27-16, after Hawai'i nearly collapsed in the third quarter. But just as they had all year, the Warriors refused to quit. Travis Laboy deflected a third-down pass on Fresno State's next possession. Rolovich marched Hawai'i straight down the field before finding Channon Harris on a perfect, over-the-shoulder 19-yard touchdown.

On their next drive, Fresno State could have ended the game, but Carr fumbled a snap on the Hawai'i 3, and safety Nate Jackson somehow recovered. Rolovich responded, directing his team *96 yards* before throwing a rope to a leaping Ashley Lelie in the back of the end zone from 11 yards out — Lelie's second on the night. On the previous play, Rolo had kept the drive alive by throwing a perfect rainbow to Lelie for a 45-yard completion.

After Carr followed up with a touchdown pass to Wright, June would find his team down by three with roughly seven minutes to play and in a very unique dilemma.

On Hawai'i's next series, Rolovich went down beneath a wave of red and white jerseys. "It was one of the hardest hits on a quarterback that I've ever seen," says Jones. "Rolo was laid out. The game was stopped for quite awhile. I finally walked out there, where I was met by the team doctor, who told me that Rolo was done for the game and probably the season." Rolovich had dislocated his shoulder, and the doctor had just popped it back into the socket moments after he got to Nick on the field.

For June, this would mean going *back* to Timmy Chang at quarterback, where an interesting subplot had developed. Jones had been told that Chang could have what is called a medical redshirt, or an additional year of eligibility, if he didn't play any more the rest of the season. However, June had always made it clear that he didn't *believe* in redshirting: His philosophy was that if *any* player can help the team win even a *single* game, he should play, if for no other reason than out of respect to the seniors on the team.

"Unless what you say and what you do are the same, then a person loses all credibility," June says. "I risked losing my credibility. I wanted the team to know that the only thing that anyone should care about is winning, and no one person is bigger than that."

June had to know if, somehow, Rolovich could gut it out and still play. "I stood there for a moment and got my thoughts together," June says. "Even though it looked dim, I felt we could still win the game. So as the doctors were still leaning over him, I leaned down and asked him, *'Rolo, can you still go?'*"

"Rolo's eyes popped open and he said, 'Coach, it's my *left* shoulder. Give me a minute, and I can go.' So I put in Jared Flint, not Timmy Chang."

Two plays later, Matt McBriar boomed a 51-yard punt, and the Bulldogs took over at midfield. All Carr had left to do was run out the clock — except that he was blindsided by Nate Jackson, fumbled and Laanui Correa recovered at the Bulldogs' 34-yard line.

Nick Rolovich came back out on the field, and Hawai'i was back in business.

Five plays later, Hawai'i had the ball on the Fresno State 14, with 13 seconds to play. June called timeout, and Rolo tipped his helmet up on his head as he approached the bench and grabbed a cup of water from the trainer.

"Here's the deal," June said, "I want you to put this ball in the corner of the end zone where nobody can get to it but Ashley." Rolo nodded. When he entered the huddle, the smiles looking back at him told the story.

"Let's win it right here," Rolo said. "We're gonna go 90 Streak, jump ball to Ashley. Ash, listen to me: This is all you. I'm gonna throw it high, *so climb up there and get it and let's go home.* Here we go . . . on two, on two."

With that, Rolovich took the snap and hung the football up in a perfect arc toward the corner of the end zone. Forty thousand people held their collective breath. Lelie pushed his hips past cornerback Devon Banks and leaped into the night sky, arms outstretched to the limit of his 6-foot-3-inch frame. Lelie wrapped his long fingers around the ball with Banks all over him, then dropped like a ballerina and tapped his toes inbounds as he fell.

Aloha Stadium exploded, as did bars and taverns across the island. June Jones had his first collegiate victory against a ranked opponent. Nick Rolovich had rebuked his demons. The Warriors were tied for first place.

And, in perhaps the oddest twist of fate, Timmy Chang would one day have Nick Rolovich to thank for his insurmountable NCAA records. Rolo's toughness and determination to finish that game would allow Timmy to enjoy an extra year at Hawai'i, a key factor in years to come in Chang's record-setting college career.

Hawai'i whipped San Jose State, then blew a chance for a share of the WAC title when another late-game rally fell short against Boise State. The Warriors rebounded with a wild win against Ben Roethlisberger and Miami of Ohio in a 52-51 shootout, winning on a Justin Ayat field goal on the last play of the game. The Warriors ran the ball only 11 times that night, while Rolovich scorched the Miami defense for 500 yards and seven touchdowns.

The next week against Air Force was more of the same, as Rolo cranked out 505 yards and five touchdowns, and Ashley Lelie turned in a nine-catch, 285-yard, three-touchdown performance. It was the ninth 100-yard game in the career of Lelie, who was shattering Hawai'i receiving records that dated back 16 years. "We have a play called Houston," says Rolovich, "where we go trips right, the outside guy basically runs a post, the inside guy runs a flag and I'm reading the safety. If he jumps the corner, I throw the post over the top. Against Air Force, I let one go just to see if Ashley could outrun the *safety and the corner.* Well, *he did.*"

Rolovich belly-laughs when he recalls the memory. "I *know* the NFL caught that on film, so allow me to take full credit for Ashley's NFL career. Seriously, though, Ashley was so good, sometimes all I had to do was throw it high and deep. He would find it. He is unbelievable."

PHOTO BY DENNIS ODA

Chad Owens sets his eyes on the prize

Way back in the spring of 2001, three weeks prior to June's car accident, Brigham Young University had scheduled a season-altering collision of its own when it agreed to play Hawai'i in December in a nonconference game.

There was no way to predict, back then, that Brigham Young would be ranked *ninth* in the nation as the undefeated (12-0) Mountain West champions, or that the Cougars would be headed to a bowl game and Hawai'i (8-3) would be snubbed completely from postseason play.

Yet BYU had little reason to fear. Hawai'i had lost its last six meetings against BYU. The Cougars averaged 46.9 points and 537.8 yards per game to lead Division I-A. Besides, the Hawai'i defense was riddled with injuries, including a stress fracture to Pisa Tinoisamoa's right leg.

"This game means *nothing* when it comes to conference championships or bowl games," said BYU head coach Gary Crowton. "This is *nothing* but a *pride* game."

Perhaps someone should have reminded Crowton that, *in Hawai'i,* pride is *all they play for* — a fact the entire mainland was about to learn. Due to the late kickoff time on ESPN, it would be the only game in the country on TV; fans could judge Hawai'i for themselves.

The Warriors huddled around their coach in the locker room in the waning minutes before kickoff. It was hard to imagine that just eight months before, no one thought June would even be there. But *there he was,* for the second time in three years, making history with *another* Hawai'i football team. This time, if they won, it would be the only time Hawai'i had ever beaten a 12-0 team.

"Guys, we talked about all this four months ago," June told the Warriors in the locker room prior to kickoff. "We thought we had a chance to get to this game right here, to be undefeated — and to be honest, we should be. But we wanted to get here and have a chance to win 9 or 10 games.

"That's where we're at," he said. "The most important thing is to go out there today and have fun like we have the last three weeks. This is a once-in-a-lifetime deal. You have an opportunity to do something that you'll keep forever. You do it for each other. You play the game with poise. You play the game smart. You leave it all out there today. If you're spent when you come back in here, we'll come back winners."

The goose is loose! Chad Owens shocked BYU – and the NCAA – with the greatest day in college-football history …

Freshman Chad Owens was overlooked in all the hoopla, he of the compact 5-foot-8 frame and the *Mighty Mouse* tattoo on his right forearm, commemorating his nickname when he had played at nearby Roosevelt High School. Owens had quietly led the WAC in kickoff returns, while finishing second on the team in all-purpose yards — but he had saved his best for last.

Whether it was Crowton crowing about *pride games* or simply Owens' relentless pursuit of respect due to his height, we'll never know. Regardless, Owens made the offense wait its turn and assured the country that this was more than just a game. Owens returned the opening kickoff 64 yards, and moments later Rolovich threw 23 yards to Channon Harris for the first touchdown of the day. When BYU punted, Owens broke the game open with a sizzling 74-yard punt return. BYU managed another field goal, only to have Owens return *the ensuing kickoff* 100 yards.

"Every time I looked up," says Rolovich, "Chad was running past our sideline with the ball."

Ashley Lelie caught his first touchdown of the day four minutes before halftime. Pisa, playing with a broken leg, made certain BYU felt his disposition. When struggling Cougars quarterback Brandon Doman tried to rally his shell-shocked team back into the game just seconds before the half, Tinoisamoa met him helmet-to-ribs at the goal line. Doman and the ball skittered across the turf as the half ended, leaving Doman on all fours and spitting up blood. Both Doman and Charlie Peterson, his back-up, would be knocked out of the game with injuries.

At the half, Jones was succinct. "They can score," he said. "Don't let up. Just keep executing. Let's put them away."

It's anyone's guess why Crowton — a former NFL assistant himself who was no stranger to Jones or the Run 'n' Shoot — would decide that man-to-man was his best option against Lelie, Colbert and Stutzmann, but he did.

"It was like stealing," says Rolovich. "June would wait to see their substi-

The Warriors rolled up 646 yards and handed 12-0 BYU the worst defeat in its history – 72-45 – after its coach referred to Hawai'i as a "nothing" game ...

tutions. Half the time, they went man-free, and we just lit them up. Everywhere I looked, guys were open." Rolo threw for four third-quarter touchdowns. Uso caught two before Stutzmann scored on a 5-yard slant, then ended his stellar Hawai'i career by punting the ball into the upper deck.

"What a way to go," Stutzmann said later. Ashley Lelie then trumped everyone with an 80-yard score.

Not to be outdone, Channon Harris caught two beautiful fourth-quarter touchdowns on perfect, down-the-chimney Christmas presents from Rolovich. Fittingly, the last play of Rolovich's Hawai'i career would be the 60 Z Go.

The game lasted four hours and 20 minutes. "I didn't have anywhere else to be," joked Rolovich, who down the stretch established himself as the hottest quarterback in the nation with 20 touchdowns in his last three games.

With time running out, June turned to Rolovich and hugged him. "Did you ever think this," he asked his quarterback, "in your wildest dreams?"

"I love you, Coach," Rolo said.

"Yeah, I love you too," June answered.

What's not to love? When the dust settled, Hawai'i had whipped BYU, 72-45.

The 72 points were a school record for Hawai'i, which amassed 646 yards. It was the worst loss for BYU in its history. The Warrior defense had six sacks, one interception and recovered six fumbles. Rolovich shattered a slew of Dan Robinson's records, passing for 543 yards and eight touchdowns. Ashley Lelie had eight catches for 262 yards. Owens set NCAA records for kickoff return yardage (249) and total kick return yardage (342).

When representatives of the Hula Bowl raced to Rolovich after the game to invite him to play in the senior All-Star game, all he could do was chuckle. *"Are you kidding me?"* Rolovich asked. *Assured they weren't,* he grinned to himself as he took another lap around Aloha Stadium, signing autographs, shaking hands, touching the fans.

"I was so proud of Nick," says June. "Nick is what happens when you refuse to let situations in your life dictate how your life is going to turn out."

Funny, but Rolovich was going to say the same thing about June.

June's accident say coaches, players and friends, was more than just a watershed turning point in his life. "I see a difference in him in everything," says Dennis McKnight, who, along with former Hawai'i coach Dick Tomey, was in the hospital room the day Jones came to. "The way June deals with stress, the way he deals with pressure, just the way he loves *people*.

"He was great before, but the way he handled the 2001 season after the

 PHOTO BY GEORGE F. LEE

Nick Rolovich threw eight touchdowns against BYU, a record even Colt Brennan can't claim ... yet ... but more importantly redeemed himself, his life and his relationship with June Jones ...

wreck . . . it was just *unbelievable*," McKnight says. "The way he handled Rolo, Timmy, Pisa . . . everything was just over the top. Then, for us to beat BYU . . . *wow* doesn't say enough."

"I don't think anyone who went through that season thinks otherwise," says Rolovich, who today is a starting quarterback in the Arena Football League. "Anyone who was there will tell you they were touched in some way spiritually by that whole season. I'm not religious. But I went from hell on earth to heaven on earth, all in a single year. Whoever is running the show up in the sky knows what He's doing, and that year, He touched all the lives in the state of Hawai'i.

"I know how this sounds, but it's like June's accident . . . was no accident," Rolo says. "We were all *blessed* to be a part of it, as crazy as that sounds."

Chapter 29

THE HIGHEST PLACE ON EARTH

Beaufort, S.C., is a sleepy seaside town, where Spanish moss beards the oak trees like aging grandfathers and fresh ocean breezes whisper through what locals refer to as "the low country." On a summer night, a galaxy of lightning bugs can be seen against the black pine trees. If it reminds you of the perfect setting in *The Prince of Tides,* that's because, well, *it is.*

Visitors come to Beaufort to relax in the warm embrace of its elegant waterfront charm, quaint shops and historic homes. Career soldiers live and work around the nearby Marine-machine of Parris Island, which is how Rene and Annetta Lelie — parents of Ashley — arrived in this most unlikely place.

On April 20, 2002, relatives and friends of the Lelie family traversed from Missouri, California, Georgia — *even Japan* — to watch and wait for Ashley to be drafted into the tight-knit fraternity of the National Football League. The draft, viewed around the world on ESPN, has become a most-American rite of passage for college players en route to what they hope will be professional stardom.

Superstar Ashley Lelie

COURTESY ASHLEY LELIE FAMILY

Every pick, every player, is built up and torn down like a roadside South Carolina fireworks stand. Ashley was no exception. He had been shuttled around to predraft appearances in New Orleans and Atlanta and surrounded by supermodels and agents. Websites trumpeted his triumphs: With the click of a mouse, you could learn that his thighs were smaller than his shoe size; that his total body fat was less than a cup of milk; or that he could run 40 yards faster than you can pluck the morning newspaper from your driveway.

On draft day, however, the people who really *knew* Ashley were in the makeshift room of his parent's garage, basically an add-on to their small split-level home. There was a couch and a bed where Ashley or the other kids slept when home. On one end was an old big-screen TV. The NFL draft was a great excuse to regale as a family. Laughter bounced off the walls and down the hallways. Childhood memories were as real as the simmering barbecue chicken and hot dogs that Rene was commandeering on the grill. Anetta threw extra love in the macaroni and spaghetti, and paper plates were piled high with Doritos, chips and salsa and cake.

The phone rang. It was the Denver Broncos. Simultaneously, NFL commissioner Paul Tagliabue took the microphone on ESPN.

"And with the 19th pick of the first round, Denver selects Ashley Lelie, wide receiver, University of Hawai'i. . . ."

Ashley Lelie had just become the *only first-round draft pick* in Hawai'i football history. Annetta began to scream — it was her proudest day since her wedding to Rene — and she had been predicting for *three months* that her son would be drafted by the Broncos.

Ashley just stared at the TV screen, numb with disbelief.

The eyes of Ashley Lelie have always been a telescope to his soul.

As a boy, his world was a lunar landscape, not visible to the naked eye. He spent his days probing, wondering, *seeking,* absorbing facts and ideas as quickly as his brain could *discover* them. His dad describes him as a "typical boy," but there was nothing *typical* about his skinny son, who wore thick glasses and engaged books with a fervor most kids reserve for an ice cream cone.

Ashley loved the Cub Scouts...

He was a Cub Scout who knew how to be quiet without being told. He was obedient, helpful and — most of all — shy. *How things worked was never enough, he also needed to know why.* This required that he ceaselessly take things apart and put them back together. In his spare time, he often would prop his chin in his little hands and stare, stare, stare at the tireless efforts of the ants in his ant farm. Their dogged work ethic amazed him.

Horsing around in the Lelie household

Other boys were *dangerous.* He was *compassionate;* rather than dissect the frog from science class, he was more likely to take it home and set it free. Other boys picked fights and found themselves in the principal's office. Ashley picked the hardest classes and found himself on the principal's honor roll. His father, a Marine, disciplined Ashley and his younger brother Justin not with spankings but with *push-ups* — with the other sibling *on their back.* The boys cried just the same.

... but he loved his dad and brother more

Ashley enjoyed his three younger siblings. Justin was his best friend. They were protective of their little sisters, LaShanda and Ciara. Rene's career in the Marine Corps required the family to move often, roughly every three years. "We never got too close to anyone, because we always knew we're moving," Ashley says. "For the most part, it was just me and Justin."

When you're as shy as Ashley, this worked to his advantage, as the family bounced around from Los Angeles, where Ashley was born, to Beaufort the first time, where Justin was born, to Louisiana, to Hawai'i the first time, back to Orange County, then back to Hawai'i, where Ashley went to high school.

One Sunday afternoon, when Ashley was 8 years old, he remembers watching Barry Sanders with his dad and brother on a TV so old it had knobs the size of golf balls. Barry was *so little,* but he could run *so fast,* and he didn't run like anyone else. Barry ran with his eyes as wide as saucers, and in a maze of giants, he danced around like one of Ashley's ants who already knew where *he was going.* Little Ashley was intrigued how Barry seemed to *figure it out as he ran.*

He turned to his dad and pointed to the TV. *"Pops, I want to do that,"* he said, mesmerized.

"You're kidding me, right son?" Rene said with a tiny smile. Marines are no strangers to pain — even the great Barry Sanders got tackled now and then, and unless you're Richard Simmons, there's nothing fun about being on the bottom of 1,200 pounds of sweaty men. Rene thought his

boy was more suited to building a rocket from scratch and landing it on the moon than putting his frail body in harm's way over a football.

"I'm going to play football," Ashley declared, just as Barry Sanders scampered into the end zone.

"Oh my," said TV announcer Dick Enberg.

Ashley stared at Barry Sanders and Jerry Rice on TV the same way a boy looks at a great span of bridge that disappears into a morning mist, hoping to discover what possibilities might exist on the other side.

It hurts to be Barry Sanders, especially when you don't know how to make the other guys miss. Ashley was in middle school in Tustin, Calif., but he might just as well have been in hell, for every time he touched the ball, somebody rocked his world. Barry could disappear like smoke through his opponents' fingers; Ashley just wanted to disappear, period, which is what he did after a few weeks of punishment. He had taken football, which counted as PE, so when report cards came out, he was shocked to see he had an F. This is how his parents found out he quit.

We'll never know how many push-ups or sit-ups that cost him. "Son, it's going to be hard," Rene encouraged. "You *have to figure it out.*"

That he could understand. Ashley and Justin had always been great basketball players and both were fleet of foot, frequently winning track meets and high jumps with ease. The nuances of football eluded him, though, until Ashley discovered that if somebody would just throw it up in the sky, he could dance like Barry and run like Jerry and go up there and pull it down like it was a pumpkin.

The Marines moved the family back to Hawai'i, where Ashley and his siblings learned to love *poi,* to take their shoes off at the front door and to not overdress for anything, including church. "In *our* culture," smiles Annetta, "you get *dressed up* for church." This meant stockings and dresses and hats for the girls and ties and three-piece suits for the boys. Steaming in the Hawai'i humidity in their Sunday clothes, they arrived at the City of Refuge Church. There they were greeted by men in

shorts and flip-flops and women in muumuus with so many color combinations it would have been startling on a tropical bird.

It's safe to say that the family must have wondered what everyone was thinking. It was here, however, where Rene and Annetta grounded their children in faith and where Ashley learned to exalt his Maker. "We told him that whenever he scores a touchdown, he better thank God first before he *thinks* about doing some silly little dance," Annetta says.

Ashley took Hawaiian history at Radford High School and made the All-Star team his junior year, only to almost throw away his senior year when he had his first brush with trouble. After a couple of freshmen harassed some seniors, those same seniors — including Ashley — took matters into their own hands. They wrapped their tormentors in duct tape and smothered their jock straps with Ben Gay.

"It burned their little *thingies* up," explains Annetta, giggling like only a mother can, perhaps at the realization she just said the word *"thingies."* "Coach got mad and kicked Ashley and the other boys off the team and told them they'd never play football again. But then the athletic director said, 'No, we'll just suspend them for two games.'"

Ashley (upper right) at his high school prom

Radford lost all nine games Ashley played as a senior. Worse, the team only threw the ball to Ashley *nine times* — and *that* burned up *his little thingy.* So he got a job at Duke's as a waiter and walked on at the University of Hawai'i, where he was more excited about being accepted to the school of engineering than he was about playing football. "I'm a student-athlete," he reassured his parents, "not an athlete-student."

Hawai'i lost all 12 games his freshman year. In Fred von Appen's various offenses, receivers were about as useless as a screen door on a submarine. The Marines moved Ashley's family back to Beaufort, and he sorely missed his family, especially Justin. Annetta would take all but $100 from her paychecks at the hospital where she worked and send the rest to her homesick son, along with special care packages that included momma's home-cooked food. Ashley rode to school on his beat-up moped, worked a second job as a part-time security officer — and barely survived.

Ashley's beat-up moped, which is how he scooted back and forth to classes

When June Jones arrived, Lelie was understandably skeptical, to say the least. "June stood up there and said we would lead the nation in receiving," Ashley says. "We were 0-12, and we had heard it all before." When Ashley learned more about Jones and his offense — and the fact that he had coached Barry Sanders — his interest was piqued. It only took a few practices before Ashley and Channon were June Jones believers.

"We barely had our basic reads down," Ashley says, "and we were *killing* the defense."

Harris played better — and more — in 1999, but in the week of the O'ahu Bowl, he ripped into Ashley for not realizing his own potential. "We got into it," Lelie says. "I didn't have a scholarship at that point. I couldn't eat with the team. I was worrying about my rent and other stuff. My focus wasn't on football. Channon really got in my face and demanded that I apply myself."

Ashley with best-friend Channon Harris

June rewarded Ashley with a scholarship the next season. Finally, Lelie could see where this bridge just might lead.

"Trust me" is something June Jones tells his players often, a fact they all usually have to figure out for themselves. Ashley remembers his first real "trust-me" moment with June during the 3-9 season of 2000.

"To be honest, this play sticks in my mind more than any other," Ashley says today. "It was the 90 Switch. June said they would line up in cover 2, and that I needed to take the deep post and I'd be wide open. I ran the post, the middle of the field parted, and I was *so* open that I was surprised when the ball got there. I dropped it. From that point forward, I believed in everything June said."

June believed in Ashley, too.

In 2000, Lelie led the Warriors in receptions (74), receiving yards (1,110) and touchdowns (11). In 2001, he finished second in the nation in receiving yards (1,713), 11th in receptions (84) and 12th in scoring (114 points). He still owns the Hawai'i records for career receiving yards and touchdowns, yards in a season and touchdowns receiving in a season.

"There was nothing that could have prepared me for the NFL better than

It's hard to wrestle a football away from Ashley Lelie, even on the sidelines

Despite his years in the NFL Ashley Lelie still sweeps the floor and washes dishes whenever he returns back home to the slow pace of Beaufort, perhaps as Rene and Annetta's not-so-subtle way of reminding their son to remember how he got there.

His brother Justin remains his best friend, as does his old teammate Channon Harris, who calls Ashley's parents "mom and dad" and shares Lelie's condo in Hawai'i. He bought Annetta a new Dodge Magnum and spoils his sisters with laptops and iPods. In the mall, when fans approach, the soft-spoken and humble Ashley often denies he is who he is, preferring to remain anonymous and enjoy time with his family.

Ashley wonders what might have become of Hawai'i football without June Jones.

"It feels so good to be part of the framework of what this whole program has become," Ashley says softly. "But every guy in that program better remember this all started with Coach Jones. He told me my first year under him that I had a chance to play in the NFL. It's hard to see it, or believe it, until it actually happens to you."

June Jones and the Run 'n' Shoot," he says. "I was always open. Go back and look at the film. The defense could play man-free, cover 2, cover 3, it didn't matter. Man, do I miss that.

"June teaches receivers to read coverages, then run to space," Ashley adds. "When I got to the NFL, I was shocked. My reads were tougher in college than in the pros. In the NFL, I usually have one pre-snap read, then I run my route. With June, you keep reading and changing the route until the ball hits your hands."

When Lelie thought about leaving to the NFL after his junior year, he was surprised when June made no attempt to talk him into staying. "He was totally selfless," says Ashley. "June told me I'd be picked in the first round and that I needed to go. He was honest. It was sad in a way, but I knew my time had come."

Ashley with mother Annetta during his time with the Denver Broncos

Ashley with his father Renee

"Without June, I'd be sitting in an office somewhere, looking out the window as a mechanical engineer, wondering what might have been. Thanks to him, I get to play a game for my life's occupation. I'm living my dream. I owe it all to him."

So it's OK to admit that you don't know where you're going sometimes, especially when the path winds you through an inadequate array of choices and circumstances. The NFL — or any other of life's destinations — might require a bus, a bridge or some other failed journey before it culminates, as with Ashley, into an alchemy of hope.

The lesson, perhaps, is to keep crying, *"Here I am! Here I am!"* until life shows up.

Beaufort might indeed be low country. But when all the Lelies are gathered here, judging from the smiles around the modest table and the clinking of spoons inside the bowls of momma's jaw-dropping seafood gumbo, it's still the highest place on earth.

Lelie uses every inch of his six-foot-three-inch frame to pluck this ball from the air against the New England Patriots

Chapter 30
BREAKING THE CHAINS THAT BIND

The trek from the Hawai'i locker room to the practice field is like a procession of circus elephants: some big, some small, helmets and shoulder pads in one hand, the sound of cleats clicking on asphalt until they hit the damp grass field. Small talk is the usual fare, except for the occasional wisecrack or practical joke; anything to ignore the soreness and fatigue brought on by yesterday's practice and last night's studies — or worse, parties or the bouncy coeds who won't leave you alone.

Far away from the bright lights and roaring fans of Aloha Stadium, practice — rain or shine — is where metal is forged. It's a mental push each day to focus, to block out what's not right in your life and to be the athlete that you keep telling yourself you can be.

Despite their hulking frames, the mental makeup of the college athlete is fragile. The young players have to be better than a very good high school player to get here, even as a walk-on. You are now usually removed from the comforts of home. You are still faced with the challenges of acne and hormones and anger and frustration, only you're learning to deal with it by yourself. You are choosing friends and making choices, some of which might affect you for a lifetime. You are fighting for a roster spot. The weak generally weed out themselves; June Jones expects you to spend *at least* six hours a day on football. If you're doing that *and* passing your classes, you have hefty lifestyle choices to consider, to say the very least.

Juniors and seniors have the distinct advantage of experience and time. Their bodies have grown. Their true personalities are catching up with

Nobody chooses to draw air into their own lungs. Nobody decides who they are or where they're born or what condition they're born with. June believes that it's up to each individual to take what God gives them and find a way to win. Your eyes see only what you want them to see.

their swollen muscles. Their inner strength — their *sheer will* — has begun to develop. The world is opening up. Better yet, their *minds* are opening up. Physical boundaries can be stretched in the same proportion as the brain's ability to accept them; and make no mistake, your place as an alpha male amidst a pack of Hawai'i Warriors is in direct correlation to your physical and mental staying power.

So it's easy to overlook the guy in the wheelchair by the fence as you push past him and onto the field to stretch. Curious fans, the groupies, the hangers-on, the weirdos somehow always find their way to practice to gawk and stare: the guy with the same t-shirt every day or the pennant you've signed 15 times already. But the guy in the wheelchair — he's different. He was invited by other players that he met in a class and isn't about to go away.

He's there almost every day. As you glance at him out of the corner of your eye, you try to feel *sorry* for whatever happened to him. But let's face it, when your abdomen and hamstrings are still screaming and burning from yesterday's up-downs, it's hard to empathize with a guy who can't even *run*.

He's actually lucky, you joke to yourself. That's your way of deflecting reality, of simply *not dealing with it,* so that you can get on with the task at hand, which is limbering your sleek, muscled frame for another day of athletic prowess that hopefully, come Saturday night, will enable you to bring tens of thousands of people to their collective feet in a single gasp.

When God has blessed you with soft hands or supple limbs; when you are fleet as a deer and strong as an ox and can force another man to do something *against his will,* why waste your time on a guy who can't button his own shirt? So, if you don't avoid him somehow altogether, you grace him with a pat that he can't even feel on your way onto the practice field or maybe on your way out. Better yet, *bless him* with your autograph one more time, just to show him how much you *really* care.

Then you'll make the same trek back to the locker room, where in a matter of minutes the pounding sound of hip-hop or reggae will be bouncing off the walls; you'll be bitching about the lack of soap in the showers, and somebody will be complaining that the deodorant in their locker is missing. You will get dressed, grab your books and head off to a class that you can hardly stay awake for, all paid for by the great State of Hawai'i, simply because you know how to catch or throw or protect or defend an oval ball.

He stares longingly at his heroes until they all disappear. He doesn't hate them for not understanding him. On the contrary, he is happy each day just to have shared vicariously in their strength, their laughter, from afar. Ah, the unmitigated *joy* of *being able* to run!

He wonders how it must feel to be tackled, so hard you *can feel it in your spine,* to run so fast that the wind dances across your cheeks and your feet barely touch the ground. In his imagination, he has winged feet, spinning through defenders, himself a mighty Warrior.

These are his dreams, and they make him gurgle with glee as he spins in his wheelchair. It bumps across the uneven grass and finally onto the smoother sidewalk. He slowly whirrs off toward classes of his own, for he knows nothing in his life will come for free. Yet, in a world where it seems that it's all people ever do, he is determined to not be judged by these chains that bind him — *this chair..*

If you haven't already had a *thalamotomy*, then drop to your knees right now and pray that you never will. That's because it's a *destructive* procedure that's *done on purpose,* and not to a knee or a hip or some other reasonably painful place.

It's done to your brain, where a tiny area called the thalamus controls

COURTESY BRIAN KAJIYAMA

The remarkable Brian Kajiyama, whom June Jones would eventually appoint as a graduate assistant coach

your involuntary movements. Generally, the person is awake during the surgery, but the scalp area where instruments are inserted is numbed with local anesthetic. The surgeon inserts a hollow probe through a small hole drilled in the skull to the target location. Liquid nitrogen, an extremely cold substance, is circulated inside the probe. The cold probe destroys the targeted brain tissue. The probe is then removed, and the wound is closed.

Surgery on one side of the brain affects the opposite side of the body. If you have tremors in your right hand, for instance, the left side of your brain will be treated. The procedure can be repeated on the other side of the brain if needed, but it greatly increases the risk of speech and cognitive problems after surgery.

But if, like Brian Kajiyama, you have cerebral palsy, and your brain is firing nonstop signals down your left arm so fast that it flies about like an unattended water hose at full spigot, and *both* of your tiny parents can't hold you down, it's a *relief* when they tell you that simply by drilling a few holes in your head they can make it stop.

On July 18, 1976, at the old Kapi'olani Women's and Children's Hospital, the umbilical cord of unborn Brian Kajiyama wrapped around his neck and choked out the oxygen to his brain for approximately 15 minutes, resulting in cerebal palsy. His parents, Bert and Grace, both of Japanese descent, were merely happy to have him alive.

It takes only minutes for this to happen to an otherwise healthy, normal child.

The medication they pumped into his skull ensured that he would always have a bald spot the size of a half-dollar on the left-hand side.

"Cerebral palsy" is a term used to describe a group of chronic disorders impairing control of movement. The disorders are caused by faulty development of or damage to motor areas in the brain that disrupts the brain's ability to control movement and posture.

Symptoms of cerebral palsy include difficulty with fine motor tasks (such as writing or using scissors); difficulty maintaining balance or walking; and involuntary movements.

It is estimated that there are 500,000 people in America that have some form of cerebral palsy. Each year 8,000 infants and nearly 1,500 preschool-age children are diagnosed with it.

By his second month, Brian was in the Easter Seals Stimulation Program, where they learned he was of normal intellect, to the relief of his parents. His mother began reading to him daily; his father would sing him to sleep at night.

By age 2, Brian had his first wheelchair; by age 10, he had his first *motorized* wheelchair, which he promptly drove knee-deep into the mud under the banyan trees at the Honolulu Zoo.

He was attending Kailua Intermediate School the first time he was laughed at, by a group of kids who used words such as "retarded," "stupid" and "mental," in spite of the fact that he was none of those. Smaller children, he learned, will blurt out anything. Humor became his coping skill at an early age. "I must be beautiful," he joked. "Everyone's staring at me."

Academics quickly became a way to prove his self-worth. Despite being rejected by "normal" schools, Brian and his parents demanded he be allowed to attend them and to be judged only by his test scores.

His parents added a fully accessible room to their three-bedroom house in Kailua to accommodate their son. From an early age, sports became his love, and Hawai'i football memorabilia and Michael Jordan posters soon framed his walls. Brian grew up watching football with his dad, a bespectacled man whose typical attire consists of an aloha shirt and slacks and who was a role model for his son. In his spare time, Brian worked on his Topps baseball card collection, like any other boy.

When Brian was 7, his mother gave birth to twin sisters. Together they formed a tight family unit, one that routinely tailgated in the Aloha Stadium parking lot while downing huge bowls of Zippy's chili.

Brian dreamed of becoming the scrambling Raphel Cherry or making circus catches look easy like Walter Murray.

His "Rudy" moment occurred after he graduated from Kailua High School and was accepted at Hawai'i. To avoid stares and gestures, Brian would hang out by himself by Kennedy Theater, away from the hustle and bustle and where he could read and study alone.

After his first thalamotomy failed and his left arm continued to thrash wildly, Brian's mind became his own worst enemy. "I was a mess," he says. "I felt that I had *no* hope. Here I had gone through a major surgery, and it had failed. I was a failure. I felt God had failed me. I actually hoped I would die during the second operation."

The night before the second surgery, Brian's Uncle Nilt — Nilton Matayoshi — prayed at his bedside. His prayers were answered: The surgery succeeded and Brian's saga would continue.

It's impossible to know if any Hawai'i football players dropped some change in the red Salvation Army kettle on the week before Christmas in 1998 outside Daiei, the Japanese supermarket in Kailua, where a boy in a wheelchair had volunteered to sit for three hours a night ringing a bell. But if they didn't, they should have.

You see, football players laud themselves on overused clichés like *"heart"* and *"you gotta play hurt"* and *"put some tape on it and go back in,"* all facts that young Brian knew well from his years of attending UH games with his dad. His heroes, he thought, would have respected his willingness to "get back out there," just barely a month removed from having *two* metal rods stuck in his brain — even if it only meant ringing this bell at each *shh-hhhhhhpppppp* of sliding glass doors to get people to hand him their spare change. With each *kerplunk* of coin, Brian swelled with pride; for this year, some family who hadn't planned on one just might have a Christmas.

He had read newspaper articles where coaches always talked about *the little things* and how they can make a difference in somebody else's life. He had read Mark Twain, too, and believed him when he wrote that "kindness is the language which the deaf can hear and the blind can see."

The sound of the bell seemed to jingle right down *through* the taped-up holes in his head, but hey, gimme a break — *he was out there,* taking his reps, and he was *happy and excited* to be there.

COURTESY BRIAN KAJIYAMA

"Humor is my greatest coping skill," Kajiyama says. *"I have so much to be thankful for."*

The class was Kinesiology and Leisure Science

or adapted physical education for students with disabilities. Dr. James Little, who taught the liberal studies class, had encouraged Brian — whose study emphasis had become advocacy for persons with disabilities — to take the course.

Brian rolled in like he did in any other class. Suddenly the room darkened as some very large guys in HAWAI'I FOOTBALL t-shirts and shorts filled the doorway, temporarily blocking the light from the hallway as they rustled in and jostled for seats.

Jeff Ulbrich. Brian's heart skipped a beat. *Forty-four was his hero!*

Then came Kaulana Noa. He couldn't believe it!

Are you kidding me?

Dedrick "Dee" Miller. Is this Christmas? Brian almost whimpered aloud!

La'anui Correa. Holy crap!

He couldn't contain himself, and he must've been obvious.

Ulbrich made eye contact and nodded in his direction. *Jeff Ulbrich nodded at me!* Brian nearly peed in his pants.

Omigosh! The Warriors!

This was the greatest day of his life. Brian couldn't wait to tell Brent Yoshikawa and Daniel Schmidt, his best friends.

It wouldn't take long before the players quickly realized that the smartest guy in the room was in the wheelchair; all of their 40-yard-dash times and remarkable bench presses *combined* weren't going to change the standard grading curve that was being set by little Brian Kajiyama.

His mobility was challenged by the chair, yes — but his mind could slip and move like Muhammad Ali.

"Hey B," Ulbrich grunted one day, smiling, "try not to do so good on the exams, OK? You're killing me. I need to *pass* this class!"

Kajiyama was impressed at how hard the players worked in the classroom — and how much they were *just like him.* Brian began to scribble notes to the guys on his steno pad; a rapport was born and a bond began.

"Do you ever go to games?" Dee Miller asked him.

"Sometimes," Brian scratched back. "If I'm not busy studying."

"B, you gotta come see us play, bro," Miller said. "I'll sign you up for tickets. Don't worry about it."

A few games later, Miller inquired what time Brian came to school. Brian scribbled back furiously on his steno pad. "I come to school at 7 a.m. . . . . my mom drops me off before her work. . . ."

Miller burst into a smile. "Listen, if *we* have to practice that early, then so can *you.* I'll see you at practice tomorrow, awright?"

Brian nodded. *They accept me for me.*

In his emails, Brian had always included a quote by Dr. Seuss: *"Be who you are and say what you feel; those who mind don't matter, and those who matter don't mind."* He so loved his Warriors — *in a box, with a fox, on a train, in the rain* — and now, they *loved him back.*

He will never forget his first Warriors' practice. He sat just outside the black chain-link fence that circles the practice field. The early morning Hawai'i sun warmed his cheeks a cherry red, but it was no match for the pulsing glow that radiated from deep within his heart.

▼▼▼▼▼▼▼▼▼▼▼▼▼▼▼

There is no smell sweeter than an official, 100 percent heavy nylon, rib knit jersey with dazzle shoulders, sleeves and sides. As he inhaled, it occurred to him that nothing really mattered at that moment outside of the people in that huddle or how they made him feel.

▲▲▲▲▲▲▲▲▲▲▲▲▲▲▲

lungs. Nobody decides who they are or where they're born or what condition they're *born with.* June believes that it's up to each individual to take what God gives them and *find a way to win.* Your eyes see only what you want them to see.

It's a coach's job to bathe in other's dreams and teach them how to take chances, accept challenges and help others meet their goals. So when June discovered all the random acts of kindness that were going on around him, he began to pay closer attention. Funny, though — they weren't directed *toward* Brian, they were being performed *by* Brian. June began to enjoy the aura of the kid with the undying spirit and tireless optimism.

You always hear about random acts of kindness, but you seldom witness someone *do* them. Talk of karma is everywhere, but how often we forget that it begins with a selfless act. When was the last time you paid for the person behind you at the Taco Bell or swept a neighbor's driveway? Or fixed a friend's bicycle, when your own feet will never pedal one?

Don't talk about it, be *about it,* Brian always heard the coaches saying at practice.

He was just taking them at their word, that's all.

Hawai'i coaches learned more about Brian Kajiyama when a classmate began filming him on the practice field for a documentary after witnessing a presentation Brian did in school. When secondary coach Rich Miano relayed to June Jones what was happening with the guy in the wheelchair, June's interest peaked.

This is because the more June listened to what his coaches were telling him, the more he began to wonder if, in fact, the *toughest* guy on the field wasn't *inside* the fence but *outside.* Each day as he stared across the field at Brian, June wasn't looking at the paint on the car; he was testing what was *under the hood.* Nobody chooses to draw air into their own

In the days before the '99 O'ahu Bowl, Dan Robinson had the wheels and seat stolen from his bicycle just outside the Hawai'i locker room.

"Why don't you just send the o-line after the thief?" Brian texted him.

Robinson's response reflected the character of his own turn-the-other-cheek values.

"Brian, I believe that the person who stole from me probably needed the wheels more than me," Dan replied.

Unbeknownst to Dan, Brian began calling local bike shops. He couldn't afford much, he had little to give, but he would offer up *all that he had.* He was pleasantly shocked when the owner of the McCully Bike Shop told him to bring in Dan's bike and that he would rectify the problem *as a gift to Brian for making the effort.*

Brian and his mom showed up at Dan's house to get the bike, where they met Robinson's stunned parents, who were in Hawai'i for the bowl game. Amidst the protests of the Robinsons, Brian's mom loaded up the bike and away they went. For an hour and a half they waited outside McCully's, when — *presto* — the bike was delivered, good as new.

And that's how the great Dan Robinson made it to practice each day before he laid a whupping on the Oregon State Beavers.

Safety David "Happy" Gilmore was the first player to ever invite Brian "inside the fence," during spring practice in 2001. "C'mon B, get your butt in here and let's go to practice," Gilmore said. Brian needed no further invitation; he put his wheelchair in overdrive and hummed right past the sign that read, "CLOSED TO MEDIA AND PUBLIC."

"Just be alert, OK?" Gilmore instructed. Brian loved his newfound freedom. He zipped around like a kid in a candy store. The day came when he noticed a change in the way the coaches spoke to him. He was no longer a visitor. After *repetition, repetition, repetition,* he learned where to park and where not to, especially after a few errant throws caromed off his chair. "Don't get hit, B!" June would yell, laughing at the kid's moxy.

Of all the players, kickers and punters intrigued him most. Their game was purely mental. They were required to do one thing only and do it right — hopefully every time. Talk about pressure. He loved watching the zeal and intensity behind their work ethic as they broke down each individual movement into a rhythm, like a golf swing. He could grasp the mechanics of the process; it reminded him of rehab.

Before Matt McBriar would become an All-Conference punter or find current NFL fame with the Dallas Cowboys, he was just a native Australian kicker who left his country to come to Hawai'i in the hopes of playing American football. Few of the players could understand McBriar's

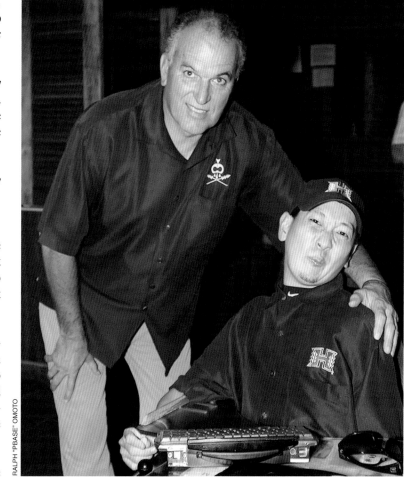

RALPH "PBASE" OMOTO

Brian with June, whom he never guessed would one day be his boss

thick cockney accent, but Brian's steno pad gave him a distinct deciphering advantage.

Brian remembers the first day McBriar positioned himself behind Hawai'i's first-team long snapper. The ball whistled back, zipped through his hands, and nailed him right in the nuts.

In case you're wondering — *MMMMmmmppphhhh!* with an Australian accent means the exact same thing as it does in American English.

Brian and Matt became fast friends. They went to movies and spent hours afterward discussing themes and plots and characters. Eventually, Matt developed a postgame ritual of seeking out Brian before he would board the team bus.

"How'd I hit it today, mate?" he'd ask.

"GREAT JOB," Brian would type.

"See you at practice, mate!"

Practice, yes, practice — inside *the fence.*

Something was wrong, evidenced by the way trainer Eric Okazaki was acting. "Hey B, you need to make sure you see Coach at the end of practice today," Eric told him. This was cause for consternation. Perhaps he'd overwheeled his boundaries. The entire practice, his stomach churned.

What did I do wrong?

When the horn sounded to mark the end of practice, June, the coaches and the players all gathered at midfield. "Brian!" Coach Jones yelled. "Get over here!"

He wheeled cautiously toward them. With no warning, June began to speak — not to him, but *to the team.*

"Fellas," June said. "For those of you who don't know yet, this is Brian Kajiyama. . . ."

Brian sat in disbelief as the head coach began to rattle off things about him that even he had almost forgotten. June knew his story, his background, his challenges, his surgery . . . eventually, it all just became a blur.

"Listen men, I need you to welcome Brian into our *ohana.*"

He paused, and Okazaki handed him a jersey: number 31.

June shook it out and held it up for the world to see. "KAJIYAMA" read the nameplate on the back.

The players gathered around his wheelchair, arms outstretched. "Kajiyama on three!" someone shouted.

"ONE . . . TWO . . . THREE . . . KAJIYAMA!" they roared.

There is no smell sweeter than an official, 100 percent heavy nylon, rib knit jersey with dazzle shoulders, sleeves and sides. As he inhaled, it occurred to him that nothing really mattered at that moment outside of the people in that huddle or how they made him feel.

Faith, like the roots of a tiny mustard seed, can move mountains.

Brian Kajiyama had made the cut.

He, too, *was a Warrior now.*

Courtesy Jeremy Spear

Chapter 31

POLYNESIAN POWER

It's amazing how often the phone rings — and the characters you meet — when you survive a "fatal" car accident, win two out of three bowl games — *beat Alabama!* — push your team into a Top 25 ranking and have your quarterback chasing the all-time NCAA passing threshold.

Times had certainly changed in the football office at the University of Hawai'i. It was no longer uncommon for June Jones to be greeted by a representative from the offices of the Hawai'i governor or the Honolulu mayor, to open a letter from the White House, read about his team in *USA Today* or take phone calls from ESPN, NFL Films or HBO's *Inside the NFL.*

June was intrigued, however, the day he got a call from Jeremy Spear, an independent filmmaker from New York. This was not your everyday sports journalist. Spear didn't care about Timmy Chang's records or Hawai'i's amazing turnaround or even the mighty Run 'n' Shoot. He wanted to chronicle the passion of the Polynesian people via a "coming-of-age" documentary on American Samoan football players.

"I'm thinking about a journey-into-manhood story," explained Spear, "a story of a couple young Samoans who are sustaining the warrior traditions through the discovery of American football."

If he wants a journey, chuckled Jones, *we'll show him a journey.*

Before you could say Pago Pago (pronounced *pango-pango*), Jones and assistant coach Rich Miano had Spear and his movie crew on a small plane fluttering over expansive ocean. Like modern-day missionaries, they were en route to American Samoa, a string of six South Pacific islands where Spear hoped to unlock the mysteries and uncover the secrets of the many Polynesian players who were now routinely filling up Hawai'i's football roster.

Hawaii standout and future NFL star Isaac Sapoaga ... literally the poster-boy for Polynesian Power

Artists *love* to throw around words like "passion" and "journey" and "discovery," but as the one-strip runway appeared in the middle of the lush, tropical island of Tutuila in the middle of the sea and the brown-skinned natives of Samoa flocked to greet the incoming aircraft — waving their arms, smiling and cheering — Spear began to feel that this experience would surpass any cliché.

Always comfortable around Polynesians, the movie director had a rush of anticipation for what lay just ahead.

Thus the journey began.

Ironically, Spear's fortuitous route to finding himself on an airplane with a couple of Hawai'i football coaches was about as auspicious as his chances of becoming an award-winning filmmaker.

A graduate of Yale, Spear had played second base on his Ivy League baseball championship team. This was before he became — *are you kidding me?* — a sculptor/painter/*shortstop* for seven years while living in the Big Apple. Yes, *shortstop:* Spear's fast-pitch softball skills had taken him all around the world.

COURTESY JEREMY SPEAR

Filmmaker Jeremy Spear

"I made art for years after college," Spear says, though he's unclear if he's taking about his painting, his sculpting, or his ability to turn a base hit line drive into a double play. "Then I had this huge leap of faith to make a film. It made so much sense to me — to be able to bridge that gap in my life . . . I don't why it took me so long to figure it out."

Artists can be so (sigh) . . . *abstract.* His first film was *Fastpitch,* which landed him on the *Today Show* with Matt Lauer, and he received critical acclaim from the *New York Times,* the *New York Post, New York Newsday,* the *Los Angeles Times,* the *Chicago Sun-Times* and NBC film critic Jeffrey Lyons.

Now if you're wondering what all of this has to do with the price of *alaisa* (rice) in Samoa, you must see for yourself what June saw: an incredible means by which to pay tribute to the Polynesian culture while promoting the University of Hawai'i and his own philosophy far outside the conventional boundaries of a normal football program. Spear, to June, was one enormous recruiting, networking and *relationship* opportunity, and he wasn't about to let it pass.

June's foresight — behind Spear's talented lens — was about to raise awareness of Hawai'i football to levels no one could have imagined. With programs like Nebraska, Michigan State, BYU and USC all competing for Polynesian players, June had come across a novel way to offset the powerful recruiting budgets of his irritating opponents.

Leave it to June Jones to figure out how to turn a documentary into a formidable, long-running media weapon that would confound and outfox his adversaries while building Hawai'i into the largest Polynesian power on the planet.

Hawai'i, New Zealand and Easter Island mark the outer corners of what is called the Polynesian Triangle, which encloses roughly 10 million square miles of water. Courageous open-water canoe migration settled the Polynesian islands over a 3,000-year period, and the entire region enjoys a rich warrior culture.

Jones and Miano did their best to bring Spear and his team up to speed. "It doesn't matter where the Polynesian kids come from," June told them, "because they've been told they're not as good as the American players. So every time we tee it up, it's also about proving *we are something special.*"

Miano explained that now *two-thirds* of the Hawai'i roster was comprised of Polynesian kids, because "we've made it our backbone in recruiting. . . . We recruit out of American Samoa, we recruit from Hawai'i, and we want all of the Polynesian kids on the mainland to come back home and play for us."

Spear chose Isaac Sopoaga and Pisa Tinoisamoa to storyline his film, perhaps because their upbringings perfectly contrast the routes most Samoan athletes traverse to get to college and, hopefully, the NFL. Isaac

June Jones speaks before a hushed audience at one of Samoa's open-air schools

hails from a remote village deep within Samoa, where his father is a speaking chief. Tinoisamoa, whose estranged father was born and still resides in Samoa, was raised by his mother in San Diego and was forced to overcome severe financial and legal hardships.

The result would be a splendid cinematic metaphor by which to illustrate the impact of colliding cultures on the Hawai'i football program — and why the Warriors, including their mainland imports, draw such great pride from their Samoan roots.

There are only two flights a week into Samoa, which explains why everyone goes to the airport when a plane arrives. "The whole village comes to celebrate the landing of the plane," says Miano. "Almost everybody has a relative or friend who is either leaving or coming back, and they celebrate." The "airport," it should be noted, is down a gravel road, including everything from baggage claim to immigration.

There are roughly 500,000 Samoans in the whole world, and only half of those have ever been exposed to American football. A little more than 60,000 live here in a place small enough to have one zip code: 96799. Spear watched carefully how the locals received Jones and Miano. "The coaches were like someone from a foreign land with a magical presence," he says. "It was obvious they knew these men could help their villages, their children and *their* children, and that football is the conduit for that to happen."

When Jones spoke before an open-air school (the only kind of school there is in Samoa), hundreds of students hung on his every word in the 90-degree heat. He immediately called upon their pride and honor. "It's my pleasure to be here," June said, as the children sat at perfect attention, beaming. "I think that in order to be the best, you have to have something *inside* you that makes you *want* to be great. I played college football four years and never played a game. Yet I made it to pro football because I was willing to *work harder* than everyone else, *not* because I was better than everyone else."

"You could have heard a pin drop," says Spear. The director made certain to pan the crowd as Rich Miano and June strode from the room. The kids were awestruck, the way American teens would stare at, well, an Eminem, or a 50-Cent.

"The first thing you notice," says Spear, "is the respect and humility these kids have, followed by their sheer athletic ability. All the Polynesian kids have a kind of showmanship to their physical prowess, whether it's fire-knife dancing or climbing trees to grab a coconut, and I don't say that with any disrespect. It's not unusual to see a 300-pound kid dancing with extraordinary skill. They are *athletes*. Then when they speak to you, they're so humble, it shocks you."

The Samoans call it *fa'a Samoa,* or the Samoan way — the ancient customs and codes of conduct that govern traditional Samoan village life. Samoans are always representing their people, their village and God.," This is the Samoan way." In Samoan culture, *respect* is the foundation of life.

Sopoaga was a rugby player in American Samoa but switched to football with hopes that his physical skills would be discovered. "The first time I saw Isaac," says June, "I walked in a gym, and he was dribbling a basketball, took it between his legs and slam-dunked it from the foul line. He didn't have an ounce of fat on him, and he was 320 pounds."

During a brief junior college career, Sopoaga had 31 sacks. "His highlight tape was unbelievable," says June, "and he didn't even know how to *play* the game. He just blew up the interior line." Miano says the coaching staff first saw Sopoaga when he was engaged in a game of *volleyball;* his opponents would cower in fear as Isaac limberly leaped *4 feet* in the air and pounded the leather ball back across the net like an exploding cannon.

"Back then," says Miano, "Isaac wouldn't talk to anybody. The only way we got him was because *we were Hawai'i,* and we were committed to the Polynesian kids."

Former Nebraska head coach Frank Solich still recalls Isaac's decision. "We've lost guys to Notre Dame, we've lost guys to Miami — but we'd never lost a guy to *Hawai'i,*" he says. "That's the first time I can remember a guy choosing Hawai'i over Nebraska."

Hawai'i over Nebraska?

Are you kidding me?

It was yet another sign of things to come.

Rich Miano and June Jones discuss the island life with Isaac's father

With cameras rolling, Spear and Robert Pennington, his coproducer and codirector, followed as Isaac took the crew deeper and deeper into the villages, where there are no street signs, no addresses and telephones are rare. "The first time I went to Isaac's home," says Miano, "it was unbelievable. It's such a small place . . . you just keep walking and knocking on doors. They all know each other's villages."

Outside of Isaac's home, an enormous pig was being raised in a screened-in cage, right in the front yard. "How much does that pig weigh?" June asks Isaac's dad.

"'Bout 300 pound," says his father. "Take long time to get that big, 'bout five, six year."

"Same as Isaac," smiles Miano.

The United States annexed most of what would become American Samoa in 1900 and had little involvement with the island after shutting down its naval base in the 1950s, other than encouraging the construction of foul-smelling tuna canneries.

But a *Reader's Digest* article titled "America's Shame on the South Seas" concluded that the simple island lifestyle was actually desperate poverty. President John F. Kennedy responded to the groundswell of public opinion over this well-meaning but ignorant outrage.

The United States aggressively — and controversially — started to modernize the island and transform its traditional village structure. Shortly after more populous Western Samoa became independent of New Zealand in 1962 — ensuring its traditional lifestyle would continue — the airport, roads, homes, schools and businesses were constructed in American Samoa.

That's when television, originally intended as a device to help educate the people, beamed in pictures of American life, thus introducing the rugby-crazed island to *American* football. That was just 30 years ago.

A Samoan boy is 40 times more likely to reach the NFL than a boy growing up in the United States, evidenced by the fact that Samoa now has more than 30 players in the league. These islands produce more NFL players per capita than any place on the globe. To define this aberration,

COURTESY JEREMY SPEAR

Kava Ceremony, University of Samoa, Apia, Samoa, June 2004 (L to R: Pisa Tinoisamoa, Isaako Sopoaga, Jesse Sapolu, Tihati Thompson)

consider that Nampa, Idaho, 12 miles west of Boise—no metropolitan hub itself—has the same population as American Samoa at 67,000. Can you imagine it producing 30 NFL players?

There are only five schools in Samoa that play football. "It's primitive the way they coach and play, but the intensity, the *passion,* the people — it's just incredible," says Miano. "The natural size of these kids, without creatine or amino acids or proteins or weight rooms. . . !"

The wheels in Miano's mind are spinning; the self-assured smirk on his face tells you there's something else burning inside him. Finally, he blurts it out: "Listen, there are what, 270 million white people in the U.S.? Another 30 million black people? And, I'm guessing, a couple of million Polynesians? I'm telling you — they are raw, but they have the best genetics of *anybody.* They are *explosive.* They are *strong.* They *can dance.* They have the God-given rhythm *of life.*"

Let's not forget *character,* either.

There is no such thing as political correctness in Samoa. You worship God; you obey your elders — *without question or hesitation;* and you serve your village. Samoan families, or *aiga,* are large, extended and hierarchical. They are headed by a chief, or *matai.* Nonconformity is frowned upon. Disrespect is not tolerated. A respect for leadership is frequently cited as the reason Samoans make good soldiers and are so well liked by football coaches.

In Samoa, there is *always* something to do, and that includes *fun.* There are no Gameboys or iPods, nor is anyone asking for one. They sing. They play. They go to school. They work in muddy fields. They gather with family and friends in the evenings, where they regale each other with stories and lessons and dancing. It is a simple yet surprisingly fulfilling lifestyle.

"These kids have so much pride in *who* they are," says Miano. "When it's translated to the football field, they are very easy to coach, because they have a solid foundation. They are old school. They understand what *respect* is."

Outside of a schoolhouse, a teacher (Samoa Samoa, aka "Sam," who played for the Cincinnati Bengals in the early 1980s) is brandishing a paddle — with a smile — and displaying it for Spear and his cameras. "This is a Samoan bat," he explains with a grin. "We use this for playing cricket, we use it to hit the ball. But in school . . . the kids think it's part of the school . . . I use it to their advantage."

"Any of our Polynesian kids," says Miano, "all we have to do, if we're having a problem, is call their fathers. That's worse than anything we can do to them. In that culture, they are far more concerned about what their family, their people, think than what we as coaches think."

In Samoa, football uniforms consist of hand-me-downs from who knows where. Slippers are used for thigh pads. Hoses become neck braces. Goalposts are 4 x 4s. Younger kids commonly use coconuts for footballs. "Sometime the kids run head first (into the poles)," laughs coach "Pooch" Taase of Fagaitua High School. "But here in Samoa, ya know that jus' part of da game."

"The Lord gave us a talent," says coach Samoa Samoa of Tafuna High School. "*God* gave us a talent. We gotta utilize that talent and we like challenge . . . we *like* go out and be a *warrior*. American Samoa don't

Coconuts are the perfect size for footballs to little boys in Samoa

have head coach like June Jones at University of Hawai'i. *He's* the one gonna pull for us. He's the one gonna give our kids a scholarship if they are good and meet all requirement. It's a big thing."

"Football is a way out of American Samoa," Sam adds. "Call it fate, you can call it anything. But it's a ticket, it's a chance."

Spear spent several years following this story, and his dedication to the project began to pay off. By the NFL draft in 2003, Pisa had blossomed into one of the nation's best linebackers, particularly after June Jones sat him down *before his senior season* and *threatened to cut him from the team* unless he dropped his weight from 248 to 213.

"You've been here three years," June told his linebacker. "You need to weigh 213 for us by opening day, and 232 pounds for the NFL Combine [workouts] in February. Either make the commitment to be the best or I'll cut you — and I mean it."

The best part of the story, says Dennis McKnight, is that June "told him 232, not 220, 225, 230. June told him exactly what he needed to do and what he needed to be to play in the NFL." Pisa followed June's direction, had a spectacular season and Combine and, by draft day, he once again looked the part of a lean, mean wrecking machine.

Now Pisa, Spear and everyone watching at home would find out if June was right.

For the draft, Pisa's family gathered at his mother Ruta's home. Spear's cameras captured it all: Pisa's family and friends; tears and cheers. "As a mother," Ruta says, "you have this unconditional love for your children, no matter what they do. No matter the hardships that we go through. There is nothing you wouldn't do for your child. In so many ways through this journey with my son, God has helped us keep the faith because really, without the faith, we wouldn't be able to get through it. But we did, with the help of the Lord."

The television blares in the background. Suddenly, NFL commissioner Paul Tagliabue announces: *"With pick number 43, the St. Louis Rams select from the University of Hawai'i, Pisa Tinoisamoa."*

Pisa Tinoisamoa returns to his roots to share his story of faith and perseverance

The phone rings, and Pisa picks it up. It's the St. Louis Rams. "I'm excited to be a Ram," he says. "I am. I am. Alright. Thank you."
He looks at his mother, who is weeping. "I love you," she says. Pisa wipes away tears. "I love you, too," he replies. The family — roughly a couple dozen or so, all of whom supported Pisa during his time in jail — gather in a circle.

"It's been a long road for you guys," Pisa says. "I remember four years ago, all you guys were there for me in court. We're on the other side of it now and it's good to see all of you guys still here and how everyone hung with me."

"I can honestly say," Ruta adds, "that what has happened has come about through perseverance, through God's grace. It's more than we ever imagined."

The family holds hands, and someone begins to pray aloud. "Thank you for so many things today, Lord Father," he prays. "We pray for a *humble spirit . . . thank you Lord Jesus . . .* and Father, we just thank you for the St. Louis Rams' organization. . . ."

Behind the camera, Jeremy Spear was misty-eyed when Pisa was drafted. "There's only been a few times in my career that's happened," he admits. "Here Pisa is, headed toward mainstream success, he's pulling the reigns, yet everybody is still on that cart. . . . It was so obvious that everyone was humbled as they shared in that experience. It was just one big wave of emotion. Wow. I was blown away."

A year later, he would relive this scene when Isaac Sopoaga was drafted by the San Francisco 49ers.

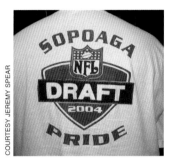

"The most amazing thing, even after they make it to the NFL, is that they are all just one generation removed from the villages," notes Spear. "It's humbling. They don't get caught up in the excesses of college football or even pro football.

"In fact, when they make NFL money, they still have the same responsibilities as anyone else — to give back to the village, the church, their family. Nothing changes. It's the opposite of the modern-day athlete, who has his hand out and hoards all he can. These kids give it all back. It's ingrained in their blood as just the way it's done."

Isaac returns each off-season to American Samoa

Isaac Sopoaga is hailed as a hero whenever he returns to American Samoa. Twice Spear and his cameras would capture it for posterity.

The first time, Spear followed Isaac, Jones and Miano into a celebratory feast with Chief Olo Letuli. Village chiefs are elected by consensus within the *fono* of the extended family and villages concerned. The second time, he would feast with King Malietoa Tanumafili II of Western Samoa (now Samoa) when he returned to the island with Pisa and a contingent of NFL players.

After the Samoa Bowl, Sopoaga picked taro leaves, retrieved coconuts from the trees and helped prepare the pigs for the feast in his family's backyard, back in Fagasa, American Samoa. "That's their way of keeping everyone on the same page," says Spear. "That is the village's way of keeping everyone humble, no matter *who* you are."

In the film, even June is noticeably nervous as he's introduced to the chief. "This deal is right out of a history book," Jones says. "It's a powerful experience."

Filming the king was the biggest shoot of Spear's cinematic career. "From a film-making standpoint, orchestrating that shoot was one of the hardest things I've ever done," he says. "The king was a ruling monarch, yet he lived very modestly. It was very humbling; one of those rare moments in making a film. I was drained; euphoric actually, to get this in the can."

His Royal Highness, Malietoa Tanumafili II, Apia, Samoa, June 2004

If you happen to hear a rumor that June Jones is still playing for the chiefs, it's true. They're just not referring to Kansas City.

When a tropical cyclone and 160-mile-per-hour winds left Spear and his crew stranded in American Samoa, they went into the streets with the locals and helped clear downed power lines, breadfruit, mango and coconut trees. "This film just continued to come to life and to put things in perspective for me," he says. "Everywhere you looked, everyone was helping out. Everybody pitched in, and life just . . . goes on."

Dwayne "The Rock" Johnson poses with co-producers Robert Pennington (left) and Jeremy Spear

Samoans sometimes refer to their land as "The Rock," which, coincidentally, is what one-time popular wrestler, actor — and part Samoan — Dwayne Johnson was nicknamed. Jeremy Spear appropriately chose him to narrate the film. The entire Polynesian soundtrack, too, was donated: "Just another example of their cultural pride," Spear says. "Everyone wanted to be involved."

The film, entitled *Polynesian Power,* was an overwhelming success, thanks to its purchase by ESPN. It now has aired several times on ESPN and continues to air on PBS and the Internet. Major credit goes to ESPN for their vision in recognizing the film's potential and for their instrumental participation in the project. As for Spear, he has now settled in Hawai'i with his wife Janu and two boys, Kainalu and Kaimana. He is clearly still moved by the experience.

"I put my whole heart into this project," he says. "I remember how June and I connected immediately. June really got it. When you watch this film, you can feel it; it has a certain karma to it. This turned out to be a personal journey for *me,* too, in many, many ways."

Isaac today starts for the San Francisco 49ers at nose tackle and lives in American Samoa in the off-season, where he continues to raise new generations of Samoan warriors. Pisa is married, with a beautiful family of

HAWAI'I WARRIOR FOOTBALL

ALOHA BOWL
1989

HOLIDAY BOWL
CHAMPION
1992

WAC CHAMPION
1999

JEEP EAGLE
OAHU BOWL
CHAMPION
1999

CONAGRA FOODS
HAWAII BOWL
2002

SHERATON HAWAII
BOWL CHAMPION
2003

SHERATON HAWAII
BOWL CHAMPION
2004

SHERATON HAWAII
BOWL CHAMPION
2006

Aloha,

As you look forward to summer and your senior year in high school I wanted to take some time to visit with you about your future and the University of Hawaii Warriors.

Even while I was playing and coaching in the NFL one of my dreams was to come back to Polynesia and become the Head Football Coach at the University of Hawaii. During my playing days at UH in the 1970's I developed a deep love and appreciation for the Polynesian culture. My aloha for the Polynesian athletes who were my teammates made me believe that one day I would return and share my vision of making Hawaii "Polynesia's Team."

Since returning to the Islands not only have we become WAC champions and a Top 25 nationally ranked football team, we have been to 5 bowl games and beaten teams from every BCS conference that has been on our schedule. Today over 75% of our football team is made up of players of Polynesian decent. No team in America has had more Polynesian players drafted to the NFL than the University of Hawaii during that time. This past year alone we had 5 guys drafted and another 2 sign free agent contracts with NFL clubs. Just as importantly 6 of those 7 Polynesian athletes had graduated from Hawaii prior to going to their first mini camps.

When Hawaii goes on the field we know we represent something much bigger than ourselves and even our state. For a feel of what it means to be a Polynesian athlete playing football at the University of Hawaii go to www.warriorsrespond.com and you will be able to view some of the national media exposure our program has gained as well as a look at the origins of the Haka here at Hawaii.

As an outstanding football player you will have many options about where you will continue your academic and athletic career. We sincerely believe that Hawaii is a place that can offer you the opportunity to not only win on the field and in the classroom but also give you a chance to reach back to your "roots" and represent your culture and your people.

We will follow your progress closely and hope that if you're ever around our program you will come visit us.

Aloha,

June Jones
Head Coach University of Hawaii

UNIVERSITY OF HAWAII • OFFICE OF INTERCOLLEGIATE ATHLETICS
1337 LOWER CAMPUS ROAD • HONOLULU, HI 96822 • (808) 956-6508 • FAX (808) 956-9552

1-800-638-3825 (TOLL FREE)

COURTESY JEREMY SPEAR

COURTESY JEREMY SPEAR

235

COURTESY PISA TINOISAMOA

Pisa at home with wife Shannon with children Mylie, Ryder and Kaleb

his own. He lives in St. Louis, where his charitable works lead the National Football League. "Pisa," says 49er linebacker and Hawai'i alum Jeff Ulbrich, "is one of the greatest human beings there is. He's really turned his life around, and I'm just proud to be his friend."

On the field, Pisa is known as one of the fiercest hitters in the NFL. Like all Hawai'i players, he carries the Polynesian chip on his shoulder with great pride. "There might be horns on my helmet," Pisa says, "but when I hit you, there's an 'H' in my heart."

Imitation is the most sincere form of flattery; more than 300 Samoans are on Division I rosters. Thirty of 32 NFL teams have at least one Polynesian player, including 23 Samoans, 4 Tongans and 12 Hawaiians. The University of Hawai'i has put more in the NFL than anyone, because *no team in the world* has more Polynesian players than the football Warriors.

June Jones reigns as the de facto don of Polynesian power, in no small way thanks to, well, *Polynesian Power.* "We are the only football team in the world," says Miano, "that lives and breathes on the shoulders of the mighty warriors of the South Pacific people. Give June credit for living up to his commitment. He said it, and he did it. Almost every kid we get has seen *Polynesian Power.* These kids know we don't just talk about it, we *are* about it."

The credits on this film, however, should include more than just Spear, Pennington, The Rock or even June Jones. Remember *Ruta,* Pisa's tiny little mom, who, when her son was in prison, prayed that God would somehow use all of her son's errant ways for good?

Read this e-mail:

> *My uncle taped this for me, sat me down, and made me watch it a lot. I was struggling in school, and kept getting in fights. But listening to the story of Pisa made me realize gangs are pointless. Ever since then, I've been doing a lot better in my academics, I quit hanging out with the bad crowd, and just focus on family. I let my anger out on the football field. It makes me so proud to know that I descend from such great people. Every time I feel like school or training isn't worth it, I just pop in this tape.*
>
> *Mali Tuiasosopo*

Mali was 17 years old when he typed that e-mail. It's just one of hundreds from kids around the world who have seen the film. "I often wonder," says Spear, "just how many more there are."

God knows, insists Ruta. *God knows.*

COURTESY JEREMY SPEAR

Pisa and Isaac are among the NFL's most popular Polynesian players

Chapter 32
THE ENIGMA OF TIMMY CHANG

Enigma.

It's human nature to love things that confound us, like a Rubik's cube; or things we cannot explain, like the huge, 450-foot Egyptian pyramids; or secrets, like who really shot John F. Kennedy.

We don't, however, like enigmas at quarterback.

When we open our Sunday sports page over a steaming cup of coffee, we want to read about a Matt or a Cade or a Billy-Joe, and we want them neatly defined behind our local sportswriters' favorite adjectives. These can include but are not limited to terms like *"gutty"* or *"mobile"* or *"daring."* If they are particularly special, we might read that they are a *"natural-born-leader"* or employ *"pinpoint accuracy,"* which results in them playing *"in a zone"* — my personal favorite.

So can somebody explain just *how* red-blooded NCAA football, by *gawd*, ended up with an all-time passing leader who is as indifferent as your mother's cat and has the surname *Chang?* Let's be honest: *Timmy Chang* sounds like the name of the kid who beat you in the fifth grade science fair with some stupid mold spores, not a *quarterback* who set a record that will *never be broken* by throwing for 17,072 yards.

Had only Chang used his *middle* name — *Keali'i'oka'āina Awa* — that would've *really* been a riot in the sports bars of Oklahoma, especially when it took Chang only a season and a half to do what took the Sooners' Jason White — their Heisman Trophy winner — a whole *career.*

Who is Timmy Chang?

The answer is as tessellating as his Hawaiian, Chinese, Scottish and Spanish heritage.

PHOTO BY GEORGE F. LEE

Had Waipahu-born Timmy Chang been accepted by the Kamehameha Schools — the superb Honolulu prep school for students of Hawaiian ancestry that was his original choice — all of this would be a moot point.

But due to Kamehameha's picky admission standards, he ended up at St. Louis High School, where he followed in the footsteps of a long list of outstanding quarterbacks, such as Jason Gesser (Washington State) and Darnell Arceneaux (Utah), which under head coach and future UH assistant Cal Lee ran an offense called the Run 'n' Shoot.

"I knew his mother, his father, his sister," says Lee. "He was a very bright boy. He came in as a wide receiver, and one of the coaches moved him to quarterback. He picked it up so fast that he became the starter. He was smart, he had a quick release, he was humble, he paid attention, he did all the right things."

Chang, like those before him, flourished in the system, where he threw for 8,115 yards and 114 touchdowns and was named a high school All-American by eight major organizations and publications. By his senior year, he was a high school hero of Texas-size proportions, where screaming girls called his name and fans loitered outside the locker room for his autograph.

California, Washington and Utah offered Chang scholarships, but the University of Hawai'i made the most sense. He could stay home, literally and figuratively; for what other team could possibly afford him the same opportunities as June Jones and, of course, the Run 'n' Shoot?

"It was the perfect fit," says Lee. "June had been a big influence on us, so when Timmy came to Hawai'i, I knew he'd do everything they asked of him."

The terminology at the college level was similar to what Timmy knew in high school, but the defenses and the reads were, of course, far faster and more complex. Still, Chang threw for 3,041 yards and rocketed to WAC freshman of the year honors in 2000, after taking the job from a shaky Nick Rolovich. He relinquished it three games into the 2001 season, after a wrist injury to his throwing arm. The NCAA granted him a medical redshirt season, allowing him an additional year. That, when

combined with his bowl games, pushed his career numbers out of the reach of most mortals.

After *five* seasons and three bowl games, Chang completed 57 percent of his passes — 1,388 to be exact — for 17,072 yards and 117 touchdowns, shattering the old mark of 14,465 yards by BYU's Ty Detmer. Four times he was an All-WAC selection.

Timmy Chang would dazzle – and confuse – Hawaii fans for four years

But who is Timmy Chang? This question *still* confounds the media *and* Hawai'i fans and *still* frustrates his ex-coaches and teammates. His 67 interceptions, also the all-time record, added a bizarre asterisk to his brilliant collegiate career. Fans point to his failure to win a WAC championship, the same way Dolphins fans shrug at Dan Marino's lack of Super Bowl hardware. Chang's 27-14 record as a starter over three seasons is as baffling as his oscillating displays of both toughness and fragility.

Few other quarterbacks in college football history have achieved such lofty numbers only to have their toughness, their ability or their *heritage* so hotly debated. Merely mention the name *Timmy Chang* in any of Hawai'i's sports bars, and you will ignite an immediate, fiery, passionate debate, with one side calling for his canonization and the other side calling for his head.

"He throws too many picks!"

"Oh yeah? Well, how many times did Babe Ruth strike out?"

And so it goes.

Chang marched the Warriors to their first-ever 10-win season under Jones in 2002, but not before a rocky start. In the season's first loss, a 35-32 heartbreaker over hated BYU, he threw four interceptions. Jones vacillated between Chang and Shawn Withy-Allen in a win over UTEP, then went back to Chang, who responded at one point by orchestrating seven consecutive victories.

"He showed what he's made of today," June praised, after Chang threw for 403 yards and four touchdowns in a win over Tulsa. In that game, Timmy became Hawai'i's all-time passing yardage and total offense leader, a place in history he would never relinquish. He then led the Warriors to 22 unanswered fourth-quarter points to beat Fresno State, and he even taunted the Bulldogs' bench from midfield. Unfortunately, few Hawai'i fans witnessed his Joe Montana–like comeback, for the game was at Fresno.

▼▼▼▼▼▼▼▼▼▼▼▼▼▼

Shouldn't any system be praised if it works, week after week, at a very high level of success against opponents of equal or greater talent? Consistent play at the quarterback position might have hushed the household-variety heretics, but, well, Timmy Chang wasn't about consistency, even if he was all about being good — sometimes.

▲▲▲▲▲▲▲▲▲▲▲▲▲▲

"Beating Fresno, he showed *unbelievable* mental toughness," says Jones. "He threw a touchdown on fourth and 12. At a point when it could have gone either way, he went for the throat and won it."

Against Cincinnati, Chang hobbled back into the game after halftime on a sprained knee and electrified the crowd with a 33-yard touchdown pass to Jeremiah Cockheran. It was an amazing display of bravado that won the game — and also ignited a postgame brawl that lasted nearly five minutes. "Timmy showed the heart of a warrior," Jones said afterward.

Then, inexplicably, Timmy tanked. With Hawai'i ranked 24th in the nation — and enjoying its first national ranking under June Jones — the Warriors faced 14th-ranked Alabama at home. Before a sold-out crowd and national television audience, Chang lobbed up four critical interceptions in a devastating 21-16 loss. In the ConAgra Bowl against Tulane, he banged his throwing hand on an opponent's helmet and left the game with Hawai'i winning 14-3. Hawai'i lost, 36-28, and Chang told reporters that he considered returning but then decided his best alternative was "to rest and sit this one out."

"Rest for what?" screamed irate fan number one on a website after the game.

"Next year!" came obliging fan number two's reassuring answer. "We need him healthy for 2003!"

"That's a year away!" huffed irate fan number one.

And on it goes.

The last thing June Jones wanted was to have Chang pigeonholed as a *"product of the system"*; extra emphasis on *system*, as in Run 'n' Shoot *system*, and thereby, Chang not being nearly as good as his conventional counterparts.

This sparked the age-old argument of whether or not Chang could succeed in any other offense. It suddenly seemed that whenever you turned on a radio or television, if the subject was Hawai'i football, an announcer was arguing that *"anybody in this offense can throw for 400 yards."* June rightfully wondered why nobody ever said *"anybody in this offense can RUSH for 100 yards,"* when the subject was the veer, or the option or the wishbone.

Shouldn't any *system* be praised if it works, week after week, at a very high level of success against opponents of equal or greater talent? Consistent play at the quarterback position might have hushed the household-variety heretics, but, well, Timmy Chang wasn't about consistency, even if he was all about being good — sometimes.

In 2003, Chang, despite leading the nation with 357.6 yards a game, went 7-for-23 against Alabama on November 30. Trailing 14-0 and amid deafening boos from the *home* crowd, Jones pulled his star again. Meanwhile, backup Jason Whieldon responded with the "product-of-the-system" game of his life, throwing for *four touchdowns* and running for another to rally the Warriors to a 37-29 victory. Jeremiah Cockheran was on the receiving end of two touchdowns and had five catches for 124 yards. It was one of Hawai'i's biggest wins ever, and Timmy Chang was watching from the bench.

"Guys have to be able to battle through their deal," June recalls. "Timmy struggled, so I went with Jason." Asked for his thoughts, Timmy replied, "No comment."

Weeks later, in the Hawai'i Bowl, Chang was hotter than the balmy 80-degree Christmas Day temperatures. He came off the bench to throw for 475 yards and five touchdowns in a thrilling triple-overtime, 54-48 win, which also ended in another brawl between the teams. Chang was named Most Valuable Player.

"Christmas Wish List: Marry Timmy Chang," read a huge sign held by an attractive young Asian fan.

Callers besieged the airwaves in postgame radio recaps. *"Why can't he play like that all year?"* wondered one aloud.

And so it goes.

RALPH "PBASE" OMOTO

The Yin and Yang is a Chinese generalization of the antithesis or mutual correlation between certain objects or phenomena in the natural world, if you believe everything you read on Wikipedia. They represent opposite ends of the universe, like Timmy, which is Greek, and Chang, which needs no explanation.

Yin is a receptive, feminine, passive force, such as referring to the padding on the small finger of your throwing hand as your "pinky pillow," as Timmy once did. Yang is a creative, masculine, bright, active force; such as laying out a linebacker on a reverse, as Chang once did.

"Timmy is both," says a former teammate. "One week, he was the toughest player you've ever met, he was our leader, and we rallied around him.

The next week, he'd be talking about his pinky, or he'd refuse to play because of a concussion, even when Coach Jones said he didn't have one."

"He's quiet, he's forgetful, that's just how he is," says Lee. "He's a true islander. He's humble, he's not mean-spirited. Most people just don't understand him."

Timmy Chang suffered frequent, but mostly minor, injuries

Who is Timmy Chang? Is he the soft-spoken, boyish kid with the pouty smile whom we occasionally observed laughing and playing with children? Or is he the player who would ask equipment men to sneak him out with the laundry after games so he didn't have to sign autographs or face the media? What is his name? At one point, his grandmother protested his being called "Timmy," so he switched to Tim. The fans stuck with Timmy.

Just when you thought you had Tim, or Timmy, pegged as a cowardly, inaccurate, selfish player, Chang "could step up at any time and virtually play a perfect game," says Dave Reardon, who covered both Timmy and Chang for the *Star-Bulletin* throughout his career.

"People booed him off the field against Alabama," Reardon says, shaking his head, "but man, you should have seen the crowd go wild against Houston when he came off the bench. He ran around like a crazy man. He was awesome that game."

And on it goes.

Peering through the lens of the Timmy Chang debate is just as frustrating as visiting your optometrist; San Diego State: *Better;* Tulane: *Worse;* Cincinnati: *Better;* Alabama: *Worse.* Anyone hoping for a clearer view in 2004 might have been disappointed.

Well, maybe. Hawai'i started out 4-5, with *humiliating* losses of 69-3 and 70-14 against Boise State and Fresno State, respectively. The Fresno State loss was the highest points yield in 54 years at Hawai'i. Chang, who broke the all-time NCAA career passing-yardage record the week before, threw for only 167 yards. "You can't put it all on Timmy," reminds June. "We had a lot of injuries that season. At one point, we were pretty much playing anyone who could walk and chew gum."

Still, whether Jones will admit it or not, his quarterback's frequent turnovers certainly never helped Hawai'i's cause. But never fear: Just when the Warriors were facing postseason extinction — *yep, you guessed it* — Chang finally sputtered back to life. Against Idaho on November 21, he lit up the Vandals for 376 yards and a career-high six touchdowns, passing Marshall's Chad Pennington for fourth on the NCAA career touchdown list.

a maniacal second-half rally. He scrambled for first downs, including one 22-yard jolt. He found Chad Owens again and again, including bombs of 51 and 36 yards. Chang even plunged into the end zone on a fourth-and-one sneak. Hawai'i did the impossible, pulling off a 41-38 win.

On Christmas Day, he closed out his NCAA career by wowing an ESPN audience with 405 yards and four touchdowns, and he ran for another score. Chad Owens — who had eight catches for 114 yards and two touchdowns — and Chang shared co–MVP honors.

The next week, heavily favored Big Ten opponent Northwestern came to Aloha Stadium. Northwestern had beaten ranked opponents Ohio State and Purdue and was expected to win easily against the much-smaller Warriors.

Timmy — of course — was intercepted on Hawai'i's first two possessions. "Then he sucked it up like a man," Jones recalls, "and played the last three quarters like he's capable of playing." Chang connected with Chad Owens alone nine times for 155 yards and four touchdowns. Owens also returned a punt 76 yards for a touchdown; Chang finished with 405 yards. "It was a battle of wits," said Northwestern safety Dominique Price, "and Chang picked up on everything and hit the holes in our zones."

Needing one more consecutive victory to secure a spot in the Hawai'i Bowl, the Warriors faced Michigan State on December 5 — its *second* Big Ten team in as many weeks. Hawai'i fell behind 21-0, then Chang led

Timmy Chang and Chad Owens were co-MVPs of the Hawaii Bowl

"He was plugged in," said June of Timmy Chang's final Hawai'i performance. "He closed the show."

Then, like the Riddler disappearing in a puff of smoke, Timmy Chang was gone, leaving behind far more questions than 17,072 yards could answer.

"We'll miss you Timmy!" wrote a fan to an online blog.

"Thank God that's over!" was the reply.

And so it goes.

How will history judge Timothy *Keali'i'oka'āina Awa* Chang? Was Hawai'i better for having him or worse? Could Jones' teams under Chang have been better or worse? Was Timmy a great quarterback — or a great *Run 'n' Shoot* quarterback?

"That four-game stretch he had at the end of 2004 was as big as any we've had since I've been here," June says. "That was enormous pressure. Nobody in Hawai'i believed we could do it. Only the guys in our locker room did. Timmy played the best four games of his life and put us in."

As for the records, Lee says, "Timmy doesn't care. In high school, he was one touchdown short of the national record and didn't care. Nothing bothers him. He's more concerned about winning than records or anything else."

June disagrees with those who ridicule his former quarterback. "Timmy played as well in some games as anyone I ever coached," Jones says. "People will always have their opinions about Timmy Chang, but as far as I'm concerned, he gave Hawai'i his best, and we will always remember his greatest moments."

Chang struggled and failed in efforts to make an NFL team before landing on his feet in Canada, where the field is big enough for both his reputation and sometimes-errant throws. In Hamilton, Ontario, where they say "out" like *"oot"* and "about" like *"aboot,"* Chang doesn't seem to care what you or I — or anyone, for that matter — thinks *aboot* his place in football history.

PHOTO BY GEORGE F. LEE

There are worse things in the world than waking up and realizing you've *done* something no one has done and *probably no one ever will*.

"Unfortunately, the legacy left behind by Timmy Chang," says Reardon, "is he's the guy that played here before Colt Brennan. I know that sounds harsh, but it's true. He was a very nice local kid. Sure, his record is great. He will be remembered fondly by most — but also with a sense of what he could have been."

Who is Timmy Chang?

Apparently, whoever you *want* him to be.

Seniors of 2001
Tui Ala, Brett Clowers, Joe Correia, Jacob Espiau,
Jared Flint, Robert Grant, Channon Harris, Mike Iosua,
Nate Jackson, Manly Kanoa, Kalae Lee,
Bronson Liana, Bobby Morgan, Chris Riccardi,
Nick Rolovich, Karman Saulsberry, Brian Smith,
Craig Stutzman, Tafiti Uso, Lonnie Williams

Chapter 33
FAITH, LOVE AND PERSEVERANCE

Mouse Davis remembers addressing a Hawai'i special teams meeting in 2004, in which he posed this question: *"Does anyone in this room know why we're going to be a great punt return unit?"*

Finally, someone spoke up. "Because we've got Chad Owens?"

"Correct!" roared Davis.

"There's an attitude that goes with a kick returner that's just special," he says, "and Chad has that sparkle. In his mind, he's invincible. There are guys faster than Chad, but he has an innate quickness that makes you miss. But the most important thing about Chad is his attitude. He has that chip on his shoulder, that belief that he can get it in the end zone."

A kick return is a short soliloquy: a one-man, dramatic expression of thought, feeling and unspoken reflection. There is no other play in football like it. Chad Owens stands alone. His initial moves decry all football instincts: He doesn't run, feint, block or tackle.

He stands virtually still. He looks skyward, eyes squinting, as he locates the football against the afternoon sun. He ignores the mass of humanity — bad intentions all — thundering toward him. Oblivious to the crowd, Owens rests in a vacuum of silence, awaiting the spotlight that will be his and his alone, as the football tumbles downward into his awaiting arms.

The touch of the ball electrifies him. His eyes pop wide open. There is no time for fear. Muscles explode with fury; his mind shoots survival instincts to his limbs. He sees only shapes, not people. He doesn't think — he *feels*. His eyes flicker in response to the tiniest peek of daylight; this is the one place in football where being *small* works to your *advantage*. When he hits the gas, you've got one chance.

RALPH "PBASE" OMOTO

Chad Owens in the open field ... an exhilarating sight for Hawaii fans

Guess right, and you've got him. Guess wrong, and he's gone, like a whisper in the wind.

Chad Owens is a kick-return *artist* and the world of football is his stage. His single-game performances stand alone in NCAA history, frozen in time like the words of a Shakespearean monologue.

For Owens, *"To be or not to be?"* is *always* the question; the answer is always just one kickoff away — not just in football but in life as well.

Chad Owens is 5-feet-7-inches tall, nearly a foot shorter than former teammate and San Francisco 49er Ashley Lelie and the same height as Woody Allen. If he were a girl, he'd be an inch too short to be a contestant on *America's Next Top Model,* but he's just the right size for Inkie's Scrambler at the Santa Monica Pier.

Could Chad's success be correlated to his lifelong battle of being stereotyped as *too short? "Do we have to go there?"* bellows a laughing Davis, himself 5-foot-8. "But yes, speaking from experience, it is."

Being short, particularly in the Pacific Island culture, isn't easy. Had Owens been cynical, pessimistic, apathetic or mediocre, he most certainly would have failed. Instead, he used his *short*coming as motivation. "I believe God had one thing in mind when he made me," says Chad. "I just had to find out what that *one thing* was."

Owens had been a hyperactive grade school kid who blossomed in high school. As a senior, he weighed 165 pounds — if you put a couple rolls of quarters in his pocket. He had the smarts: He was an honor roll student who graduated magna cum laude from Roosevelt High. He was strong — eventually, he would be able to bench-press 225 pounds 26 times. He lettered in track and football and led his *basketball* team to a state championship.

But he found his niche returning kicks, where he was more elusive than an Indian mongoose — and shocked would-be tacklers with his overwhelming strength.

"In high school, people told me I had no chance at the next level," Owens says. "I used it for motivation."

AP PHOTO

He *walked on* at Hawai'i and immediately made his mark on special teams. By 2002, he had earned a full scholarship. "Had I not been willing to return kicks," Owens says, "I never would have had the chance to get a scholarship."

June quickly discovered that while Chad might be only as tall as the leprechaun on a box of Lucky Charms, Owens was magically propitious. As a nonscholarship freshman, he blistered BYU with a punt and kickoff return for touchdowns, en route to setting two NCAA return-yardage records in a 72-45 victory.

He fought his way into the lineup as a clutch wide receiver with sticky hands and proved to be fearless over the middle. Better still, he was a shining example for others to follow. "Nobody works harder than Chad," says Nick Rolovich. "He never misses an opportunity in the weight room. He is never late for a meeting. If he isn't playing, he is helping in some other way."

At Hawai'i, Owens scored touchdowns the first time he ever ran the ball, the first time he ever caught a ball, and the first time he returned a punt. At Hawai'i, his kickoff return average of 29.4 yards set a Western Athletic Conference record, breaking the old career mark of 27.2 yards by Chris Farasopoulos of Brigham Young (1968–1970). His six punt returns for scores topped the old WAC career record of five, set by Arizona State's Lenny Randle (1968–1969).

Owens returned 46 kickoffs for 1,354 yards, two touchdowns and the 29.4-yard average already noted, which was also, of course, a school record. He gained a school record 1,014 yards on 85 punt returns (an average of 11.9 yards per return) and set another Hawai'i mark with four touchdowns. His 5,461 all-purpose yards set another school all-time record, eclipsing the previous mark of 4,558 yards by Gary Allen (1978–1981).

More importantly, Owens used his role on special teams to work his way into a starting wide receiver role as a slotback in the Run ' n' Shoot, where he became Timmy Chang's favorite target. Casual fans are surprised to learn that *Owens* is Hawai'i's career reception leader — not Lelie or any of Colt Brennan's current corps of wideouts. Owens closed out his career as Hawai'i's all-time leader with 239 receptions, good for

3,031 yards (12.7 average) and 29 touchdowns in 44 games. His 5,461 all-purpose yards are still the most in Hawai'i history.

Before he was finished, the "littlest" Warrior received the biggest praise: Associated Press All-America honors as an all-purpose player and winner of the Mosi Tatupu Award, presented annually to the nation's best senior special-teams player.

"Chad motivates everyone around him," says June Jones. "His attitude, his work ethic, his passion was a big part of our success."

AP PHOTO

Chad Owens … still catching 'in the noose' …

Why the Tampa Bay Buccaneers signed Owens is obvious: In their 31-year franchise history, the Bucs have *never* returned a kick for a touchdown. Once again, Chad finds himself playing special teams, waiting for the opportunity to prove he can also be a breakout wide receiver at the highest level.

Tattoos in the Polynesian culture are a rite of passage. Owens flashes a toothy white smile as he raises his shirt: His body is a mosaic of art that tells his life's story. Mighty Mouse, his nickname, is on his right bicep. On his lower right abdomen is a heart, where the words *"faith, love, perseverance and family"* flow forth.

"My family is everything," Owens says of his wife Rena and two children, Chad and Areana. "They are why I persevere. I've always been one of the smaller guys. I've always been told I wouldn't make it. I've had to prove it all my life.

"I can't wait every time the ball is in the air," he says, "to prove it all over again."

Seniors of 2002
Alapa'i Andrews, Omar Bennett, Keith Bhonapha, Chris Brown, Sean Butts, Justin Clobert, Laanui Correa, Lui Fuata, Josh Galeai, Neal Gossett, Jonathan Kauka, Greg Kleidon, Vince Manuwai, Mat McBriar, Keiki Misipeka, Thero Mitchell, Viliami Taufa, Pisa Tinoisamoa, Colin Wills, Shawn Withy-Allen, Matt Wright

Seniors of 2003
Keali'i Aguiar, Houston Ala, Keani Alapa, Jeremiah Cockheran, David Gilmore, Clifton Herbert, Kevin Jackson, Shayne Kajioka, Chad Kalilimoku, Travis Laboy, Kelvin Millhouse, Michael Miyashiro, Hyrum Peters, Lance Samusera, Isaac Sopoaga, John West, Jason Whieldon, Gary Wright

Seniors of 2004
Justin Ayat, Mike Bass, Michael Brewster, Timmy Chang, Abraham Elimimian, Iui Fuga, Patrick Lavar Harley, Watson Ho'ohuli, Chad Kapanui, West Keliikipi, Britton Komine, Uriah Moena, Chad Owens, Se'e Poumele, Gerald Welch, Ikaika Blackburn, Jonathan Ekno, Matt Faga, Thomas Frazier, Blake Harano, Patrick Jenkins, Chad Kahale, Phil Kauffman, Paul Lutu-Carroll, Matt Manuma, Lincoln Manutai, Daniel Murray, Kilinahe Noa, Darrell Tautofi

Chapter 34

BE CAREFUL WHAT YOU PRAY FOR

There was trouble in paradise.

After the 2004 season, June Jones was frustrated and exhausted, both mentally and physically. Some days, he felt like he was holding the program together with Scotch tape and prayer —and *wow*, had his prayers *changed* through the years! It didn't seem too long ago that he'd been asking God for the strength to *rebuild* Hawai'i. Then, in a classic example of *"be careful what you pray for, you just might get it,"* June was now asking God to give him the strength to *improve* the program he'd *rebuilt*.

The car accident had taken a toll on his body, which remained wracked with pain. Twenty-three other seniors had walked out the door alongside Timmy Chang and Chad Owens. Kevin Lempa, his defensive coordinator, had already left for his hometown and Boston College before the 2004 season. Then offensive line coach Mike Cavanaugh pulled a Chang of his own and inexplicably was picked off by Oregon State.

June's conference opponents had clearly grown tired of the rising Warriors: Within a two-year period, Boise State spent $35.9 million on new facilities; Utah State, $10 million; and New Mexico, $9 million. Anyone who thought the Western Athletic Conference was a second-class act clearly hadn't seen the 38 new luxury suites in Boise, the new indoor training facility in Utah or the modern locker rooms, weight rooms and medical facilities in New Mexico.

Part of the irony is that *Hawai'i's success* and television exposure *had created* the groundswell of the WAC's exploding popularity.

▼▼▼▼▼▼▼▼▼▼▼▼▼▼

Perhaps the most amazing thing about prayer is that you never know who's praying to meet you on the other end. How was June to know at that very moment, three different series of completely unrelated events from all around the world had already been set in motion, and soon all paths would point to Mānoa?

▲▲▲▲▲▲▲▲▲▲▲▲▲▲

And Hawai'i? Since changing the uniforms and logos, June had managed to get the deadly Astroturf at Aloha Stadium replaced with field turf, and . . . well, that's about it. When his coaches watched film, they still relied on VHS, not DVDs. Only three coaches had working VHS players, and only one had a DVD player that he'd won that in a golf tournament. Nothing else — zilch, nada, zero. Cook Field, the practice turf, had been *condemned* for six years.

"When a kid comes out on a recruiting trip, he's got about 48 hours to make a decision," says Rich Miano. "We're selling Hawai'i. We're selling a winning tradition. We're selling June Jones. Trust me, we're *not* selling facilities. In fact, if they actually *see* our facilities during their visit, it *impedes* our efforts."

More than once June would ponder his next move while watching the sunrise through his third-floor office window — which, like the rest of the Athletic Department windows, hadn't been washed on the outside since 1999. Yet he *believes* that God works in mysterious ways. Whether you choose to embrace that is up to you, but June is unshakeable in his faith. So each time he reaches an impasse, he resorts back to the one constant in his life: *He simply prays.* "Prayer is very personal to me," he says, choosing his words carefully. "It's not just *wishing* for something. It's the comfort of knowing when you hit low points in your life, God is out there, working in ways you could never imagine."

June desperately needed, as he says, "a big-time," play-making quarterback. He needed a big-time, play-making receiver. He needed a play-making defense, and someone who knew how to coach one. Hawai'i had slipped to dead-last in the nation in total defense, which had made the Warriors' success, records and bowl wins even that more remarkable.

However, you don't just look up "quarterback" or "defensive coordinator" in the yellow pages. Recruiting players *and* coaches is an arduous process, one that takes months —even years. So with chaos swirling around him, June turned it over to God. Prayer helps Jones maintain *perspective:* This is *football* — not a car accident, not death or divorce or suicide or cancer or the *real* issues of life.

He asked God for inspiration and direction. *"Amazing, God, your love . . . how can it be? To know my King would die for me . . . it's my joy to honor You . . . in all I do . . . there's a lot of worse stuff in the world than this . . . but if somehow you can use this situation, my life, this program, for your good . . ."*

Perhaps the most amazing thing about prayer is that *you never know who's* praying *to meet you* on the *other end.* How was June to know at that very moment, *three different series of completely unrelated events* from *all around the world* had already been set in motion, and soon all paths would point to Mānoa?

June was about to get not only the answers he desperately sought — but also to discover true forgiveness, healing and hope in the process.

PHOTO BY DENNIS ODA
June credits his deep faith for keeping him centered through life's toughest trials

The tape flickered to life on the big screen: The quarterback rocketed a ball effortlessly 35 yards for a touchdown. June instantly sat upright in his swivel chair and leaned forward on his desk. He grabbed the remote and backed up the film, just to the point where the quarterback sets and throws. He rewound it again and again: *set, throw —set, throw — set, throw.*

"Un-be-liev-able!" June muttered. *"This guy looks like Jeff George."*

Set, throw. Someone let out a low whistle. Had you been standing *outside* the office, you might've thought they were watching a beach-bounding Pamela Anderson episode of *Baywatch,* for that's *exactly* what the sight of a great quarterback does to a real coach's blood pressure.

"That's the best release I've ever seen on film," gushed Morrison.

"His name is *Colt Brennan,*" Miano said. "He's been in some trouble in Colorado; he's got some personal baggage. That's why he's at Saddleback. But personally, I think the Saddleback coaches haven't sent out his tape because they want to keep him another year."

"Can you blame them?" grinned June. "When can we talk to him?"

We're on top of it, assured his coaches, as they charged from the room.

Rich Miano and receivers coach Ron Lee were reviewing film of a wide-out from Saddleback, a junior college in Orange County, Calif. The receiver looked pretty good, but the quarterback caught Lee's eye. "Who's *he?*" Lee asked.

They corralled quarterbacks coach Dan Morrison from down the hallway, and all of the coaches headed into June's office where they plugged in the tape. "June, take a look at this . . . we think we might have something here," Miano said.

It was 2 a.m. in Hawai'i, and June was staring in disbelief at his computer screen. An admitted sports junkie, he was clicking through stories on ESPN.com when he saw an unthinkable headline:

Ex-NFL Coach Jerry Glanville Vies for Northern State Job

The Jerry Glanville?

Jones scrolled down further.

Are you kidding me?

Jerry Glanville, who hadn't coached since 1993, was contacting schools like Northern State (South Dakota), New Mexico, San Jose State and the University of Nevada–Las Vegas, inquiring about their respective head coaching positions. Glanville was quoted in the media as saying he'd had some sort of epiphany during an NFL–sanctioned trip to Iraq to visit the Gulf War troops. On the other side of the world, he had decided to return to coaching as some battlefield pledge he'd made to U.S. soldiers.

You can't be serious!

Jones hadn't spoken to Glanville since 1993, when Jerry had been fired by the Atlanta Falcons and June, who was his offensive coordinator, had replaced him as head coach. Though they had been best friends for years, Glanville felt betrayed by June and the pair parted ways. June had tried unsuccessfully to call Glanville; for whatever reasons, they had failed to connect. That night on the computer, *"Something just came over me,"* June says. *"I felt like God was giving me the opportunity to correct something in my life that just wasn't right."*

So Jones started making phone calls until he found a mutual friend who had a working number for Glanville.

"I was basically packing my bags for South Dakota and the phone rang," Glanville says. "It was June. He said, *'Why would you coach somewhere else when I need you here?'* He said, 'The tickets will be waiting for you at the counter, so get over here immediately.' He hung up. I unpacked my suitcase, which was full of winter clothes, and started repacking shorts and t-shirts."

Keith Bhonopha, a graduate assistant, came into June's office. "You're not going to believe this," he said.

"Try me," answered June.

"Do you remember Davone Bess?"

"Big-time receiver, right . . . went to Oregon State?" June said.

Only pro wrestlers have bigger belt buckles than Glanville, here with June Jones during their tenure with the Houston Oilers

"That's him. Well, he's not at Oregon State. He's sitting in jail in Oakland for possession of stolen goods."

Bess, in fact, *was* serving out a one-year sentence for possession of stolen goods. He had played at Skyline High School in Oakland under John Beam, Bhonopha's high school coach. Bess had signed a scholarship with Oregon State, which, of course, withdrew its offer once he had been arrested and sentenced.

"There's a lot of extenuating circumstances, Coach," Bhonopha said. "I know his people. All this kid is asking for is a second chance."

"Well," June smiled, "he's looking at it. Find out what we need to do. Tell him I said if he's *serious about turning his life around,* then we'll make him the best receiver in the nation."

Before you could even question the power of prayer — and chalk all of this up to mere *coincidence* — June Jones was on an airplane to California to meet with Colt Brennan and his family. Paperwork was being drafted on behalf of Davone Bess in the hope of setting him free. And Jerry Glanville — who the late *Bill Walsh* once called the *greatest defensive mind in football* — was in transit to Hawai'i to give June and his ailing defense an overhaul.

Are you kidding me?

Chapter 35
THE "BESS" IS YET TO COME

Every boy, in his journey to become a man, takes an arrow in the center of his heart, in the place of his strength. Because the wound is rarely discussed and even more rarely healed, every man carries a wound. And the wound is nearly always given by his father.

— *John Eldredge, Wild at Heart*

We'll never know how much better a kid Davone Bess might have been had his father chosen to be one, but we do know that by July14, 2003, Davone was doing pretty doggone well on his own.

Bess had established himself as a wide-open, game-breaking escape artist, and his on-field heroics at Skyline High School in Oakland, Calif., had college coaches from all over the PAC-10 swooning over him like schoolgirls.

In the open field, Bess was a 5-feet-11, 185-pound magician; he bobbed around like a beach ball in the ocean on a gusty day. Coaches couldn't believe his raw skills — *Man, can this kid dance!* — each time he touched the ball, he was spinning, weaving and infuriating diving opponents who repeatedly were left with nothing but empty fistfuls of air.

Bess had the thick glutes of Walter Payton, which allowed him to stop, start and change direction on a dime. He had more speed and gears than a Porsche with a tiptronic transmission. *"If he's even,"* said John Beam, his high school coach, *"that boy's leavin',"* and when he *left,* he'd glance over his shoulder and flash his million-dollar smile as he kicked away.

Football was Davone's ticket out of the mean inner-city streets of Oakland — and Skyline High in particular. Decades had passed since actor Tom Hanks had graduated there; by the time Bess arrived, the school had become one of the most dangerous in the country. Six full-time police

"When I catch the ball in the end zone, and my momentum takes me to the wall, I start giving the kids high-fives, and I love the joy I see in their faces," says Bess, who can be found every day at 6:15, working out on Hawaii's practice fields alone, in the dark …

officers were called upon daily to quell the violence, which included a student shooting in a classroom in 2001.

But Davone was above the clashing of crime and culture. He had never been in trouble and had never been arrested — not once. He never did anything underhanded, except make those boys over at Lincoln High

"PBASE" OMOTO

wish they knew how to tackle a ghost. His name had never been in the newspaper, other than the front page of the sports section as he scored touchdown after touchdown. He was going to *college, dawg.* The coaches at Oregon State had convinced him of his place at the top of the world the day he signed his scholarship. Not only was he going to break every receiving record in the PAC-10, but he was going to get his degree *and* go to the NFL. In two weeks, he'd be moving on to training camp in Corvallis.

That's what he was telling all his homeboys the day they asked him to help them move some boxes of "stuff." He didn't ask — it would only take a few minutes. They loaded up his car and were headed to a friend's house when the 5-0 appeared from nowhere and almost rammed his rear bumper before bathing his car with flashing blue lights. *"Wassup?"* Davone asked his boys. He didn't like it one bit when they got deathly quiet, slumped in their seats and stared straight ahead.

"Oh, *crap!"* Davone said, as he pulled over. He pounded the steering wheel. *"Oh crap, oh crap, oh crap!"*

COURTESY DAVONE BESS

The Bess brothers

"Everybody put your hands where I can see them and step away from the vehicle," the police officer said, gun drawn.

"Most people would have called their dads at a time like this," Davone says. "I didn't have a dad. I mean I had a dad, but he was never there. And my other dad, my brother's dad, he was in jail a lot, too. I was worried, real worried, for my mom, my brother . . . I was their income . . . I didn't know what to do."

"Don't worry," everyone told Davone. The public defender, the court counselors, the juvenile people assigned to him all agreed that everything was going to be OK. He had simply helped friends move some boxes from one place to another. He had no idea it was stolen merchandise. He hadn't participated in the theft of the property; he didn't have any on his person, at his house, or anywhere else, and his fingerprints weren't on any of the boxes.

He was telling the truth, and even the arresting officers had written in their reports that they believed him. So after five days in jail, Davone was ready to get the whole mess over with, apologize to the judge, get in his car and drive to Corvallis and forget this ever happened.

The day he stood before the judge, Davone remembers his attorney explaining *who* he was, his scholarship, his poor judgment and asking that he be released on his own recognizance. "You're charged with two counts of residential burglary and two counts of possession of stolen property," the judge said.

As a first-time offender, Bess couldn't wait to be released. It was only when the judge reacted sternly, shaking his head as he read the charges, that Davone realized the gravity of the situation. *"I'm ordering you held* indefinitely *in the Martinez County Detention Facility."*

Any hope of a quick release disappeared when, four months later, Bess was sentenced to a year in jail *with no time served.* He had spent his 18th birthday in jail, believing all the while that soon the nightmare would end, only to have his faint hopes dashed *again.* He was relieved, however, to learn he had been tried and convicted as a juvenile; at least in years to come, it wouldn't appear on his record.

Sports had come easy to Davone and his little brother, who had kept out of trouble by playing in every league available — football, basketball, baseball — you name it. Hardly a week went by where, between them, there weren't 5 to 10 practices and several games. Davone had become the de facto man of the house; growing up, he didn't even *meet* his dad until his senior year in high school, and by that point there was little to be said. Bess credits Lamont Prince, a boyfriend of his mom's, for helping when he could, even before Prince fathered Davone's little brother into what was obviously a complicated home life.

But it was Coach Beam who had kept Davone focused and academically eligible. Now, in less time than it takes to snap your fingers, a single moment of bad judgment had made his whole life go up in smoke.

Shackled with dozens of other inmates, Bess was herded onto a county bus en route to a detention center. As he stepped on the rubber platform and ascended up the three steps, he was scared and lost. He had *vowed* to his young mother, who had given birth to him when she was only 15 years old, that this day would *never* come.

He thought of the time he had found her on her bedroom floor; crying, sobbing to God. She was tired of being hurt. She was tired of being lied to. She was tired of being *alone.* He had held her that night — rocked her, actually. He called her *momma;* told her not to worry. He promised that one day, everything was going to be OK, that he was going to play football and fix all this mess that was their lives and that she would never, ever hurt again.

Davone looked through the metal mesh screen windows of the bus, which bumped and banged its way down the smoggy Oakland interstate. Tiny little faces of kids in the backseats of other cars stared back at him. He felt the promises he'd made to his mother dissipating, like the hot, dirty exhaust all around him.

Davone Bess
COURTESY DAVONE BESS

If he was going to survive, Davone Bess was going to have to embrace the wound in his heart left behind by his father. Despite the fear lumped in his throat, the pain in his heart and the *loneliness* that was caving in on top of him, he was going to have to fight the urge to give up . . . and find power in something far greater than himself to do so.

When the pressure is most severe, whatever you have in you — *good or bad* — rises to the surface and either works *for* you or *against* you. In jail, Bess realized he had a choice: Fight the system or accept his mistake and face his consequences with dignity and courage.

So each day, he began spending time with other inmates, for *two* reasons. "Well, I would teach the guys who hadn't been to school, who didn't have any knowledge of any other type of life, that there was more to life than committing crimes," Davone says. "I would teach these guys

that if you expect to *have a life,* then you've got to mentally hop on the other side of the fence *right now* and start doing something about it." His second reason was more personal: "I had to keep myself *motivated* every day, and that helped *remind me* that I didn't belong there and I never wanted to go back there."

So he kept a journal, which literally became his life plan. His four-year scholarship, he thought, was gone. So in his journal, he wrote down what his height, weight and 40-yard-dash time *should* be by the time his sentence expired. He maintained a strict prison-house workout plan and diet that would make his goals attainable. Bess then listed 10 colleges that he would approach upon his release, and he assumed he'd have to go to a junior college first in order to get there.

For the record, Hawai'i was *nowhere* on that list. "I would have never thought of Hawai'i, not in a million years," Davone says. "I didn't even know they *had* a football team." When you're in jail in Oakland, a magazine cover is about the closest you ever get to Hawai'i . . . unless, of course, God already has you a plane ticket and just hasn't told *you* yet.

"I found myself praying a lot," Davone says. "In jail, you have a lot of time to think. I was never a bad person. I never got caught up in any of the stupid stuff, like gangs or robbing people or doing drugs, but somehow, I was sitting here with the kids that *did.* I read the Bible, prayed, talked to God and kept asking Him to forgive me and give me a second chance. I kept saying, 'God, you give me that second chance, I will never let you down. I promise you that. Just give me that second chance.'

"Sometimes you don't think God's listening. Then that call came, and I was like, 'Man, there's *hope.* Maybe He *is* listening.'"

Incidentally, the "call" Davone is referring to came from — *yep, you guessed it* — June Jones. You see, Jones had learned long ago that the best way to *receive* amazing grace and mercy is to *practice it yourself, and in the course of doing so, you unlock the most powerful principles of faith.*

Now you understand why Jones was so incredulous the day Keith Bhonopha walked into his office and asked him to give Davone Bess a second chance. These things just don't happen every day in college football, and June was literally astounded at what he calls "the handiwork of God working in the lives of so many people," meaning Coach Beam, Bhonopha and now Davone himself.

June personally wrote a letter to the judge and asked that Bess be released — Pisa style — into the custody of the University of Hawai'i.

That was the first time Davone Bess had ever *heard* of June Jones. "I learned real quick," he smiles. "He was the only one reaching out to me. Keith said Coach Jones was the kind of guy who genuinely cares about people. Everyone else had blown me off." Then, in a devastating setback, the judge *denied* Jones' request: Bess would have to serve out his entire sentence. Still, Davone wrote Jones a letter to thank him for his initial efforts, and a relationship was born.

"The fact that Coach Jones *cared* . . . that sealed the deal for me," Davone says. "That showed me everything about him as a person."

Within weeks of his release, Davone was fidgeting in June's office for the first time, waiting for the coach to bring up his troubled past. Instead, June spoke only of the future.

"The choices you make from this day forward will determine the rest of your life," June said. "You have a chance to be not only the greatest wide receiver to *ever play here,* but you have a chance to be one of the *best human beings to ever play here.*"

Bess was amazed. "He didn't mention my past, not once," says Bess. "He didn't even tell me to stay out of trouble. Coach Jones kept it real brief. We both had a very positive vibe with each other, and he gave me the ins and outs of the situation and the offense. The whole time, I was just looking at him, thinking this man is about to turn me *loose,* I've been set *free,* I'm a million miles away from whatever happened in the past.

"I thought, 'This is a *miracle* . . . I was truly *blessed.* I got my second chance. I remember reading that God will never leave you or forsake you.

RALPH "PBASE" OMOTO

Bess captures the ball 'in the noose,' like Chad Owens, Ashley Lelie and all great Run 'n' Shoot receivers before him . . .

I remember just thinking that I was a walking miracle. One day I'm in jail in Oakland, and now I'm going to live and play football in Hawai'i?"

Are you kidding me?

Bess had just *received the gift of a new life* from June Jones — and Davone was going to *grab* it, right *in the noose.*

Chapter 36
ROPING COLT

Beagles have unstable temperaments, which is why every college coach prior to June Jones who stepped foot in the Brennan residence didn't trust Colt's dog. When it leaped on the sofa and laid his head down next to June, however — without so much as a whimper — the Brennans would later say it was a "sign" that they finally had encountered *someone* they could *trust*.

Trust had become an elusive commodity in the Brennan household, especially after Colt had literally been caught with his pants down in the middle of a sex scandal at the University of Colorado during his freshman year. This had led to his embarrassing arrest and trial, and eventually he was found guilty of first-degree trespassing and second-degree burglary and sentenced to seven days in jail and four years of probation.

While it seemed everybody on the planet had their own opinion of what *really* happened that night in Boulder, there was *zero debate* about the fact that his football career had been left dangling. Colorado cut him *immediately* following the incident, so he transferred to Saddleback Junior College, just a few miles from his house in Orange County, Calif. He was having a breakout junior college season when he finally went to trial and was convicted, newspapers *wrongfully* blaring that he had been found guilty of *unlawful sexual trespassing*. Every major college considering Colt — Syracuse in particular — immediately withdrew their interest.

Suffice it to say that by the time Jones arrived at the Brennans' immaculate, ornate home, Colt had been publicly shamed, blamed and defamed. June patted the dog and took in the breathtaking view of the Laguna Hills through the giant plate-glass windows. He was startled to

PHOTO COURTESY OF THE BRENNAN FAMILY

A feisty little Colt

see a giant falcon fly past and settle into a nearby tree. It broke the ice, and they all admired the hawk for a moment. June, a former Falcon himself, hoped it was an omen.

"I can't offer a scholarship," Jones told Colt and his family matter-of-factly, "but if Colt will walk on at Hawai'i, I promise he'll be a first-round NFL draft pick. Colt, there are no guarantees in life, but you're going to have to *trust me* on this one, and we can get this thing turned around."

Saturdays at Saddleback had become the only release for Colt's fears, the pressure and the nonstop ridicule. Watching his little beagle fall asleep against the arm of June Jones, Colt couldn't help himself — he actually managed to laugh for the first time in a long time. If you can't trust man's best friend, who can you trust?

Laguna Beach is a pristine little ocean town, roughly an hour south of Los Angeles and an hour north of San Diego, nestled quaintly into the breathtaking southern California hills that flow seamlessly into the surrounding cities of Irvine, Santa Ana and Newport. Ocean spray from crashing waves creates chilly morning mists, as miles of faultless beaches wrap cozily around sprawling hills and rock formations, painting landscapes seldom seen this side of . . . Hawai'i.

Divers probe the icy clear water to investigate fish-filled reefs; world-class surfers divide territories between streets named Brooks and Thalia. The beaches, beauty and restaurants draw international visitors who far outnumber its 25,000 residents, 15 percent of whom are working artists with household names like Wyland and Ruth Mayer and Richard McDonald.

Colt through the years

same results, decided Colt needed another year of grooming and opted to spend $37,541 for a year of preparatory, postgraduate work at the exclusive, private Worcester Academy in Massachusetts. Through the years, his parents, teachers, classmates and teammates used words like *"respectful . . . a leader . . . a friend"* to describe him. He rewarded everyone by becoming the All–New England Prep Quarterback of the Year.

Colt was squeaky clean: never suspended, never in trouble, never even missed a *class*. As with most thoroughbreds, the making of Colt Brennan had been a team effort, with little left to chance. Numerous people, including family, friends and coaches, had invested countless hours in his tutelage — not to mention thousands of dollars. Colt worked harder than anyone, pushing himself through endless practices, games and clinics.

In 2003, he appeared dressed, groomed and ready to ride the rail against the best quarterbacks college football had to offer when he became a red-shirt freshman in Boulder at the University of Colorado. He was expected to compete the following season for the starting job and, with a little luck, earn the same celebrity achieved by Leinart, his old high school teammate.

Main Beach sits dead-center on Pacific Coast Highway and Ocean Avenue, where the sun sets on a glittering, endless horizon. Across the street at Starbuck's Coffee, picture-perfect people enjoy their café lattes as they gaze out over their picture-perfect world. In Orange County, blue-chip prosperity gives birth to blue-chip children pedigreed with blue-chip dreams, evidenced by the number of teens zipping past in late-model BMWs, Mercedes and Porsches.

In 2002, none were more blue chip than high school quarterback Colt Brennan.

July 27, 2003, was like any other Tuesday — and a typical party night for college kids. Brennan, the hotshot rookie *surfer* quarterback had been enjoying his freshman year at Colorado until he was given *unthinkable* news by the girl he was dating: *She wanted to date other people! Omigod! Of all her nerve!* No sooner had he escaped to the school cafeteria to grab some chow and process this over in his 19-year-old brain when lo and behold, he was approached by *another* fair-haired beauty, she of the sultry eyes, pouty lips and a bosom that beckoned his name. She approached Colt and informed him that her dorm was "down the hall" from his and flirtatiously invited him to *"come by later."*

With a cannon arm and maverick leadership, Brennan tingled the spines of college scouts who visited Mater Dei High, the nation's second-largest Catholic school, where his family paid $9,257 a year for him to be one of its 2,312 students. Effortlessly flipping footballs 50 yards in the warm Santa Ana winds, the chiseled, stubbled Brennan looked as ready for Calvin Klein commercials as he did for the NCAA.

Brennan had apprenticed under superstar Matt Leinart for several seasons, until Leinart graduated to USC, where he would win the Heisman Trophy and become a first-round NFL draft pick. Brennan's family, hoping for the

While this might have been enough to make any boy's fantasies flutter, you must know that Colt Brennan was hardly just *any* boy. From what seemed like birth, this middle child had been ordained to be a big-time quarterback, and his well-heeled father from Orange County — the *real O.C.!* — had spared no expense in making sure this dream came true. Colt grew up surfing the icy curls of the Pacific, and catching another girl was as easy to him as catching the next wave. You fall, you get right back on.

Colt considered his possibilities; he opted instead to go hang out with some other friends, where the alcohol flowed freely. Someone then suggested they go to a club, where the underage Colt was turned away. Finally, after a frustrating evening and way too much drinking, he pounded down what he describes as a "a giant glass of wine" and went back to his dorm room. He picked up the phone, ordered up some fast-food delivery, threw on a pair of sweats and was just about to settle in for the night when — *voila!* — his now-foggy 19-year-old brain offered up the recollection of the bouncing cafeteria coed.

If this were a horror movie, it's where the audience starts screaming, *"Don't do it! Don't do it!"* — only the actors on the screen can't hear us. Minus the alcohol, Colt might have felt his conscience bouncing back-flips like a Chinese gymnast — *It's not worth it! Nothing good happens after midnight!* — but alas, it was no match for his saturated liver and leaping libido.

He hadn't even asked her *which* dorm room was hers. So he stumbled down the hall, just on the off chance that he might actually *find* it, when — *voila!* — as *luck* would have it, there's an open door with a whiteboard with her *name* on it. Colt tapped on the door, and she invited him in. What happened next, Colt claims, was consensual. Regardless of *who* was telling the truth, the next five minutes would live with him forever. Sometime after Colt had returned to his room, eaten his food, and gone to bed, the girl filed a complaint with police.

After a brief investigation by the Boulder Police, Brennan — who had already been dismissed from the football team — was arrested and charged for unlawful sexual contact and trespassing. Sitting in jail, he indiscreetly tore his name out of the newspapers that were lying around the cell and wadded the clippings into his pockets, for fear his fellow inmates might take justice into their own hands against yet another prima donna athlete.

Why did I even go down to her room? Colt wondered from his cell. *Why? Why? Why?*

In the same millisecond it took Barbaro to snap a right rear ankle on the front stretch of the Preakness, Colt's dream for a picture-perfect college career was shattered. How could a kid from Laguna Beach who had been

blessed with money, power and privilege wind up *here?* He couldn't believe just how fast bad things can happen when a man finds himself alone in the darker regions of his soul, where his struggles and addictions collide.

Stupidity, Colt told himself. *Drunken, arrogant, cocky stupidity.*

He made bail, but he couldn't escape the headlines and Web sites that were quick to draw their own conclusions. "This entire time," Colt says, "I just kept thinking, *if I had only gone to bed, none of this would've happened,"* which is something perhaps all of us should write somewhere in permanent ink.

When the case finally came to trial, he was acquitted on all sexual charges but pled guilty to lesser charges and was sentenced to seven days in jail and four years of probation. One major newspaper erroneously printed on the *front page* that Brennan had pled guilty to illegal sexual contact. The very next day it retracted the story, but the correction was buried in a tiny paragraph *on page 11, no less.*

The damage was done. All that was left of Brennan's character, reputation and career was his sheer determination and desire to show the world it had judged him too soon; that he was far from the monster he'd been made out to be.

But who on earth would believe Colt now? How on earth could a coach relate to what he had been through? The mainstream media was painting Brennan as a guilty gangster of ill repute — and no college coach he knew desired to be married to the mob.

Michael Franzese was called the "Long Island Don" by the media and members of New York law enforcement. Franzese was once the primary target of a massive, 14-agency government task force that had one assignment: to bring down the mafia's youngest and most financially powerful new superstar. *Fortune* called him the "biggest money earner the mafia has ever seen since Al Capone" and included him among its survey of "The Fifty Biggest Mafia Bosses."

While Colt Brennan was in a Colorado courtroom pleading his case, Franzese was in the football locker room at the University of Hawai'i

June Jones (center) with former Mob boss Michael Franzese (second from right) and family

He explained to June's players how this single verse had led to his personal transformation. The players were stunned; that day in the Hawai'i locker room, you could have heard a pin drop. Players approached Franzese afterward with tears in their eyes; many had given him a long embrace, for they understood exactly what the inside of a jail cell felt like. "God is no 'flash' out of the sky," Franzese warned. "Every time you have a challenge, you must reinforce your faith in God. Your life is a process. With pain comes surrender, and in surrender, you will find peace."

Jones and Franzese had become fast friends, and they spent hours talking about grace, mercy and second chances. Grace, he told the coach, is bigger than a man's history. Grace, he told June, must consistently be given for free.

pleading his. Surrounded by the "gangsta" mentality of modern culture, the forward-thinking June Jones had sought out a *real* gangster — rehabilitated tough-guy Franzese — to speak to the Warriors about the wiles of crime. Furthermore, Hawai'i is a gambling mecca, with wagers available on everything from cockfighting to high school football.

"I didn't even know June Jones," says Franzese, in thick New York staccato. "He contacted me and flew me in on his own dime to speak to his kids. He told me how prevalent crime was on the islands, and that some of his boys had been in some trouble. I was really moved by how much *passion* he had for these kids. He told me when I spoke to them to not hold *anything* back, and trust me — that was a first."

Franzese shared his life of crime. He had narrowly escaped the mafia contract that called for his execution; he had faced 50 years in prison for racketeering; he had served 29 months in solitary confinement. At one point, when a prison guard shoved a Bible through a slot in his jailhouse door, Franzese hurtled it against the wall in anger. When he picked it up, it fell open to Proverbs 16, where his eyes fell upon this verse:

"When a man's ways are pleasing to the Lord, even his enemies can be at peace with him."

Sitting on the sofa in the Brennan's living room, with Colt's dog asleep on his thigh, Jones listened intently with great compassion as the family laid out what seemed like an insurmountable mess of circumstances. Looking at Colt, and with Franzese's words echoing in his mind, June saw a broken, humbled young man who needed more than just touchdowns. Colt needed something that all the money in the world couldn't *buy* — and that was *hope*. June knew from experience that there was no better place than Hawai'i to get away from the scrutiny, to study to be quiet and to do your own business.

Even his enemies, June thought, *can be at peace with Colt.* Jones also understood the media backlash he would probably endure for taking a chance on Colt Brennan. But he was willing once again to forego being *popular* for being *right*. If Colt would meet him halfway and *walk on without a scholarship,* then June was going to rally around this kid and give him a new lease on life.

As he got up to leave, Jones touched the young quarterback's shoulder. "If you're as smart as I think you are," Jones said, "then *I'll see you in Hawai'i.*"

June walked out the door, got into his car and backed down the driveway. Colt's beagle ran to the window and, tail wagging, barked as the coach drove away.

Chapter 37

THE MAN IN BLACK

PHOTO BY CRAIG KOJIMA

There will never be another Jerry Glanville in all of football, and some will tell you that one Glanville is plenty ...

Rekindling a relationship is a difficult deal, especially when you were *hired* to do the job for which one of your best friends was just *fired*.

So forgiveness and healing between Glanville and June were serious business, especially after the rift had simmered for a good dozen years.

There were numerous dynamics at play *prior to their phone call*: everything including *job security, loyalty, perceived betrayal, resentment, guilt, anger* — even *jealousy.* Now imagine the split second of tension when Glanville realized it was June on the other end of the phone.

June's willingness to *reach out to Glanville* triggered something in Jerry, who was willing to reengage the relationship. "Without June, there'd be no Jerry Glanville," Jerry says. "He helped me out twice. I took the Hawai'i job for no other reason than June."

Imagine how stunned the dead-last Hawai'i defense must have been to hear that an NFL legend was headed in their direction. "Coach Glanville affected a lot of people by coming here," says former Hawai'i defensive end Ikaika Alama-Francis. "He really helped all of us. We went from having no defensive coach to having an NFL head coach as our coordinator. It was an incredible experience." Glanville's decision to coach with Jones would have a far-reaching impact, not only on the history of Hawai'i football but also on the numerous lives of dozens of coaches and players, many of whom would use his tutelage to springboard to the NFL.

▼▼▼▼▼▼▼▼▼▼▼▼▼▼▼

What June and Jerry would accomplish in two short years makes one wonder: How much could be accomplished in the world if we all were so willing to put the past aside, pick up the phone and just call an old friend?

▲▲▲▲▲▲▲▲▲▲▲▲▲▲▲

Here's the reality: *Relationship* is nourished by contact, kingship is maintained by reciprocity — but friendship requires *love.* There is no relationship that can be compared with friendship, for it is in learning the laws of friendship that one understands ethics and morals and the relation between God and man. Gold is gold. It doesn't change. So when June finally spoke to Jerry and the perceived daggers were cast aside and the relationship ignited again, it proved something both men already knew: They genuinely loved each other, and they wanted the friendship restored.

Asking Jerry Glanville to join a coaching staff alongside Mouse Davis was like asking Bill Clinton and George W. Bush to put aside their philosophical differences and run on the same party ticket. Yet that's exactly what June Jones did to both of his mentors in the spring of 2005; if his goal was to stimulate stereotypes and flagellate free speech, well, it worked immediately.

"*I totally* understand how things can get a little stale when you've been coaching in the same place for a long time," wisecracks Mouse, who nearly fell out of his chair when he learned that Glanville, the "Man in Black," was en route to Honolulu. "But I told the June-er that there was no need to jump to such *ridiculous* conclusions."

Jerry, forever set in his defensive ways, was equally facetious about working with the godfather of the Run 'n' Shoot. "Anytime Mouse and June want to come down and help me coach the defense on the other end of the field," Glanville said laughing, "I don't foresee any problems whatsoever."

Playful pokes aside, Jones had done something all great coaches do, which is to know when and how to delicately reshuffle and shake up a staff, thereby preventing any extended period of apathy. The proof of leadership is found in the followers, and the message was clear to the rest of the staff and team: If Jerry and Mouse could follow June and work together, *nothing* was sacred; winning took precedence over personalities, and every job was up in the air.

"Football is supposed to be fun," Mouse says. "June knows this. Things had gotten to him just a little bit, and he has a little bit of both Jerry and I in him. What he did was really a smart move to make things *fun* again. The more you scratch and laugh, the more fun football becomes, and when it's fun, that's when you love doing it."

With a solid-black wardrobe rivaled only by the late Johnny Cash and a belt buckle big enough to make Hulk Hogan blush, Glanville is to defense what June and Mouse are to offense. His defenses harassed the NFL for decades, where he succeeded with undersized and less-talented players behind his outrageously aggressive blitzing schemes and vicious, helmet-shattering hits that became a Glanville trademark.

He was known equally as much for his biting candor, which often hit harder than his players; Glanville is very, very funny, which merely added insult to his opponents' injuries. Glanville was a rolling road show; he left tickets at will call for Elvis Presley, left his opponents swearing and left reporters wishing they had more ink. He told referees that the NFL stood for "*Not For Long*, which sums up my career if you keep making bad calls." After a game at the old, dilapidated Cleveland Stadium, Glanville said, "This place really brings us together. It's not so much the game, but when you have 55 guys and only two showerheads, it brings out a sense of camaraderie that we don't feel anywhere else."

His act didn't sit well with some coaches. Former Cincinnati head coach Sam Wyche was once a division rival who had to face Glanville teams twice a year. "Glanville's teams are the stupidest, most undisciplined teams we've ever played," he once said, this after another Glanville team had run roughshod over the Bengals.

History, however, doesn't agree with Wyche. Paul Zimmerman, pro football editor for *Sports Illustrated,* once asked the late Bill Walsh (and three-time Super Bowl winner) to name the best defensive coordinator he ever faced in the NFL. "I had already penciled in the name *'Buddy Ryan'* in my notebook when Walsh said, *'Jerry Glanville,'*" says Zimmerman. "I was stunned, but not after I thought about it for a minute."

While Mouse spent decades drawing up wild offenses on chalkboards from Portland to Houston to Detroit, Glanville was scribbling radical defensive concepts of his own, from Western Kentucky to Georgia Tech to Detroit to Atlanta. He plucked theories from other coaches like Rick Forzano, Bud Carson and Leeman Bennett, while forming ideals that would become, well, *uniquely* his.

He joined Atlanta in 1977, a bit out of control. Zimmerman said that Glanville was *"given to strange and unpredictable innovations on the field."* Jerry worked his way up to coordinator, then head coach. Zimmerman, once looking at the defensive schemes, admitted that even he *"could see where his concoctions would have given Walsh fits."*

The Jerry Glanville defenses of the 1970s looked much like his defenses of the 1980s and '90s, when he served as head coach of the former Houston Oilers and the Atlanta Falcons. Glanville's teams were always noted for their undersized players, clawing and fighting to stay alive, relentless and seemingly tireless, but never as tired as their opponents. It was Glanville who created Atlanta's "Gritz Blitz," where he would send every defensive player but the cornerbacks — nine guys in seemingly ridiculous fashion.

"He would send them all," said Zimmerman. "Anybody on the team with a heartbeat, he would blitz them. He'd send 'em all in, pull 'em off the street if he could, meter maids with their notepads, policemen with billy clubs, sportswriters with typewriters, all in wild-eyed pursuit of the quarterback."

Unlike many of today's blitzes, where defensive players *show* blitz only to back into coverage at the snap, Glanville's players *showed* blitz but came anyway, pouring through holes like ocean water through the *Titanic.* When Glanville blitzed, there was no turning back. In pregame interviews, opposing quarterbacks would talk glibly about finding their "hot" reads, about finding the uncovered receiver, about play-action screens and draws and other methods they intended to use to slow down the Glanville onslaught.

Except that *nothing* worked. Glanville learned that quarterbacks didn't remember much about what to do when they were running for their lives. "You know you've been watching too much football," quipped comedian David Letterman during a late-night monologue, "when, during sex, you accidentally call out Jerry Glanville's name."

There's no question that a few offensive coordinators screamed Glanville's name at night, but rest assured: These were nightmares, not fantasies. The 1977 Falcons set a modern record, allowing just 129 points over a 14-game season, a better per-game average than the Baltimore Ravens had during their 2001 Super Bowl season — and a record that still stands today.

That same Glanville unit led the league in pass defense with fewer than 100 yards allowed per game; opposing quarterbacks completed only 44 percent of their passes for only *nine* touchdowns all season. "It's much more difficult to throw the football," Glanville once surmised to the media, "when you're on your ass." Glanville would leave his corners exposed, man-to-man, often with no help from the safeties, who were too busy having staff meetings on the quarterback's head.

Corner Rolland Lawrence led the NFL in interceptions that season — and holds the Falcons all-time record with 39 — before the NFL slowly

"He couldn't say their names, but he could say their numbers, and Jerry had them hitting from day one," says Jones

began to catch up with Glanville, using max-protection schemes to slow the barrage. Glanville was the first coach to ever run Zone Blitz — the Falcons called it *Safety 4* — when Atlanta used it to pick off Philadelphia quarterback Ron Jaworski for an easy touchdown after he correctly made the hot read but failed to see it was *zone*.

As Glanville's career progressed to Houston and finally Atlanta again as head coach (and the NFL progressed into conservative, safety-first passing), he would occasionally dust off the Gritz Blitz, forsaking the double

zones prevalent today. Like a blacksmith or wagon master, Glanville would take a page from the past to apprentice young men to a football future.

A staple of Glanville's career has been great safeties. In Detroit, he had Charlie West; in Atlanta, Ray Easterling, Tom Pridemore and Bob Glazebrook; and in Houston, Jeff Donaldson and Bubba McDowell. Kenny Johnson played for Glanville in both Atlanta and Houston. *"Mass times acceleration,"* wrote Isaac Newton, *"equals force."* If there is a familiar sound on a Glanville-coached team, it's the *thwack* of a safety applying said force to a ball carrier, and with devastating results — so devastating, in fact, that players renamed the Houston Astrodome *"The House of Pain."*

"There is no finer a defensive coach in all of football," the late Bill Walsh concluded, "than Jerry Glanville." In 1993, the Atlanta Falcons fired Glanville after a losing season, and he would bounce around doing whatever fit his quirky personality. He raced at NASCAR and was nearly killed in a fiery crash. He covered the NFL as a TV announcer for FOX, CBS and HBO. Finally, he seemed to disappear altogether.

For a moment, some thought we had seen the last of Jerry Glanville. Our last memories, it seemed, would be those captured on NFL highlight reruns at midnight on ESPN: Jerry Glanville stalking the sidelines, harassing officials, haranguing opponents and squeezing every drop of talent from every one of his defensive players.

However, the exploding war in Iraq changed everything.

I would rather live one year with the lions than a thousand with the lambs.

Jerry Glanville was hurriedly urinating in a latrine in March 2004 when he glanced up to read the magic-marker graffiti scrawled across the wall. Eleven years removed from the tempest of the National Football League, Glanville had been asked by the NFL Alumni Association to join six other former players and coaches on a secret mission to Iraq. So secret was the mission that Glanville had no idea who was joining him; he was not even permitted to tell others he was going. He had joined a convoy in the desert dust of the Middle East when an officer had ordered the men not to waste a last-chance opportunity for relief.

When he read the graffiti on the wall, it brought tears to his eyes. The motivator had become the *motivated.*

It was signed: *"An American Soldier."*

The NFL is a violent place, but nothing prepared Glanville for the realities of actual combat. He was numbed by the 36-hour firefights, when soldiers would return, shower and head back out on two hours sleep. Even "off-time" was surreal: machine gunners protecting off-duty soldiers during

pick-up basketball games; the haunting memories of beautiful male and female soldiers, still in the formative hope of youth, staring blankly ahead as they ate precombat "meals" of cheese sandwiches and chocolate shakes. "You felt like you were at the Lord's Last Supper," says Glanville, because everyone knew one or more might not return.

Right there, on the war-torn streets of Baghdad, Glanville made himself a promise. "I said to myself, 'If I do get home alive, then I am going back to coaching and work with these kids who are 18, 19, 20 years old,'" Glanville says. "I truly believe they are the greatest generation of Americans today."

Few could dream, however, that the University of Hawai'i football program would be the benefactor of Glanville's landmark decision to return to the game.

No one quite knows for sure how much the University of Hawai'i spends to maintain its authentic Japanese teahouse and garden, which is located on the East-West Center grounds, or the studies center, which architects designed to resemble a Korean king's throne hall, or the serene and peaceful taro patch, symbolic of the islands' native sustainable teachings.

One thing is certain: Whatever it is, it's more than it spends on *defense.*

The first time Glanville trotted out to the Hawai'i practice field — sporting his trademark cowboy hat — he could hardly hide the culture shock: In addition to transitioning back to the college game, Glanville would be working with Asian, Samoan and Hawaiian players for the first time in his life, some of whom had never stepped foot on a college field. Worse, he had the stiffer challenge of *pronouncing* names like Tanuvasu Moe, Kila Kamakawiwo'ole and Solomon Elimimian.

For a man whose coaching resume included three members of the NFL Hall of Fame, a shut-down corner named Deion Sanders and man-eating All-Pro pass rushers like Sean Jones, Chuck Smith and Ray Childress, Hawai'i football was going to be a bit of an adjustment. Nevertheless, Glanville's trademark *thwack* could be heard on the field from day one, as he taught his young Warriors their own native concept of *ho'okauka'eha,* or "placing pain on to others," a Glanville specialty. "He

"Two quarterbacks and 11 running backs didn't finish the game against us, and those are the only two stats I care about," says Glanville

couldn't say their names," Jones says, "but he definitely could call them by number, and he had them hitting to the whistle on the first day."

When Hawai'i opened at home against USC in 2005, *5* of its 11 defensive players *had never started a game.* USC, behind quarterback Matt Leinart, shellacked Hawai'i, 63-17. "It's a good thing they didn't bring the horse," Glanville said, speaking of USC's white stallion that gallops down the sidelines following Trojan touchdowns in Pasadena, "because he would've died from exhaustion."

There was Glanville at his finest, using humor to salvage the start of the season and to take the pressure off his troops. Meanwhile, the *real*

Glanville could be found on the field. Coaching is teaching, he declared, "and I want to be the best teacher on this campus." Glanville announced that he would be at practice at 10 a.m. on a Sunday, an off day, if anyone wanted to prepare for the opponent.

"Fifteen kids showed up," Glanville says. *"Fifteen.* We can only play 11 at a time. What does that tell you? I may not have had the most talented players, I may not have had the greatest athletes, but if you hustle and have great courage, you have a chance to play at Hawai'i."

Chuck Smith, the stalking former Atlanta Pro Bowl defensive end, wasn't the least bit surprised by Glanville's immediate impact on the Hawai'i program. "Jerry's personality and the side show he brought

Glanville with now-graduate assistant coach Bryan Kajiyama

overshadowed the great defensive mind he has," says Smith. "He was all about the blitz before coaches *started* blitzing. What sets Jerry apart from everyone is that his defenses will hustle and bring it on every play. They will always come with bad intentions, they will run their tails off and they will hit someone in the mouth."

The percussion of Jerry Glanville's high-pitched, raspy voice became a practice mainstay, but with an obvious difference. The "new" Jerry was very emotional. Mention the troops in Iraq, the passion of his boys on the field, get him going on *"these kids, the greatest generation of Americans,"* and tears would flow behind his obnoxious black sunglasses.

Though Glanville was now in his mid-60s, the Hawai'i coaching staff compared his energy to that of "two 30-year-olds." In the NFL, Glanville had been a macromanager, leaving the micromanaging — such as teaching fundamental reads and assignments — to his assistants. Reborn in Hawai'i, he relished his role as a teacher, never showing for a moment that he missed the grand stage.

"I witnessed a whole new 'him,'" says Jones. "He was *influencing* the kids. He changed his coaching personality. He really proved that he loves the kids and he loves teaching."

Ahem. *Love? Teaching? Influencing? Are you kidding me?* Had the "Man in Black" grown soft? Are we talking about the same coach who once challenged his NFL team to break 100 facemasks in a season, only to reach that goal in *six weeks?* Is this the same man who referred to his Houston unit as the "stand-up" defense, *"because we hit so hard, the crowds stand up,"* or once referred to injured players who refused to play as *lassies?*

Glanville deflects the questions, pointing only to the fact that he restored the roar in the Hawai'i defense. "All I know," he says, "is that I promised June our defense would give us a chance to win and that we'd have fun. We accomplished both."

Though Hawai'i finished 2005 with a losing 5-7 record, Jones called it the "most fun year I ever had in coaching," thanks largely to the influence of his two mentors, Mouse and Jerry, who became close friends themselves in the process. In 2005, they laid the framework for 2006, which became one of the best seasons in Hawai'i football history. Mouse Davis and Jerry Glanville, in the most improbable leap of faith, would leave *together* in 2007 to resurrect the football program at Portland State University, the old haunt of Mouse and June.

There is no replacement for healing and forgiveness in a close relationship. Glanville, no question, is a controversial, hard-charging character. He is a perfectionist and fiercely independent. Yet his humor and all-black veneer hides a wonderfully soft human being who cherishes relationships and cares about others.

What June and Jerry would accomplish in two short years makes one wonder: How much could be accomplished in the world if we all were so willing to put the past aside, pick up the phone and *just call an old friend?*

Now the beat goes on, as Mouse and Jerry carry the torch back to Portland State, the very place where all this madness began. "I still kind of wish June hadn't called Jerry," deadpans Mouse Davis. "June got to stay in Hawai'i. I'm stuck with Jerry. Now, you tell me . . . who got the best end of this deal?"

Mouse roars with laughter. It is a rich, healing laugh, one that flows like honey.

Chapter 38
THE 60 DIVIDE SPECIAL

Though Davone Bess chuckled when he first saw "the All-American–looking quarterback" at spring practice of 2005, he still wanted to talk to him afterward. Brennan had yet to become the starter and was trading snaps with Tyler Graunke; it was unclear who would quarterback the season opener against Southern California. Bess was betting on Brennan, based on what he called the "nice little pop" Colt put on the ball. He was also partial to how the pair quickly synchronized on timing routes.

"Hey Colt," Davone said, "we stay around the corner from school. Come check it out . . . we got big things coming up together, so let's talk."

Colt agreed, and the two exchanged numbers. A few hours later, Bess was outside on his porch talking on his cell phone when Colt appeared from nowhere. They hugged and slapped palms like old friends. Their eyes gave them away: They looked at each other like spies from opposite sides of the world — but bearing the same secret

"I heard about your deal," Colt smiled.

Bess grinned. "I heard about *your deal,* too, bro. Sounds like yours sucked a lot more than mine, unless *you* count time served."

They laughed at the joke, which really isn't funny unless you've *been there.* Their journey *to begin* had been an arduous one. Their faithfulness had yet to flourish. Their futures were yet to be written. They sat

▼▼▼▼▼▼▼▼▼▼▼▼▼▼

"I'm going to take all the blame and all the responsibility for everything we do," Colt told him. "I'm going to be totally up front with everyone. Whether it's a receiver or lineman, I'll treat everyone equal and let people know if I'm not comfortable. I'm going to get the team behind me, get the team positive and take the leadership role when it comes."

▲▲▲▲▲▲▲▲▲▲▲▲▲▲

down on the steps and began to talk. A few minutes went by, then a dozen. They talked about family, Coach Jones, fresh starts and second chances. They talked about basketball, competition, training harder than anybody else, having fun, watching film and engulfing their whole lives with football.

"I've got a lot to prove," Colt said.

"Me, too," Davone answered, "and I don't want to let JJ [June] down. Ten years from now, I want people to remember me and say, 'That dude worked his butt off.'"

Colt shook his head in agreement. Never before had a guy from Laguna Beach had so much in common with a guy from inner-city Oakland. "It was weird," Bess recalls. "But I said, 'I *really* like this dude.' We were honest with each other about everything." Colt laid out his plan for becoming the Hawai'i starter, and he didn't mince words.

"I'm going to take all the blame and all the responsibility for everything we do," Colt told him. "I'm going to be totally up front with everyone. Whether it's a receiver or lineman, I'll treat everyone equal and let people know if I'm not comfortable. I'm going to get the team behind me, get the team *positive* and take the leadership role when it comes."

Bess marvels at the memory. "It was like he already could see the future," Davone says. "It was like Colt could see what was coming, and he hadn't played a game yet."

Colt and Davone wasted no time living up to their promises to one another. Davone began a tradition — which he continues to this day — of catching balls in the dark each morning at *precisely* 6:15, just before sunrise. Whether it is Colt or a complete stranger throwing him the ball, Davone can be found running routes, swerving through imaginary tacklers and dancing his way to the end zone. "When everybody else is sleeping in," Davone says, "I'm out there in the dark, finding a way to beat you."

Likewise, Colt was relentless in his quiet pressure of Graunke. "Tyler and I became good friends," Brennan says, the same way a sniper talks about

RALPH "PBASE" OMOTO

Tyler Graunke was a record-setting high school quarterback … and with Colt's surfing and ocean-cliff-jumping antics, is always just one shark away from leading the Warrior attack …

eating ice so you can't see his breath — or the ensuing bullet that kills you. "But I laid low. I kept my easy-go-lucky attitude and waited for my opportunity. In the meantime, though, everything I did, I made *sure* I led by example, even if it was a pick-up game of basketball with the guys after practice."

Graunke started against USC but soon gave way to Colt in the 63-17 loss. The Warriors traveled 4,000 miles the next week to play in East Lansing against Michigan State, and Graunke started again. At halftime, June turned the reigns over to Colt, who went the rest of the way in the 42-14 loss. Brennan would never relinquish the helm again.

A new era of Hawai'i football was born. "Everything went exactly like I hoped — pretty much how I planned," Colt says of his progress. Meanwhile, Brennan was being put through Quarterback U by Professor Dan Morrison, digesting the exact same steps — *hips, eyes, repetition* — that the lineage of Robinson, Rolovich and Chang had in years past.

The inherent challenge was that no prior Hawai'i quarterback could *run like Colt.* "Our quarterbacks read 1-2-3-4 progressions," explains June. "Colt would go 1-2 and take off running. He never *made it* to number 3. I'd close my eyes and pray he didn't get killed. He'd move the chains; we'd tee it up and do it again."

The venerable, understated Cal Lee agreed, but with a caveat. "Colt gives you more problems because he can run," says Lee, and you realize he could be talking about both the Hawai'i coaches *and* the opposing defense. "There was an immediate difference between Timmy [Chang] and Colt in the beginning, because Colt had this uncanny ability to *feel* pressure, move and escape. He was also really accurate."

Brennan was distributing the ball and finding open targets. The receiving corps — Ryan Grice-Mullins, Ross Dickerson, Ian Sample — quickly demonstrated that it had the potential to be among the nation's best. Still, the whole team was very young, and all the coaching and sheer ability in the world couldn't replace . . . time.

Losing games isn't fun; Mouse remembers never seeing June more frustrated or thrilled all at once. "He could see that Colt had pizzazz, that

By the time the 2005 season ended at home against San Diego State, Hawai'i had won just four games, but the team was now showing spurts of excellence on both sides of the ball. Fans remember seasons by individual games. Coaches remember individual *plays*, for they are privy to tiny nuances the fans can't see, and they also have a teacher's instincts for when the tide is *actually turning*, even when it's not reflected by the score.

This is what happened in the first half against San Diego State, which had only given up five touchdown passes *all year* and earlier in the season had held national champion Ohio State scoreless for two quarters. First, Brennan hit Grice-Mullen in stride on a crossing route over the middle, who then scooted the final 50 yards untouched up the hash for a touchdown. When the Aztecs scored twice to resume a comfortable 21-7 lead, Brennan patiently went back to work, *staying in the pocket* and hitting Dickerson on a skinny post for a 17-yard touchdown. Glanville called for Cover 4 to slow the Aztecs' aerial assault, and Ryan Keomaka obliged with an interception at the Hawai'i goal line. Five plays later, Brennan sliced the SDSU defense again, this time with a 13-yard touchdown to Grice-Mullen. When the Aztecs fumbled the ensuing kickoff, Hawai'i recovered at their opponents' 10-yard line with 19 seconds left.

"Let's go 60 Divide Special here," June told Colt, who nodded.

The play that followed will never appear on a Colt Brennan highlight film but will live forever in the memory of June Jones.

"What do you think, Dan?" June barked into his headset as Colt trotted out toward the huddle. Upstairs in the press box, *yes,* Morrison *was sensing* it too. "I agree with you, June . . . the lights are really coming on for Colt today."

Colt was actually seeing his progressions unfold for the first time!

"Yeah, and he actually looked off the safety, too, on that last touch," June chuckled. Inwardly, he couldn't contain his glee, for these are the moments coaches *live* for. "Let's see what he does on the Divide Special . . . if Colt hits this, then we'll *know* he's seeing it for the first time."

Colt took the snap, paused and threw an effortless pass to the exact spot where it was called to go and Grice-Mullen yanked it into his chest with

Colt Brennan led the nation in passing under Jones, "before he even knew what he was doing," says June . . .

he was accurate, that he worked hard — all the stuff you want, and that he was going to be pretty special," Mouse says. "But you also realized you just had to keep playing him until he caught on."

The team had replaced 25 seniors, and "the learning curve was pretty steep," Jones says. "It wasn't just Colt, it was everybody at once. Offense, defense, special teams — everywhere you looked, we were learning on the job. But it was evident that Colt still didn't have any idea what he was doing out there — and he was *still completing* 70 percent of his passes."

Bess hauled in 89 catches and earned WAC freshman of the year honors. When the coaches reviewed the film as a complete body of work, they loved what they saw at the end.

There was Colt Brennan: *reading,* then throwing; *reading,* then throwing. One-two-three-*four,* throw. *"I think he's got it,"* June said. He backed up the film one more time, and the coaches watched carefully as Brennan checked down through his progressions, then fired another frozen rope down the seam. "Man, when he *sees* it, he *delivers it,*" June said. *"Wow!* I don't think I've ever had anybody — and that includes Jimmy [Kelly] or Jeff [George] — who throws like this kid."

When Colt delivered another perfect strike — this time to the inside shoulder of a receiver and *just behind* the defender's turned back — Rich Miano couldn't contain himself. "If you're a cornerback," said the former NFL safety, who witnessed firsthand the likes of John Elway, Dan Marino, Joe Montana and Dan Fouts, "Colt is going to make you wish you never got out of bed."

RALPH "PBASE" OMOTO

Ryan Grice-Mullens: another thoroughbred in Colt's stable of receivers

19 seconds left in the half. *Touchdown.* "He keeps that up and we might stay employed," June joked.

On the day, Colt completed 25 of 37 passes for 326 yards and five touchdowns, doubling what San Diego State had given up *all year.* Hawai'i won, 49-38. For most, the season ended with little fanfare. Up in the video room of the football offices, however, June and his coaches were glued to the big screen like meteorologists tracking the biggest hurricane of their lives.

In his first season under Jones, Colt led the nation in total offense, passing for 4,301 yards and 35 touchdowns, against just 13 interceptions.

UNIVERSITY OF HAWAII ATHLETICS

There may be no finer head coach-quarterback relationship in college football than Colt Brennan and June Jones

Chapter 39
PLENTY OF HEROES AND PLENTY OF HOPE

Excitement was building prior to the 2006 season, and June was as optimistic as he'd ever been since taking the Hawai'i job. Unlike 1999, when he had built the entire program from scratch, or even 2001, when he was forced to start anew after his car accident and with a quarterback controversy, this team was a working model that reflected nearly a decade of hard work, as well as the greatest attribute a head coach can achieve: *consistency.*

That 2006 off-season, a single passage from a book June was reading jumped out at him. It read: *"A hero is a person who, when tested, excels, and in doing so, inspires others."* He scrolled down his 2006 roster the way a conductor looks at a sheet of music, and he wondered which of his players would be the new impresario.

Everyone expected to see more of Brennan. When the *entire team* stepped to the fore, Jones was as pleasantly surprised as anyone, though his coaches saw it coming.

"June is consistent, week in and week out, year in and year out," says Miano, who has remained at the core of the Hawai'i coaching staff. "That's how you have seasons like 2006. It was the culmination of everything he's done. Guys just *emerged, week after week.* You know what he expects from you, and you know what you can expect from him. There is an enormous relationship of trust among the coaches — and between us and the players."

Call it trust, call it consistency or call it the culmination of hard work. The bottom line was this: Never before had Hawai'i enjoyed such a dominant quarterback *and defense* at the same time, and it resulted in one of the wildest — and most exhilarating — rides in program history.

First, three key players — safety Leonard Peters, receiver Ian Sample and 250-pound running back Nate Ilaoa — were each granted a

PHOTO BY GEORGE F. LEE

Like father, like son: Future NFL star Samson Satele 'strikes a pose' in the shadow of his head coach

sixth season of eligibility by the NCAA. Offensive lineman Samson Satele elected to stay for his senior season and was moved to center. Davone Bess, Ian Sample and Ryan Grice-Mullins were joined at receiver by Jason Rivers, who had missed 2005 due to personal reasons.

June quietly had assembled one of the finest coaching staffs in the nation, with nearly 200 years of NFL experience on his sidelines. Best of all, everyone was having *fun,* and usually, Glanville could be found in the middle of it, along with sidekick Jeff Reinebold, who had joined the team as a graduate assistant in 2005 before Jones moved him to defensive line coach in 2006. Right down to his sun-streaked, crazy blonde hair, Reinebold was doing his part to strip Glanville of his title as undisputed champion of "crazy," epitomizing all of the coaches on June Jones' eclectic staff.

Calling himself a "Hawaiian trapped in a haole's body," Reinebold was a 25-year coaching veteran with stops at five different colleges, two Canadian Football League clubs and several teams in NFL Europe. He was earning six figures with the NFL in international player development when he called June prior to the 2005 season and begged to join Mouse and Jerry Glanville on the Hawai'i sidelines. "I don't care if I have to hand out jockstraps, I want to be part of your team," he told June.

A surfer who had fallen in love with Hawai'i and the Polynesian people during various scouting trips to the islands, Reinebold was suffering from a June Jones–like epiphany. "I could understand where he was coming from," June says, "but all I had to offer him was a graduate assistant's position." June was shocked when Reinebold *accepted* the whopping salary of $842.23 a month and showed up to work, dressed in slippers, aloha shirt and carrying an ukulele and an *ipu*. "At that point," says June, "you couldn't question his *desire* to be here."

Seated, from left, Larry Sauafea, Mel Purcell, Jeff Reinebold, Ikaika Alama-Francis, Kahai LaCount. Standing is Renolds Fruean

Glanville loved his new assistant — but for different reasons than just his knowledge of football. "Reinebold brought in a fresh credit card," Glanville smirks. His voice drips with sarcasm. "See, we didn't have a recruiting budget or a scouting budget. So I put scout-dot-com on my credit card, and Reinebold put rivals-dot-com on one of his." Glanville pauses before erupting in laughter. "That just goes to show you how two assistant coaches who refuse to be denied can single-handedly turn around an entire program," he quips.

It's a 4,495-mile flight from Hawai'i to Atlanta, Ga., which is where the Warriors opened the 2006 season. They trained in Atlanta for several days before busing over to Tuscaloosa, home of the vaunted Crimson Tide, Hawai'i's first opponent of the season. Although Alabama had appeared in 54 bowl games and won 12 national titles, the Warriors felt they were up to the test, having already faced Southern Cal and Michigan State the year before.

"We fully expected to beat Alabama," says Glanville. "In fact, we were so sure we were going to win, our guys didn't wear shoes all week. The media, the Friday before the game, kept saying, 'Your players don't have shoes.' I said, 'Our guys don't *wear* shoes.'"

The hotel staff marveled over the players singing, dancing, piano and ukulele playing — some even asked if the Warriors were a traveling Polynesian musical act. "There have been times on the road," says Jones, "our guys will start singing in the lobby, and hotel guests try to tip them."

What about fire-knife dancing? "Probably a felony in Alabama," says Glanville.

In front of 92,138 fans at Bryant-Denny Stadium, Hawai'i came within a touchdown of beating the Crimson Tide. Dave Rader, Alabama's offensive coordinator, didn't mince words after the team's narrow 25-17 escape. "If Glanville wasn't there," he said, "they might sneak up on people. If you don't prepare well against these guys, they are going to make you look bad." Hawai'i held Alabama to only 21 yards rushing in the second half, and the game ended when Brennan — trying to tie the game — was picked off in the end zone.

Glanville's swarming defense engulfed UNLV the following week in a 42-13 victory, allowing only six first downs in the first half and 39 yards rushing. A week later against Boise State, Brennan threw five touchdowns, including three to Jason Rivers and two to Davone Bess, who became the first receiver to break 100 yards against the Broncos. Still, Hawai'i lost in a shootout by a touchdown, and the players sat in somber silence on the six-hour flight home, realizing that for all their talent, they were still 1-2 on the year.

Hawai'i righted the ship against Eastern Illinois, when Jones nearly pulled off his dream game by calling only *nine* running plays in a 44-

Keoni Steinhoff (78), Aaron Kia (77) and Timo Paepule (10) take the field

9 romp. Brennan was *ridiculously* magnificent in *less than three quarters*, completing 30 of 41 passes for 409 yards and five touchdowns. Talk in the stands, however, was about safety Michael Malala, who on Hawai'i's opening kickoff attempted to leap *over the wedge in a full somersault* and hit the return man in the head with his foot.

The next week, Nate Ilaoa rushed for 151 yards in a thrilling 41-34 win against Nevada. Davone Bess caught 10 passes for 139 yards and a touchdown; Ian Sample caught two touchdowns. Colt threw for four touchdowns and rushed for another, while adding 419 yards to his growing season totals. But again, it was the defense that saved the game, when it stuffed the Wolf Pack in *four tries from the Hawai'i 3-yard line* to preserve the win.

When the game ended, 300-pound nose tackle Mike Lafaele sought out Brennan. "You have to learn to trust us, brah," he said.

"I think I just did," Brennan told him.

In Brennan's first visit to Fresno State, he threw for another five touchdowns — including 10 passes for 115 yards to senior Ross Dickerson — to lead Hawai'i to an overwhelming 68-37 win. Brennan's

Adam Leonard (44), Mel Purcell (99), Fale Laeli (96) and a high-flying Leonard Peters hold a staff meeting on a hapless ballcarrier

Nate Ilaoa punished tacklers ... especially near the goal line

weeks, Brennan threw for a whopping 1,200 yards and 15 touchdowns, as Hawai'i matched the school record for *consecutive victories in a season.* Now ranked 25th in the nation, the Warriors were tied with Purdue at 35 points, with the clock winding down. Facing second and 6 at the Purdue 23, Jones called for the wide receiver screen to Ian Sample. Brennan double-clutched and Dane Uperesa cut the defensive end. Colt hit Sample, Jason Rivers threw his best block of the year against the safety and Hawai'i won again, 42-35.

Colt finished with 434 yards and three touchdowns, but again it was the defense that kept Hawai'i alive with two critical interceptions. One by Gerard Lewis set up Sample's winning touchdown, while the second by linebacker Adam Leonard sealed the game. "This team is amazing," Sample said afterward. "There are no words to explain it."

The regular season ended with a heartbreaking three-point loss to Oregon State, when Colt Brennan underthrew Rivers as time ran out. Three weeks later, Hawai'i whipped Arizona State to complete its best season in history.

Hawai'i's three losses were by a total of just 18 points.

best throw of the year might have been a 47-yard, deep-stride post to Ian Sample, who scored two touchdowns for his third consecutive game. Not to be outdone, Leonard Peters returned an interception 54 yards for a score.

When the Warriors rolled into Las Cruces, N.M., the defense again stole the show from Brennan when defensive end Melila Purcell laid a thundering hit on Chase Holbrook, which knocked the quarterback out of the game. Hawai'i won easily, 49-30. "During the time I was at Hawai'i," Glanville says, "eight quarterbacks and 11 running backs didn't finish against us. Those are the only two stats I care about." The defense also forced two fumbles, both resulting in Hawai'i touchdowns.

Against Idaho, Colt continued to pour it on, throwing for five more touchdowns and taking over the national lead for passing efficiency in a 68-10 pounding. Ross Dickerson returned a kickoff 100 yards for a touchdown. More important to June, however, was that Colt extended his streak of passes *without an interception* to 158. Over the next three

Melila Purcell (98) embraces Samson Satele

"By the end of the year, we could really hit and totally take over a football game," says Glanville. "To be honest, we played somewhat unbelievable."

Brennan would win WAC Offensive Player of the Year and finish sixth in the Heisman Trophy voting. June Jones was named WAC Coach of the Year, even though his team failed to win the conference. Hawai'i again led the nation in total offense.

Brennan was among a school-record nine Warriors to earn berths on the All-WAC first team, including slotback Davone Bess, who led the Warriors with 91 catches for 1,155 yards and 14 touchdowns. The others were running back Nate Ilaoa, , offensive linemen Tala Esera and Samson Satele, defensive linemen Melila Purcell and Ikaika Alama-Francis, safety Leonard Peters and kick returner Ross Dickerson. Named to the second team were wideout Jason Rivers, right tackle Dane Uperesa, nose tackle Michael Lafeaele and linebacker Adam Leonard.

Dennis McKnight

Every player had a story, and each one seemed more remarkable than the last. Ilaoa, who finished with 1,674 all-purpose yards and 18 touchdowns, had played through a significant heel injury. Esera had been a walk-on, little-known defensive tackle, only to be one of the country's best offensive tackles. Peters played in spite of chipped cartilage in his rib cage and partially torn ligaments in his right knee. Purcell had weighed only 208 pounds as a freshman before blossoming into a man-eating defensive end.

Jones had even plucked Francis from the basketball team, and Reinebold and Glanville had turned him into one of the WAC's most feared pass rushers. "Francis weighs 272 pounds dripping wet," says Glanville, "and 270 of those pounds is his *heart*."

Colt has been known to audible in Samoan to confuse opponents

Barely had the season ended than fans wondered: Which Warriors were better, those of 1999 or the 2006 version? Dan Robinson warns that such comparison is unfair.

"You're comparing apples and oranges," the former quarterback says.

"The program in 2006, and today, has come so far that it enjoys tradition, history and a foundation of winning. We were the guinea pigs. We didn't even know if we were going to *have a team*." This is in addition to the fact, reminds former linebacker Jeff Ulbrich, "that we won a share of the conference."

"That's funny," says Dennis McKnight, "because June, psychology professor that he is, used the '99 team to motivate the '06 team. He told them the 1999 team would be remembered for the next 50 years, that they had left a legacy. The result was the 2006 kids set out to leave their own mark. Regardless, it was fuel for the fire, and both teams will be remembered forever."

Hawai'i fans should just smile, for it is *they* who *own both teams*. Still, the fact that such a debate can be had must bring June tremendous satisfaction; for when he arrived at the University of Hawai'i, there was *nothing to argue*. Not even a decade has passed since Hawai'i was *"out of heroes and out of hope,"* yet today, thanks to June Jones, Hawai'i has *both*, everywhere you look.

Are you kidding me?

Jacob Patek emerged as one of the best defensive backs in the Western Athletic Conference

This is battle, and Warriors (from left) Dane Uperesa, Marques Kaonohi and Timo Paepule are ready to respond

Seniors of 2005
Kainoa Akina, Tony Akpan, Lamar Broadway, Ikaika Curnan, Brandon Eaton, Derek Faavi, Justin Faimealelei, Omega Hogan, Landon Kafentzis, Kila Kamakawiwoʻole, Bryan Maneafaiga, Lono Manners, Tanuvasa Moe, Turmarian Moreland, Jeffrey Rhode

Seniors of 2006
Ikaika Alama-Francis, Ross Dickerson, Tala Esera, Victor Fergerstrom, Renolds Fruean, Nate Ilaoa, Marques Kaonohi, Kahai LaCount, Michael Malala, Reagan Mauia, Kurt Milne, Chad Mock, Kenny Patton, Leonard Peters, Melila Purcell, Ian Sample, Samson Satele, Dane Uperesa, Lawrence Wilson

Chapter 40
"THEY DIDN'T GET MY SHOES"

It is Saturday, April 29, 2007, and June Jones' cell phone is ringing as he drives through traffic on the H-1 in Honolulu near the university, preparing for tonight's spring game. The caller is Ikaika Alama-Francis, a former member of the UH basketball team whom June – out of urgent necessity -- had to convince to walk on to the football team just a few years before. He had just been drafted with the 58th overall pick by the Detroit Lions, and he is literally sobbing.

Samson Satele was picked in the second round by the Miami Dolphins

Converted basketball player Ikaika Alama-Francis was drafted by the Detroit Lions

"Coach, I can't believe they took me in the second round," Francis said. *"How do I say thanks? I owe you my life . . . I don't even know what to say. You told me this day would come if I worked hard, but I cannot believe it has happened."*

Within minutes, the phone rings again. It's a newspaper reporter from Miami, who informs Jones that center Samson Satele has just been taken in the second round *two picks later* by the Miami Dolphins and is already projected to fight for the starting job. The reporter asks June for his opinion. "He's probably as good or better than anybody starting for them right now," Jones says.

Both players are instant millionaires. The phone rings again. "Yeah, I believe it," Jones says to whoever just asked. "I'm eager to see who goes next."

"Who" went next would stun even *who went next,* for *nobody* saw this one coming.

Reagan Mauia's cell phone rang, and it was a scout with the Miami Dolphins.

"Reagan?"

"This is him."

"How do you pronounce your name?"

"MA-WE-UH. Why?"

"Uh, Coach Cam Cameron wants to talk to you."

"Who's Coach Cameron?"

"Reagan, this is the Miami Dolphins. We're about to draft you in the sixth round. Are you watching the draft on television?"

Reagan smiled. It was almost funny how his teammates. . . .

"Reagan, say hello to Coach Cameron."

The phone jostled around, and Cam Cameron of the Miami Dolphins came on the line.

"Reagan? Hey, I *love* your style of play, and I used to coach a pretty special guy in San Diego named Lorenzo Neal, and I think you're going to be our Lorenzo Neal here in Miami. . . ."

Reagan almost dropped the phone. He *did* drop to his knees, and his eyes filled with tears. Across the bottom of the screen on ESPN, Reagan saw his name scroll past.

He *really was* a Miami Dolphin.

Nobody was a longer shot to play in the National Football League than Reagan Mauia.

Just a few years earlier, Mauia had been a 6-foot-tall, 380-pound junior-college offensive guard. He was weighing his options and realizing that

RALPH "PBASE" OMOTO

Reagan Mauia grew up in a village in American Samoa

few Division I programs would give him a serious opportunity. "I was lost," Reagan says. Ironically, it was the *month of June;* his son had just been born; and he was working two jobs — as a bouncer at night and for Sears during the day — while trying to play football at the same time.

Reagan sat down in front of the television to think when — *are you kidding me?* — a show entitled *Polynesian Power* caught his attention. Mauia had been *born and raised in American Samoa* and had been in the continental United States only since his freshman year in high school. He watched with awe "at the love June had for the Polynesian people," Reagan says, his voice barely above a whisper. "I felt like if I even had the *slightest* chance to make it at the next level, it would be with June Jones. So I prayed about it and decided to take a chance. I picked up the phone and called. At first, I couldn't get through. I was about to give up when Coach [Mouse] Davis called me back and asked me to send some film.

"I had seven game tapes, all on one reel," Reagan continues. "I even put a *high school* film in there. Then, I put a picture of me and my son in there, along with a note, thanking them for the opportunity to walk on and earn a scholarship."

Are you kidding me?

Growing up in Samoa, Reagan had lived in a village like everyone else. His family had "running water," if you count a PVC pipe as "running." There was no faucet or sink. *Hot water* was not a luxury, it was *totally unheard of.* The kids took cold showers in the morning before school and cold showers at night before bed. There were no phones. Half of his childhood, the family lived without power or lights, and food was cooked outside in a pit. Dinner was served just before dark, and after sunset the kids were put to bed on woven mats.

"Back in Samoa, if we had a package of Top Ramen, we thought we were rich," Reagan says. "If I had a hot dog, I felt like the rich kids who had lunchboxes. As embarrassing as it is, we didn't even have toothpaste. I brushed my teeth with soap."

In hopes of giving him a "better chance at life," Reagan was flown to Oakland when he was 10 years old. He *didn't own a pair of shoes* and was given a pair of girl's slippers — *"with butterflies on them," Reagan says* — for the flight. He moved into a three-bedroom home, which he shared with 13 other brothers, sisters and cousins. The boys slept in the garage, which was still a step up from the woven mats in the village. The first time he felt hot water, he jumped. He also jumped for joy when someone bought him a new pair of shoes.

"I had never worn tennis shoes in my life," he says. "Man . . . I *was proud of those shoes!*"

Even though he was just in the fifth grade, because of his size Reagan was often mistaken as someone much older. Such was the case one day on the way home from school, when he was jumped by drug dealers who attempted to take his brand-new shoes. The fight was hellacious. They broke his jaw, his nose and split his lip.

"I was bleeding everywhere," he says. "I was only three blocks from home. I was with my little brother, and I yelled at him to run before they got him, too. I stood my ground and fought, but they busted me up pretty good."

What about the shoes?

Reagan chuckles. "Oh, they didn't get *my shoes*," he says. "I'd never had shoes in Samoa. They busted me up, but they weren't *getting my shoes*."

Perhaps the greatest discovery of Reagan's life was football. He had played it in the park but had never seen kids in full pads. The first time he walked on a junior high field to inquire about playing, the coaches looked at his size and immediately pointed to another field.

"Varsity's over there," said the coach. Eventually he wound up in a locker room, carefully watching the other boys get dressed. "I had no idea which pads to put where," he says. "I didn't know how to put my pads on. I didn't know a center from a guard. All I knew was a running back, a quarterback, and a receiver."

Reagan also knew how to hit, and in no time he was crushing teammates so ferociously that some guys *quit* rather than get blown up by the big Samoan. "I was just a big, happy kid," he says. "I'd never had the experiences these kids had. Looking back, I must've looked like an idiot, because I went full speed on every drill. But I was proud of myself."

So proud was he, in fact, that he would stay in full pads, helmet and all, for the public bus ride home, oblivious to the stares around him.

His sophomore year, he moved to varsity. As a senior, he had no idea about SAT scores and failed it twice, which landed him at San Joaquin Junior College as a bull-rushing noseguard. When the team needed an offensive lineman, he moved to guard, where despite weighing "way too much," he says, his nimble feet, balance and Samoan rhythm caught the eyes of coaches, including June Jones the day he opened Reagan's envelope and looked at his tape.

June called Reagan and invited him to walk on when camp opened in August. Mauia neglected to tell Jones his weight had swelled to 380 pounds, and if he had, "I might have told him not to bother," June says today. Reagan began shedding pounds — through a strict diet of chicken and salads — but due to his weight and the team's depth at the position, it seemed he had little hope to play.

Eight games into the 2005 season, while Hawai'i was in preparation for Wisconsin and its enormous fullback, Jeff Reinebold asked Mauia to simulate their opponent by playing fullback in practice. "It was ugly," Reagan says. "I ran over people like a train running over a child. So I had a passing play, and I caught the ball, turned up and destroyed more people."

The next thing Mauia knew, June told him to go get a different jersey number, and he was switched to fullback. "You've got good feet, good hands, good athletic ability," June told him. "I think we can build a fullback out of you."

During the season's last game against San Diego State, he carried 12 times for 69 yards, including his first touchdown. "The play was 32 belly," he says. "I took the handoff and was supposed to go front-side A gap and cut back. Instead, I took out three guys. They were just bouncing off of me. June said, 'Wait until your junior college coaches see this deal!'"

By spring of 2006, Reagan was down to 315 pounds; June shocked him by offering him a scholarship. "I had tears in my eyes," he says. "I never thought Coach would do that, especially my senior year. *Why would he give a scholarship to a senior?* I was so overwhelmed, because kids in Samoa just don't get this opportunity."

Reagan's father suffered a heart attack just prior to the Alabama game. When Hawai'i got within scoring distance against the Crimson Tide, June replaced starter Nate Iloa with Reagan and called the 261 Screen. "He said, 'This one's for you and your dad, Reagan. They're never going to expect it.'" Alabama *didn't* expect it, and Mauia scored the first touchdown of the game.

RALPH "PBASE" OMOTO

In a shocking draft-day surprise, Reagan Mauia was selected by the Miami Dolphins

He wore the numbers 684 and 685 in eye-black under his eyes — the area codes of American Samoa. Against UNLV, on a play called Tampa Left, Reagan took the handoff and followed the right guard to the outside. When the safety — all 200 pounds of him — roared to meet him, the 300-pound Mauia delivered a devastating blow, shattering his would-be tackler's nose. After the game, Reagan apologized when he saw him. "His eyes were black, almost swollen shut, he had cotton swabs in his nostrils — but I give him credit; he said, 'Thank God it was my nose. *I thought you broke my neck.*'"

More than once teams would blitz a safety in pursuit of Colt, only to be viciously met in the hole by Reagan Mauia. "They'd be coming full speed," says Brennan, "then they'd see Reagan and start pumping the brakes. I'd never seen safeties pull up in my life, but trust me, they did."

The day after the Dolphins drafted Reagan he was asked what he would do with his newfound wealth from the NFL. His answer was immediate and sincere.

"It won't change me," he says. "But it will change my parents. I will move my parents to a nicer place. I'm not a big spender. I've spent most of my life in poverty and to be honest, I don't need a million dollars to make me happy. My life is all about two H's — hungry for my dreams and hungry for my parents and their well-being. I will stay humble, take care of my son and take care of my family. I plan to keep God first in my life in everything I do, and it will all continue to fall in place for me."

Running backs coach Wes Suan called Reagan shortly after he was drafted, and the two cried together on the phone. "I told him, 'Coach, so many guys get things handed to them,'" Reagan says. "I've always seemed to have an uphill battle — but don't feel sorry for me. I'll find a way to make it, somehow. Like June says all the time, *this is battle, we must respond.*"

One gets the feeling that in Miami, he'll be running *downhill* for the first time.

Ironically, Hawai'i's *starting* tailback and All-WAC running back Nate Ilaoa was drafted by the Philadelphia Eagles in the seventh round, *after* Reagan Mauia. Defensive lineman Melila Purcell went to the Cleveland Browns in the sixth round. Tackle Tala Esera joined Reagan and Samson in Miami as a free agent. Tackle Dane Uperesa signed with Cincinnati. Lawrence Wilson signed with the Baltimore Ravens, Kenny Patton with the Oakland Raiders and Leonard Peters with the New York Jets.

It was the greatest windfall of NFL players in a single weekend in Hawai'i football history, and *half of them* came to the Warriors as walk-ons. Only Texas, Tennessee, Michigan, Ohio State and Florida had more players drafted.

RALPH "PBASE" OMOTO

Nate Ilaoa was drafted by the Eagles; Tala Esera signed with the Dolphins

RALPH "PBASE" OMOTO

Leonard Peters (left) signed with the New York Jets; Mel Purcell was drafted by the Cleveland Browns

Greg McMackin, as you might recall, was the defensive coordinator back in 1999 when Jones first took over the Hawai'i program. McMackin left Hawai'i to coach at Texas Tech, primarily because the Red Raiders offered him so much money he couldn't refuse the job. Like so many others, however, he couldn't resist the call to return to the islands; when Jerry Glanville left the Warriors to take the head coaching job at Portland State, McMackin leaped at the opportunity.

"I was shocked when I got back here," says McMackin, whose prior coaching stops also include the University of Miami and the Seattle Seahawks as assistant head coach. "I've recruited at Miami. They get their pick of the players. The top five schools in the nation — they get their pick of the players. But how does June put 10 guys in the NFL in a single weekend? It's a miracle. The budget here is the same as it was when I left. Some of these kids weighed 180 pounds when they got here.

Now they weigh 230 and they're an NFL prospect. They are all products of the product."

Dennis McKnight agrees. "Compare our facilities. Compare our budgets. It's *impossible* what June has done. When the NFL scouts are here, June personally goes into those meetings. He knows exactly what the NFL is looking for, and the scouts know they can trust him when he tells them what we have.

"When June tells a kid, 'Drop 80 pounds and you'll be drafted,' they don't question him. They drop 80 pounds. If you don't believe it, stick around. Don't be surprised if we have that many guys drafted again next year."

More guys drafted? Are you kidding me?

282

Chapter 41
THE COLT NOBODY SEES

Colt Brennan *will be signing autographs for an hour! Colt Brennan will be appearing at the Quarterback Club luncheon! Colt Brennan, film at 11! Check out Colt Brennan on ESPN! Colt Brennan quoted in USA Today! Colt Brennan appearing at local foundation for charity!*

Everywhere you look in Honolulu, you find Colt. The governor of Hawai'i declared August 16, Brennan's birthday, as *Colt Brennan Day.* He was even invited to the State Capitol to receive a proclamation from Lieutenant Governor James "Duke" Aiona for his "outstanding contribution to college football."

If you *still* just *aren't satisfied,* either at the newsstand, your car radio or TV, then *by all means,* click on the university's Web site. Then you can eat breakfast with Colt; ride around with him in his SUV; hit the beach with Colt for some bodysurfing; even join him as he leaps carefree from an array of jutting cliffs — *are you kidding me?* — into the frothy, pounding surf below. Tyler Graunke must find solace in the fact that he

RALPH "PBASE" OMOTO

Surf's up for the Laguna Beach-bred Colt Brennan

is always just one shark away from starting against Boise State, something the backup quarterbacks *certainly* can't say at Notre Dame.

There are several places, however, where the general public doesn't see Colt. One is at local elementary, intermediate and high schools, where weekly he shares a story of faith and the importance of making good decisions. "I was a typical Southern California kid," he tells students. "I wanted to make a bunch of money and all that stuff. Hawaii has helped me focus more on family, friends and relationships, and less on money and fame."

Another place you actually don't want to meet Colt is at Hale Ho'omalu, a detention center that he and Davone Bess have been known to visit and share their personal stories with the inmates. Brennan, whose apartment is across the street, drops by so often that he refers to Rita Bongon, the deputy superintendent, as Auntie. Colt's message: Hope. "I hope they can see us and say, 'God, my life is not ruined. I can make things better. I can make things right.'" In one three-day stretch before the 2007 season, you could find spreads on Colt in *Sports Illustrated*, *The New York Times*, and *The Los Angeles Times*, proving, says Rich Miano, that "there's never been anybody in the history of Hawaii football with a greater platform than he has."

Yet Colt remains humbled by the one blemish on his record, the incident in Colorado which nearly made all of what he enjoys today impossible to imagine. When asked by Pete Thamel of *The New York Times* how he found peace during his time of trial, Colt unabashedly shared his faith with the country's largest newspaper, relating a verse in Romans 12 that reads, "Do not be conformed to this world, but be *transformed* by the renewing of your minds, so that you may discern what is the will of God – what is acceptable and perfect."

"If you work hard to be a better person," Colt says, "you no longer have to worry about what people think about your past. What I try to prove

PHOTO COURTESY OF THE BRENNAN FAMILY

RALPH "PBASE" OMOTO

From left, the making of a racehorse: Colt in little league (left); high school ; and as a Heisman Trophy candidate

every day is that my actions will clear up everything in the past -- and everything in my future. Each day I get another chance to show who I really am, whether anybody sees me or not."

Another place you don't get to see Colt is here, in June's office. "If he sinks," June tells Colt, freezing the film on the screen and highlighting the safety with a red laser pen, "then throw the swing. If we know he's gonna do that, we'll go scissors, but throw the post *first*. If we don't read it this way, then we take more sacks."

Colt nods. June freezes another throw. "Now, on this one, you're a little flat on the throw. When the pro scouts grade this throw, they're going to tell you it's *under*thrown. You need to hit the buckets. Put them at 39 yards, 44 yards, 46 yards and throw a *million* balls. You need to make sure your deep ball is *consistent* — not flat, but over the top."

Time and again, June rewinds and plays the tape, ensuring that it's engrained in Colt's mind. Patiently, Jones moves on to the next topic,

which is the choice route. The highlighter finds C.J. Hawthorne, who has been converted from defensive back to wide receiver for 2007 and can be seen streaking up the screen. "The *whole* choice route is going to take on a new dimension because he's so fast," Jones tells Colt. "File this information away in your mind. It's good against teams like Fresno State."

Again and again, he shows Hawthorne's speed as the receiver races past a defender. "C.J. looks a lot like Michael Haynes," June says. "Do you know who he is? I had him in Atlanta. Chris Miller hit him for an *unbelievable* amount of choice routes, just the same way. Drop the left shoulder, open your hips up, pop your eyes, *stretch the eyes deep* and hit that out, OK?"

And so it goes, player to coach, coach to player, glued together by a matrix of X's and O's and passing formations that will soon be wowing Saturday afternoon viewers on ESPN.

Down the hall, however, is another film, one that few people have seen. In a drawer, deep in the wooden desk of quarterback coach Dan Morrison, is a *hidden* tape that will live for posterity — one that could serve as a constant reminder to all of us when it comes to who we *think* we are; or who we *plan* to be; or how we *think* we'll get there.

It's difficult to fool the godfather and Mouse Davis should have known better. Still, when someone tells Mouse, *"You need to take a look at this quarterback,"* his heart palpitates and his palms sweat, for discovering quarterbacks to Mouse is the equivalent of Indiana Jones looking for the Ark of the Covenant.

Rich Miano, Dan Morrison and Dennis McKnight were acting like high school boys one day back during the 2006 season when they urged Mouse to the overhead projector in the Hawai'i film room. Morrison, in particular, unveiled the videotape as if it contained the launch codes to a nuclear sub.

"You won't believe this," he promised. *"Wait until you see this guy . . . and we can get him!"*

The high school film was a little grainy, but it made Mouse whistle nonetheless. Throw after throw, long, short, underneath, it mattered not. The quick release, the arm strength — *my gosh, the mobility* — "This kid can do it all," Mouse said, eyes glued to the screen. "Danny, this is the *best tape you've ever brought me! He's throwing rockets! Look at the velocity on that humdinger! What's his deal?"*

"He's only got one offer," Morrison reassured Davis. The film continued.

"You're kidding me!" said Davis. Finally, the money question: "Who *is* this kid?" Mouse asked.

Morrison and the other coaches erupted with laughter.

"It's Colt's high school tape," Morrison said.

None of the Hawai'i coaches had seen the tape before, until somehow Morrison had fetched a copy. Watching the "old" Colt, however, wasn't like watching the mature, humble, *poised* Colt of modern Hawai'i football. It was just another great high school quarterback, one who could make all the throws but was cocky and naïve to the wiles of the world lying in wait to consume him alive.

It's surreal — freaky even — to go back and watch the film. Every great high school quarterback should watch it once, if for no other reason than to realize what Colt's lived through since those high school games; it makes you recognize how close he came to the flames. Every young kid eventually hurts himself and other people with his actions and behavior. We've all done things that were ill-tempered, ill-advised, hypocritical or judgmental. Most of us have found ourselves in some pretty dark places; we're lucky — ask Colt — if we don't get caught. Some of us have been fortunate enough to fall into the hands of a June Jones, who was able to correct our behavior and set us back on our way.

Seeing just what Brennan has *become,* you realize the vulnerability of our fallen world, where danger lurks in every shadow. Colt is living proof that — although we sometimes choose to walk life's most dangerous paths — God still worries where we place our feet.

"Colt is never rattled," says June Jones of his quarterback, pictured here 'hanging loose' ...

Conclusion: Who Cares?

Recently I had lunch with several sports editors from the *St. Petersburg Times,* including one who asked me with all seriousness, *"Who cares about June Jones and Hawai'i football?"* They regaled themselves with laughter after several stereotypical Hawai'i football wisecracks, all of which were factually dead wrong. In Florida, where I live, any mention of June Jones or Colt Brennan is met swiftly with a verbal pick-axe assault, usually having something to do with Tim Tebow and Urban Meyer.

For the record, I'm still confused about why it's OK for a Florida quarterback to rack up huge numbers running a system that has not been proven to work in the NFL but *not* OK for a Hawai'i quarterback to the do the same using a *proven* system. It is unfortunate that Hawai'i's scheduled game with Florida in 2008 couldn't have occurred in a year in which Colt Brennan was pulling the trigger.

But who, indeed, cares? It is a fair question. For the record, I didn't protest. I sat quietly, eating my ham and Swiss on rye, and listened to them with interest, the same way an astronaut listens to someone tell him he's an idiot for thinking he'll ever leave the earth's atmosphere.

This book, like most, became a journey, starting at one place and ending at quite another. It is far more than just a book about "Hawai'i" or "football," but rather it is a collection of essays, mostly about June Jones and how he has navigated the circumstances of time, people and events to reach the most unlikely of places: Hawai'i, now, can actually *be included* in a debate of top college teams.

To me, that says more about the *man* than it does about the school, the program or the team; for when taken as an entire body of work — wins, records, championships, awards, draft picks — he has accomplished more than even the most doubting pundit ever dreamed — and far more than the average football coach could hope to do. Otherwise, it would have already been done before.

I always believed, however, even before I began, that the *real measure* of the story would wind up beyond the lines of football — in *people.* When I delved into the *generations* of lives that have been touched by Jones, I was stunned to learn how a man could navigate so effortlessly in a world of egos and chest-thumping arrogance to selflessly affect so many *people.*

As a journalist, I've always believed in the question, *"Who cares?"* It's a great, great question.

I found some clues; ultimately, you can be the judge.

John C. Maxwell is considered America's foremost expert on leadership, with more than 12 million books in print and the author of *The 21 Irrefutable Laws of Leadership.* He has worked with S. Truett Cathy, founder and chairman of Chick-Fil-A; former Dallas Cowboys coach Tom Landry; and Zig Ziglar, renowned author and motivational speaker.

Maxwell says that the legacy of *all great leaders* — Robert Goizuta of the Coca-Cola empire, Jack Welch at General Electric, even Mother Teresa — boils down to the following criteria, the legacy by which Jones will ultimately be judged:

A legacy of succession. Lasting value, or *legacy,* is measured by *succession.* "Leadership cannot be delegated," Maxwell says. "You either exercise it, or abdicate it."

Long view. Any coach can make a program look good for a year, maybe two, by launching flashy new initiatives or drawing crowds to a *single* event. "Leaders with legacy take a different approach," says Maxwell. "They lead with *tomorrow,* as well as *today,* in mind."

Create a leadership culture. The most stable football programs have strong coaches at every level of the organization. "The only way to develop such widespread leadership is to make leaders a part of your culture," he says.

Pay the price to assure success tomorrow. There is no success without sacrifice. "Each team or organization is unique, and that dictates what the price will be," he says. "Any leader who wants to help his organization must be willing to pay that price to ensure lasting success."

Value team leadership above individual leadership. No matter how good a coach might be, no leader can do it all alone. "The larger the organization, the stronger, larger, and deeper the team of leaders needs to be," he says.

Jones found a place in relative obscurity — Hawai'i — where he could build out a program that met such criteria. The result is that he is now a father of both a culture and a system of winning — one that performs at such consistently high levels that it refutes scrutiny from even its fiercest critics.

Who cares? The answer lies in all of the people who have followed June Jones. "Look at the people that follow you," says Maxwell. "Whatever character *you* possess, you will find in all of the people who follow you."

Chris Mortensen isn't a critic; on the contrary, he is among an array of media personalities who believe in June Jones and the meteoric growth of the Hawai'i program. An award-winning journalist, Mortensen appears weekly alongside Dan Marino, Bob Costas, Cris Carter and Cris Collinsworth on HBO's *Inside the NFL.* His insight, relationships and investigative reports have graced sports pages for 25 years.

"Whether anyone wants to acknowledge it or not," Mortensen says, "there's been a surge in offensive production everywhere June has been. People seem to forget the Oilers were a pretty darn good football team. Can the Run 'n' Shoot win a Super Bowl? Yes, if the defense is dominant — which, by the way, is what it takes for *any* offense to win a Super Bowl.

"June is a coach who is well regarded at every level," he says. "The NFL people are uncomfortable with the moniker of Run 'n' Shoot, but what

he has done at Hawai'i speaks for itself. As a parent, I trusted my son to June. My *own* son almost went to Hawai'i to play for June, and I'm not so sure he doesn't regret it now that he didn't. In fact, if I'm a big-time college that needs to have immediate success, June Jones would be at the top of my wish list."

ESPN's Neil Everett agrees, saying that until Jones arrived at Hawai'i, "the patient was dead . . . and now there's a sense of ownership between the people of Hawai'i and the football program that is unique beyond any other program's relationship with its community. The future of the program might have depended on June Jones, and he delivered, way beyond anyone believed he could."

Larry Beil, an ABC sports anchor in San Francisco, sees Jones as a coach who has "done something that is just not supposed to happen. . . . Who can say they took a program that was going down the drain and instantaneously turn the whole thing around, then continue to build on it at a pace that none of us in the media believed he could maintain? On the very face of it, for June to actually *have* a Heisman candidate at Hawai'i is simply ridiculous."

Sporting News sent reporter Matt Hayes to Hawai'i to do a simple college football preview story; he was incredulous at what he discovered. "I think *we* care," Matt says, when I pop the question. "The theme of our college football preview this season was *'What Matters Most in Football,'*" and the centerpiece became *"Hawai'i Matters Now."* Hawai'i helped open the door for non–BCS teams. They are a legitimate, non–BCS school, with a legitimate Heisman Trophy candidate.

"I was pretty shocked, to be honest," he says. "June is winning with players nobody else wants. He is giving people second chances, where nobody else would. He told me, 'I've got a mission here.' There is no doubt in my mind, after talking with June, that he's there for more than just football."

In my search for *who cares* I moved on from the media and took my place among football coaches. I was puzzled as to *why,* if *nobody cares,* did Michigan State pay $250,000 to remove itself from Hawai'i's schedule this year, joining the ranks of Notre Dame, Virginia, Iowa State and Texas as schools that have pulled out of games since June took control of the program.

"Hawai'i has been an easy mark for a lot of the big-time schools before June got there," says Joe Haering of the NFL's Buffalo Bills, which is about as far east of Hawai'i as one can get and *still care*. "It used to be that these schools would advertise Hawai'i on their schedules as a second bowl game, an easy win, where they could bring the alumni and have fun at the school's expense. June ruined that for everybody. Surfing isn't nearly as fun when you go to Hawai'i, get beat and have to get back on the plane and go home with your record ruined."

Haering, long a respected coach and personnel scout whose football career spans four decades, cuts to the chase. "Anybody who might say 'Who cares?' regarding June or the Run-and-Shoot or Hawai'i or the whole deal in general must understand something," he says. "Five years from now, *nobody will care* who the coach at Hawai'i was or who the coach of the Tampa Bay Buccaneers was or who won the Heisman. What it all comes down to is: What mark did June leave as a *man?*

"Answer that question," Haering says, "and you'll find out *who cares.*"

Honolulu Mayor Muffi Hannemann replied to my email, and boy, *does he care!* Here, verbatim, is his e-mailed response:

The University of Hawai'i's Warrior football program is perhaps the most prominent among island sports, by virtue of football's tremendous popularity across the nation, and partly because the UH fields the only collegiate team in the state and we lack an NFL franchise.

Coach Jones has built on the foundation begun by former coaches Larry Price, Dick Tomey, and Bob Wagner, by introducing a unique and exciting brand of Jonesian football that's a delight to everyone — whether it's someone with an intimate knowledge of the game or just the casual fan.

June has quite literally transformed the Warriors into not just Hawai'i's team, but Polynesia's team and a team for the entire

Asia-Pacific region. His ability to attract and mold student-athletes from multicultural, if not multinational, upbringings and backgrounds, and build them into champions, is making him a household name in Samoa, Australia, New Zealand, Japan, and the mainland United States. The growing success and profile of the UH Warriors means that Coach Jones is fast-becoming more than a local football legend, he's becoming an influential leader in the region much like the storied college coaches of the past and present.

I know June has faced adversity and pain in his life. I also know he embraces the power of prayer and faith, as I do, and that those themes guide and inspire him and the team. During a particularly challenging period early in my term as mayor, June stood beside me and bolstered my spirit and reaffirmed my confidence in my decision. It's a gesture I've never forgotten, and indicated the measure of the man; that he'll stand by you through even the most difficult of times.

It's that kind of trust and confidence you want and expect in a leader, that motivates you to succeed, and that's exactly what we're seeing on the football field. June's example is now reaching beyond the stripes on the field; he's become more than the UH Warrior football coach, he's becoming a leader in the Pacific.

Yet it was the last place I looked that I *think* I finally found *who cares.*

It was *in June's office.* June is looking away, out the dirty plate-glass windows, toward the practice fields below. Men are gathered all around; on the sofa, in a chair, on the floor. I spot coaches Jeff Reinebold and George Lumpkin, who I recognize. I don't know Anthony Holyfield, a former lineman who played under June in the pros, or Norman Nakanishi, a tiny middle-aged man of Asian descent, who I would learn about later.

I look around the room, and everyone is . . . *crying.* June wipes his face, again and again. Tears stream down the brown cheeks of *George Lumpkin,* who actually hides his eyes behind dark sunglasses. Anthony Holyfield, all 300 pounds, is sniffling like a child.

Between sobs, the thickly muscled Reinebold is telling a story . . . *about how he was interviewing with the Oakland Raiders but had the opportunity to be in Hawai'i, for a purpose he can't fully understand . . . about how he had temporarily lost, then regained custody of his precious baby boy . . . about divorce, and disappointment and how he trusts that God will make all of the pain in his life worth something. . . .*

"It's in God's hands," June says. He doesn't move, left or right, he just stares out the window. *"Why did I live through my accident?* This isn't about football. . . . I feel God didn't take me because of so many kids who have come to know the Lord *through* football."

"God is in complete control, and nothing else matters to me anymore," says Lumpkin, in a whisper. "I keep telling people that God has a plan for this football team. . . . God is healing so many people, touching so many lives . . . each day I'm here, I'm amazed at how much bigger it gets."

Seconds tick by. Norm, the team chaplain, puts his hand on Jeff Reinebold and begins to pray.

"Father, we thank you today, for your grace, your love and your mercy, for we know, O God, when it feels like no one else cares, we know that you cared enough to send your Son to pay the ultimate price so that we might live abundantly. . . ."

Are you kidding me?

RALPH "PBASE" OMOTO

Prayer Warriors: June Jones leads his team as they return thanks

About the Author

J. DAVID MILLER is a celebrated author whose work has appeared in major national magazines and newspapers, as well as television and radio. Miller earned the New York Newspaper Guild's coveted *Page One Award* for investigative journalism, as well as best feature honors for The Southeastern Writer's Council. Two of his other eight books were highly praised, including *Elvis Don't Like Football*, with Jerry Glanville, and *The Super Book of Football*, for *Sports Illustrated*. He makes his home in St. Petersburg, Florida. He can be contacted at author89@gmail.com.

The Miller family on a football weekend …

J. David and Laurie Miller … The jersey on the wall is Miller's, where it was retired by restaurant owner Franc Urso -- in honor of Miller's brief playing days as a Pittsburgh Gladiator in the Arena Football League. Miller, however, refuses to relinquish his leather helmet.

The gang at Beef 'O' Brady's – Mary Williams; owner Franc Urso; Laurie and J. David; and John and Cheryl Slivick … "Beef's, believe it or not," says Miller, "has it all – faith, friends, and football."

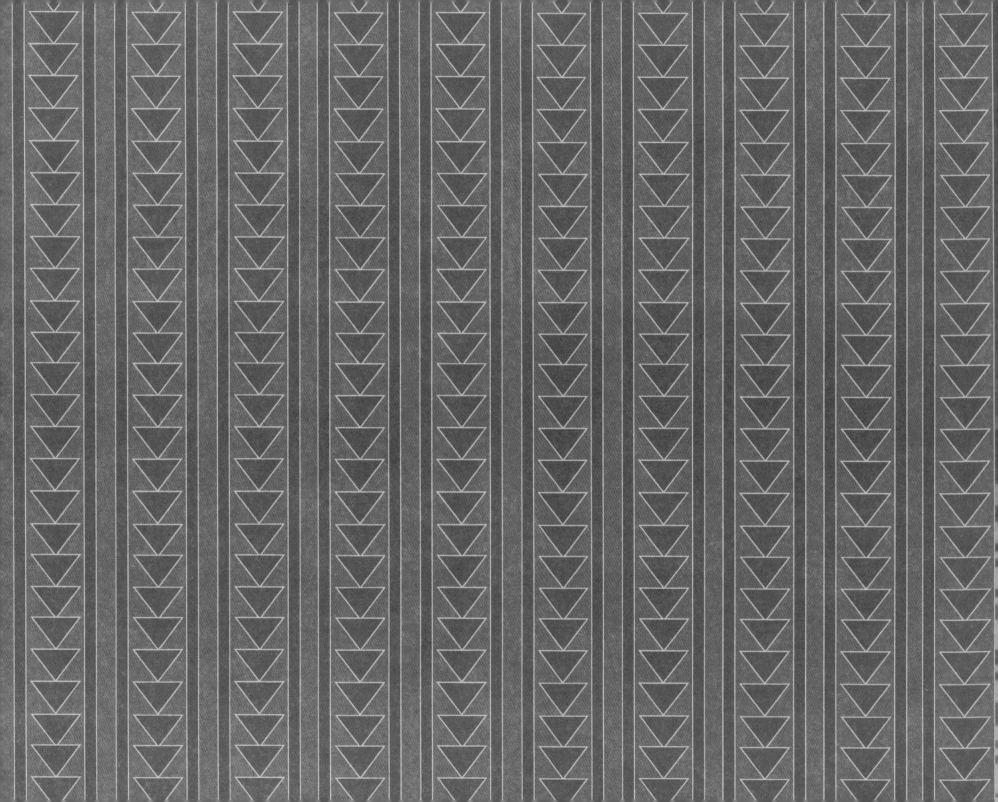